S0-BHT-770

™

BESTSELLING BOOK SERIES

Certification for the Rest of Us!™

Are you intimidated and confused by computers? Do you find that traditional manuals are overloaded with technical details you'll never use? Do your friends and family always call you to fix simple problems on their PCs? Then the *...For Dummies*® computer book series from IDG Books Worldwide is for you.

...For Dummies books are written for those frustrated computer users who know they aren't really dumb but find that PC hardware, software, and indeed the unique vocabulary of computing make them feel helpless. *...For Dummies* books use a lighthearted approach, a down-to-earth style, and even cartoons and humorous icons to dispel computer novices' fears and build their confidence. Lighthearted but not lightweight, these books are a perfect survival guide for anyone forced to use a computer.

> *"I like my copy so much I told friends; now they bought copies."*
>
> — *Irene C., Orwell, Ohio*

> *"Quick, concise, nontechnical, and humorous."*
>
> — *Jay A., Elburn, Illinois*

> *"Thanks, I needed this book. Now I can sleep at night."*
>
> — *Robin F., British Columbia, Canada*

Already, millions of satisfied readers agree. They have made *...For Dummies* books the #1 introductory level computer book series and have written asking for more. So, if you're looking for the most fun and easy way to learn about computers, look to *...For Dummies* books to give you a helping hand.

IDG BOOKS WORLDWIDE ®

MCSE TCP/IP

FOR

DUMMIES®

2ND EDITION

MCSE TCP/IP FOR DUMMIES®

2ND EDITION

by Cameron Brandon, MCSE, A+

**Foreword by Eckhart Boehme,
Marketing Manager
Certification and Skills Assessment,
Microsoft Corporation**

IDG Books Worldwide, Inc.
An International Data Group Company

Foster City, CA ◆ Chicago, IL ◆ Indianapolis, IN ◆ New York, NY

MCSE TCP/IP For Dummies,® 2nd Edition

Published by
IDG Books Worldwide, Inc.
An International Data Group Company
919 E. Hillsdale Blvd.
Suite 400
Foster City, CA 94404
www.idgbooks.com (IDG Books Worldwide Web site)
www.dummies.com (Dummies Press Web site)

Library of Congress Catalog Card No.: 99-63114

ISBN: 0-7645-0613-7

Printed in the United States of America

10 9 8 7 6 5 4 3 2 1

2O/QY/QW/ZZ/IN

Distributed in the United States by IDG Books Worldwide, Inc.

Distributed by CDG Books Canada Inc. for Canada; by Transworld Publishers Limited in the United Kingdom; by IDG Norge Books for Norway; by IDG Sweden Books for Sweden; by IDG Books Australia Publishing Corporation Pty. Ltd. for Australia and New Zealand; by TransQuest Publishers Pte Ltd. for Singapore, Malaysia, Thailand, Indonesia, and Hong Kong; by Gotop Information Inc. for Taiwan; by ICG Muse, Inc. for Japan; by Norma Comunicaciones S.A. for Colombia; by Intersoft for South Africa; by Eyrolles for France; by International Thomson Publishing for Germany, Austria and Switzerland; by Distribuidora Cuspide for Argentina; by Livraria Cultura for Brazil; by Ediciones ZETA S.C.R. Ltda. for Peru; by WS Computer Publishing Corporation, Inc., for the Philippines; by Contemporanea de Ediciones for Venezuela; by Express Computer Distributors for the Caribbean and West Indies; by Micronesia Media Distributor, Inc. for Micronesia; by Grupo Editorial Norma S.A. for Guatemala; by Chips Computadoras S.A. de C.V. for Mexico; by Editorial Norma de Panama S.A. for Panama; by American Bookshops for Finland. Authorized Sales Agent: Anthony Rudkin Associates for the Middle East and North Africa.

For general information on IDG Books Worldwide's books in the U.S., please call our Consumer Customer Service department at 800-762-2974. For reseller information, including discounts and premium sales, please call our Reseller Customer Service department at 800-434-3422.

For information on where to purchase IDG Books Worldwide's books outside the U.S., please contact our International Sales department at 317-596-5530 or fax 317-596-5692.

For consumer information on foreign language translations, please contact our Customer Service department at 1-800-434-3422, fax 317-596-5692, or e-mail rights@idgbooks.com.

For information on licensing foreign or domestic rights, please phone +1-650-655-3109.

For sales inquiries and special prices for bulk quantities, please contact our Sales department at 650-655-3200 or write to the address above.

For information on using IDG Books Worldwide's books in the classroom or for ordering examination copies, please contact our Educational Sales department at 800-434-2086 or fax 317-596-5499.

For press review copies, author interviews, or other publicity information, please contact our Public Relations department at 650-655-3000 or fax 650-655-3299.

For authorization to photocopy items for corporate, personal, or educational use, please contact Copyright Clearance Center, 222 Rosewood Drive, Danvers, MA 01923, or fax 978-750-4470.

About the Authors

Cameron Brandon (MCSE, CNE, CNA, MCPS: Internet Systems, A+) is a Network Engineer/Administrator living in the Portland, Oregon, area and working with Capstone Technology Corporation. His networking specialty is Windows NT with BackOffice Integration. Cameron participated in the Intel migration to Windows NT in Oregon, the largest migration of its kind in history. He completed his MCSE, CNE, CNA, MCPS: Internet Systems, and A+ certifications in just five months.

Syngress Media is a Boston-area firm that creates books and software for Information Technology professionals seeking skill enhancement and career advancement. Its products are designed to comply with vendor and industry standard course studies and are geared especially to certification exam preparation.

ABOUT IDG BOOKS WORLDWIDE

Welcome to the world of IDG Books Worldwide.

IDG Books Worldwide, Inc., is a subsidiary of International Data Group, the world's largest publisher of computer-related information and the leading global provider of information services on information technology. IDG was founded more than 30 years ago by Patrick J. McGovern and now employs more than 9,000 people worldwide. IDG publishes more than 290 computer publications in over 75 countries. More than 90 million people read one or more IDG publications each month.

Launched in 1990, IDG Books Worldwide is today the #1 publisher of best-selling computer books in the United States. We are proud to have received eight awards from the Computer Press Association in recognition of editorial excellence and three from Computer Currents' First Annual Readers' Choice Awards. Our best-selling *...For Dummies®* series has more than 50 million copies in print with translations in 31 languages. IDG Books Worldwide, through a joint venture with IDG's Hi-Tech Beijing, became the first U.S. publisher to publish a computer book in the People's Republic of China. In record time, IDG Books Worldwide has become the first choice for millions of readers around the world who want to learn how to better manage their businesses.

Our mission is simple: Every one of our books is designed to bring extra value and skill-building instructions to the reader. Our books are written by experts who understand and care about our readers. The knowledge base of our editorial staff comes from years of experience in publishing, education, and journalism — experience we use to produce books to carry us into the new millennium. In short, we care about books, so we attract the best people. We devote special attention to details such as audience, interior design, use of icons, and illustrations. And because we use an efficient process of authoring, editing, and desktop publishing our books electronically, we can spend more time ensuring superior content and less time on the technicalities of making books.

You can count on our commitment to deliver high-quality books at competitive prices on topics you want to read about. At IDG Books Worldwide, we continue in the IDG tradition of delivering quality for more than 30 years. You'll find no better book on a subject than one from IDG Books Worldwide.

John Kilcullen
Chairman and CEO
IDG Books Worldwide, Inc.

Steven Berkowitz
President and Publisher
IDG Books Worldwide, Inc.

Eighth Annual
Computer Press
Awards ≥1992

Ninth Annual
Computer Press
Awards ≥1993

Tenth Annual
Computer Press
Awards ≥1994

Eleventh Annual
Computer Press
Awards ≥1995

Dedication

From Cameron: I would like to thank my wife Sallye for her patience and support.

Authors' Acknowledgments

We would like to thank some people at IDG Books who worked to make this book happen. They include Diane Steele, Jill Pisoni, Mary Corder, Mary Bednarek, Nancy DelFavero, Christy Beck, and Elizabeth Kuball.

Publisher's Acknowledgments

We're proud of this book; please register your comments through our IDG Books Worldwide Online Registration Form located at http://my2cents.dummies.com. Some of the people who helped bring this book to market include the following:

Acquisitions, Editorial, and Media Development

Project Editors: Nancy DelFavero, Ryan Rader

Acquisitions Editor: Joyce Pepple

Copy Editors: Christine Meloy Beck, Elizabeth Netedu Kuball

Technical Editors: Nickolas Landry, MCSD and Microsoft Regional Director; Bassam Alameddine, MCSE; Nils Dussart, MCSE

Media Development Editor: Joell Smith

Associate Permissions Editor: Carmen Krikorian

Media Development Coordinator: Megan Roney

Editorial Manager: Leah Cameron

Media Development Manager: Heather Heath Dismore

Production

Associate Project Coordinator: Maridee V. Ennis

Layout and Graphics: Linda M. Boyer, Angela F. Hunckler, Brent Savage, Janet Seib, Michael A. Sullivan

Proofreaders: Christine Berman, Nancy Price, Marianne Santy, Rebecca Senninger, Janet M. Withers

Indexer: Rebecca R. Plunket

CD-ROM Exam Reviewer: Joe Wagner, MCSE, Systems Engineer, ST Labs, Inc.; Steven A. Frare, MCP, Network Engineer, ST Labs, Inc.

Special Help: Kelly Ewing; Seta K. Frantz; Richard Graves; Pat O'Brien; Barry Pruett; Prime Synergy; Tina Sims; Development of the QuickLearn game by André LaMothe of Xtreme Games, LLC; CD-ROM Exam authored by Raul A. Jimenez, MCSE, MCT; Beth Parlon; Jamila Pree; Sento Corp.

General and Administrative

IDG Books Worldwide, Inc.: John Kilcullen, CEO; Steven Berkowitz, President and Publisher

IDG Books Technology Publishing: Richard Swadley, Senior Vice President and Group Publisher

Dummies Technology Press and Dummies Editorial: Diane Graves Steele, Vice President and Associate Publisher; Mary Bednarek, Director of Acquisitions and Product Development; Kristin A. Cocks, Editorial Director, Branded Consumer; Mary C. Corder, Editorial Director, Branded Technology

Dummies Trade Press: Kathleen A. Welton, Vice President and Publisher; Kevin Thornton, Acquisitions Manager

IDG Books Production for Dummies Press: Michael R. Britton, Vice President of Production and Creative Services; Cindy L. Phipps, Manager of Project Coordination, Production Proofreading, and Indexing; Shelley Lea, Supervisor of Graphics and Design; Debbie J. Gates, Production Systems Specialist; Robert Springer, Supervisor of Proofreading; Debbie Stailey, Production Control Manager; Tony Augsburger, Supervisor of Reprints and Bluelines

Dummies Packaging and Book Design: Patty Page, Manager, Promotions Marketing

◆

The publisher would like to give special thanks to Patrick J. McGovern, without whom this book would not have been possible.

◆

Contents at a Glance

Cartoons at a Glance

By Rich Tennant

page 367

page 5

page 355

page 153

page 101

page 257

page 321

Fax: 978-546-7747 • E-mail: the5wave@tiac.net

Table of Contents

Foreword

● ●

*M*icrosoft certification makes you stand out as an expert. In the ever-changing computing environment, the Microsoft Certified Professional (MCP) designation shows that you're one of the technical elite, a proficient professional who understands and can use Microsoft products to their fullest potential. In short, you're someone in the know.

That's why picking this book from the ...*For Dummies* series is an appropriate way to reach your potential. The ...*For Dummies* series stands out for being in the know, and for giving readers exactly the information they need. This MCP approved study guide continues that legacy, helping you prepare for the exams by addressing critical exam objectives. And, because Microsoft regional directors have reviewed this study guide for technical accuracy, we know that this book is among the best available on the topic.

You've chosen an exciting and dynamic career path. Microsoft training and certification will help prepare you to face the many challenges ahead. Let this book be your guide.

Eckhart Boehme, Marketing Manager
Certification and Skills Assessment,
Microsoft Corporation

Introduction

· ·

*O*nce upon a time, I was where you are right now. I knew that an MCSE designation would help to jump-start my career in the networking industry, but I felt overwhelmed at the thought of having to cram volumes of information on networking technology into my head and then hoping to remember it all when I got to the testing center. If only I knew what I really had to study. What was actually going to be on the exam? How would I know when I was ready to be tested?

I didn't need a book that included every detail ever written about TCP/IP. I just needed a book to help me pass the exam and, at the same time, brush up on the TCP/IP tools and technology. It turns out that what I needed was *MCSE TCP/IP Certification For Dummies.* This book was written to help you zero in on precisely what you need to study to pass exam number 70-059, *Internetworking with Microsoft TCP/IP on Microsoft Windows NT 4.0.*

About This Book

You can use this book as your sole source of exam-preparation information, or you can use it to supplement your other reading on the TCP/IP protocol, such as Microsoft's Technical Information Network (TechNet). Or you can use it in tandem with classroom-based training.

I've written this book to be easy and quick to use. You won't find excess technical jargon or complex processes covered in excruciating detail. You simply find what you need to know in a nutshell.

This book is especially handy for the test-taker who's only a week or two away from taking the exam and who wants to do some extra, last-minute preparation. If a concept is likely to be tested on the exam, I make sure to cover it thoroughly here, which makes this book an ideal place to begin studying for the exam. A number of user-friendly features are included in the book:

 ✔ Every chapter starts off with a page-long preview of what's to come, including a list of exam objectives and chapter highlights.

 ✔ Chapters 3 through 16 offer Quick Assessment quizzes to test how much you already know about the exam objectives. Then you can just concentrate on the areas where you may be weak. If you get all the Quick Assessment questions right, you can skip to the end of the chapter and have a go at the Prep Test.

✔ Each chapter ends with a Prep Test. Each question in the Prep Test gauges your understanding of a particular topic. If you miss a question, the answer tells you which section of the chapter to review.

When a question can be answered with more than one choice, check boxes appear next to the answers. If only one answer is right, the check boxes are circles (just like on the real exam and in the Practice Exams at the back of the book).

✔ Step-by-step Lab exercises walk you through a number of administrative and networking tasks that are likely to be tested.

✔ Tables of facts and figures provide critical information at a glance, material that I strongly recommend you commit to memory.

How This Book Is Organized

This book into divided into seven parts, each of which contains several chapters in logical order. You can read this book cover to cover, or you can skip to what you need right *now*. Part I provides some basic information on the exam and the TCP/IP technology itself, Parts II–V roughly follow the content of the TCP/IP exam, and the last two parts provide an assortment of helpful reference materials.

Part I: The Basics: Exam Facts and TCP/IP Fundamentals

Studying your opponent so that you know exactly what you're up against is always a good idea. Chapter 1 tells you what to expect on the test — the number of questions, the question structure, and other important information designed to prepare you for Test Day. The remaining chapters provide a solid overview of the components of the TCP/IP technology.

Part II: Planning

I've given special attention to the planning aspect of configuring a network to use the TCP/IP protocol. You'll find loads of information on IP addressing, sub-netting a network, and IP routing — important topics that are likely candidates for those tricky scenario-type questions you can expect to encounter.

Part III: Installation and Configuration

Four heavily tested topics — DHCP, WINS, DNS, and SNMP — each earn their own chapter in this part of the book. I clue you in on the important aspects of installing and configuring these TCP/IP components and services, and I provide methods for troubleshooting an installation that's gone wrong.

Part IV: Connectivity

This part of the book presents a variety of situations in which a TCP/IP-based client can take advantage of resources on a network. You'll find information on how Windows NT computers must be configured to share resources on a network with non-Microsoft clients and which utilities are used for connections, browsing, file transfer, and printing when you have a mixed bag of devices on a network. Expect to see a number of questions about these utilities on the exam.

Part V: Monitoring, Optimization, and Troubleshooting

Besides having to know how to monitor network performance by using the various tools that come with TCP/IP and Windows NT 4.0, you also need to know how to diagnose and resolve specific networking problems. In this part of the book, I focus on using the TCP/IP and Microsoft monitoring utilities to troubleshoot certain TCP/IP-based problems — especially the ones that crop up with IP addressing and name resolution.

Part VI: The Part of Tens

Here you'll find my personal Top Ten lists of useful bits of information to use in preparing for the exam. Included are ten online resources guaranteed to help you pass the exam and become an MCSE, and ten test-taking strategies gathered from those who have been there and won.

Part VII: Appendixes

Want to know whether you're really ready for prime time? This part of the book includes two complete practice exams with questions just like the ones you'll see on the test. Also included is a guide to Microsoft certification and how the TCP/IP exam fits into the big picture of MCSE certification. In addition, you can find out about this book's companion CD-ROM, which is packed with study aids and other resources.

Icons Used in This Book

When you flip though this book, you'll notice some eye-catching icons. They appear in the margins to draw your attention to some important information.

Stop here for insights on how to save precious time while studying for the exam or while you're taking it.

Make a point of carefully reviewing the material next to this icon. It provides information you need to instantly answer a question correctly.

Maybe you already know this information. This icon is just a gentle reminder that you better not forget it for the exam.

This icon alerts you to potential problem areas and limitations of the TCP/IP technology that may appear on the exam.

This icon points out some insider advice or a little-known technique that may come in handy.

Part I
The Basics: Exam Facts and TCP/IP Fundamentals

In this part . . .

The first chapter of this part of the book provides you with some basic information on the Internetworking with Microsoft TCP/IP on Windows NT 4.0 exam, including how to prepare for it, the number of questions you can expect to find, the amount of time allotted to answer the questions, and a few hints on how to pass this exam with flying colors. The information presented is unique to the TCP/IP exam, so make sure you spend some time reviewing Chapter 1, even if you're a veteran of other Microsoft exams.

The other four chapters in this part give you a solid foundation in the fundamentals of the TCP/IP protocol. Chapters 2 through 5 provide a general overview of the history and workings of TCP/IP, and information on some of its basic elements, including IP Address Resolution Protocol, Host Name Resolution, and the Network Basic Input/Output System (a.k.a. NetBIOS).

Chapter 1

The TCP/IP Exam

. . . .

In This Chapter

▶ Reviewing the test objectives and other stuff you'll be tested on

▶ Getting familiar with the structure of the test questions

▶ Putting together a killer game plan

. . . .

*E*xam Number 70-059, *Internetworking with Microsoft TCP/IP on Microsoft Windows NT 4.0,* is the most popular elective exam in the MCSE certification path. It also has a reputation of being one of the most difficult of all the Microsoft exams available. This chapter gives you an insider's view of how the exam is built, the types of questions you can expect to see, and how you can put together a sure-fire game plan to ace this test.

Most Microsoft certification exams have a number of features in common, such as the number of questions and their basic setup. But each exam also has characteristics that are unique to the technology being tested. Therefore, you need to be aware of some TCP/IP exam specifics, such as the required passing score, the study objectives being tested, and the topics most likely to be covered. Having this information in advance can make the difference between success and your having to make another visit to the exam center.

What to Study? The Microsoft Exam Objectives

The exam measures your ability to implement, administer, and troubleshoot information systems that incorporate Microsoft TCP/IP. The following are Microsoft's testing objectives, all of which are covered in later chapters of this book:

✓ **Planning**

- Given a scenario, identify valid network configurations.
- Configure subnet masks.
- On a Windows NT Server computer, configure Microsoft TCP/IP to support multiple network adapters.
- Configure a Windows NT Server computer to function as an IP router.

✓ **Installation and Configuration**

- Configure scopes by using DHCP Manager.
- Install and configure the DHCP Relay Agent.
- Given a scenario, select the appropriate services to install when using Microsoft TCP/IP on a Microsoft Windows NT Server computer.
- Install and configure a WINS server.
- Run WINS on a multihomed computer.
- Import LMHOSTS files to WINS.
- Configure static mappings in the WINS database.
- Configure WINS replication.
- Configure HOSTS and LMHOSTS files.
- Install and configure the Microsoft DNS Server service on a Windows NT Server computer.
- Integrate DNS with other name servers.
- Connect a DNS server to a DNS root server.
- Configure DNS server roles.
- Configure SNMP.

✓ **Connectivity**

- Configure and support browsing in a multiple-domain routed network.
- Given a scenario, identify which utility to use to connect to a TCP/IP-based UNIX host.
- Configure a Windows NT Server computer to support TCP/IP printing.
- Configure a RAS server and Dial-Up Networking for use on a TCP/IP network.

✔ **Monitoring and Optimization**

- Given a scenario, identify which tool to use to monitor TCP/IP traffic.

✔ **Troubleshooting**

- Diagnose and resolve IP addressing problems.

- Diagnose and resolve name resolution problems.

- Identify the correct Microsoft TCP/IP utility to use to diagnose IP configuration problems.

- Use Microsoft TCP/IP utilities to diagnose IP configuration problems.

You absolutely *must* review the list of exam objectives provided by Microsoft. Although the objectives can be somewhat vague, they nevertheless provide a fairly close approximation of the areas you'll be tested on. However, Microsoft doesn't give you any indication of the number of questions you get on each objective, nor does it give you any indication of the depth of the questions.

Throughout this book, I tell you which areas of the TCP/IP technology are likely to be more heavily tested than others, and which areas will be covered with just a question or two. I also fill you in on the kind of information the questions are seeking, including the amount of detail you're expected to provide, depending on the objective.

Other Must-Study Topics

Most test-takers I've talked with think that the *Internetworking with Microsoft TCP/IP on Microsoft Windows NT 4.0* exam truly reflects the skills required by an administrator in a TCP/IP-based network. Although these test-takers say that the exam doesn't heavily emphasize any one topic, a few areas of TCP/IP technology tend to crop up more often than others. The general consensus is that you'd better brush up on the following topics:

✔ Dynamic Host Configuration Protocol (DHCP)

✔ Windows Internet Name Service (WINS)

✔ NetBIOS

✔ Host Name Resolution

This book devotes an entire chapter to each of these four topics. It's worth noting that most of these are Microsoft-created Windows-based technologies. The TCP/IP protocol is a vendor-neutral industry standard, and Microsoft has contributed a number of enhancements to the protocol. These enhancements, not surprisingly, are well represented on the exam.

For nearly every Microsoft exam I've taken, I made it a point to copy the exam objectives to a text file and continually update the file with information that I needed to remember for the test. After a few weeks of doing this, you should have a sizable file of pointers that you can print out and read during your lunch hour or while you're commuting (but not when you're behind the wheel, of course).

Self-testing software is available that parallels the Microsoft exam objectives. You can use this software to identify those areas where you may be weak. See Chapter 18 for more information on Web sites that offer self-testing software — some of which is free!

How the Exam Is Structured

The *Internetworking with Microsoft TCP/IP on Microsoft Windows NT 4.0* exam consists of 58 questions. You will have 90 minutes to complete them all. You need a score of at least 750 to pass, which works out to a minimum of 44 correct answers.

The multiple-choice format

Most of the questions on the exam are in a multiple-choice format. Approximately 80 percent of the exam will probably consist of multiple choice questions with four possible answers. (I cover two types of multiple-choice questions — the scenario-based question and the diagrammed question — later on in this section of the chapter.)

Only a couple of questions on the exam will list five possible answers from which to choose the correct answer (or answers). I found those questions to be no more difficult than the questions with four possible answers. In either case, you can almost immediately narrow down the possible correct answers to one of two choices.

Questions with more than one correct answer

Some of the questions have multiple correct answers. Those questions can be difficult to deal with because it always seems that at least one of the choices is never clearly right or wrong. Fortunately, you shouldn't see more than three to five questions of this type.

Those questions that allow you to choose multiple answers use square instead of circular check-off areas and tell you to "Choose all that apply." But beware: Just because you see square check boxes doesn't necessarily mean that the question has more than one correct answer.

Diagrammed questions

A few multiple-choice questions include a diagram, usually of a network, that you need to decipher in order to answer the question correctly. Those questions tend to be relatively difficult because of the large amount of information presented in the diagram. (Luckily, most of the questions you'll get are the standard multiple-choice type with no diagrams or scenarios.) In addition, some of the information in the diagrams may be hard to read if your testing center uses smaller-sized monitors.

The secret to answering this type of question correctly is to rewrite the information shown in the diagram on the scratch paper provided. Then, work out the answer from your diagram. First, determine what information is absolutely necessary in order to arrive at the answer; and second, eliminate the information that's included just to trick you.

Scenario-based questions

The scenario-type questions are composed of a fairly lengthy description of a problem situation, followed by two or more questions you need to ask yourself in order to solve the problem and a proposed solution to each question. The same situation applies to each question; only the proposed solutions change.

Scenario-type questions start out by listing required networking results that must be achieved and other results that are optional; for example:

Required results

You must increase security.

Fault tolerance must be present.

No software should be installed on the workstations.

Optional results

Users should be able to log on from any domain.

User authentication times should be minimized.

Next, the scenario-type questions list proposed solutions, such as

Install the Microsoft TCP/IP printing service on each computer.

Create a mapping for each domain controller in the LMHOSTS file.

Finally, you must choose among possible answers to these scenario-based problems, for example:

The proposed solution produces the required result and produces both of the optional desired results.

The proposed solution produces the required result and produces only one of the optional desired results.

The proposed solution produces the required result but does not produce any of the optional desired results.

The proposed solution does not produce the required result.

Putting all this together, you end up with a typical scenario-type question that reads something like the following:

1.   Your company has just moved to a new office building. You are responsible for setting up the network for the company's 20 employees. Each employee's computer must be connected to the network.

Required results: You must choose an extremely reliable network topology with built-in redundancy.

Optional desired results: The initial setup costs and ongoing maintenance costs should be kept to a minimum.

Proposed solution: Implement a bus topology.

Which results does the proposed solution produce?

A. The proposed solution produces the required result and produces both of the optional desired results.

B. The proposed solution produces the required result and produces only one of the optional desired results.

C. The proposed solution produces the required result but does not produce any of the optional desired results.

D. The proposed solution does not produce the required result.

To maximize your chances of getting a scenario-type question correct, you must examine the required and optional results one step at a time to determine whether the proposed solution has generated either type of result. This process can be time-consuming because you have to determine whether each action in the proposed solution fulfills any of the requirements.

I recommend using your scratch paper to write out each required and optional result, and then put a check mark next to each requirement that's met by the proposed solution. After reviewing the list of results, refer back to your scratch paper. You can see at a glance how many of the optional desired results have been met.

If the required result is not met, you're finished with that question. You don't need to determine optional results if the required result isn't met.

Have a Plan in Mind to Avoid Running Out of Time

Most test-takers tackle the Microsoft exams in one of two ways:

- ✔ They spend the majority of their allotted time on a thorough first pass through all the questions and then do a quick double-check of their answers after they've completed the entire exam, or
- ✔ They make a quick pass through all the questions first, with the intent of returning later to examine more closely and reconsider each answer they weren't absolutely sure of.

I prefer to spend most of my time on the first pass, concentrating closely on each question as I go. Besides, after I've finished answering all the questions, I'm usually so excited to be done that I really don't feel like digging into another review of the questions.

A single pass through the previous TCP/IP exam, *Internetworking with Microsoft TCP/IP on Microsoft Windows NT 3.51,* took up almost all the allotted time. With the Windows NT 4.0 exam, you should have enough time to read through each question two or three times before answering, and not feel rushed. The TCP/IP on Windows NT 4.0 exam has fewer complicated subnetting questions, and the scenario-based questions are easier to evaluate. (In the previous version of the exam, you had to rate a proposed solution based upon whether it was a great solution, a solution that worked but was not desirable, or a solution that simply didn't work.)

If you find yourself spending more than three to four minutes on one question, you should note the question and return to it later. You'll probably have the answer to that question narrowed down to one of two choices, so simply jot down the question number and the letters of the possible answers on your scratch paper. Then, when you return to the question, you can pick up right where you left off.

Because you may not have enough time to review every question, make note of those questions that stumped you the first time around. Another question you encounter down the road may jolt your memory or provide a clue to answering an earlier question.

Some test-takers say that you should never change any answers while going through your test on the second pass; others say it's okay to change your mind the second time through. Arguments exist for both sides:

✔ You'll be more relaxed and have more time to think on your second pass-through. Therefore, you're more likely to come up with the correct answer.

✔ You may fool yourself into thinking you're being tricked, and change a perfectly correct answer to be incorrect. Trusting your first choice usually proves wise.

The experts say that you should change an answer only if you're absolutely sure that your original response was incorrect. Your initial instincts are usually right on track.

How Much Time Should You Spend Studying?

When figuring out the amount of time you should spend preparing for the exam, you must first assess your current skill level. The more you already know about TCP/IP, the less time you need to get up to speed.

Do keep in mind how much time you have every day to devote to studying. A beginning TCP/IP student should be able to pass the exam after three weeks of study with a couple hours of homework each weeknight and a few more hours on the weekends. You may want to extend your study period to one month if you feel uncomfortable with some of the material you need to know. Then again, you can spend weeks preparing for the exam and not be ready if you're studying inefficiently. By focusing on the exam topics presented in this book, you can make the best use of your study time — and have more time left for sleeping, eating, and your other favorite pursuits.

If TCP/IP is new to you, it may be helpful to read through this book once to get a general understanding of the concepts presented here. You can then go back and reread the chapters in order to focus on each exam objective. Along the way, take notes on anything you think is important. I guarantee you'll end up poring over those notes in the parking lot just before you head into the exam center.

With all the techno-terms and acronyms that must be memorized, learning TCP/IP is almost like studying a foreign language. Try the old flash-card technique your schoolteachers used. Write out the term or acronym on one side of a card, and the definition on the other. I guarantee that this time-tested study aid makes it easier to memorize that alphabet soup of TCP/IP acronyms.

Some Final Tips and Advice

How you prepare for the TCP/IP exam depends on your current skill level, the amount of material you have to study, and the amount of time you plan to devote to passing the exam. No matter what plan of action you choose, you can benefit from the following strategies.

You're looking for the Microsoft solution

The TCP/IP exam tests your knowledge of planning, configuring, and trouble-shooting networks by using Microsoft solutions. Therefore, if you've narrowed down an answer to one of two possible choices, ask yourself: "Which answer is the *Microsoft* answer?" This approach may sound silly until you remember you're taking a Microsoft test on a Microsoft product.

Use this book to determine what is and isn't tested

In each chapter of this book, I tell you the number of questions you can expect to see on a given topic. The coverage of topics in this book, by and large, parallels the exam in terms of what is and isn't emphasized. (Loads of information on TCP/IP is floating around out there, most of which won't be tested.) I made every effort to eliminate unnecessary material (in terms of the exam), which saves you some study time and reduces the amount of information you have to remember.

Practice using the tables in each chapter

You're allowed to use a calculator during the exam, although some folks say you shouldn't use one unless you have to. You can't bring your own calculator to the test, but you can use the calculator on the Windows desktop. If you have the subnetting tables from Chapter 6 memorized, you may not even need a calculator. If you do choose to use one, spend some time using it on practice questions so that you can calculate answers quickly.

Opt for the practice exam

You have the option of taking a practice test before your real exam begins, which many test-takers recommend. Taking the practice exam doesn't subtract time from your actual exam; the time for the actual exam begins when the first real exam question is asked. Some people take the practice exam *not* to get warmed up, but to buy a few minutes before the test begins to write out the subnetting tables they have crammed away in their heads. If you skip the practice test while the clock is running in order to scratch out the tables, consider it time well spent. I used my tables to answer at least five questions and shaved the time it took me to answer the questions in half!

Registering for the Exam

So, are you ready to schedule your test? Some people schedule a week or two ahead of time; others wait until a few days before. The exam fee is $100, but it's well worth every penny when you pass!

You can register for the exam by contacting either of the following two companies:

- ✔ Sylvan Prometric at 1-800-755-EXAM, or you can register online at www.sylvanprometric.com/testingcandidates/register/reg.asp

- ✔ Virtual University Enterprises at 1-888-837-8618, or at their Web site www.vue.com

Test Results on the Spot

The exam program stops automatically when your time is up. Your test is graded right then and there. The results are displayed on the computer screen and printed out for you. Your test coordinator notarizes the printout or gives you an ID number for verification, and there you have it — your official *Internetworking with Microsoft TCP/IP on Microsoft Windows NT 4.0* report card.

Chapter 2
A TCP/IP Primer

*T*he exam for internetworking on Windows NT 3.51 was notorious for being one of the most challenging tests offered by Microsoft. The newer version, *Internetworking with Microsoft TCP/IP on Microsoft Windows NT 4.0*, although not as difficult as its predecessor, nevertheless requires you to know many TCP/IP-related skills, such as subnetting, name resolution, and troubleshooting.

If you don't have years of experience working with TCP/IP or Internet technologies, or if you're just rusty on the subject, you need to get up to speed in a hurry — and this chapter can help you do just that. This chapter covers the basics of the TCP/IP protocol, the Internet, and related technologies and introduces the numerous protocols and their functions in the TCP/IP suite.

More Than Just Good Manners: The TCP/IP Protocols

The Internet is based on the Transmission Control Protocol/Internet Protocol (TCP/IP for short), which is actually a complex suite of many different protocol "modules." TCP/IP is the glue that holds the Internet together. You can think of it as the language that every computer on the Internet speaks — whether it's a PC, a Mac, a UNIX system, or a giant mainframe computer. The TCP/IP protocol enables millions of computers worldwide to communicate with each other. If your computer isn't configured with the TCP/IP protocol, then you're living in a cold and lonely world.

TCP/IP is not the smallest, fastest, or easiest-to-configure protocol out there, but it is the most common. And, Microsoft puts its own little twist on TCP/IP. It has created some additional features that take advantage of the Microsoft operating system. Knowing "the Microsoft way" is to your advantage, so this book offers whole chapters devoted to each of the Microsoft enhancements, including the Dynamic Host Configuration Protocol (DHCP) and the Windows Internet Name Service (WINS).

You may be wondering how to install TCP/IP on Windows NT. You can install it when you first install Windows NT, or you can install it later. Just open the Network window from the Control Panel, click the Protocols tab, and then click Add. Select TCP/IP Protocol from the list shown in the Select Network Protocol dialog box and click OK.

This chapter contains plenty of acronyms (as does the entire book, for that matter). Some of the acronyms aren't important for the test, while others are vital, so I tell you which ones you definitely need to memorize. For example, you should definitely memorize the acronyms for the various protocols, and you may want to have at least a passing acquaintance with the acronyms listed in Table 2-1. The list tells you what those letters stand for and provides a brief definition of each term.

Table 2-1   A Guide to TCP/IP Acronyms and Their Meanings

Acronym	What It Stands For	What It Means
ARP	Address Resolution Protocol	A protocol used to determine the hardware address from the IP address of the destination computer.
DHCP	Dynamic Host Configuration Protocol	A protocol that enables a computer to obtain an IP address and other information from the DHCP server during booting.
DNS	Domain Name Service	Translates host names into IP addresses. One example of a host name is microsoft.com.
DOD	The Department of Defense model	A term sometimes used to describe the layers involved in the TCP/IP protocol.
FTP	File Transfer Protocol	A protocol used to transfer files between two computers; requires user authentication.
ICMP	Internet Control Message Protocol	A maintenance protocol used between two systems to share status and error information.

Acronym	What It Stands For	What It Means
InterNIC	Internet Network Information Center	Registers domain names and assigns valid IP addresses to users and companies on the Internet.
IP	Internet Protocol	One of the two main parts of the TCP/IP protocol. Delivers TCP and UDP packets across a network.
OSI	Open Systems Interconnect model	One of the oldest and most popular reference models. It was created in the late 1970s by the International Standards Organization (ISO).
RARP	Reverse Address Resolution	Required when a computer must Protocol determine an IP address when it already has a physical hardware address.
RFCs	Internet Request for Comments	A proposal presented by an individual or company to the Internet community to debate.
SMTP	Simple Mail Transfer Protocol	Protocol used to send and receive mail over the Internet.
SNMP	Simple Network Management Protocol	Protocol used for managing SNMP-compliant network devices, such as hubs and routers.
TCP	Transmission Control Protocol	A connection-oriented protocol that ensures the data from the source will arrive at the destination in the correct order.
TFTP	Trivial File Transfer Protocol	Similar to FTP, but doesn't require user authentication.
UDP	User Datagram Protocol	A protocol that's built for speedy transmissions and is mainly used for broadcasts. However, UDP can't guarantee that data will arrive in order, if the data arrives at all.
WAIS	Wide Area Information Server	A server that maintains an index of documents on hundreds of servers.

Make flash cards to help you memorize those TCP/IP acronyms and what they stand for. You may be asked what purpose a particular protocol serves, so knowing that information brings you one step closer to passing.

One of the most difficult challenges in preparing for a test as rigorous as an MSCE exam is pinpointing what you definitely need to study and what you can safely bypass. With that in mind, I suggest the following:

✔ **Make sure you know what each of the acronyms listed in this chapter stands for.** You may get hit with a question in which all the possible answers are nothing but acronyms.

✔ **Know the basic purpose of each protocol in the TCP/IP suite.** You won't have to answer an essay question on the complete inner workings of any one protocol, so don't spend every spare hour poring over textbooks on the TCP/IP protocol components. Just knowing the basics is fine.

✔ **Don't spend a lot of time studying the OSI model.** The model won't be covered in depth on the test, but studying it does provide a good understanding of networking concepts.

✔ **You don't need to worry about the Wide Area Information Server (WAIS), Gopher, or Archie being tested.**

✔ **Don't spend a lot of time on FTP or the World Wide Web.** You may receive a question or two on these topics, but don't expect anything too complicated. The exam tests your knowledge of TCP/IP, not the Internet. However, in case you get a question or two on either of these topics, the information in the rest of this chapter has you covered.

✔ **Know the basic purpose of every layer of TCP/IP model.** The section "How the Protocols Stack Up: The OSI and TCP/IP Reference Models" later in this chapter tells all.

TCP/IP and the File Transfer Protocol

You may end up with a number of exam questions that pertain to the *File Transfer Protocol (FTP),* and you can also count on seeing FTP mentioned elsewhere in this book. If you see a reference to FTP in an exam question, it may be there in an attempt to confuse you. For example, you may see a question such as the following:

> You are using an FTP utility to connect to a remote file server. You type in the name of the server and receive an error message saying that a connection can't be established. However, when you type in the IP address of the file server, a connection is made. What is the problem?

Even though the question refers to FTP, you aren't really dealing with an FTP problem. In this case, you need to ignore the references to FTP and concentrate on the problem of name resolution, which involves other protocols in the TCP/IP model. (Those protocols are covered in the section "TCP/IP Protocols," later in the chapter.)

You can use FTP to transfer files across the Internet or download information. FTP sites are everywhere on the Internet. You may not even realize that
you're downloading via FTP when you click a file from your Web browser.
Nevertheless, FTP is working in the background.

You can also use an FTP utility at the DOS-like command prompt to access
the many servers on the Internet. This method requires some practice,
however, because the FTP programs aren't terribly intuitive. Windows
comes with its own command-line FTP utility, shown in Figure 2-1.

```
Command Prompt - ftp                                          _ □ ×

C:\>ftp
ftp> open ftp.microsoft.com
Connected to ftp.microsoft.com.
220 ftp Microsoft FTP Service (Version 3.0).
User (ftp.microsoft.com:(none)): user cameron
331 Password required for user cameron.
Password:
530 User user cameron cannot log in.
Login failed.
ftp> user anonymous
331 Anonymous access allowed, send identity (e-mail name) as pass
Password:
230-This is FTP.MICROSOFT.COM
 230-Please see the dirmap.txt file for
 230-more information. An alternate
 230-location for Windows NT Service
 230-Packs is located at:
 230-ftp://198.105.232.37/fixes/
230 Anonymous user logged in.
ftp>
```

Figure 2-1:
The
Windows
Command
Prompt FTP
utility at
work.

If you have older computers in your organization that lack the horsepower
to run a Web browser, you can take advantage of the more efficient FTP
program that is included in Windows NT. Or you can find a shareware
graphical FTP program (like the one shown in Figure 2-2) that makes
connecting, navigating, and downloading files from FTP sites much easier.

The left side of the screen in Figure 2-2 shows the contents of the local hard
drive from which you can select files to upload. On the right side is the
remote computer that you are browsing. You can navigate through the
directories by clicking around as you normally would in Windows Explorer.

You can gain access to an FTP server in either of two ways: with a user name
and password, or anonymously. Remember the two ways of accessing an
FTP server for the exam because you may be presented with a scenario
involving security and FTP.

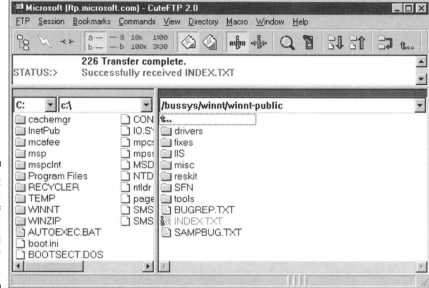

Figure 2-2:
The main
window of
CuteFTP, a
graphical
FTP
application.

If you can type in a user name and password to gain access, that means you have some sort of account on the server that can be used for authentication. For example, you have an account on a server if you're a paid member of the site, or if you bought some software over the Internet and the site you bought it from gave you a user name and password for downloading.

As shown in Figure 2-1, I first tried to log on to `ftp.microsoft.com` as `cameron`. I was rejected because no user account exists for `cameron` or because the server only accepts anonymous access. With an anonymous FTP server, you enter the user name `anonymous` and your e-mail address as the password.

Which method of authentication do you think is the most secure? You're probably thinking, "The one that requires a valid user name and password, because you must be a valid user to log on." In fact, the opposite is true. If a server requires your user name and password and that information is sent using clear text, a hacker can steal your credentials. With anonymous access, however, the server doesn't require users to send any confidential information over the Internet. If private information isn't sent, it can't be intercepted.

FTP information is sent in clear text, otherwise known as *unencrypted* text.

Although the Internet and the World Wide Web are held together by the TCP/IP protocol, it is highly unlikely that you will encounter questions on the exam about the World Wide Web. You are much more likely to see a question concerning the FTP protocol because FTP is a part of the TCP/IP model, whereas the WWW and Hypertext Transfer Protocol (HTTP) are not.

How the Protocols Stack Up: The OSI and TCP/IP Reference Models

In order to make sure that vendors and manufacturers are on the same page when it comes to designing compatible hardware and software, the industry uses *reference models* to describe the layers of each protocol. These models enable product creators to fashion their products to be compatible with all other products that follow the same model. The computer world would be in chaos if companies didn't adhere to these standards.

The many networking models and protocols are important to review for the TCP/IP exam — some more so than others. The reference models are composed of functional components — known as *layers* — and you need to be familiar with many of them for the exam. You may have gotten along so far without a thought about the TCP/IP or OSI models, and you may not remember all the layers in each of them a year from now, but for the day of your test, you need to know what they are.

If you've already taken the Microsoft Networking Essentials exam, you've seen plenty of information on the reference models while studying — and on the OSI model in particular. In that case, you can consider this section a refresher course. If you haven't taken the Networking Essentials exam, I suggest reviewing each reference model and its layers. I point out the items you need to memorize.

The OSI model

The *OSI model* is tested on the Networking Essentials exam but isn't a significant part of the Internetworking TCP/IP exam. I illustrate it here so that you can compare the OSI model of communication to the TCP/IP protocol suite, which may help to demystify TCP/IP.

The *Open Systems Interconnect (OSI)* model is one of the oldest and most popular reference models. It was created in the late 1970s by the International Standards Organization (ISO) to standardize protocols used for communication between computers. The OSI model maps to seven *layers* that perform specific tasks in cooperation with the layers immediately above and below (see Figure 2-3). After each layer performs its specific function, it hands off the task to the next layer. From bottom to top, the layers of the OSI model are as follows:

Physical layer

The physical layer is in charge of sending the data out onto the network, and the way this layer accomplishes that task depends on the electrical, mechanical, or optical interface used. In this layer, data is converted into binary format.

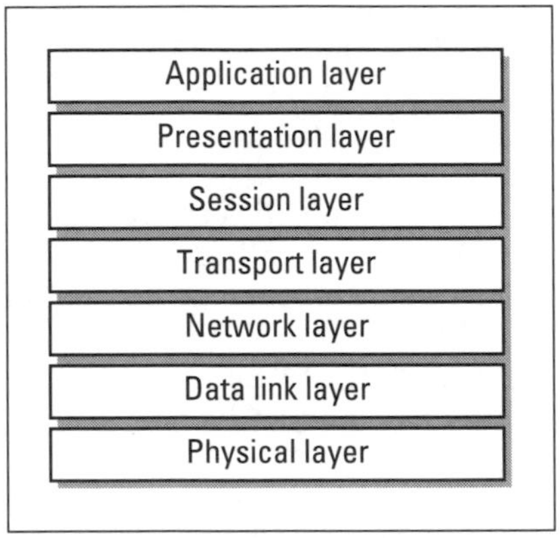

Figure 2-3:
The seven
layers of
the OSI
model.

Application layer
Presentation layer
Session layer
Transport layer
Network layer
Data link layer
Physical layer

Data link layer

The data link layer manages *frames,* which are small packets of data in binary format. This layer provides for error-free transfer of frames.

Network layer

The network layer determines the path that the frames will take. It hides all the complicated stuff, such as the route to the remote network, from the higher layers in the OSI model. A hardware device called a *router* works at the network level to route packets according to their addresses.

Transport layer

Like the data link layer, the transport layer deals with frames to enable efficient data transmission over a network. This layer breaks long messages into the correct frame size, which can vary depending on the way the message is to be transmitted.

Session layer

The session layer enables applications on different computers to start, use, and end a type of connection called a *session.* The layer ensures that the sending and receiving computers using the session know which computer is transmitting and for how long.

Presentation layer

The presentation layer translates information sent between two computers. Here the data is formatted and converted into a recognizable character code, if possible. It also uses *encryption* (the scrambling and unscrambling of data) for security reasons. Data can also be compressed at this level to reduce the amount of information being sent.

Application layer

The top layer of the OSI model and the final protocol in the communication process between two computers is the application layer. Communication between two computers really begins here at the application layer when information is sent through the layers and out to the destination computer. When the information arrives at the destination computer, each layer strips off the information required for its particular function and passes the leftovers up to the next layer. Eventually, the information arrives at the destination computer's application layer.

You can use a number of mnemonics to remember the order of the layers in the OSI model. One that I recommend to recall the order of the layers from top to bottom is **All People Seem To Need Data Processing.** Another memory aid that can help you remember the order from the bottom layer to the top is **Please Do Not Throw Sausage Pizza Away.** (As for the anchovy pizza, well, that's another matter.) You'll be surprised at how these seemingly silly mnemonics help you remember the OSI model layers at test time.

The TCP/IP model

The TCP/IP model was created almost a decade before the OSI model was developed. It describes the layers involved in the TCP/IP protocol. The TCP/IP reference model is divided into four conceptual layers, instead of seven like the OSI model. The functionality of the two models is roughly equivalent; the TCP/IP model simply packs it into fewer layers.

The TCP/IP model enables vendors and manufacturers to make their TCP/IP-based products, such as network interface cards, compatible with other TCP/IP-based products on the market. This model describes the purpose of each layer in the TCP/IP protocol and what service each layer provides to the layer directly above or below it. Figure 2-4 shows the layers that constitute the TCP/IP model. The following sections describe each layer, from bottom to top.

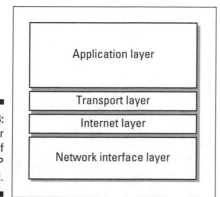

Figure 2-4:
The four layers of the TCP/IP model.

Network interface layer

The network interface layer is the bottom layer of the TCP/IP architecture, just above the hardware. This layer is responsible for putting frames of data onto the network and picking data off the network via the network adapter card.

Internet layer

The Internet layer determines the route from the source to the destination computer. The Internet layer must use the Internet Protocol (IP) to obtain the correct physical hardware address or *logical address,* such as an IP address or host name.

Transport layer

The transport layer provides communication between hosts and provides data delivery for the layer above it. Although it may sound like a duplicate of the Internet layer, the transport layer also provides frame sequencing, error detection, and acknowledgments.

The transport layer has two protocols that it can call upon, depending upon the nature of the application being used. If an application requires speed rather than guaranteed delivery, the transport layer uses the User Datagram Protocol. If data must arrive intact, then the Transmission Control Protocol is used.

Application layer

The application layer contains the most important protocols and applications. This is the layer that the user and the applications interact with. Applications that are run in this layer determine how the lower layers perform their jobs and, at the same time, require the services of the lower layers to function. For example, the `ping` command makes use of the Internet layer's ICMP protocol.

Despite its name, the application layer is not where your applications, such as those in Microsoft Office, run. This layer really should be called the "application helper layer" because it provides services that certain applications may need, such as printer support, resource sharing, and remote file access.

Protocol Components of the TCP/IP Model

A number of TCP/IP protocols are components of the TCP/IP model. These protocols are divided among the various layers of the TCP/IP architecture based on the tasks they perform. Some of the components of the TCP/IP model, such as FTP, are also utilities; other components, such as the DNS, are considered services. In the following sections of this chapter, I cover the most significant protocols in the TCP/IP suite.

The protocols listed here map to the layers in the TCP/IP communications model, with the exception of the network interface layer. No specific interface protocols are defined for the network interface layer. It is designed, rather, to adapt to a variety of network types.

Application layer protocols

The protocols that constitute the application layer are utilities or services that you interact with directly. These protocols are procedures that you actually have a hand in, as opposed to all those activities that go on behind the scenes, like breaking messages into frames and frames into binary digits. Every layer below the application layer does its job to get to this point.

Many of the protocols within the application layer are also utilities. Keep this point in mind, because you not only need to be aware of the placement of the protocols within the TCP/IP model and their functions, but also how to use each utility for monitoring and troubleshooting. This is especially true for FTP, ping, and Telnet. You may have to spend some hands-on time with these utilities to become familiar with their capabilities.

   ✔ **File Transfer Protocol (FTP)** is used to send and receive files or programs across a network or across the Internet. The computer from which you are receiving files must have FTP server software running.

   The concept of FTP is somewhat confusing because it is a protocol, but it is also an *application,* which can trick you on the exam. The context in which FTP is being used determines whether the question is referring to the FTP protocol or to the FTP application.

   ✔ The **Trivial File Transfer Protocol (TFTP)** won't show up on the exam, so don't fret over it. TFTP is much like FTP, with some differences that are, well, trivial. With TFTP, you use the User Datagram Protocol (UDP), which you can read about in the section "Transport layer protocols."

   ✔ **Simple Mail Transfer Protocol (SMTP)** is used to transfer e-mail over the Internet. Although it sounds like a very important protocol in the TCP/IP suite, it isn't covered in the exam and can be safely ignored (at least in regard to the exam).

   ✔ The **Domain Name Service (DNS)** is a TCP/IP solution to the problem of using text files to resolve host names to IP addresses. DNS turns up frequently during the exam. DNS and name resolution have apparently replaced custom subnetting as the major focal point for the new TCP/IP exam.

DNS is used heavily on the Internet, primarily to resolve a host name to an IP address. (An *IP address* is a 32-bit number that uniquely identifies a computer on the Internet or on a network.) DNS servers store host names and IP address information and are queried by clients. Therefore, if a client has just the name of your computer, the client can still reach you through a DNS server. (DNS is covered in much greater detail in Chapter 10.)

✔ The **Simple Network Management Protocol (SNMP)** is used for network administration. Through this protocol, you can get information on the status of devices on the network, which is helpful in troubleshooting and configuring the network. With Microsoft's SNMP implementation, you have only client software that can be queried by a central management computer; the management software is not included.

Judging from some newsgroup discussions I've seen, a number of people besides myself were surprised to see so many SNMP questions on the exam. One individual said that the SNMP questions were so ambiguous that he recommends focusing on this area so that you aren't confused during scenario questions on the exam. (Chapter 11 is devoted to the subject of SNMP services.)

✔ Ping is a utility that sends special packets (ICMP echo request and echo reply packets) to a destination. If the destination responds, you have a good TCP/IP connection. If it doesn't respond, you have some work to do to fix the problem.

The ping utility may appear on the troubleshooting portion of the exam. You won't be questioned on the ping utility itself, but it may be included as part of a statement of a problem. For example, a question may begin with, "You have just configured your workstation with TCP/IP. When you ping the computer, the following happens . . ."

✔ **Telnet** is a connectivity command that provides terminal emulation for PCs and computers. Telnet dates back to the mainframe days when clients were simple, "dumb" terminals that couldn't do much of anything independent of the mainframe. Dumb terminals typically accessed the powerful mainframe, which did all the processing.

I hadn't used Telnet in a long time until I bought a router and had to Telnet into it to configure it. Using Telnet isn't very difficult, so work with it once or twice and you should do just fine. By the way, it's free with Windows NT.

Transport layer protocols

Despite what they're called, the purpose of the transport layer protocols isn't really about transporting information. The transport layer provides frame sequencing, error detection, and acknowledgments. So you can say that these protocols deal with information that has already been transferred and now needs to be inspected.

On the other hand, you can also think of the transport layer as the place where information is processed before it's sent to the destination computer. The protocols in this layer make a difference in how the layer inspects the received data or prepares the data to be sent to the destination computer. The transport layer contains two protocols: the User Datagram Protocol and the Transmission Control Protocol.

✔ The **User Datagram Protocol (UDP)** is a protocol that, unfortunately, doesn't guarantee that the data transmitted between two computers will arrive in the order it was sent, if the data arrives at all. On the positive side, UDP is fast because it doesn't have to wait to receive acknowledgments from the destination computer before the next packet is sent out from the source computer.

Using UDP can be compared to mailing a letter. When you post the letter, you hope it arrives at its destination. In the meantime, you have no idea whether it's lost in the mail, in transit, or delivered. Only after you receive a reply do you know for sure that your letter arrived safely. The UDP protocol is used for broadcasting, which is not very common on the Internet. UDP is also used in place of TCP when the information doesn't require a reliable delivery, such as in broadcasting of real-time audio and video. Most Internet applications don't use UDP.

✔ The **Transmission Control Protocol (TCP)** is a protocol that ensures that data will arrive at its destination in the correct order. The TCP protocol is a reliable, connection-oriented protocol between two communicating devices for sending and receiving data. If data is received out of order, TCP reorders the information. If the expected information is not received, the destination computer makes another request for the information from the source computer.

You can think of the TCP protocol as being similar to a telephone conversation. A connection is made between the source and destination devices (this connection is sometimes referred to as a *virtual circuit*). Files or programs can be transferred between the two computers during the connection, just like a two-way phone conversation. After the information transfer is complete, both sides can agree to terminate the connection, or one computer can just drop the connection on its own.

Internet layer protocols

You should definitely know about the protocols within the Internet layer because they will be tested. These protocols get ample coverage in later chapters of this book, but for now you can make note of the material here before diving into the rest of the book.

✔ The **Internet Protocol (IP)** is at the core of the TCP/IP suite. The Internet Protocol is responsible for putting the source and destination IP addresses in the packet and then sending the packet to its destination. (You can find out in Chapter 6 how the IP address is used to route packets across the network.)

Although I saw many questions concerning IP on my exam, they primarily covered the IP address and not the protocol itself. This book provides a great deal of coverage on the IP address, which is a unique numeric address that is used to get packets of information to their destinations.

Basically, the IP address works like this: Source and destination IP addresses are "glued" to the beginning of packets of information so that the packets know where to go. The part of the packet that contains this information is called the packet *header*. The packet is then routed around the network, and other computers examine the header to determine whether the packet is intended for them.

✔ The **Internet Control Message Protocol (ICMP)** is essential to performing diagnostics and error reporting for the TCP/IP protocol suite. The ICMP protocol uses *echo request* and *echo reply packets,* which request a computer to respond to the packets and return updates on the route to the destination. The `ping` and `tracert` commands use this protocol. (`Tracert` is a cool utility, because after typing `tracert` at the command prompt, you can actually watch in real time as your packet zips around the world, passing through routers and possibly satellites.)

✔ **Address Resolution Protocol (ARP)** enables another computer to communicate with your computer with just the name of your computer and not necessarily its physical address.

If your computer needs to send information to another computer on the network, your computer first checks to see whether it has sent information to that computer before. Your computer looks in its cache for the destination computer's network card address. If it can't find the address there, ARP sends the IP address out on the network and asks all the computers on the network to examine the address to see whether it belongs to any of them.

If any computer on the network recognizes the IP address as its own, it sends its network card address back to ARP on your computer. When ARP knows the destination computer's network card address, it holds the address in cache for a few minutes. After that, ARP deletes the address in order to maintain an up-to-date list of computer addresses.

✔ **Reverse Address Resolution Protocol (RARP)** is exactly the opposite of ARP; when you supply the hardware address, RARP determines the proper IP address. Microsoft uses Dynamic Host Configuration Protocol (DHCP) instead of RARP for determining an IP address when given a hardware address, so you probably won't find RARP mentioned on the exam.

✔ **Dynamic Host Configuration Protocol (DHCP)** is used to configure TCP/IP on a workstation. This is the method of choice for medium- to large-sized Windows-based networks. Without DHCP, you have to visit every workstation personally and configure the complex TCP/IP protocol. (DHCP is covered in more depth in Chapter 8.)

✔ **Internet Group Management Protocol (IGMP)** provides routers on a local network with information on multicast groups of hosts. Multicasting is a technology that enables data to be routed to multiple hosts simultaneously.

Chapter 3

IP Address Resolution Protocol

● ●

In This Chapter

▶ Getting familiar with the hardware address

▶ Resolving a local address

▶ Resolving a remote address

▶ Viewing and consulting the ARP cache for speedier resolution

▶ Troubleshooting common ARP problems

● ●

*I*P Address Resolution Protocol (ARP) may be the least understood protocol in the TCP/IP suite. Nevertheless, this protocol has a very important purpose. ARP enables IP to determine the hardware address of a destination computer from a given IP address.

If you're less familiar with the address resolution protocol than the other TCP/IP protocols, you may find yourself guessing on some questions instead of answering them with confidence. To make sure that doesn't happen, this chapter explains the purpose of ARP and fills you in on the whole address resolution process, making you prepared to answer any challenging hardware address resolution questions that come your way.

For the exam, you should be familiar with a number of aspects of ARP, including the following areas, which are covered in this chapter:

✔ **Make sure you know the function of the ARP protocol.** Then those ARP questions will be a "gimme" and not a "gotcha."

✔ **Know why, where, and how ARP is brought in to resolve addresses.** Pay special attention to how ARP deals with determining the hardware address of a remote host.

✔ **Understand how the ARP cache is used to resolve addresses.** When is the cache consulted? How often are entries purged?

✔ **Understand what can go wrong during the address resolution process.** In this chapter, I show you the most common problems that occur and how to go about fixing them.

Quick Assessment

1 (True/False). Another name for the hardware address is the Ethernet address.

2 The most common term for the hardware address of a network card is the _____ address.

3 If an address is not in a cache, ARP sends a _____ to determine the address.

4 On a local network, ARP appends the destination's hardware address to the header of the _____.

5 If you are communicating with a remote host, ARP needs the hardware address of the _____ in order to send the packet.

6 The parameter to view the contents of the ARP cache is ARP _____.

7 An address in the ARP cache is purged after _____ minutes if not accessed again.

8 The _____ command is helpful for troubleshooting ARP addressing problems because you can view the computer's hardware address.

9 (True/False). You need ARP only when you are communicating with remote hosts.

Answers

1 *True.* Review "Identifying the hardware address."

2 *Media Access Control (MAC).* Review "Identifying the hardware address."

3 *Broadcast request.* Review "Resolution on a local network."

4 *Packet.* Review "Resolution on a local network."

5 *Router.* Review "Resolution on a remote network."

6 *-a or -g.* Review "Viewing the ARP cache."

7 *Two.* Review "Dynamic entries."

8 *ipconfig /all.* Review "Solving ARP problems with the ipconfig /all command."

9 *False.* Review "Exploring the IP Address Resolution Process."

Playing Post Office: The Hardware Address

In this section of the chapter, I explain how the whole routing process takes place. I start with an explanation of the hardware address, which is an essential element of Address Resolution Protocol.

Identifying the hardware address

When a network card is manufactured, it comes equipped with its own address that uniquely identifies the card on the network. The address contains six two-digit hexadecimal characters separated by hyphens — for example, 00-E0-98-00-DE-D5. You can view this address through the `ipconfig /all` command, which is covered in the section "Troubleshooting duplicate address and subnet problems with the Big Three commands," later in this chapter.

A number of terms are used interchangeably for the hardware address of network cards, and you should be familiar with all of them. The exam may refer to the hardware address by any of these terms:

- ✔ Network Interface Card (NIC) address
- ✔ Media Access Control (MAC) address
- ✔ Physical address
- ✔ Network Adapter card address
- ✔ Ethernet address

The most common term for the hardware address is the *MAC address*. Chapter 2 covers the OSI model Data-Link layer, which has two sublayers. One of those two sublayers is called the Media Access Control sublayer, which deals with the network interface card. Therefore, you'd be correct in calling the hardware address of the network interface card the MAC address.

Because hardware addresses are unique, they can be used as source and destination addresses throughout the world. However, those addresses can't be changed — they are hard-coded into the network adapter.

Going beyond the hardware address

You need more than the hardware address to deliver and receive packets on a TCP/IP network, for several reasons:

✔ A hardware address is difficult for humans to remember — much more so than an IP address.

✔ A hardware address doesn't clearly indicate which network the host is located on.

✔ A hardware address can't be modified, as an IP address can.

To bridge the gap between the hardware address and the rest of the TCP/IP protocol, your computer uses Address Resolution Protocol (ARP) to translate the hardware address to the easier-to-use IP address.

When a packet of data is being constructed on a source computer, the destination's hardware address must be included in the packet header. Therefore, ARP must ascertain this hardware address prior to sending the packet. The basic steps involved in the process are as follows:

1. TCP/IP attaches the destination's hardware address to the beginning (header) of each IP packet that is sent out.

2. TCP/IP also attaches the source of the packet so that the destination host can reply after the packet has been received and processed.

3. Each host on the network scans the header to determine whether the hardware address is its own.

   • If a packet isn't intended for a particular host, it doesn't process the packet.

   • If the destination hardware address in the packet header is the host's own, it sends the packet up through the other layers of the TCP/IP protocol for processing.

4. The subnet mask determines which network the destination host is on to ensure that the packet is sent to the correct network. (See Chapter 6 for more information on subnet masks.)

   • If the destination host is on the local network, the destination's hardware address is attached to the packet header. (Refer to the section, "Resolution on a local network," for more information on this process.)

   • If the destination host is on a remote network, the hardware address for the router used to reach the remote host is attached to the packet header. (Refer to the section, "Resolution on a remote network," for more information on this process.)

5. After the IP packet arrives at the network where the destination host is located, ARP completes the delivery by resolving the destination hardware address from the IP address.

Each step of the process I just listed is described in more detail later in this chapter.

Exploring the IP Address Resolution Process

You can expect to see at least one question on the exam about address resolution on both local and remote networks. This type of question can be tricky because you have to know the differences in how ARP works for both local and remote resolution. This section compares the two so that you can feel confident answering any ARP resolution questions that crop up. (The exam may have a number of questions on other types of resolution, such as name resolution with the Windows Internet Name Service [WINS] or resolution through a Domain Name Server [DNS]. See Chapters 9 and 10, respectively, for more information on WINS and DNS.)

Some address resolution preliminaries

You need to keep a few things in mind about the start of the address resolution process:

You must know another computer's hardware address before you can begin communicating with it. When you *resolve* an address, you are obtaining the hardware address of the destination computer from the host's IP address.

The first step of the ARP process occurs when a host initializes itself on the local network. At that point, a couple of events take place:

1. An ARP broadcast is sent out containing the IP and hardware address of the new host to determine whether another host is using the same IP address on the network.

2. If another host is using the IP address, TCP/IP fails to initialize on this new host.

ARP is used to resolve addresses on both local and remote networks. The following sections explain how ARP works on either network type.

Resolution on a local network

In Chapter 6, I explain that a destination host is considered *local* if the subnet mask indicates that the network portion of the host and destination IP addresses are the same. After the destination is judged to be local, ARP takes the IP address of the destination host and determines the hardware address that will be attached to the packet header while the packet is being constructed on the source host.

As you review the following steps to resolving a local IP address, keep in mind that in order to begin communicating between the two hosts, the IP address of the destination machine must be resolved to a hardware address. This resolution requires an ARP request and an ARP reply.

In these steps, I describe what happens in the ARP process when a host tries to communicate with another host on the local network (you can follow along with Figure 3-1, which illustrates the process):

1. The source machine uses the `ping` command to communicate with another host. (You can find more information on the `ping` command in Chapter 13.)

2. When it is determined that the IP address is on the local network, the ARP cache on the local machine is checked to see whether a mapping exists for the destination computer.

3. If no mapping is found in the local ARP cache, an ARP request is sent out.

    This request asks, in essence: "Who does this IP address belong to, and whoever you are, what is your hardware address?" Because the ARP request is a *broadcast,* it is received by every host on the network for processing. This broadcast is at the Data Link layer, not at the network layer or IP.

4. Each host checks the IP address of the data packet to determine whether it matches its own.

    If the address does not match, the request is ignored.

5. The destination host determines that the IP address being requested matches its IP address.

6. The ARP reply is sent directly back to the source host that originated the request with the destination's hardware address that was just found.

    The reply can be sent back because the source IP and hardware address are contained in the ARP request.

7. The ARP cache on both machines is updated with the correct mapping.

8. Communication is now established between the two hosts.

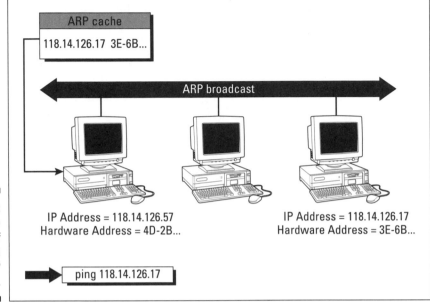

Figure 3-1:
The process of resolving a local IP address.

Resolution on a remote network

A remote network is one that needs to be reached through one or more routers. Whether a network is remote is determined by comparing the source IP address and subnet mask with the destination's IP address. After the destination host is determined to be remote, the ARP process on a remote network doesn't differ too much from the resolution process on a local network.

An important point to remember for the exam in regard to remote ARP is the special part that routers play in the resolution process. I had a question on my exam about the correct hardware address to use when routing to a remote network. Luckily, you have more than enough information in this section to answer any surprise questions on the ARP protocol as it applies to remote resolution.

ARP must resolve the address of each router that stands between the source and destination host. Each stop through a router is called a *hop*. When a packet is to be sent out on the network, the destination is not the final destination host's address, but the address of the next router that will continue to route the packet. ARP adds the hardware address for the first router by using the steps I describe in the preceding section of this chapter.

As you review the next set of steps to resolving a remote IP address, keep in mind that in order to begin communication between the two hosts, the IP address of the destination machine must be resolved to a hardware address. The destination machine may be the next router used to reach the host.

In the following steps, I describe what happens in the ARP process when a host tries to communicate with another host on a remote network (you can follow along with Figure 3-2, which illustrates the process):

1. The IP address of 118.14.33.187 is determined to be remote from the ping.

2. The routing table on the source machine is checked to see whether the known route exists to the network that the host is on.

    • If a route is found, the ARP cache is checked to see whether the mapping to the router that's needed to reach the destination host is in place.

    • If no route to the host is found, the source machine checks the ARP cache for the mapping of the default gateway for the second machine; in this example, the gateway is 118.14.126.1.

3. If a mapping is not found in the ARP cache for the default gateway, an ARP request is broadcast, *not* for the destination host, but for the hardware address of the default gateway.

4. The router responds to the ARP request with its hardware address.

5. The source host sends the final destination address to the router in order for the router to determine which network the destination host is on.

6. The router determines whether the IP address it was just given for the destination host is local or remote.

7. If the destination is remote, the router consults its own routing table for a route to the network the destination host is on. The router also has to consult its own ARP cache to determine the hardware address for the next router.

8. If the hardware address is not found in the cache, the router has to do a broadcast request.

    Now the packet can be sent to the next router.

9. The destination host receives the packet and replies back to the source host.

10. The source host was on a remote network, so the destination host has to consult its own routing table for a path back to the source. Again, ARP has to consult the local cache or broadcast a request for the hardware address of the router that will get the packet back to the source host.

11. The address mapping is not in the ARP cache, so a broadcast request has to be sent out on the network to determine the router's hardware address.

12. When the router's hardware address is found, the packet is well on its way back to the originating host.

    All the packet has to do now is travel through the router back to the network that the original host was on.

When a packet arrives at the router on the destination network, the hardware address is changed in the packet to the destination host's address. Many people think that the final destination host is always specified in the packet header, no matter what. This is wrong, however, and this assumption can cause you to miss a question on the exam.

ARP must determine the hardware address for the next router or the destination host (if the destination host is on the local network). The router also checks the contents of the ARP cache for the next destination, just as the source host did when the packet was being created.

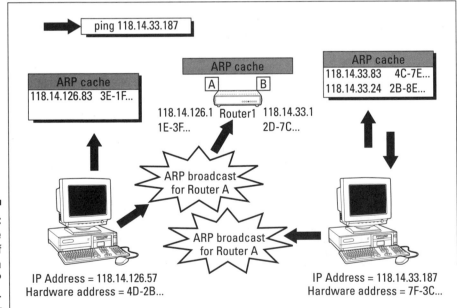

Figure 3-2:
The process of resolving a remote IP address.

Using the ARP Cache for Faster Resolution

The *ARP cache* is a table on a local machine containing all the address mappings that the ARP protocol has completed during the current session (the ARP cache may be the subject of an exam question). Every hardware address that has been determined from an IP address is stored in the ARP cache. Storing these addresses makes for increased performance if the same address needs to be resolved in the future.

When a TCP/IP packet is being prepared to be sent out on the network, the source and destination IP addresses are attached to the header of the packet. In addition to those addresses, ARP must provide the IP address resolution to the hardware address. After the hardware addresses are found, the source and destination hardware addresses are also appended to the packet.

The ARP cache is not permanent. The contents in the ARP cache are lost when the computer is turned off because the cache information is stored in temporary RAM.

Consulting the ARP cache for address resolution

The ARP cache can be consulted instead of using the normal address resolution method of broadcasting. Not only does the ARP cache decrease the time it takes to resolve an IP address, but it also decreases the amount of broadcast traffic on the network.

The ARP cache on the local machine is consulted when the destination's hardware address needs to be resolved. Most likely, the ARP cache doesn't contain the destination's hardware address, so ARP sends out a broadcast request to determine the destination's hardware address. After it is found, the address is added to the ARP cache, where it can be used again during subsequent address resolutions.

The ARP cache is consulted at several critical stages of the ARP process. These stages may be tested on the exam, so make sure you remember them. The ARP cache is consulted

　　✔ Before the packet is sent out.

　　✔ After the packet has arrived at a router.

　　✔ When the packet has arrived at the destination and the host must reply.

Each router along the way to a remote host consults its ARP cache for a mapping to the destination host or to the router that will send the packet to the destination host. This process can happen several times during the course of routing the packet to the destination.

When the destination host receives the packet, the host replies and consults the ARP cache again. The source IP and hardware address are encapsulated within the packet, but the destination host doesn't know the hardware addresses of the router that will get the packet back to the source host. Therefore, the ARP cache is consulted for the next router.

Viewing the ARP cache

You can view the contents of the ARP cache for your local host by using the ARP utility. Just enter the ARP command at the command prompt along with the -a parameter.

Additional *parameters* (which are simply switches used to change the output of a command) besides -a are associated with the ARP command. However, those parameters aren't tested on the exam, so I don't cover them in this section. Incidentally, the parameter -g works the same as -a — they both enable you to view the contents of the ARP cache.

Differentiating static and dynamic ARP entries

The entries you see in an ARP cache are either static or dynamic. Knowing the difference between the two types of entries may help you handle a tricky question or two.

Static entries

Static entries are added manually to the ARP cache by using the ARP command-line utility. I won't go into the details of adding these entries to the ARP cache because the exam won't go into it. Nevertheless, you should know why you need to add a static entry to the cache.

Hosts that are accessed frequently are likely candidates for static entries because the entries eliminate the need for ARP broadcasts on a regular basis. A static address remains in the ARP cache until you restart the computer or you manually delete the entry. The static entry also can be automatically updated if a different resolution is found for that entry.

Static entries are updated manually, as opposed to routing table entries, which are updated dynamically. You can manually update a static entry in the ARP cache if a newer address resolution is found for an entry that already exists in the ARP cache — one of the few times you can actually update a static entry in Windows NT. This is unlike the static entries in the routing table, which can't be updated dynamically if a new path is found.

During the exam, you may be presented with a scenario about updating static entries in the ARP cache. Look for an answer that says something like "the static entry will be dynamically updated." It's a good bet that's the right answer.

The steps in Lab 3-1 show you how to add a static ARP entry and how to view the contents of the ARP cache to determine whether the static entry has been added.

Lab 3-1   Adding and Viewing a Static ARP Cache Entry

1. **Open a command prompt window by selecting Start⇨Programs⇨ Command Prompt.**

2. **Enter the following command:**

```
arp -s 12.12.12.12 00-00-00-00-00-00
```

This command adds a static entry in the ARP cache for the IP address of 12.12.12.12, which will be mapped to the hardware address of 00-00-00-00-00-00.

3. **Enter the following command to verify that the static entry was added:**

```
arp -a
```

You see a listing of Internet addresses (IP address) to physical mappings similar to this:

```
Interface: 206.129.249.204 on Interface 2

   Internet Address        Physical Address        Type

   12.12.12.12             00-00-00-00-00-00        static

   206.129.249.193         00-c0-7b-7b-5a-f8        dynamic

   206.129.249.194         00-40-05-40-8a-d2        dynamic
```

4. Enter the following command to remove the static entry that was just added:

```
arp -d 12.12.12.12
```

This step removes the static entry from the ARP cache. Notice that you do not have to enter the physical address when removing the mapping.

Dynamic entries

Dynamic entries in the ARP cache remain in the ARP cache for about two minutes. If they aren't accessed within two minutes, they are purged from the ARP cache. If they are accessed within the two-minute period, they remain in the ARP cache for a total of ten minutes.

Whether or not the entry is accessed again, it is purged after the ten-minute period expires. If the contents of the ARP cache aren't purged on a regular basic, the list of IP-address-to-hardware-address entries grows very large and slows down querying of the ARP cache significantly.

Troubleshooting Common ARP Problems

Microsoft loves to include troubleshooting problems on its exams, so pay close attention to the following sections. The two most common address resolution problems involving ARP are problems with duplicate IP addresses and incorrect subnet masks.

Duplicate IP addresses

If you receive a question on the exam regarding duplicate IP addresses, keep in mind that the second host to come up on the network won't have TCP/IP initialized correctly. This second computer will simply refuse to function on the network. Other operating systems and devices are not so unforgiving. All in all, however, having ongoing communication problems when the network contains duplicate IP addresses is much worse than having one stalled computer.

Using the Dynamic Host Configuration Protocol (DHCP) greatly reduces the chance of duplicate IP addresses on the network. If you need to manually assign some IP addresses to important devices on the network, such as servers or printers, you can exclude these addresses from the pool of valid addresses on the DHCP server. (See Chapter 8 for more information on DHCP.)

Incorrect subnet masks

A subnet mask determines whether a host is local or remote. I guarantee that you will see a number of questions on the exam regarding the subnet mask; however, they may not be ARP-related (more information on subnet masks in Chapter 6). An incorrect subnet mask can cause an ARP request broadcast to search continually for a host. Continual broadcasting decreases performance on the network because every host has to receive and process each broadcast message to determine whether the message is intended for it.

Troubleshooting duplicate address and subnet problems with the Big Three commands

If you have either duplicate address or subnet problems, a few troubleshooting techniques are advised. Exam questions dealing with ARP problems may include those techniques, which make use of the following three commands: ipconfig /all, ARP, and ping.

Solving ARP problems with the ipconfig /all command

The ipconfig /all command displays all the important TCP/IP-related information needed to verify a problem. This command can determine whether a problem is related to the ARP process. You can also use this command to determine the destination IP and hardware address for static mappings of the ARP cache.

The following is an example of ipconfig /all command output:

```
Windows NT IP Configuration
Host Name . . . . . . . . . . :
        cbrandon.capstonetechnology.com
DNS Servers . . . . . . . . :
Node Type . . . . . . . . . : Hybrid
NetBIOS Scope ID. . . . . . :
IP Routing Enabled. . . . . : No
WINS Proxy Enabled. . . . . : No
NetBIOS Resolution Uses DNS : No

Ethernet adapter LECARD5:
Description . . . . . . . . : PCMCIA Ethernet Card
Physical Address. . . . . . : 00-E0-98-00-AA-D5
DHCP Enabled. . . . . . . . : Yes
```

(continued)

(continued)

```
IP Address. . . . . . . . . : 198.113.21.248
Subnet Mask . . . . . . . . : 255.255.255.0
Default Gateway . . . . . . : 198.113.21.1
DHCP Server . . . . . . . . : 198.113.21.23
Primary WINS Server . . . . : 198.113.21.23
Secondary WINS Server . . . : 198.113.21.38
Lease Obtained. . . . . . . : Thursday, February 12, 1999
          5:19:13 PM
Lease Expires . . . . . . . : Sunday, February 15, 1999
          5:19:13 PM
Ethernet adapter NdisWan4:
Description . . . . . . . . : NdisWan Adapter
Physical Address. . . . . . : 00-00-00-00-00-00
DHCP Enabled. . . . . . . . : No
IP Address. . . . . . . . . : 0.0.0.0
Subnet Mask . . . . . . . . : 0.0.0.0
Default Gateway . . . . . . :
```

The `ipconfig /all` command is used for troubleshooting many other TCP/IP problems in addition to those for address resolution. You can use the command to determine which IP address a host is using and whether you manually configured your IP address or received the IP address via DHCP. If you're having addressing problems, you may want to verify that your IP address is unique on the network. (Be sure to check out Chapter 13 for more information on the `ipconfig /all` command.)

Solving ARP problems with the ARP -a command

The `ARP -a` command shows the contents of the ARP cache and is useful for determining which mappings are invalid. The following is an example of what you see when you enter `ARP -a` at the command prompt:

```
C:\>arp -a
Interface: 116.123.21.63
Internet Address      Physical Address     Type
116.123.21.60  00-4C-C0-3B-E6-6C    dynamic
116.123.21.49  2B-00-3F-D4-00-2A    dynamic
116.123.21.13  AA-00-04-00-EC-E7    static
116.123.21.112 E4-1B-00-DD-8C-3B    dynamic
116.123.21.93  3D-00-5B-EE-AC-5B    dynamic
```

Use the `ARP -a` command utility to add, modify, view, or delete entries in the ARP cache. If you're having trouble communicating and you've tried everything else, check the ARP cache for the correct IP-address-to-hardware-address mapping. You may also have to use the `ipconfig /all` command on the destination computer to determine its hardware address.

If you regularly communicate with the same few hosts, those hosts make good candidates for a static mapping. You can use the `ipconfig /all` command to gather the proper IP and hardware addresses, and then enter the static entry for the mapping by using the `ARP` command at the command prompt.

You may have to delete an entry in the ARP cache if the mapping is not correct. An incorrect entry causes the source host with the incorrect mapping to send packets to the incorrect hardware address of the destination host continually.

Solving ARP problems with the ping command

The `ping` command can be used to communicate with a destination host. What follows is an example of the most common use of the `ping` command — pinging a destination computer by its IP address to determine whether connectivity exists between the two computers. If connectivity exists, the destination computer replies, as it does in this example:

```
C:\>ping 187.21.135.33

Pinging 187.21.135.33 with 32 bytes of data:
Reply from 187.21.135.33: bytes=32 time<10ms TTL=128
Reply from 187.21.135.33: bytes=32 time<10ms TTL=128
Reply from 187.21.135.33: bytes=32 time<10ms TTL=128
Reply from 187.21.135.33: bytes=32 time<10ms TTL=128
```

The `ping` command is extremely useful for verifying connectivity between two hosts. You can use it with the utilities I describe in the preceding sections of this chapter to determine whether you have a physical network problem, an addressing problem, or a name resolution problem.

Prep Test

1 How many hexadecimal numbers are separated by hyphens in a network card hardware address?

A ○ 4

B ○ 5

C ○ 6

D ○ 8

2 A destination hardware address is not needed in which situation?

A ○ When the destination host is local.

B ○ When the destination host is remote.

C ○ When the destination host is a router.

D ○ The destination hardware address is always needed.

3 You are trying to communicate with another host. You enter the IP address of the destination. A mapping does not exist in the ARP cache for this host. What happens first in the ARP resolution process?

A ○ The ARP cache is consulted.

B ○ The IP address is checked with the subnet mask to determine whether the host is local or remote.

C ○ The route table is consulted.

D ○ An ARP broadcast is sent out on the network.

4 When an ARP request broadcasts an IP address, how does the host with a matching IP address send the hardware address information?

A ○ As a broadcast

B ○ As a broadcast to the source host

C ○ Directly to the source host

D ○ Directly to the source host, only if it resides on a remote network

5 You are sending information to a remote host. The IP address is determined to be remote, so the route table on the source host is consulted. An IP-address-to-hardware-address mapping is not found in the route table for the remote host. What happens next?

A ○ An ARP request is broadcast to determine the destination host's hardware address.

B ○ An ARP request is broadcast to determine the next router's hardware address.

C ○ The ARP cache is consulted for the next router's hardware address.

D ○ The ARP cache is consulted for the default gateway's hardware address.

6 You are sending a packet to a host on a remote network. This packet has to pass through two routers to reach the destination host. How many times is the ARP cache consulted before the packet reaches the host?

A ○ 1

B ○ 2

C ○ 3

D ○ 4

7 Why is the ARP cache consulted on the remote destination host when a packet is received?

A ○ The destination host has to determine the IP address from the hardware address for the host that was appended to the packet header.

B ○ The destination host has to determine the next router to send information back to the source host.

C ○ The hardware address for the source host specified in the packet header is no longer correct.

D ○ The ARP cache is not consulted when the packet is received.

8 You are having excessive broadcasting problems on your network. You have made sure that all the hardware is functioning correctly. What could be a possible cause of the problem?

A ○ An incorrect subnet mask

B ○ An incorrect route table

C ○ A duplicate IP address

D ○ An incorrect ARP hardware address mapping

9 You have added a few static entries to the ARP cache, and you now believe that you may have entered an incorrect mapping. What should you do to verify the problem?

A ○ Ping the destination host.

B ○ Use the ARP -v command to view the contents of the ARP cache.

C ○ Use the ipconfig /all command on the destination host to determine the proper address for mapping.

D ○ Delete the questionable ARP entry and let it be dynamically added to the ARP cache.

Answers

1 C. An example of a network card hardware address is 3E-00-8B-4C-00-2B — a group of six two-digit hexadecimal numbers separated by hyphens. *Review "Identifying the hardware address."*

2 D. The ARP protocol is required to ascertain the destination host's hardware address every time a packet is being constructed. Therefore, the hardware address of the destination computer must be appended to the packet header. *Review "Going beyond the hardware address."*

3 B. This is the first step in the process. If the host is determined to be local, the ARP cache is consulted. If the host is determined to be remote, the route table is consulted. *Review "Some address resolution preliminaries."*

4 C. This is the case when the host with the matching IP address is found on the network. *Review "Resolution on a local network."*

5 D. If the route table doesn't indicate a path to the network that the destination host is on, the packet is sent to the default gateway. Therefore, the hardware address of the default gateway has to be determined. *Review "Resolution on a remote network."*

6 C. The ARP cache is first consulted on the source machine. For each router in line to the host, the ARP cache is consulted. Therefore, the ARP cache is consulted three times. *Review "Resolution on a remote network."*

7 B. Because the source host is now remote, the hardware address of the next router has to be determined, just as the hardware address of the first router was needed by the source host in order to route the packet to the destination. *Review "Resolution on a remote network."*

8 A. The source host continues to broadcast because it can't determine whether the destination is on a local or remote network. *Review "Incorrect subnet masks."*

9 C. Although the `ping` command tests for connectivity between the two stations, it may not use the correct-IP-address-to-hardware-address mapping. The `ipconfig /all` command on the destination host gives you accurate information in which to add the correct static mapping in the ARP cache. *Review "Solving ARP problems with the ipconfig /all command."*

Chapter 4

Host Name Resolution

● ●

In This Chapter

▶ Becoming familiar with the host name concept

▶ Understanding the host name resolution methods

▶ Troubleshooting using host name resolution methods

● ●

*H*ost name resolution constitutes a significant portion of the TCP/IP exam. The exam covers host name resolution even more extensively than it covers subnetting, which comprised the bulk of the old *Internetworking TCP/IP on Windows NT 3.51* exam.

Some unlucky test-takers have been surprised by (rather than prepared for) the amount and depth of the host name resolution questions, and suffered for it. *You,* on the other hand, should be ready to answer just about any exam question on host name resolution after reading this chapter. To help prepare you for the exam, I suggest boning up on the following topics:

✔ What a host name is and how it is combined with a domain name to create the Fully Qualified Domain Name.

✔ The order of the steps in the host name resolution process. You may be asked which step will be tried next by TCP/IP in order to resolve the host name.

✔ What can go wrong during the host name resolution process. Sections of this chapter describe the steps in the resolution process and offer tips for troubleshooting.

The following pages provide an overview of the host name resolution methods, the order in which they are used, and the problems associated with host name resolution.

Quick Assessment

1 A host name can match the computer's _____ name, but doesn't necessarily have to.

2 In a properly configured _____ file, the host name always corresponds to an IP address.

3 (True/False). A Fully Resolved Domain Name is formed by adding the host name to the domain name.

4 The _____ command displays the name of the local host.

5 (True/False). Parsing the HOSTS file is the first step of the host name resolution process.

6 One of the steps in the host name resolution process is to check the _____ name cache.

7 (True/False). The HOSTS file is located in the `<systemroot>` `\system32\drivers\etc` directory.

8 A Domain Name Service (DNS) server resolves _____ to IP addresses.

9 (True/False). If another method hasn't yet resolved the host name, a p-node broadcast is sent out on the local network.

10 (True/False). Check the Use LMHOSTS for Host Name Resolution box to enable LMHOSTS lookup.

11 A common error when using the _____ file is not using case-sensitive naming.

12 LMHOSTS is the predecessor to _____.

Answers

1 *Machine* or *NetBIOS.* Review "What's in a Name? Host Name Basics."

2 *HOSTS.* Review "What's in a Name? Host Name Basics."

3 *False.* Review "What's in a Name? Host Name Basics."

4 *HOSTNAME.* Review "Configuring Host Names."

5 *False.* Review "Examining the Host Name Resolution Process."

6 *NetBIOS.* Review "Examining the Host Name Resolution Process."

7 *True.* Review "Locating the HOSTS file."

8 *Host names.* Review "Domain Name Service (DNS) and host name resolution."

9 *False.* Review "Broadcasting and host name resolution."

10 *False.* Review "Enabling the LMHOSTS file."

11 *HOSTS.* Review "What's in a Name? Host Name Basics."

12 *WINS.* Review "Understanding the LMHOSTS file."

What's in a Name? Host Name Basics

Even if you have been working with host names and the TCP/IP protocol for some time, as far as the exam goes, you'll probably want to brush up on a few pointers for using host names in a Windows-based environment.

Host names provide a method of assigning an alias to a computer so that the user doesn't have to remember lengthy, number-filled host addresses. When you use a friendly host name, such as `cbrandon` to identify your computer, the host name has to be resolved to an IP address, which then has to be resolved to a hardware address.

First, in order to fully grasp the concept of a host name as it applies to a TCP/IP-based environment, it helps to keep the following guidelines in mind:

- ✓ The host name uniquely identifies computers on a network. The host name doesn't have to match a computer's NetBIOS name, although it can. You can also use multiple names to reference a host.

- ✓ The host name can be used in place of the IP address when using TCP/IP utilities.

- ✓ A host name is a user-friendly alias associated with a computer that makes it easier for users to remember an address. A host name is much easier to recall than a 32-bit IP address or a 48-bit hardware address.

- ✓ A host name can still be used to reference a host when the corresponding IP address has changed.

- ✓ A host name can contain up to 256 characters, including any combination of the following: the letters *a* through *z* and *A* through *Z,* the numerals 0 through 9, the hyphen (-), and the period (.). If any invalid characters are used, these characters are mapped to a hyphen. For example, the host name `c_brandon` is invalid, so the underscore character is mapped to a hyphen, as such: `c-brandon`.

- ✓ The host name always corresponds to an IP address in a HOSTS file or on a dynamic name server, such as a Windows Internet Name Service (WINS), or a Domain Name Service (DNS) server.

The terms *Domain Name Server, Domain Name System,* and *Domain Name Service* are all variations on the full spelling of the *DNS* acronym. Be aware that you may see DNS used interchangeably to mean any one of the three in some other books and reference materials. In this book, however, when I refer to DNS, I mean the *Domain Name Service,* which is what it stands for on the exam. (Chapter 10 covers DNS in depth, but DNS also warrants some coverage here as it applies to host name resolution.)

When I use the term *domain* in this chapter, I'm referring to the DNS domain, not to the Windows NT domain.

A DNS domain name (for example, `microsoft.com`) is conventionally entered in all lowercase letters, although a DNS domain name can be entered in mixed-case characters. DNS domain names and HOSTS files are not case-sensitive. (HOSTS files for some products, such as UNIX, are case-sensitive. But Microsoft HOSTS files, which are covered on the exam, are not case-sensitive.)

The DNS acts as a database for resolving host names to IP addresses. DNS is the primary means of resolving host and domain names on the Internet and can also be used for host name resolution on a local intranet. DNS uses a *Fully Qualified Domain Name (FQDN)* to uniquely identify a host on the domain (a *domain* is a logical, as opposed to physical, grouping of TCP/IP hosts).

The FQDN is formed by adding the host name, such as `sapphire`, to the domain name. If the domain name was `capstonetechnology.com`, the resulting FQDN would be `sapphire.capstonetechnology.com`. Notice the periods that separate the host name from the domain name and the domain name from the domain type.

Subdomains can also exist under the root domain — for example, `sapphire.engineering.capstonetechnology.com`. Again, periods are used to separate the host from the subdomain and the subdomain from the root domain.

Configuring Host Names

When it comes to implementation of name resolution, Microsoft wants to make sure that you know how and where to configure the host and domain names in its operating system. A question on the exam may ask you which button or tab you should select to configure a host name.

You should know that Windows NT uses the machine name (also called the NetBIOS name) as the default name for the host. As I indicate earlier in this chapter, invalid characters (including underscores) are mapped to the hyphen (-) and should not be used. The NetBIOS name, which is, by default, all uppercase, is transformed to the lowercase equivalent for the host name.

In Windows NT 4.0, host names are set in the Network dialog box of the Control Panel, as follows:

    1. Click the Protocols tab.

2. Select the desired TCP/IP protocol on the Protocols page.

3. Click the Properties button.

The Microsoft TCP/IP Properties dialog box appears. Clicking the DNS tab gives you the DNS properties page, which you can see in Figure 4-1.

Many of the elements of the TCP/IP Properties dialog box are explained further in Chapter 10. In Figure 4-1, you can see that in Windows NT 4.0, the DNS host name and domain name need to be specified (see the text boxes at the top of the figure).

As an alternative to using the Network dialog box under the Control Panel for viewing the current settings, you can use the HOSTNAME and IPCONFIG / ALL command-line utilities.

Issuing the HOSTNAME command at the command prompt displays the name of the local host. (This name is identical to the host name seen in Figure 4-1.) The HOSTNAME utility enables you to view only the current host name.

The IPCONFIG /ALL command is very useful for determining TCP/IP information. When this command is entered, you see the host name represented as a Fully Qualified Domain Name (FQDN), with the host name appended to the domain name. As with the HOSTNAME command, you cannot modify any values presented through the command in regard to the host name or the FQDN; the values are read-only.

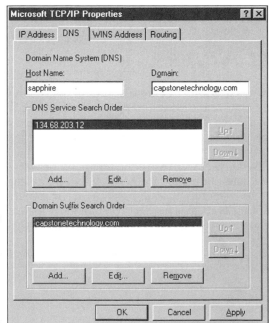

Figure 4-1:
The DNS page in the TCP/IP Properties dialog box.

Examining the Host Name Resolution Process

Many people, including myself, were surprised to see so many host name resolution questions on the exam. I had prepared for plenty of subnetting questions, but I felt uncomfortable with the amount and depth of name resolution questions. The rest of this chapter ensures that you walk into the testing center feeling confident that you can tackle any question on name resolution.

Host name resolution is the process of resolving the destination host name to an IP address. It can be accomplished in any number of ways, as I soon describe. A host continues to search for a destination IP address until the host name is resolved. A number of sources are searched, and the searching is done in a specific order.

The order in which the sources are searched is extremely important to know for the exam. You are likely to receive a host name resolution question that gives you the name of one source and then asks you to name the next source, such as the WINS or DNS server, to be queried for the destination's host name. This process can be quite lengthy because seven possible sources, from text files to servers, can be searched. The sources and the order in which they are searched are as follows:

1. The computer checks its local name to determine whether it is the destination host.

2. The local HOSTS file is consulted.

3. A DNS server, if specified, is queried multiple times. Multiple DNS servers are specified in the DNS Service Search Order (found in the TCP/IP Properties dialog box under Network in the Control Panel) in the event that the previous DNS server could not resolve the host name.

4. The local host checks its own NetBIOS cache for the name of the destination host.

5. A WINS server is queried, if specified, to see whether a NetBIOS name exists for the destination host.

6. The source host uses b-node broadcasts to see whether the destination host responds.

7. The local LMHOSTS file is consulted for a matching NetBIOS name.

   After any one of the various sources resolves the destination host name, the name resolution process ends.

The *first* IP address that is found is used to communicate with the destination host, which can cause problems. If the HOSTS or LMHOSTS files are outdated, the incorrect mapping continues to be used. This situation happens when you are renaming a host or changing its IP address and forget to update one of the static text files with the new mapping. So for the exam, you need to remember that the first source is used to resolve the host name, whether or not the host name is correct.

The situation I just described is a likely candidate for a host name resolution troubleshooting question on the exam. For example, you may be presented with a problem in which one IP address is not correct, but another one is. You are then asked to say which IP address is used first. After you have the resolution order memorized, questions such as this one should be no problem for you.

If none of the sources contain the correct mapping for the destination host name, the following error message is generated:

```
Bad IP address hostname
```

This message doesn't mean you can't communicate with the host. It just means you can't communicate using the host name. You have to use the IP address, which bypasses all host name resolution processes.

Try using this very helpful mnemonic device for memorizing the order in which sources are queried in the host name resolution process: *L*et's *H*ave *D*inner *N*ext *W*hen *B*aby *L*eaves.

> *L*et's = The source host's *local name* is checked to make sure that it isn't the destination.

> *H*ave = The *HOSTS* file is consulted on the local machine.

> *D*inner = A *DNS* server is queried.

> *N*ext = The *NetBIOS* name cache on the local machine is consulted.

> *W*hen = A *WINS* server is queried.

> *B*aby = Broadcasts, or *b-node broadcasts,* are used on the local network to try to reach the destination host.

> *L*eaves = The *LMHOSTS* file is consulted on the local machine.

Methods for resolving host names

Host names can be resolved in a number of ways on the network, and all those methods are very likely to be on the exam. Some of those methods, such as the standard resolution methods, were in existence years before Windows NT, and some were introduced by Microsoft to support Windows-based machines. They're all capable of resolving the host name to an IP address.

Standard resolution

A few name resolution methods are common for many different computer
platforms, such as UNIX and Macintosh, as well as for Windows-based
computers. Those methods include

  ✔ Local host name

  ✔ HOSTS file

  ✔ DNS, if enabled

These standard methods are the first ones used by the TCP/IP protocol in
the host name resolution process. If the host name is not resolved using one
of these three methods, then the methods in the specific resolution process,
which are listed next, try to resolve the host name.

Specific resolution

In addition to supporting the standard methods of host name resolution,
Windows NT supports more resolution methods that are Microsoft-specific,
such as the use of the NetBIOS name cache and the LMHOSTS file. For the
most part, non-Windows clients such as a UNIX machine can't use these
methods. However, some exceptions to this rule exist, such as the WINS
server proxy, which can forward requests from non-Windows clients to the
WINS server.

Because these methods are unique to Microsoft, you can guarantee that
they are thoroughly tested on the exam:

  ✔ NetBIOS name cache

  ✔ NetBIOS name server, if enabled (WINS)

  ✔ NetBIOS broadcast

  ✔ LMHOSTS file, if enabled

The standard name resolution methods, combined with the Microsoft-
specific resolution methods, make up the complete name resolution process. In general, the standard resolution methods are tried first to resolve a
host name before the specific resolution methods are used.

Trying the standard methods first makes sense because the standard
methods apply to clients whether they are Microsoft machines or not. If a
name is not resolved using the standard methods, the process continues
with the Microsoft-specific methods until the host name is resolved or an
error message is generated. (The following sections of this chapter describe
each step of the resolution process in the order in which the source host
attempts to resolve the host name to an IP address.)

Determining whether the local host and source host are the same

The first step of the host name resolution process, and probably the simplest, is checking the name of the local host to determine whether the source host and the destination host are the same. A host name in Windows NT is specified in the DNS host name section of the TCP/IP Properties dialog box. A host name does not have to be the NetBIOS machine name; however, the host name defaults to the NetBIOS name when Windows NT TCP/IP is installed.

If the destination host name is the same as the source host, you don't need to continue with the name resolution process. However, the local host name is rarely the same as the destination name, so the process usually moves on to the next step.

Understanding the HOSTS file

The HOSTS file is one of the most complex components of the host name resolution process. You can expect to see a number of questions on the HOSTS file, including those that ask for the proper syntax and where the syntax lies in the host name resolution process. (In Chapter 9, I tell you how to format a HOSTS file so that you can see how it compares with configuring an LMHOSTS file.)

A *HOSTS file* is a text file that contains the host-name-to-IP-address mappings. The entries in the HOSTS file start with an IP address and are followed by one or more host names that map to that particular IP address. The following is an example of a HOSTS file entry:

```
127.33.102.200        RUBY
```

The HOSTS file is the predecessor to DNS, which uses a large, central database of host names. DNS has become the preferred tool for name resolution because you need to add, modify, and delete mappings in only one place — the DNS database. A lot of work is involved in creating and maintaining a functional HOSTS file for each client. Not only must the entries be technically accurate, but they must also remain up to date for all computers on a network. This can become a sizable task on a large network, so DNS was created to ease the workload. I talk about DNS in the resolution process in the section "Domain Name Service (DNS) and host name resolution," later in this chapter.

Locating the HOSTS file

On the exam, don't rule out the possibility of being asked where the HOSTS file resides on the local computer. The HOSTS file is located in the `<systemroot>\system32\drivers\etc` directory. A sample HOSTS file included with Windows NT called `HOSTS.SAM` has been provided for you to view, which also has instructions on how to use the HOSTS file.

Because the HOSTS file contains text entries, you can use any text editor to view and modify it. Be sure to save the file *without* an extension; for example, do not save the file as `HOSTS.TXT`.

Parsing the HOSTS file

Lab 4-1 demonstrates what happens when a HOSTS file is parsed as part of the name resolution process. *Parsing* the HOSTS file refers to the process by which the TCP/IP protocol progresses line by line through the HOSTS file searching for a match for the host name. If no entry exists for the host name, the TCP/IP protocol continues with the next step in the host name resolution process.

Lab 4-1   Parsing the HOSTS File

1. **You can open the HOSTS file by either double-clicking the filename or by opening it from Notepad. The file is located in the** `<systemroot>\system32\drivers\etc` **directory**.

   If you choose the first method listed in Step 1, Windows NT doesn't know what application to use to open a file of that type. You have to specify a text editor, such as Notepad, in order to open it.

2. **Read through the comments provided at the beginning of the file.**

3. **At the line in the text file that contains the mapping for the local host** (127.0.0.1 localhost)**, change the name of** localhost **to** testhost.

4. **Open a command prompt window by choosing Start➪Programs➪ Command Prompt or by clicking Run from the Start menu and typing the command** cmd.

5. ping **the name** testhost **by entering** ping testhost.

   You see a reply from the loopback address of 127.0.0.1 under the command you just entered, which maps to the testhost name in the HOSTS file.

6. **Close the command prompt window.**

7. **Change the host name back to** localhost **by reopening the HOSTS file and finding the line that you previously changed.**

   The original line should appear as 127.0.0.1 localhost.

Solving common HOSTS file problems

Take the time to memorize the following HOSTS file problems and their solutions for the exam. They can provide the answers to some complicated scenario-based questions.

If you receive a `Bad IP address hostname` message, any number of things may be wrong:

- ✔ **The HOSTS file is not in the correct directory.** Make sure it's in the `<systemroot>\system32\drivers\etc` directory.

- ✔ **The HOSTS file is not using the correct format.** Make sure the IP address is listed first, with at least one space between the host name and IP address. Make sure comments are not listed to the left of mappings.

- ✔ **The HOSTS file may be corrupt.** Make sure it's *not* saved to a text file format (`HOSTS.TXT`). If it is, you can resave the file without an extension.

- ✔ **An incorrect or duplicate mapping may be present.** Make sure the correct host mapping is listed first.

- ✔ **An entry may be misspelled.**

Domain Name Service (DNS) and host name resolution

Domain Name Service (DNS) is an important part of the *Internetworking TCP/IP on Windows NT 4.0* exam. Although DNS is covered in depth in Chapter 10, I bring it up here as it relates specifically to the name resolution process.

If an IP address for the host name is not found after the HOSTS file is consulted on the local machine, a DNS server is queried for an IP address that corresponds with the host name. Being able to query the DNS server depends upon whether DNS has been configured for the host. A Windows NT client must have at least one server specified under DNS Service Search Order in the DNS Properties dialog box found under Network in the Control Panel. The DNS Service Search Order specifies the DNS servers to use for host name resolution.

At the time of this writing, the DNS database is still not dynamic; entries must be manually entered into the database by using DNS Manager in the Administrative Tools (Common) program group. Microsoft is working on improving this situation because manually updating entries is especially difficult on very large networks. A dynamic database would not need an administrator to add, modify, and delete mappings; that would be done by the clients when they register their names with the DNS server, as clients do now with the Windows Internet Name Service (WINS) server.

The DNS database conforms to a tree structure with the root domain at the top of the tree hierarchy. This structure is referred to as the *domain name space*. The top level of the domain space consists of the DNS components, such as `.com` for a commercial organization, `.mil` for a branch of the military, and so on. The *root domain name* of a commercial organization appears as `microsoft.com`, for example.

Because the domain name space is hierarchical, it can contain many subdomains below the root domain that represent certain divisions of an organization. However, subdomains are not required. For example, you can have just the domain name of `guitarsgalore.com` for a guitar retailer, and skip having any subdivisions, such as `repair.guitarsgalore.com` for the store's repair department. Hosts can be present in the top-level domain, or they can exist within their respective subdomains, as illustrated in the following sample DNS database hierarchy:

Organization:	`microsoft.com`	
Subdomains:	`engineering`	`sales`
Network ID:	`130.45.22`	`130.45.32`
Hosts:	`eng1`	`sales1`
IP addresses:	`130.45.22.118`	`130.45.32.61`

In this example, the fully qualified domain name (FQDN) `eng1.engineering.microsoft.com` is created for the host in the `engineering` subdomain. The FQDN is resolved from right to left, as follows:

1. When a request is made to the DNS server for this particular destination host, the highest level of the domain hierarchy, `microsoft.com`, is queried.

2. After `microsoft.com` is found, a server on the next level of the `engineering` domain is found and queried, as indicated in the FQDN.

   The host name `eng1` is found on that level.

3. The IP address of the `eng1` host is found in the engineering sub-domain's DNS database and returned to the source host that initiated the name resolution request.

4. The DNS server is queried multiple times.

   If the DNS server doesn't respond, any other DNS servers specified in the DNS Service Search Order are queried next for the IP address that corresponds with the host name.

Network Basic Input/Output System (NetBIOS) and host name resolution

The Network Basic Input/Output System (NetBIOS) is an often misunderstood feature of TCP/IP technology that may catch you off guard during the test if you're not familiar with it. NetBIOS questions pop up all over the exam, but not as you may think. You probably won't be tested on NetBIOS directly; nevertheless, NetBIOS is essential for establishing TCP/IP sessions. Chapter 5 is devoted to the subject of NetBIOS, but for now, you need to understand how NetBIOS applies to host name resolution.

A name such as `eng1`, shown in the example in the previous section of this chapter, is a NetBIOS name. When you map a network drive, you are also using NetBIOS. For example, examine the following command. This line is a NetBIOS command that uses the server name `fileserver` and the directory share name `files`:

```
net use R: \\fileserver\files
```

A host name that needs to be resolved is most likely the machine name of the destination computer, which is also a NetBIOS name. This name is set by default when Windows NT is installed, but it can be changed. Non-Windows clients do not use NetBIOS names, so the step of checking to see whether the host name is the same as the machine name is not required for non-Windows clients.

Viewing the NetBIOS name cache

The *NetBIOS name cache* consists of all the NetBIOS names that have been resolved by your computer from the time the computer was initialized. This cache is intended to limit the use of broadcasts on the network and decrease the need to query a WINS server repeatedly for name resolution. You can view this cache from a command prompt by using the `nbtstat` utility, which involves running the NetBIOS software interface over TCP/IP (NBT) statistics. (*NBT* stands for *NetBIOS over TCP/IP.*)

Lab 4-2 demonstrates the use of the NetBIOS name cache and explains how to view the data contained within it.

Lab 4-2   Viewing Data in the NetBIOS Name Cache

1. **Open a command prompt window by choosing Start⇨Programs⇨ Command Prompt or by clicking Run from the Start menu and entering the command** cmd.

2. **Enter the** nbtstat -n **command at the command prompt.**

   The following is an example of the output of the nbtstat -n command on my machine:

   ```
   Node IpAddress: [0.0.0.0] Scope Id: []
            NetBIOS Local Name Table
      Name                                    Type
          Status
   ------------------------------------------------------
          HAL-LCBRANDON  <03>  UNIQUE      Registered
   CBRANDON        <03>  UNIQUE      Registered
   ```

   In the example in this step, the machine I am logged on to is HAL-LCBRANDON, and I am logged on as CBRANDON.

3. **Enter the** nbtstat -c **command at the command prompt.**

   The results of entering this command are NetBIOS names of other hosts that have been resolved on your machine. You may see a large number of names in the cache if you're on a network, or you may see no names if you are not on a network. The following is an example of the output from the nbtstat -c command on my computer:

   ```
   Node IpAddress: [198.113.221.109] Scope Id: []
            NetBIOS Remote Cache Name Table
   Name              Type  Host       Address
            Life[sec]---------------------------------
            -------
   HAL-WLAMUNDSON1   <20>  UNIQUE     198.113.221.226
            600
   HAL_SDATABASE2    <20>  UNIQUE     198.113.221.45
            60
   HAL-WDRYENDER1    <20>  UNIQUE     198.113.221.236
            600
   HAL-WJSIMMONS     <20>  UNIQUE     198.113.221.220
            600
   HAL-WH2FSCALE     <20>  UNIQUE     198.113.221.80
            600
   HAL-PFINANCE      <20>  UNIQUE     198.113.221.34
            600
   HAL_SSECFIBER1    <20>  UNIQUE     198.113.221.25
            60
   HAL_SSUPPORT1     <20>  UNIQUE     198.113.221.28
            60
   ```

What was just listed are all the entries from other hosts at this point in time; these entries change quickly as the computer continues to resolve more names. The cache changes often as old names are purged and new names are added. Each entry has a Life column that tells you how long the entry has to live (in seconds) before it is purged from the cache.

A fellow test-taker in an MCSE newsgroup made the following observation after finishing the *Internetworking TCP/IP on Windows NT 4.0* exam: "You must be clear on the difference between a NetBIOS name and host name. That distinction is very important." A host name is used in the TCP/IP environment and can identify a host on any type of TCP/IP machine, such as a UNIX, mainframe, or Windows-based machine. NetBIOS names are used strictly in Windows-based environments. And there you have the primary difference between the two.

Making connections using host name resolution versus NetBIOS

Host name resolution is used for resolving TCP/IP resources that do not connect through a NetBIOS interface. One example of a TCP/IP connection to a non-NetBIOS resource is the interface between a Web browser and the Internet. The browser enables a user to navigate through the Web, which is used by more than just Windows machines. This process requires using host names and not NetBIOS names. The Internet comprises more than just Microsoft machines; therefore, you can't use NetBIOS names for Internet connections.

TCP/IP utilities such as ping and Telnet do not connect to other hosts using NetBIOS. In order to make a connection, ping and Telnet use *sockets,* which are IP addresses used in conjunction with port numbers. An example of a socket is 103.58.221.12(132) — the IP address is 103.58.221.12 and the port number is 132.

NetBIOS is used, for example, when a client connects through a Windows-related resource, such as File Explorer, to another Windows computer. A Windows NT network employs NetBIOS in a number of situations: mapping a network drive, browsing in a Network Neighborhood, or connecting to a printer. All of these situations use NetBIOS names to make the connection, and these NetBIOS names need to be registered and resolved on the network by a WINS server or an LMHOSTS file.

Windows Internet Name Service (WINS) and host name resolution

If each of the previous host name resolution methods has been tried — checking the source host's *local name,* consulting the *HOSTS* file on the local machine, querying the *DNS* server, and consulting the *NetBIOS* name cache on the local machine — without successfully resolving the host name, the *WINS* server is then queried for the host name. (See Chapter 9 for more on WINS, the Windows Internet Name Service.)

WINS is a Microsoft Windows-based technology that maps NetBIOS computer names to their IP addresses. A WINS server can be queried in the same way that a Domain Name Service (DNS) server is queried to return an IP address mapping for a host name. (See Chapter 10 for more on DNS.)

Also like DNS, a client must be configured to use WINS before it can take advantage of the service. Configuring a client to use WINS is done in the Network window of the Control Panel. Select the desired TCP/IP protocol, click the Properties button, and then click the WINS Address tab. Figure 4-2 shows the page that appears next. Here you can specify WINS properties.

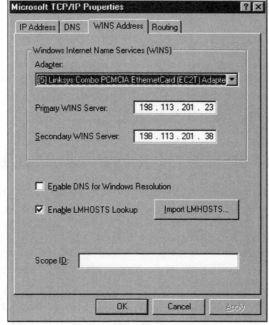

Figure 4-2:
You can use this page to specify WINS Address properties.

The WINS server has the advantage over any of the other name resolution methods by having many more IP address to host name resolutions because its primary purpose is to register NetBIOS information when a computer initializes on the network. That's pretty much all the WINS server does — resolve NetBIOS names to IP addresses — so it always has numerous mappings in its cache. If a WINS server is queried, it can reply with the correct IP address for the given host name if one exists in its dynamic database.

The components that are available in the WINS system for host name resolution include the following:

- ✔ The WINS server, which fields name registration requests from WINS clients and registers the clients' names and IP addresses.

- ✔ The WINS client, which registers its name with the WINS server when it initializes on the network. The WINS client also queries the WINS server to resolve host name addresses.

- ✔ The WINS proxy, which resolves names for non-WINS clients on the network by forwarding requests to the WINS server. The WINS proxy doesn't maintain its own database, but it does keep a cache of recently resolved host names.

A primary WINS server can be specified by entering the IP address of the server (refer to Figure 4-2). A secondary WINS server can be specified in the event that the primary WINS server is unavailable. (This is important to remember for the exam.) These are the two most important client configurations in WINS.

If the primary WINS server doesn't reply to the client's name resolution request on the first attempt, the host tries two more times, and then continues on to the secondary WINS server if one is specified in the client's TCP/IP Properties in the Control Panel. If none of the WINS servers respond, or if the requested name is not found, the client begins to broadcast, which is the next step in the host name resolution process.

Broadcasting and host name resolution

You are likely to see a question or two on broadcasting on the exam. You'll probably be asked about the various types of broadcasting and when broadcasting occurs in the host name resolution process. You also need to know that broadcasts are next in line when a WINS server, or any of the other previous methods used, fails to resolve the host name. (A few different methods of name resolution involve broadcasting, and those methods are covered in Chapter 5.)

Broadcasting is a method of NetBIOS name registration and resolution used on a local network. Broadcasts can resolve host names to IP addresses on the network, but not as efficiently as WINS and DNS, which are covered in previous sections of this chapter. Because broadcasting uses so much bandwidth on a network, it is less efficient than other name resolution methods and is therefore lower in the host name resolution order.

A broadcast (and, more specifically, a b-node broadcast) asks every machine on a local network whether it has a mapping for the requested host name. (B-node broadcasts are covered in more detail in Chapter 5.) The source host sends a maximum of three b-node broadcasts. If the destination host hears the broadcast, it then sends the appropriate IP-address-to-host-name mapping to the source host. However, this process is dependent on the host name being the same as the NetBIOS machine name.

Broadcasting has two significant disadvantages when compared with the other name resolution methods, such as WINS and DNS:

- ✔ Broadcasts can result in excess traffic on the network. All the hosts on the network have to examine the packet to determine whether it is destined for them. This process uses up computer resources.

 Having numerous hosts on the network broadcasting name registration and resolution information is not recommended. This practice slows down the network and increases user response times.

- ✔ Broadcasts do not cross routers, which means you are limited to the local network only. WINS, LMHOSTS, and DNS, on the other hand, can all cross routers.

 Broadcasts, by nature, do not and should not cross routers. Configuring a router to pass the b-node broadcasts to a remote network is possible, but that defeats the purpose of segmenting the network. Therefore, broadcasts are limited to hosts on the local network. You have to use a method other than broadcasting to reach a host on the opposite side of a router. This information can come in handy during the exam when you are presented with scenarios involving different methods of name resolution.

Understanding the LMHOSTS file

The *LMHOSTS file* is one of the static text files used for host name resolution. Parsing the LMHOSTS file is the final step in the host name resolution process. If an LMHOSTS file cannot resolve a host name, then nothing else can, and an error message appears on the source machine.

The LMHOSTS file accomplishes the same tasks as a WINS server. But whereas WINS servers are dynamic, an LMHOSTS file needs to be maintained by an administrator. The LMHOSTS file, much like the HOSTS file, contains static mappings. However, the difference is that an LMHOSTS file contains NetBIOS-name-to-IP-address mappings and a HOSTS file contains host-name-to-IP-address mappings. (Be careful not to get these two file types mixed up.)

Incidentally, grasping the concept of the LMHOSTS file is more time-consuming than absorbing the concept of the HOSTS file because it has features not present in a HOSTS file, such as the capability to parse files on remote computers and find domain controllers located on remote domains. Knowing this may not save you any time, but it is encouragement to understand the LMHOSTS file more fully, which you can do by reading Chapter 9.

Knowing how and where the resolution methods covered in this chapter (WINS, DNS, LMHOSTS, HOSTS, and the rest) are configured in Windows NT would be wise. A number of times in my test-taking experience, I've been asked which menu, tab, screen, or button is used to configure a setting. Try to spend some time playing around with the Windows NT user interface before taking the exam.

The following quick summary of the LMHOSTS file as it applies to the host name resolution process may come in handy for the test:

- ✔ The LMHOSTS file contains NetBIOS-name-to-IP-address mappings.
- ✔ The LMHOSTS file is a text file with no extension.
- ✔ The LMHOSTS file is located in the `<systemroot>\system32\drivers\etc` directory.
- ✔ In an LMHOSTS file, the IP address is to the left, followed by the NetBIOS name, with at least one space in between them.
- ✔ The LMHOSTS file is not case-sensitive. `RuBy` works the same as `RUBY`.
- ✔ LMHOSTS file comments are preceded with a pound (#) sign.
- ✔ A central LMHOSTS file can be used.

Enabling the LMHOSTS file

In order to use an LMHOSTS file, you must configure Windows NT to use it. Lucky for you, this is a simple process. Figure 4-3 illustrates where LMHOSTS is enabled in Windows NT. I have heard from test-takers that questions relating to this area are on the exam. Enabling LMHOSTS lookup is done in the WINS Address page of the Microsoft TCP/IP Properties dialog box in the Network window (see Figure 4-3).

LMHOSTS lookup is enabled by default in Windows NT. To disable LMHOSTS, simply deselect Enable LMHOSTS Lookup (see Figure 4-3). This is *not* recommended, however, because LMHOSTS serves as a backup if a WINS server fails.

Because the LMHOSTS file can become very large with all the mappings entered for every computer on your network (not to mention that it's very tedious to create), you have the option of importing an already-existing LMHOSTS file from another computer. Clicking the Import LMHOSTS button

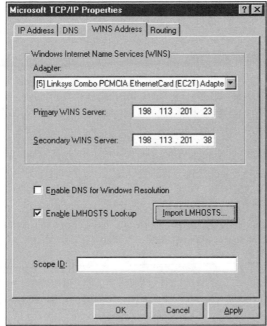

Figure 4-3:
You
configure
Windows
NT to
use the
LMHOSTS
file here.

on the WINS Address page enables you to browse for the LMHOSTS file that you have already configured on another computer. This can prove to be a great time-saver because an LMHOSTS file must be error-free in order to work correctly.

Locating the LMHOSTS file

The LMHOSTS file can be found in the same location as the HOSTS file: <systemroot>\system32\drivers\etc. You may be asked this location on the exam so it's definitely worth remembering. A sample LMHOSTS file called LMHOSTS.SAM is included in that directory to illustrate the proper usage and format of the file.

Comparing the LMHOSTS and HOSTS files

A number of similarities exist between the LMHOSTS and HOSTS files that you should remember for the exam:

- ✔ They are both text files.
- ✔ They are stored in the same directory.
- ✔ They do not have extensions associated with them.
- ✔ The IP address is listed first in both.

✔ The IP address and name must be separated with at least one space.

✔ The IP address must contain four octets, each separated by a period.

✔ Comments are prefaced with a # sign.

You must also remember some differences between HOSTS and LMHOSTS files. The most important (other than knowing exactly what each file is used for) is that a HOSTS file is case-sensitive, whereas an LMHOSTS file is not. This is a very important point and can cost you a question on the exam if you forget it. For example, if you have an entry of 143.13.87.211 raspberry and the name of the host is actually Raspberry, you will not be able to connect.

Using the LMHOSTS file

The LMHOSTS file, although declining in popularity by those favoring dynamic WINS, still has some advantages for name resolution. The following plusses make an LMHOSTS file a viable alternative or enhancement to WINS and present reasons why you'll see questions on LMHOSTS on the exam:

✔ It can be used to resolve host names on subnets without a WINS server.

✔ It can be used as a backup resolution method if a WINS server fails.

✔ It can be used in place of a WINS server for smaller networks.

✔ It will decrease the number of broadcasts required for name registration and resolution. Machines have to use broadcasts on the local network to register their names if a WINS server is not present.

✔ One central LMHOSTS file can be used for an entire network.

Solving common host name resolution problems with the LMHOSTS file

The problems that exist with the LMHOSTS file are the same as those that exist with the HOSTS file. (However, using the LMHOSTS file may introduce other complications that I talk about in Chapter 9.) Make sure that you know the most common LMHOSTS problems and their solutions for the exam.

The following information can provide the answers to complicated scenario-based questions involving the LMHOSTS file:

✔ **Problem:** The LMHOSTS file is not in the correct directory.

   Solution: Make sure it's in the <systemroot>\system32\drivers\etc directory.

✓ **Problem:** The LMHOSTS file is not in the correct format.

Solution: Make sure the IP address is listed first, with at least one space between the NetBIOS name and IP address. Make sure comments are not listed to the left of the mappings.

✓ **Problem:** The LMHOSTS file may be corrupt.

Solution: Make sure it's not saved to an improper format, such as a text file format (.txt, for example).

✓ **Problem:** An incorrect or duplicate mapping may be present.

Solution: Make sure the correct NetBIOS mapping is listed first.

✓ **Problem:** An entry is misspelled.

Solution: Verify the spelling of the host and correct the spelling in the HOSTS or LMHOSTS file.

Summing up the resolution process differences

After you compare HOSTS files with LMHOSTS files, DNS versus WINS, and host names versus NetBIOS names, Table 4-1 may help you sum up the differences in a nutshell.

Table 4-1	Host Name Resolution Methods and Their Functions
Method	*Function*
Host name	Uniquely identifies a TCP/IP host
HOSTS	Resolves host names to IP addresses through a static text file
DNS	The central source for resolving host names to IP addresses through a database
NetBIOS name	Uniquely identifies a Windows-based host
LMHOSTS	Resolves NetBIOS names to IP addresses through a static text file
DNS	Resolves NetBIOS names to IP addresses

Prep Test

1 You have entered the name of your DNS server in the Host Name portion of the DNS Configuration dialog box. You have also entered the domain for this particular DNS server in the Domain portion. What else must you do to enable DNS resolution on this computer?

A ○ Restart the computer.

B ○ Enter the IP address for the DNS server in the IP Address portion.

C ○ Enter a Domain Suffix Search Order.

D ○ Nothing. This configuration is invalid.

2 Which command shows the contents of NetBIOS name resolutions other than on your local machine?

A ○ nbtstat -S

B ○ nbtstat -s

C ○ nbtstat -c

D ○ nbtstat -C

3 The correct location for the LMHOSTS file on a Windows NT machine is

A ○ *<systemroot>*\drivers\system\

B ○ *<systemroot>*\system32\driver\etc

C ○ *<systemroot>*\system\drivers\etc

D ○ *<systemroot>*\system32\drivers\etc

4 Which source is checked next when the WINS server fails to resolve the host name to an IP address?

A ○ The LMHOSTS file

B ○ Broadcast

C ○ The HOSTS file

D ○ The NetBIOS name cache

5 Which source is checked next when the DNS server fails to resolve the host name to an IP address?

A ○ The NetBIOS name cache

B ○ The WINS server

C ○ The HOSTS file

D ○ The LMHOSTS file

6 You are trying to communicate with another Windows-based machine on the same network. You have not yet been able to receive a response when you `ping` the destination computer, even when trying the IP address and the host name. You can `ping` another computer on the same network and receive a reply. What should you check to determine the problem?

A ○ Verify that your host has DNS properly configured.

B ○ Verify that your host has WINS properly configured.

C ○ Verify that the destination host has a valid entry in the HOSTS file.

D ○ Verify that the destination host is functioning on the network.

7 How do you enable LMHOSTS lookup on a Windows NT 4.0 computer?

A ○ Check the box labeled Enable LMHOSTS Lookup for Host Resolution on the DNS page.

B ○ Check the box labeled Enable DNS for Windows Resolution on the WINS Address page.

C ○ Check the box labeled Enable LMHOSTS Lookup for Host Resolution on the WINS Address page.

D ○ Check the box for Enable LMHOSTS Lookup on the WINS Address page.

8 Which of the following is not a component of the WINS system?

A ○ WINS Relay Agent

B ○ WINS proxy

C ○ WINS server

D ○ WINS client

9 You have just finished installing an NT Server that also substitutes as your WINS server. However, you are not sure whether WINS has been configured correctly. You open a command prompt and `ping` a computer on the local network by host name, and you receive no response. You do, however, receive a response when you `ping` the IP address of the host. What is most likely the problem?

A ○ A mapping does not exist in the HOSTS file for the destination host.

B ○ You have configured your WINS server incorrectly on the server.

C ○ A mapping does not exist in the LMHOSTS file for the destination host.

D ○ You have configured WINS incorrectly on the source host.

10 Which is *not* a feature of the LMHOSTS file?

A ○ You can use just one LMHOSTS file for an entire network.

B ○ You can map multiple IP addresses to one NetBIOS name.

C ○ You can reach a host on another subnet.

D ○ It can decrease network traffic.

Answers

1 D. When specifying a DNS server to be used by the client, the DNS server's IP address is entered in the DNS Service Search Order portion of the DNS Properties dialog box. *Review "Domain Name Service (DNS) and host name resolution."*

2 C. Because the parameters used in the nbtstat command are case-sensitive, there is no parameter -C. Nbtstat -n displays the names that have been registered to the local host. *Review "Viewing the NetBIOS name cache."*

3 D. This is also the location for the HOSTS file. *Review "Locating the LMHOSTS file."*

4 B. Remember the mnemonic? The host sounds three b-node broadcasts on the local network, if the host name has not been resolved yet. *Review "Examining the Host Name Resolution Process."*

5 A. The NetBIOS name cache is the first of the Microsoft-specific host name resolution methods that are unique to Windows-based computers. *Review "Specific resolution."*

6 D. All the signs indicate that the destination host is not functioning or currently is not on the network. Pinging the destination host with both the IP address and host name and still receiving no reply is evidence of this. *Review "Solving common HOSTS file problems."*

7 D. This is the only configuration requirement needed to enable local LMHOSTS lookup, in addition to having the file in the correct location. *Review "Enabling the LMHOSTS file."*

8 A. The WINS server, proxy, and client are all components of the WINS system. There is a relay agent, but it is the DHCP Relay Agent, which has nothing to do with WINS. *Review "Windows Internet Name Service (WINS) and host name resolution."*

9 A. Because it's a TCP/IP utility, the ping command uses sockets and not NetBIOS, which means that name resolution problems using the ping command can be isolated to the HOSTS file or DNS. Make sure you have a correct mapping in the HOSTS file for the destination, or make sure DNS is configured correctly. *Review "Network Basic Input/Output System (NetBIOS) and host name resolution."*

10 B. Although you can map multiple NetBIOS names to one IP address, you cannot map multiple IP addresses to one NetBIOS name with the LMHOSTS file. *Review "Understanding the LMHOSTS file."*

Chapter 5

NetBIOS

In This Chapter

▶ Configuring NetBIOS names and service types

▶ Identifying the NetBIOS name resolution process

*T*he Network Basic Input/Output System (NetBIOS) is a critical component of a Windows-based network and a big part of the *Internetworking with TCP/IP on Windows NT 4.0* exam. In Chapter 4, I cover the topic of host names, including host name features and the host name resolution process. In this chapter, I discuss NetBIOS and the steps required to resolve a NetBIOS name to an IP address.

If you're armed with the following information (which is supplied in this chapter), you should be able to ace just about any question you encounter on NetBIOS and the NetBIOS name resolution process:

✔ A general understanding of NetBIOS, which is also extremely helpful in dealing with NetBIOS-related technologies, such as the Windows Internet Name Service and the LMHOSTS files (both of which are covered in Chapter 9).

✔ The three most common NetBIOS service types

✔ The NetBIOS name resolution order

✔ What each NetBIOS node type is used for

Quick Assessment

1 _____ total characters make up a NetBIOS name.

2 (True/False). The `net view` command displays the computer name, the domain name, and the current user.

3 The NetBIOS suffix for Server is _____.

4 You can view your own computer's settings for the computer name, domain name, and current user with the `net` _____ command.

5 (True/False). The first step in the NetBIOS name resolution process is the local broadcast.

6 The NetBIOS node type that can consult the LMHOSTS file if the first b-node broadcast is unsuccessful is the _____ b-node type.

7 (True/False). The hybrid node type uses broadcasts to resolve the name first and then resorts to p-node if an answer is not received.

8 The last step in the NetBIOS name resolution process is to query a _____.

9 A source host sends up to _____ b-node broadcasts to request a mapping for a particular host name from every machine on a local network.

10 Checking the local host name in the NetBIOS name resolution method is a _____ resolution method.

Answers

1 *16.* Review "Configuring NetBIOS Names."

2 *False.* Review "Net view."

3 *<20h>.* Review "The NetBIOS suffix."

4 *config.* Review "Net config."

5 *False.* Review "Recognizing the NetBIOS Name Resolution Methods."

6 *enhanced.* Review "NetBIOS over TCP/IP node types."

7 *False.* Review "NetBIOS over TCP/IP node types."

8 *DNS Server.* Review "Ordering of NetBIOS Name Resolution Methods."

9 *Three.* Review "Method 3: B-Node broadcasts."

10 *Specific.* Review "Specific NetBIOS name resolution."

The Ins and Outs of NetBIOS

Network Basic Input/Output System (NetBIOS) is a mystery to most administrators. No dialog box or window exists in which to configure it, it isn't a protocol in and of itself, and it isn't even part of the TCP/IP protocol. Nevertheless, NetBIOS works very closely with TCP/IP to establish sessions between computers and to enable applications to communicate over a network.

NetBIOS is an *Application Programming Interface (API).* Therefore, it's considered both a naming convention and a program interface. NetBIOS enables two-way conversations between hosts on a network. This type of connection, called a *session,* requires the communicating computers to have logical NetBIOS names in order to talk to each other.

NetBIOS can establish reliable connection-oriented data transfer. In a *connection-oriented data transfer,* the two computers are opening a session for the duration of the data transfer, as opposed to *connectionless-oriented data transfer,* in which the two computers do not need to maintain a session for communication. An example of a connectionless transfer is electronic mail — you do not need to establish a session with the destination computer to transfer mail.

NetBIOS is not a protocol, such as TCP/IP or IPX/SPX, but it requires the use of an underlying protocol in order to enable communication between machines. Therefore, NetBIOS is said to be *bound* to the protocol. In order to communicate, two computers must use the same protocol and have NetBIOS bound to that protocol. After NetBIOS is bound to the protocol, the hosts can send and receive requests to other computers. Protocols that NetBIOS supports include the following:

- TCP/IP
- NetBEUI
- IPX/SPX

Although you may only encounter one or two questions specifically related to NetBIOS names, many questions are NetBIOS-related. The following example test question illustrates how understanding NetBIOS naming can help you at exam time:

> You are mapping a drive to another server, and you receive a message that the requested server can't be found. What should you check first to rectify the situation?

To answer this question, consider the following: You know that NetBIOS names are specific to Windows-based computers. To map a drive, you need to use NetBIOS names to make the connection. Therefore, you can eliminate answers that reference the HOSTS file or Domain Name Service (DNS), which are used in resolving host names to IP addresses. (If you're unfamiliar with host name resolution, see Chapter 4.) You can then think about troubleshooting with the LMHOSTS file and Windows Internet Name Service (WINS) servers, which are used for resolving NetBIOS names to IP addresses. Without a basic understanding of NetBIOS naming, the answer to this question can slip right past you.

Configuring NetBIOS Names

In order to recognize a NetBIOS name when you see one in an exam question, you need to know how a NetBIOS name is constructed:

- ✔ The NetBIOS name consists of 15 characters, with a 16th hexadecimal character reserved to indicate the service type being used. (Service types are explained in the section "The NetBIOS suffix,"section later in this chapter.)

- ✔ If a NetBIOS name doesn't contain 15 characters, blank spaces fill the rest of the 15 character spaces, and the 16th character is added as usual.

- ✔ Although a NetBIOS name is usually written in uppercase characters, NetBIOS names are not case-sensitive.

Table 5-1 provides examples of the common NetBIOS naming standards used on most Windows-based networks. These are just examples, though, so you don't need to memorize this information for the exam.

Table 5-1 Examples of Common NetBIOS Naming Standards

Usage	Example
computer name	RUBY
server name	DATABASE1
domain name	CAPSTONE
user name	KHANSON
printer name	HP4ENGINEERING
shared directory name	PC_APPS

Commands using NetBIOS names

A number of important commands use NetBIOS names. You may be tested on some of the most common ones, including `net config`, `net view`, and `net use`, which are covered in the next sections. All the following commands use NetBIOS names.

Net config

You can view your own computer's settings for the computer name, domain name, and current user with the `net config` command. The following is example output from the `net config` command:

```
C:\>net config workstation

Computer name                        \\SFAIN
User name    SFain

Workstation active on
Software version                     Windows NT 4.0

Workstation domain                   CAPSTONE
Logon domain                         CAPSTONE

COM Open Timeout (sec)               3600
COM Send Count (byte)                16
COM Send Timeout (msec)              250
The command completed successfully.
```

With the `net config` command you can also specify a server, rather than a workstation, to use to view server statistics, as the first line of the following example illustrates:

```
Server Name                          \\RBALDUS
Server Comment
Software version                     Windows NT 4.0
Server hidden                        No
Maximum Logged On Users              10
Maximum open files per session       2048
Idle session time (min)              15
The command completed successfully.
```

You can see that the `net config server` command displays some additional server-related information, such as the maximum number of users and open files per session and the amount of time a workstation can be idle before it's disconnected.

Net view

Another useful tool for viewing NetBIOS information is the `net view` command. Again, the results consist entirely of NetBIOS names.

For the exam, keep in mind that the output from the `net view` command is similar to what you see when you browse the Network Neighborhood; however, you issue the `net view` command at the command prompt. You must also specify the domain you want to view.

An example of the output of the `net view` command follows:

```
Server Name            Remark
-----------------------------------------------------------------
                  -----------
\\DATABASE1     SQL Server
\\ENGINEERING          Engineering Server
\\SHIPPING1     Shipping File Server
\\PROXY1               Proxy Server
\\CAPSTONE      Main File Server

The command completed successfully.
```

Net use

The most popular of the NetBIOS commands is probably `net use`. You're likely to see a question on the exam covering its application. You use this command for mapping drives and printers, a task that creates a NetBIOS session using the NetBIOS names. The following example shows a `net use` command used to map a network drive:

```
C:\>net use S: \\SQLSERVER\BACKUP
The command completed successfully.
```

In this example, the `net use` command maps drive S to the BACKUP shared directory on the SQLSERVER server. A NetBIOS session begins when the matching server is found.

The NetBIOS suffix

The 16th character in the NetBIOS name is called the *suffix,* and it uniquely identifies the service type being used for the transmission. Table 5-2 lists the three most common NetBIOS suffixes that you are likely to encounter for the exam and the usage for each.

Table 5-2	The Most Widely Used NetBIOS Suffixes	
Suffix	*Name*	*Description*
<00h>	Workstation	Specifies messages from the Workstation service
<03h>	Messenger	Specifies messages from the Messenger service
<20h>	Server	Specifies messages from the Server service

Recognizing the NetBIOS Name Resolution Methods

Computers can't communicate with host names if they aren't resolved to IP addresses. Many different resolution methods are employed to resolve a host name. If one method is unsuccessful, the resolution request is passed to the next method.

Like host names, NetBIOS names must be resolved to IP addresses. The NetBIOS name resolution process also involves as many alternative methods as the host name resolution process. The standard resolution types are tried first, and if those methods fail, the specific Microsoft Windows-based resolution methods, which are unique to Windows-based networks, are used to resolve a NetBIOS name.

Figure 5-1 illustrates the order for resolving the NetBIOS name to an IP address. Using the example shown in the figure, if you're mapping a drive to the MSSQL share on the CAPSTONE server, which uses NetBIOS names, the resolution methods are tried in the NetBIOS name resolution order to resolve the NetBIOS name.

You need to memorize the NetBIOS resolution order for the exam. You stand an excellent chance of seeing an exam question that asks you to identify which resolution method is tried next when a given method is unsuccessful at resolving the NetBIOS name.

Because the NetBIOS and host name resolution processes are relatively similar, if you know the resolution process for host names you should have no trouble comprehending the resolution process for NetBIOS names on the exam. However, the NetBIOS name resolution process follows a different order than the host name resolution process.

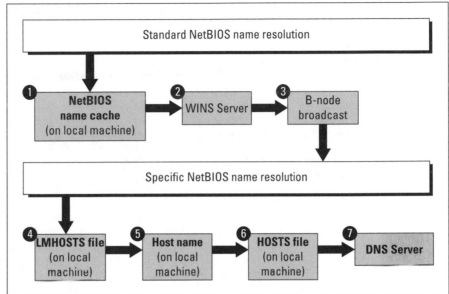

Figure 5-1:
The
NetBIOS
name
resolution
order.

Standard NetBIOS name resolution

The standard NetBIOS name resolution methods, in the order in which they are summoned to resolve a NetBIOS name, are as follows:

1. The NetBIOS name cache method (on the local machine)
2. The WINS server method
3. The b-node broadcast method

If these methods fail to resolve a NetBIOS name to an IP address, the specific NetBIOS resolution methods attempt to resolve the NetBIOS name. These name resolution methods, such as DNS and the HOSTS file, are explained in more depth in Chapter 4.

Specific NetBIOS name resolution

When the standard resolution methods fail to resolve a NetBIOS name, a number of additional methods are used, if they are enabled. If they're not enabled, they are skipped. Those additional methods are as follows, listed in the order in which they're tapped on the local machine to resolve the NetBIOS name:

1. The LMHOSTS file method (on the local machine)
2. The host name method (on the local machine)
3. The HOSTS file method (on the local machine)
4. The DNS server method

If you read Chapter 4, you may notice that the standard and specific NetBIOS name resolution methods are set up differently than the standard and specific host name resolution methods. For example, checking the local host name in the NetBIOS name resolution method is a *specific* resolution method, whereas checking the local host name in host name resolution is a *standard* resolution method.

Remember this: The standard resolution methods in NetBIOS name resolution are the specific resolution methods in host name resolution, and vice versa. The reason for this has to do with the fact that NetBIOS names are specific to Windows-based networks. In host name resolution, the standard types of resolution are used first because most clients, including Windows-based clients, use those methods. If none of those methods work, the specific Windows-based methods are used.

Because NetBIOS name resolution is mostly for Windows-based computers, it makes sense that the resolution methods are flip-flopped so that those methods that use NetBIOS names are tried before those that use host names.

NetBIOS over TCP/IP node types

Don't make the mistake of ignoring this section when studying for the exam. I encountered a question asking which NetBIOS node type should be used, and you stand a good chance of being asked the same thing.

You know now that the NetBIOS name resolution process uses methods such as LMHOSTS, WINS, and the NetBIOS name cache. However, a number of resolution types exist *within* NetBIOS broadcasts. The different ways you can configure the NetBIOS broadcasts can be thought of as "mini" name resolution methods within the larger NetBIOS name resolution process.

You can use any one of the following NetBIOS *node types,* which are the different types of broadcasts within the NetBIOS broadcast process, to configure the NetBIOS broadcasts:

- ✔ b-node
- ✔ p-node
- ✔ m-node
- ✔ h-node
- ✔ enhanced b-node
- ✔ Microsoft enhanced node

You don't need to memorize the order of the NetBIOS node types. However, you absolutely should memorize the characteristics of each method (which are described in the following sections). I haven't heard of any test-takers receiving questions on enhanced b-node or Microsoft enhanced node types, but you certainly should remember the four other node types.

b-node

A b-node broadcast is used to resolve and register NetBIOS names. It's a broadcast on the local network and normally doesn't cross routers. Broadcasts by nature must be processed by each computer on a network. They also eat up valuable bandwidth and therefore should be avoided. Other methods are preferred to b-node broadcasts.

p-node (peer-to-peer or point-to-point)

A p-node uses a WINS server to attempt to resolve a NetBIOS name. No broadcasts are used. A name resolution query is sent directly to the WINS server by means of the server's IP address. Remote hosts can then be reached across routers that b-node broadcasts can't cross. With this method, costly broadcasts are avoided; however, non-WINS clients are unable to query the WINS server. Additionally, if the WINS server fails, NetBIOS names can't be resolved, a catastrophe for Windows-based networks.

m-node (mixed)

An m-node combines the benefits of both p-node and b-node. The m-node type uses broadcasts first to resolve a name and then resorts to p-node if an answer isn't received. *Note:* This method doesn't reduce the number of broadcasts on the local network.

h-node (hybrid)

The most efficient node type is h-node, which is the reverse of m-node. The h-node method uses the WINS server for registration and resolution but switches to the less efficient b-node broadcast when a WINS server can't be contacted. The secondary WINS server is also tried, if the WINS client is configured to use one, before the broadcasting begins. Up to three b-node broadcasts are sent on the network in order to resolve the NetBIOS name. The h-node host switches back to the WINS server automatically when the primary WINS server becomes available again. H-node is the default for WINS clients.

Because the m-node and h-node modes are easy to confuse, you can bet that Microsoft takes advantage of the possible mix-up by testing you on them. I had a question on my exam that asked which of the node types query the NetBIOS name server first. (The answer is h-node.) Be prepared for questions like these regarding node types.

enhanced b-node

A Microsoft-based TCP/IP client can use enhanced b-node to consult a LMHOSTS file, if the first b-node broadcast is unsuccessful. LMHOSTS must be enabled in the Networking dialog box of the Control Panel in order for the LMHOSTS file to be parsed.

Microsoft enhanced node

The Microsoft enhanced node type makes use of LMHOSTS, WINS proxies, and TCP/IP sockets in addition to the standard node types. The Microsoft enhanced type is not as popular as the previously mentioned node types, and you're unlikely to find it on the exam.

Examining NetBIOS Name Registration

The way that NetBIOS names are registered on the network is important to remember for the exam. Although you won't receive as many questions about name registration as about name resolution, you can still expect to see a couple.

A NetBIOS computer on a network must have a unique NetBIOS name and one or more unique IP addresses. The process of name registration is what makes those names unique. Name registration can be implemented whether WINS is enabled on the client or not.

Registration when WINS is enabled

Name registration information is sent directly to the WINS server when WINS is enabled on the client. The information is then added to the database of NetBIOS clients. The WINS server is responsible for determining whether the computer name is unique to the database. The WINS server accepts or rejects the registration request based on its findings.

Certain conditions must exist for this process to work, and I strongly suggest that you memorize these conditions for the exam:

- ✔ If the WINS database contains a different IP address for the NetBIOS name that a computer is trying to register, the WINS server challenges the computer that already has that name to claim that name.

- ✔ If the NetBIOS name that is trying to be registered already exists in the WINS database, the WINS server rejects the new name registration request.

- ✔ If the NetBIOS name that a computer is trying to register doesn't exist in the WINS database, the WINS server accepts the new registration and adds the entry to the database.

Registration when WINS is not enabled

A client must send out on the local network a *name registration request* with its IP address and NetBIOS name when WINS is not enabled on the client because the non-WINS client can't directly query the WINS server. If a computer that already has the requested name exists on the network, that existing computer sends a *negative name registration response* back to the non-WINS computer. If the NetBIOS name doesn't exist on the network, the non-WINS computer can use this NetBIOS name and IP address.

The non-WINS computer is responsible for challenging attempts from other hosts to use its existing NetBIOS name or IP address when another host broadcasts a name registration request on the network. All hosts must also respond in a timely manner to the WINS server's update requests, which are used to verify that they still exist on the network.

Using the nbtstat command for name registration statistics

You can use the nbtstat command to determine the number of successful name registrations for each method. The nbtstat -r command displays the statistics for the NetBIOS name registration and resolution, as illustrated in the following example:

```
NetBIOS Names Resolution and Registration Statistics
Resolved By Broadcast      = 0
Resolved By Name Server    = 375
Registered By Broadcast    = 0
Registered By Name Server  = 9281
```

This `nbtstat -r` command example demonstrates that a large number of registrations and name resolutions are made possible through a WINS server. The high volume of registrations and resolutions is the direct result of the absence of non-WINS clients on a Windows NT network. Every client is configured to use the WINS server for registration and resolution, as evidenced by the absence of broadcasts on the network.

After a computer's NetBIOS name has been registered, that computer can then take part in NetBIOS sessions with other machines on the network using NetBIOS.

Ordering of NetBIOS Name Resolution Methods

The most important aspect of NetBIOS name resolution (as far as the test goes) is the order in which the various resolution methods are tried by the TCP/IP protocol to resolve the NetBIOS name to an IP address.

The following mnemonic makes memorizing the order of NetBIOS name resolution methods (for h-node machines) easy. Just remember this phrase: Neil Won Because Learning Let Him Develop.

Neil = NetBIOS name cache is examined on the local machine.

Won = WINS server is queried.

Because = Broadcasts (more specifically, b-nodes) are sent on the local network.

Learning = LMHOSTS file is examined on the local machine.

Let = Local host name is examined.

Him = HOSTS file is examined on the local machine.

Develop = DNS server is queried.

This memory aid is helpful when you need to recall which method is used next in the resolution process.

Method 1: NetBIOS name cache

The NetBIOS name cache holds all the resolved NetBIOS names from the time a computer was initialized.

The NetBIOS name cache has two main purposes:

- ✔ To limit the number of broadcasts on the network
- ✔ To decrease the need to continually query a WINS server for name resolution

The cache contains two types of entries, which you can access by entering the nbtstat command at the command prompt, using one of two different parameters:

- ✔ The NetBIOS names that belong to the local host, which are viewed using the nbtstat command with the -n parameter.
- ✔ The NetBIOS names that belong to hosts other than the local host, which are viewed using the nbtstat command with the -c parameter.

NetBIOS names belonging to the local host

The NetBIOS names that belong to the local host, viewed with the nbtstat -n command, look similar to the following example. In this example, the computer name, domain name, and username are HAL-CBRANDON, HAL_DOMAIN, and CBRANDON, respectively.

```
Node IpAddress: [198.113.221.109] Scope Id: []
            NetBIOS Local Name Table
        Name                Type            Status
    ---------------------------------------------------------
    HAL-CBRANDON    <00>    UNIQUE          Registered
    HAL_DOMAIN      <00>    GROUP           Registered
    ‾HAL-CBRANDON.  <00>    UNIQUE          Registered
    HAL-CBRANDON    <03>    UNIQUE          Registered
    HAL-CBRANDON    <20>    UNIQUE          Registered
    HAL_DOMAIN      <1E>    GROUP           Registered
    CBRANDON        <03>    UNIQUE          Registered
```

As a veteran of many Microsoft certification exams, I've rarely seen a question that asks for the specific parameter, such as -s or -c, that should be used with a command. Instead, the test is likely to ask which utility you use for specific situations (for example, "Which command would you use to view the contents of the NetBIOS cache?"). Knowing which utility you use in which situation should be easy to remember. My advice: Don't stay awake at night memorizing command-line parameters.

NetBIOS names belonging to another host

The NetBIOS names that belong to hosts other than the local host, viewed with the `nbtstat -c` command, look something like the following:

```
Node IpAddress: [198.113.221.109] Scope Id: []
         NetBIOS Remote Cache Name Table
Name                Type      Host Address        Life[sec]
-----------------------------------------------------------
RKOHLTFARB   <20>   UNIQUE    198.113.221.226     600
RBALDUS      <20>   UNIQUE    198.113.221.45      60
KHANSON      <20>   UNIQUE    198.113.221.236     600
MMYERS       <20>   UNIQUE    198.113.221.220     600
SFAIN        <20>   UNIQUE    198.113.221.80      600
GCRAMER      <20>   UNIQUE    198.113.221.34      600
SBRANDON     <20>   UNIQUE    198.113.221.25      60
MEDLAND      <20>   UNIQUE    198.113.221.28      60
```

Method 2: WINS server

Windows Internet Name Service (WINS) is a Microsoft Windows-based networking solution that's used to map NetBIOS names to IP addresses. A WINS server can be queried in the same way that a DNS server is queried to return an IP address mapping for a host name. As with DNS, a client must first be configured to use the service. The host can then send requests directly to the WINS server for name registration and resolution.

If the NetBIOS name resolution process has not resolved the NetBIOS name via the previous methods, the WINS server is queried next. If the WINS server is queried, it replies with the correct IP address for the given host name, if one exists in its dynamic database. (The WINS server has the advantage over the other sources that are being queried by having many more IP-address-to-host-name resolutions in its database because it functions primarily to register the NetBIOS information when a computer initializes on a network.) As a result, a broadcast is not needed, and network traffic is reduced.

If the primary WINS server does not reply, the client resends the request two more times before switching to the secondary WINS server, if one is specified on the client machine. If neither of the WINS servers responds, or if the requested name is not found, the client begins broadcasting, which is the next step in the NetBIOS name resolution process. (This same order is also followed in the host name resolution process.)

Method 3: B-node broadcasts

A broadcast (more specifically, a b-node broadcast) requests a mapping for a particular host name from every machine on a local network. The b-node broadcast is a registration and resolution method for NetBIOS over TCP/IP (NetBT). (The various methods of name resolution that involve broadcasting are covered in the section "NetBIOS over TCP/IP node types" earlier in this chapter.)

A source host sends up to three b-node broadcasts. If the destination host hears the broadcast, it sends the appropriate IP-address-to-host-name mapping to the source host. This process depends on the host name being the same as the NetBIOS machine name.

Method 4: LMHOSTS

The LMHOSTS file, in addition to resolving NetBIOS names to IP addresses, contains extensions such as #DOM, which can be used to specify remote domain controllers, and #INCLUDE, which can include LMHOSTS files on remote computers for fault tolerance.

If the LMHOSTS file fails to resolve the NetBIOS name, the name is stripped of its 16th service type character and stripped of any zeros used to pad the name to 15 characters. The result becomes the host name. (More information on configuring LMHOSTS files can be found in Chapter 9.) The next three resolution methods — local host name, HOSTS file, and DNS — then attempt to resolve the host name.

Method 5: Local host name

The local host checks its own local host name to determine whether the name that is attempting to be resolved matches. If the name doesn't match the local host name, the next NetBIOS name resolution method is tried.

Method 6: HOSTS

The new host name is checked in the HOSTS file to see whether a match can be determined for the NetBIOS name that is attempting to be resolved. If a mapping exists, the IP address is returned, and the quest is finally over. If a mapping for the host isn't found, the NetBIOS name resolution process has only one method left to resolve the name, which is to query a DNS server.

Method 7: DNS

A DNS server can attempt one last chance to resolve the NetBIOS name. A NetBIOS name query is sent to a DNS server, which checks its local database for an entry. If a mapping for this NetBIOS name is found in the DNS database, the NetBIOS name is finally resolved to an IP address. If a mapping isn't found, the entire process of resolving the NetBIOS name is tried by TCP/IP again, or an error message is generated.

Prep Test

1 Which is not a rule concerning the NetBIOS name?

A ○ The NetBIOS name has 15 characters with an additional one-byte service type.

B ○ If the name does not include 15 characters, zeros are appended to the name to equal 15 characters total.

C ○ If the name does not include 15 characters, zeros are appended to the name to equal 15 characters total, and it is given a service type that specifies that zeros have been appended.

D ○ The name is not case-sensitive.

2 Which NetBIOS name resolution method is not a standard resolution method and is considered a specific name-resolution method?

A ○ Local NetBIOS name cache

B ○ Local broadcast

C ○ LMHOSTS

D ○ WINS server

3 Which NetBIOS over TCP/IP node type consults the LMHOSTS file if the first b-node broadcast is unsuccessful?

A ○ enhanced b-node

B ○ p-node

C ○ h-node

D ○ m-node

4 Which is the most efficient NetBIOS over TCP/IP node type that uses the WINS server before it begins to broadcast?

A ○ m-node

B ○ h-node

C ○ Microsoft enhanced

D ○ p-node

5 What happens if the name registration database contains a different IP address for a computer name when a NetBIOS name is being registered?

A ○ The WINS server rejects the new name registration request.

B ○ The WINS server overwrites the existing name.

C ○ The existing computer is challenged.

D ○ The existing computer has its name modified in the database.

6 Which command produced this output?

```
NetBIOS Names Resolution and Registration Statistics
Resolved By Broadcast    = 0
Resolved By Name Server  = 375
Registered By Broadcast  = 0
Registered By Name Server = 9281
```

A ○ nbtstat -r
B ○ nbtstat -R
C ○ nbtstat -s
D ○ nbtstat -n

7 What is the first step of the NetBIOS name resolution process?

A ○ The local computer name is checked to see whether it is the destination.
B ○ The WINS server is queried.
C ○ The NetBIOS name cache is consulted.
D ○ The LMHOSTS file is consulted.

8 Which of the following are specific NetBIOS name resolution methods?
(Choose all that apply.)

A ❑ The LMHOSTS file method (on the local machine)
B ❑ The HOSTS file method (on the local machine)
C ❑ The DNS server method
D ❑ The host name method (on the local machine)

9 When is the NetBIOS name stripped of its 16th service type character and any
zeros used to pad the name to 15 characters?

A ○ Before the LMHOSTS step in the name resolution order
B ○ Before the DNS step in the name resolution order
C ○ Before the WINS step in the name resolution order
D ○ Before the HOSTS step in the name resolution order

10 What is the last method used in the NetBIOS name resolution process?

A ○ DNS
B ○ LMHOSTS
C ○ HOSTS
D ○ WINS

Answers

1 *C.* Zeros are appended to the end of a NetBIOS name that doesn't include a total of 15 characters, but a service type isn't given to reflect this. *Review "Configuring NetBIOS Names."*

2 *C.* The LMHOSTS method of NetBIOS name resolution is considered specific. An easy way to remember the specific name resolution methods is to remember that they must be enabled in order to be used, such as DNS, LMHOSTS, and HOSTS. *Review "Recognizing the NetBIOS Name Resolution Methods."*

3 *A.* In order to use this resolution method, LMHOSTS lookup must be enabled in the Networking dialog box of the Control Panel. *Review "NetBIOS over TCP/IP node types."*

4 *B.* This method uses the WINS server for registration and resolution, but switches to the less efficient b-node broadcast when a WINS server cannot be contacted. *Review "NetBIOS over TCP/IP node types."*

5 *C.* The WINS server challenges the computer with the existing name to claim the name that is being registered by the new computer. *Review "Registration when WINS is enabled."*

6 *A.* The `nbtstat -r` command displays the statistics for the NetBIOS name registration and resolution. **Remember:** The parameters of the `nbtstat` command are case-sensitive, so the output from `-r` and `-R` differ. *Review "Using the nbtstat command for name registration statistics."*

7 *C.* The NetBIOS name cache consists of all the resolved NetBIOS names from the time the computer was initialized. *Review "Method 1: NetBIOS name cache."*

8 *A, B, C, D.* Notice how every one of the specific NetBIOS name resolution methods, with the exception of the LMHOSTS file, uses the host name. This is the key to determining which methods are specific and which are standard. Remember, the specific and standard resolution methods are opposite in host name resolution. *Review "Specific NetBIOS name resolution."*

9 *D.* If LMHOSTS fails to resolve the name, the NetBIOS name is stripped of its 16th character and any zeros used to pad the name to 15 characters. The result of the NetBIOS name being stripped of its service type is now the host name. The next three resolution methods (local host name, the HOSTS file, and DNS) then attempt to resolve this host name. *Review "Method 4: LMHOSTS."*

10 *A.* If all other methods have been unsuccessful in resolving a name, DNS is tried. If DNS doesn't resolve the name, the entire process is tried again or an error message is generated. *Review "Method 7: DNS."*

Part II
Planning

"Please Dad—do we have to hear the story of Snow White's OSI model and its 7 layers again?"

In this part . . .

The topics I cover in this part of the book, the workings of IP Addressing and IP Routing, are notoriously challenging for even the most skilled TCP/IP users. To make life easier for you come exam time, Chapters 6 and 7 include tips, insights, and solid advice that will help you prepare for the test.

In these chapters, I've included charts and tables that include information essential to your breezing through those tricky IP Addressing questions. As for IP Routing, the exam questions can include just about anything that involves routing, but I narrow the topics down to just those that you need to review for the exam — such as static routing, the default gateway, and configuring your Windows NT computer as a router.

Chapter 6

IP Addressing

• •

Exam Objectives

▶ Configuring subnet masks

▶ Given a scenario, identify valid network configurations

▶ Identifying the correct utility for diagnosing IP configuration problems

▶ Diagnosing and resolving IP addressing problems

• •

*B*ecause the subject of IP addressing covers a lot of territory, you can safely expect a good 30 percent of the exam to deal in some way with IP addressing issues. You're going to see numerous IP addresses referenced on the exam, as well as a number of questions on related subjects, such as the subnet mask and default gateway.

The questions related to subnetting a network probably won't be as complicated as they were in the previous version of the exam. Nevertheless, they still require you to memorize a sizable chunk of information, which I supply in this chapter in a handy table format. I show what you need to commit to memory and how to use that information come exam time.

The exam preparers assume that you have a background in IP addressing, so you need to get up to speed on those IP addressing details that until now may have eluded you (or that you've forgotten). In boning up for the exam, you'll want to concentrate on the following areas, which are covered in the following pages:

✔ **The IP address itself.** The structure of an IP address should be no mystery to you.

✔ **The address classes.** Make sure you have them memorized!

✔ **Subnetting and the subnet mask.** You should have a complete understanding of both these topics. Commit the subnetting tables to memory so that you can replicate them quickly right before the testing starts.

✔ **Troubleshooting IP addressing.** Make sure you understand the troubleshooting methods described in this section because I guarantee you'll see a couple of questions on this area of TCP/IP.

Quick Assessment

Configuring subnet masks

1 The binary digit 10100011 is a Class _____ address.

2 The IP address of 126.26.213.75 is a Class _____ address.

3 (True/False). The .240 subnet mask gives you 14 possible subnets.

4 (True/False). The 255.255.228.0 is a valid custom subnet mask.

5 The subnet mask that gives you 254 available subnets is _____.

6 The subnet mask that leaves eight bits for the host ID is _____.

Given a scenario, identify valid network configurations

7 (True/False). You are using the IP address of 127.35.112.96. This is a valid IP address.

8 You are having trouble communicating with a certain host on the network. The host with the IP address of 102.45.78.213 with a subnet mask of 255.255.0.0 is on the _____ network.

Diagnosing and resolving IP addressing problems

9 The parameter used in the `ipconfig` command that gives very detailed information is _____.

Identifying the correct utility for diagnosing IP configuration problems

10 You are having problems with one computer on the network. If the computer's IP address is 120.64.213.17, and the default gateway is 120.64.213.1, then _____ is the subnet mask.

Answers

1   *Class B address.* Review "Assigning Network Classes."

2   *Class A address.* Review "Assigning Network Classes."

3   *True.* Review "Defining custom subnet masks."

4   *False.* Review "Defining custom subnet masks."

5   *255.* Review "Using default subnet masks."

6   *255.255.255.0.* Review "Using default subnet masks."

7   *False.* Review "Assigning Network Classes."

8   *102.45.0.0.* Review "Determining whether the host is local or remote by examining the subnet mask."

9   */all.* Review "Indentifying the Correct Utility for Diagnosing IP Configuration Problems."

10 *255.255.255.0.* Review "Solving a communication problem scenario."

A Bit of Preliminary Information on IP Addresses

The TCP/IP protocol uses an *IP address* to uniquely identify a computer on a network. An IP address comprises 32 bits, or 4 octets (for example, 198.113.201.23). If you're wondering why an IP address is a 32-bit number, the answer lies in breaking down the address to bit level. The number 198 in binary digits equals 11000110. Eight binary digits are in the decimal number 198. If you continue converting the remaining 3 octets, you end up with 32 bits total, or 4 bytes.

You don't know how to convert binary numbers to decimals in your head? That's okay. You've gotten this far in life without knowing how, and you probably won't need to remember how after the exam. In Lab 6-1, I show you how to convert a decimal to a binary number, just in case it comes up on the test.

Lab 6-1   Converting Decimal Numbers to Binary Numbers

Because you'll be afforded the luxury of using the calculator provided with Windows during the exam, I'm making use of the calculator in this Lab exercise.

1. **Open the Windows calculator from the Accessories program group.**

2. **Make sure the View menu has Scientific, and not Standard, selected.**

3. **Select the Dec option and enter the decimal number of** 240 **in the text box.**

4. **Select the Bin option.**

   The binary number 11110000 now appears in the text box.

   If you want to see the decimal conversion of a binary number:

5. **Clear the number just entered and enter a new binary number.**

6. **Select the Dec option and view the result.**

   Knowing you have the option of using the calculator to perform these steps is useful, especially if you have time to double-check your answers.

Assigning Network Classes

You may be asked on the exam to name the address class that an IP address belongs to. Address classes were created in order to be used for networks of various sizes. A larger network can benefit from having an address class that provides a larger number of hosts, whereas a small network that doesn't require as many hosts may use another address class more efficiently.

You must be familiar with some network address classes for the exam. These address classes are defined by the first octet of the IP address. Table 6-1 lists the classes and their address ranges.

Table 6-1	Network Classes and Their IP Address Ranges
Class	*Range*
A	001.a.b.c to 126.a.b.c
B	128.a.b.c to 191.a.b.c
C	192.a.b.c to 223.a.b.c

A couple of Class A addresses cannot be used on a TCP/IP network. The first octet starting with 127.x.x.x is reserved for loopback testing. More specifically, the IP address of 127.0.0.1 is used to test that the TCP/IP protocol is properly configured by sending information in a loop to the computer that originally sent the packet without traveling over the network. Remember these reserved addresses for the exam!

The first octet of the network ID cannot be 0 or 255. If all bits are set to 0, it indicates a local network. If all bits are set to 1, it represents a broadcast address. You can avoid some incorrect answers if you remember these invalid octets.

Table 6-2 lists the binary representation of each class according to what are called *high-order bits*. High-order bits tell you which class an IP address belongs to, based on the far-left bits in an address. Memorize Table 6-2 for the three network classes because the exam may give you binary representations of numbers, rather than their decimal representations.

Table 6-2	The High-Order Bits for Network Classes
Class	*High-Order Bits*
A	0
B	10
C	110

By keeping Table 6-2 in mind, you can answer a question concerning, for example, which class the 10110011 octet belongs to just by looking at the first few bits. The answer in this case is Class B, which you know from the two high-order bits. And you don't need to convert it to a decimal to answer the question!

Two other network address classes exist: Class D and Class E. Class D addresses are used for broadcasting messages to several host computers, a process known as *multicasting*. Class E addresses are experimental and are not being used. Microsoft supports only Classes A through C. As such, those are the only classes capable of being assigned to hosts. So don't expect any questions on the exam concerning any Class D and Class E addresses.

Subnetting a Network by Configuring Subnet Masks

The topic of subnetting is probably the most difficult portion of the TCP/IP exam. *Subnetting* involves taking one IP network and subdividing it into many smaller, logical networks. This is made possible by the subnet mask, which I tell you more about later in this section of the chapter.

The *Internetworking TCP/IP on Windows NT 4.0* exam does not cover subnetting as much as its predecessor, the Windows NT 3.51 TCP/IP exam, did. On that test, subnetting comprised around 30 percent of the test questions, which were very challenging. I was surprised to see the number of subnetting questions drastically reduced in the newer test, which is good news for you! I provide enough information in this section so you can tackle any subnetting questions you may run across.

Many of the questions on the exam regarding subnetting deal with planning. You likely will be presented with a scenario in which you're asked to subnet a network in the most efficient way. As a network administrator, you must maintain a balance between available network IDs and host IDs. You can have a greater number of networks with fewer hosts per network, or you can have fewer networks with a greater number of hosts. Expect to see questions on how to maintain a correct balance between the number of network and host IDs, while leaving room for network expansion.

Applying the subnet mask to an IP address

The subnet mask, in addition to the IP address, is the mandatory TCP/IP value that you must configure to enable your computer to communicate under the TCP/IP protocol. A *subnet mask* is applied to an IP address to "mask" a portion of the address in order to distinguish the network ID from the host ID. Determining which network a TCP/IP address is on without the use of a subnet mask is impossible. (The subnet mask is configured in the TCP/IP Properties dialog box in the Network window within the Control Panel.)

For the exam, you need to be able to quickly determine whether two TCP/IP-based computers are on the same network. You make this determination for two main reasons (which also illustrate the importance of the subnet mask):

✔ If a destination IP address is found to be on the same network as the source address, then the computers are both local, and these two computers can communicate via broadcast or normal address resolution on the network.

✔ If a destination IP address is found to be on another subnet, the information has to be routed to the other subnet before these computers are able to communicate.

If you can determine whether a host is local or remote by just looking at the IP address and subnet mask, you can make things simpler for the exam. To see how you can figure out whether a host is local or remote by examining the subnet mask, you need to use some binary notation, as I note in the following section.

Determining whether the host is local or remote by examining the subnet mask

The decimal number 255 is expressed as 11111111 in binary notation, which can be used in the subnet mask but not the IP address. Zero is, of course, expressed as 0 in binary notation and can also be used in the subnet mask but not the IP address. If you take a subnet mask of 255.255.255.0 and apply it to an IP address of 198.113.201.23, you have a network ID of 198.113.201 and a unique host ID of 23. You can see how the decimal 255 is used to cover up the network ID of the IP address if the IP address and subnet mask are converted to binary notation, as I demonstrate in the next two lines:

IP address: 11000110.01110001.11001001.00010111

Subnet mask: 11111111.11111111.11111111.00000000

Using the Windows calculator, I converted each of the decimals in the IP address to binary form. I did the same with the subnet mask. Remember that the decimal number of 255 yields all 1s, and the decimal number of 0 will yields all 0s.

As I mention earlier in this chapter, the subnet mask is applied to the IP address in order to separate the network number and the host number. In the example I just listed, the bits in the IP address that are covered, or masked, by the binary digit 1 in the subnet mask belong to the network ID (they are the first three octets in the IP address). The remaining bits that are not covered by the binary digit 1 belong to the unique host ID. You should now be able to look at a subnet mask and IP address and determine which portion is the network ID and which portion is the host ID.

From the information I've presented so far in this section of the chapter, you can make a few important conclusions based on your knowing the subnet mask and IP address:

✔ Everyone on this network has the same network ID of 198.113.201 (the first three octets were masked by the 1 bits in the subnet mask; therefore, they become the network ID).

✔ You can't use 0 or 255 as the unique host ID. You can choose from the remaining 254 valid IP addresses.

✔ A possible 254 unique IP addresses exist on this network.

✔ A unique IP address, such as 198.113.201.1 or 198.113.201.2, is required for each computer on the network.

If you know the IP addressing rules that I covered earlier in this section, such as octets with 0 or 255 and the reserved address class of 127.x.x.x, you can eliminate a number of wrong answers and figure out when you're being tricked by a test question. For example, if you know you cannot use the numbers 0 or 255 in the IP address, it is easy to spot invalid IP addresses (such as 184.0.21.116 or 112.210.255.36) on the test.

Using default subnet masks

Default subnet masks are used on TCP/IP networks that are not divided into subnets. They're used when you don't specify a subnet mask. You need to know the default subnet mask values in case a question includes an IP address and you are asked to provide the correct default subnet mask. (And don't be surprised if you're asked, for example, which class to use for a network of 30,000 hosts with room for future expansion.)

The default subnet mask used depends on the address class. Each IP address class (Class A, B, and C) has its own a default subnet mask, as Table 6-3 shows. In addition, each network class allows for a maximum number of networks and a maximum number of hosts per network, as Table 6-4 shows. For the test, keep in mind the following about the network classes:

✔ The Class A default subnet mask uses the 8 far-left bits of the IP address for the network ID, which leaves 24 of the 32 total bits for the host ID. As you can see from Table 6-4, the A address class allows for a tremendous number of hosts.

✔ The Class B default subnet mask uses the 16 far-left bits of the 32 total bits for the network ID, which leaves 16 bits for the host ID. This address class has a total of 65,534 available hosts.

✔ The Class C default subnet mask uses the 24 far-left bits of the 32 total bits for the network ID, which leaves 8 bits for the host ID. This address class allows for a large number of available networks, but only a relatively small number of host IDs per network.

Table 6-3   Default Subnet Masks for Each Address Class

Class	Default Subnet Mask
A	255.0.0.0
B	255.255.0.0
C	255.255.255.0

Table 6-4   Maximum Number of Networks and Hosts per Address Class

Class	Number of Networks	Number of Hosts per Network
A	126	16,777,216
B	16,384	65,534
C	2,097,152	254

It's a good idea to memorize the information contained in the tables in this chapter and be ready to scribble them out before the test starts. Then you can use them as handy references during the exam.

Defining custom subnet masks

If the default subnet mask does not provide the required balance of available networks and hosts, you have to define a *custom subnet mask* that meets your internetworking needs. With the custom subnet mask, additional bits are masked from the host ID in order to define subnets.

I strongly recommend that you memorize the information in Table 6-5; I used it at least a few times during my exam. The table lists the eight possible custom subnet mask values and the binary equivalents of these custom subnet masks.

Table 6-5	Binary Equivalents of the Available Custom Subnet Masks
Custom Subnet Mask	*Binary Equivalent*
128	10000000
192	11000000
224	11100000
240	11110000
248	11111000
252	11111100
254	11111110
255	11111111

If you memorize the entries in Table 6-5, you don't have to use the calculator during the exam for converting the subnet masks from decimal to binary, which saves you some time. I can guarantee that you will see more than a few questions on the exam that requires use of the custom subnet masks listed in Table 6-5.

You're likely to encounter subnetting questions on the exam that provide an IP address that you are supposed to subnet. You have to determine which class the IP address belongs to and then determine the default subnet mask for a particular gateway. The address class the IP address belongs to and the default subnet mask are *not* provided. The number of subnets you need for a network may be all the information you're supplied, so you really have to know this stuff before going into the exam.

Tables 6-6 through 6-8 list additional information you need to memorize in order to whiz through the custom subnet mask questions. With these tables, you can see the maximum number of subnets you can create and the maximum number of hosts that can be on a network, based on the particular subnet mask you choose. Before I took the exam, I had tables like these taped to my monitor. That's how critically important it is that you commit this information to memory.

Table 6-6 is based on the Class C address, which is the address class that I found most of my subnetting questions were based on. Tables 6-7 and 6-8 illustrate the number of networks and hosts for Class A and Class B address classes.

If you're faced with a scenario question in which you must determine the proper subnet mask for your network, you may want to apply the following type of analysis. The otherwise complicated subnetting scenario that follows is simplified if you use the information in Table 6-6:

- If you have to subnet a network into five smaller networks, you need to use the .224 subnet mask. Your subnet mask appears as 255.255.255.224. You then have a total of six subnets, which leaves you with one subnet for future expansion. But you have only 30 hosts available on each subnet.

- If you want the greatest number of possible hosts with only two subnets, you need to use the .192 subnet mask. Your subnet mask appears as 255.255.255.192. This leaves no room for future expansion of subnets but does give you 62 hosts per subnet.

You want to keep a couple of things in mind as you examine Tables 6-6 through 6-8:

- The column labeled Bits shows how many of the far-left bits are one (1), rather than zero (0), for the eight bits of the first octet. For example, 2/6 equals 11000000 in binary numbers and 192 in decimal numbers.

- The Number of Subnets column may not appear to follow a pattern, but it does. It's just that the two invalid subnets were subtracted from each entry. If they were included, you would see the sequence 4, 8, 16, 32, and so on, from top to bottom in that column.

Table 6-6   Subnet Mask Information for Class C Networks

Bits	Subnet Mask (fourth octet)	Number of Subnets	Number of Host Addresses
2/6	192	2	62
3/5	224	6	30
4/4	240	14	14
5/3	248	30	6
6/2	252	62	2
7/1	254	126	0
8/0	255	254	n/a

Table 6-7   Subnet Mask Information for Class A Networks

Bits	Subnet Mask (second octet)	Number of Subnets	Number of Host Addresses
2/6	192	2	4,194,302
3/5	224	6	2,097,150
4/4	240	14	1,048,574
5/3	248	30	524,286

(continued)

Table 6-7 *(continued)*

Bits	Subnet Mask (second octet)	Number of Subnets	Number of Host Addresses
6/2	252	62	262,142
7/1	254	126	131,070
8/0	255	254	65,534

Table 6-8   Subnet Mask Information for Class B Networks

Bits	Subnet Mask (third octet)	Number of Subnets	Number of Host Addresses
2/6	192	2	16,382
3/5	224	6	8,190
4/4	240	14	4,094
5/3	248	30	2,046
6/2	252	62	1,022
7/1	254	126	510
8/0	255	254	254

I've found that digesting the Class A and Class B address information in Tables 6-7 and 6-8 is made easier by using the following memorization technique. Basically, you need to memorize just the bottom number in each column. Here's how it works:

✔ In the Class B addresses, for example, the value of 254 at the bottom of the "Number of Host Addresses" column is 256 minus the two unusable values of 0 and 255. Double this number to get 512, and double that to get 1,024, and so on. As the values get higher, just round off the numbers to the nearest thousand (for example, 8,190 becomes 8,000, and 16,382 becomes 16,000). The exam doesn't require you to cite an exact number. For example, you may be asked which Class B address gives you at least 4,000 available hosts per subnet.

✔ For the Class A addresses, start doubling the values beginning with 64. The bottom figure in the "Number of Host Addresses" column is actually 65,534, but rounding to 64 makes your values easier to calculate. Don't worry; it won't affect the accuracy of your chart during testing. It's extremely unlikely that the exam has you choose among answers such as 65,534, 65,535, and 65,536.

Identifying Valid Network Configurations, Given a Scenario

You will be presented with scenario questions during the exam in which you are supposed to identify valid network configurations. A scenario of this type includes determining whether the IP address your Internet Service Provider gave you is valid for the subnet mask you're given. Answering questions that require you to find the valid subnets that a custom subnet mask creates requires some additional steps beyond looking up numbers in a chart.

Finding valid subnets

The first half of the process of finding valid subnets is the same as that described in the section "Subnetting a Network by Configuring Subnet Masks" earlier in this chapter, with some additional steps.

You can use Table 6-9 to determine the increment value for each of the custom subnet masks. The larger the increment value, the smaller the number of subnets that are created. For example, an increment value of 64 creates only four subnets: x.x.x.1 –x.x.x.63, x.x.x.64–x.x.x.127, x.x.x.128–x.x.x.191, and x.x.x.192–x.x.x.256.

Although the subnet mask of 192 with an increment value of 64 creates four subnets, only two of the subnets are valid. You see why in a moment. Lab 6-2 shows you how to find valid subnets when you're supplied with the subnet mask.

Table 6-9	Custom Subnet Mask Increment Values
Subnet Mask	**Increment Value**
192	64
224	32
240	16
248	8
252	4
254	2
255	1

Lab 6-2   Finding Valid Subnets When You Have a Subnet Mask

1. **Be ready to work with a subnet mask (you'll be provided with one during the exam).**

   For this exercise, use 255.255.240.0.

2. **Use the information in Table 6-9 to determine the increment value for the subnet mask.**

   The increment value for the subnet mask of 255.255.240.0 is 16.

3. **Start at zero and increment using the proper value (in this case, it's 16) — 0 through 15, 16 through 31, and so on.**

   This incrementing creates a block of addresses equal in number to the increment value (0–15 equals 16 addresses). The subnets should be x.x.x.0–x.x.x.15, x.x.x.16–x.x.x.31, with the x's substituting for the real numbers.

4. **Eliminate the first and last subnets from the subnet groups you just created.**

   Therefore, you must eliminate x.x.x.0–x.x.x.15 and x.x.x.240–x.x.x.255; additionally, any IP address with 0 and 255 is invalid.

If the exercise in Lab 6-2 left you scratching your head, you can try the whole process again with a different IP address and subnet mask:

1. Assume that a Class A address of 67.1.1.1 has a default subnet mask of 255.0.0.0. If you choose to subnet the network with the .255 mask, the subnet mask equals 255.255.0.0.

2. A .255 subnet mask provides 254 available subnets. The increment value is 1, which makes it fairly easy to find the valid subnets. The new subnets (254 total) are 67.1 through 67.254.

3. At this point, 65,534 hosts are available per subnet. For example, an IP address of 67.1.100.100 is a valid IP address on the first subnet, and an IP address of 67.2.200.200 is a valid IP address on the second subnet.

   Using this example, the exam may ask you whether the IP addresses of 67.1.100.100 and 67.2.200.200 are on the same network if your subnet mask is 255.255.0.0. You now know that they aren't.

Because the application of the .255 subnet mask is relatively easy to understand, I continue with another example, this time using a custom subnet mask.

1. **Assume that you're using a Class B address of 132.1.1.1, which has a default subnet mask of 255.255.0.0.**

2. **Subnet the address using the third octet.**

3. **Subnet the network with the .240 mask.**

   The subnet mask now equals 255.255.240.0.

4. Look up the custom subnet mask in Table 6-9 to find the increment value, which is 16.

5. Start at zero and increment using the value of 16, and then discard the first and last subnets.

You finish with subnets 132.1.16 through 132.1.239.

The following list shows all 14 subnets that are provided with the 255.255.240.0 subnet mask just used in the previous steps. The first (0–15) and sixteenth (240–255) subnets were eliminated because of the routing rules (that is, 0 and 255 are not used).

Subnet 1: 16–31 (112.1.16–112.1.31)

Subnet 2: 32–47 (112.1.32–112.1.47)

Subnet 3: 48–63 (112.1.48–112.1.63)

Subnet 4: 64–79 (112.1.64–112.1.79)

Subnet 5: 80–95 (112.1.80–112.1.95)

Subnet 6: 96–111 (112.1.96–112.1.111)

Subnet 7: 112–127 (112.1.112–112.1.127)

Subnet 8: 128–143 (112.1.128–112.1.143)

Subnet 9: 144–159 (112.1.144–112.1.159)

Subnet 10: 160–175 (112.1.160–112.1.175)

Subnet 11: 176–191 (112.1.176–112.1.191)

Subnet 12: 192–207 (112.1.192–112.1.207)

Subnet 13: 208–223 (112.1.208–112.1.223)

Subnet 14: 224–239 (112.1.224–112.1.239)

Given this list of 14 subnets, an IP address of 112.1.182.34, for example, is on the eleventh subnet. What if the exam were to ask you whether the IP address of 112.1.194.48 is on the same subnet as 112.1.182.34? You could check out the list of subnets you just created and quickly determine that the two IP addresses are not on the same subnet.

Defining host IDs for a subnet

You may be asked on the exam whether a particular host address is valid or invalid for a certain subnet. You may also be given some IP addresses and a subnet mask, and asked whether the IP addresses are valid for that particular subnet mask. These questions may seem impossible to answer at first, but you'll find that they're no problem if you memorize the information in Tables 6-6 through 6-9, found in the previous two sections of this chapter.

For example, the subnet mask of .248 has an increment value of 8. With this in mind, I've drawn up a scenario for you, such as you may see on the exam, and then provided the steps that you can follow to solve a question based on this scenario:

> You are assigned three IP addresses and the subnet mask of 255.255.255.248 by your Internet Service Provider, and you want to verify that they are valid IP addresses for that subnet mask. The three IP addresses are
>
> 219.35.86.116
>
> 219.35.86.117
>
> 219.35.86.118

I'll tell you the easiest way I know to arrive at the answer: Because you already know that the subnet mask of .248 has an increment value of 8, you can start at 0 and increment using the value of 8. The incrementing creates a block of addresses, the number of which is equal to the increment value (0–7 equals 8 addresses). Here's an example of what the incrementing will look like:

> 219.35.86.0
>
> 219.35.86.8
>
> 219.35.86.16
>
> 219.35.86.24, and so on

You can use the Windows calculator to add 8 plus 8, and then press the equals sign repeatedly until you arrive at the subnet in which your IP addresses reside. (In this example, the IP addresses from the ISP are 219.35.86.116, 219.35.86.117, and 219.35.86.118.) You will arrive at the subnet that contains the IP addresses of x.x.x.112–x.x.x.119. When you add the network ID, you get 219.35.86.112.

Pressing the equals sign again on the calculator gives you 120, indicating that you're at the beginning of a new subnet, which does not contain the host IDs of the three IP addresses assigned by the ISP. Now you have a valid range of 219.35.86.112 through 219.35.86.119. Therefore, the answer to this example scenario question is *Yes,* the IP addresses assigned by the ISP are correct.

When using the Windows calculator, entering the increment value and pressing the equals sign gives you the *beginning* of the next subnet. For example, an increment value of 16 produces subnets beginning at 16, 32, and so forth. The subnet range, however, is not x.x.x.16 *through* x.x.x.32, because 32 is reserved for the beginning of the next subnet.

Another way to think of the increment value is to equate it with the number of hosts per subnet, based on the subnet mask. Earlier in this section of the chapter, I noted that the .240 subnet mask yields 14 subnets with 4,094 available hosts on each subnet (assuming that the third octet is masked). The number of subnets that were created just happens to be equivalent to the increment value — that is, 14 for the .240 subnet mask.

The two minutes you spend at the beginning of the exam writing out the information contained in Tables 6-6 through 6-9 will save you time in the long run when you encounter subnetting questions. I must have used the information in those tables ten times during the exam for questions asking which subnet mask to choose for the right balance of subnets and hosts. Because I had the charts written out beforehand, I could answer a number of questions in a matter of seconds just by referencing them!

The exercise in Lab 6-3 shows you how you can save some time when answering questions that involve verifying whether certain hosts are on the same subnet.

Lab 6-3	Verifying Whether Hosts Are on a Valid Subnet

1. **Be ready to work with a subnet mask and IP address (you'll be provided with each in the exam question).**

2. **Use the information in Table 6-9 in this chapter to look up the increment value for the subnet mask.**

3. **Start at zero and increment using that value — 0 through 15, 16 through 31, and so on — to create a list of subnets, such as x.x.x.0– x.x.x.15, x.x.x.16–x.x.x.31, and so on.**

4. **Eliminate the first and last subnets from the list of subnets that you just created.**

5. **Find the subnet that the IP address belongs to.**

   Now that you know which valid subnet your IP address (the one assigned to you by the ISP in the scenario question) is on, you can determine whether the other IP addresses are in the same subnet. For example, if your IP address is on the x.x.x.16–x.x.x.31 subnet, does the other IP address of x.x.x.90 that the ISP gave you also fall within this subnet? The answer is *No.*

Identifying the Correct Utility for Diagnosing IP Configuration Problems

If you had a question about the ipconfig command utility, could you look at the example ipconfig output and know which TCP/IP configuration is wrong? I bet you'll see a question on the exam that asks you to do just that.

The ipconfig command is great for monitoring and troubleshooting problems you're having with IP addressing. ipconfig is a command prompt utility that displays everything you need to know about your TCP/IP configuration. This information is especially helpful, and just about mandatory, if you are running Dynamic Host Configuration Protocol (DHCP) because you'll be receiving TCP/IP configuration settings, including the IP address, from the DHCP server. (Note that Windows 95/98 uses winipcfg.exe.)

Typing ipconfig at the command prompt gives you the primary TCP/IP information — the current IP address, subnet mask, and default gateway. The ipconfig switches are used to release and renew addresses that were assigned via DHCP. (A few other parameters can be used with the ipconfig command, which are covered in Chapter 8.) The following is sample output generated after entering the ipconfig command:

```
Windows NT IP Configuration

Ethernet adapter E190x2:


        IP Address. . . . . . . . . : 198.113.201.109

        Subnet Mask . . . . . . . . : 255.255.255.0

        Default Gateway . . . . . : 198.113.201.1
```

The most frequently used parameter (or switch) for the ipconfig command, other than no parameter at all, is the /all switch. (I provide more information on the ipconfig /all switch in the next section of this chapter.) You may see a question on the test with sample ipconfig /all information that asks you to determine which setting is *incorrect* based on the information provided.

Entering the ipconfig /all command displays much more information than entering the ipconfig command, as you can see from the following:

```
Windows NT IP Configuration

Host Name . . . . . . . . . :
               cbrandon.capstonetechnology.com
DNS Servers . . . . . . . . :
Node Type . . . . . . . . . : Hybrid
NetBIOS Scope ID. . . . . . :
IP Routing Enabled. . . . . : No
WINS Proxy Enabled. . . . . : No
NetBIOS Resolution Uses DNS : No

Ethernet adapter E190x2:

Description . . . . . . . . : 3Com 3C90x Ethernet Adapter
Physical Address. . . . . . : 00-60-97-58-50-63
DHCP Enabled. . . . . . . . : Yes
IP Address. . . . . . . . . : 198.113.201.109
Subnet Mask . . . . . . . . : 255.255.255.0
Default Gateway . . . . . . : 198.113.201.1
DHCP Server . . . . . . . . : 198.113.201.23
Primary WINS Server . . . . : 198.113.201.27
Secondary WINS Server . . . : 198.113.201.32
Lease Obtained. . . . . . . : Thursday, January 15, 1998
             2:55:34 PM
Lease Expires . . . . . . . : Sunday, January 18, 1998
             2:55:34 PM
```

Diagnosing and Resolving IP Addressing Problems

The subject of troubleshooting covers a lot of territory in TCP/IP, and more information on troubleshooting is supplied throughout this book. This section addresses troubleshooting only as it applies to IP addressing.

You may see a question on the exam that includes a printout of the ipconfig /all command. The question will likely tell you that a problem exists with communicating with another host and, based on the ipconfig information, you must decide which setting is incorrect. A question such as this one often includes two printouts of the ipconfig /all command — one from the source and one from the destination computer. Attempting to answer this question may seem overwhelming at first because of the volume of numbers in the ipconfig /all output: the IP address, default gateway, subnet mask, DHCP server, hardware address, and more.

Solving a communication problem scenario

To give you an idea of how to handle a question such as the one I just described, I put together the following sample scenario with example source and destination ipconfig /all configurations. (I left out the nonessential settings so you can immediately get to the root of the problem.)

The two computers in the following example are not able to communicate and you have to figure out why. You are trying to transfer files from one computer to another on the same subnet, but you are unable to connect to the destination computer. You ran a printout of the ipconfig /all command on both computers, with the following results:

```
Windows NT IP Configuration
Host Name . . . . . . . . . :
        computer1.capstonetechnology.com
IP Address. . . . . . . . .: 207.149.40.112
Subnet Mask . . . . . . .: 255.255.255.0
Default Gateway . . . . .: 207.149.40.242
Host Name . . . . . . . . :
        computer2.capstonetechnology.com
IP Address. . . . . . . . .: 207.149.40.28
Subnet Mask . . . . . . .: 255.255.0.0
Default Gateway . . . . .: 207.149.40.242
```

The subnet mask of computer two appears to be incorrect, which is preventing communication. The subnet mask creates the impression that the two computers are on different networks. Computer1 is on the 207.149.40 network because of the 255.255.255.0 subnet mask. Computer2 is on the 207.148 network because of the 255.255.0.0 subnet mask. You can attempt to send packets all day long with these settings, and nothing will end up arriving where it should. If you fix the subnet mask error for Computer2, everything should be fine.

Solving another problem, with a different scenario

The following is another example using this same scenario, but with different ipconfig /all information. (I have again omitted nonessential information.)

You are trying to transfer files from one computer to another on the same subnet, but you are unable to connect to the destination computer. You ran a printout of the ipconfig /all command on both computers with the following results:

```
Windows NT IP Configuration
Host Name . . . . . . . . . :
        computer3.capstonetechnology.com
IP Address. . . . . . . . .: 221.54.214.17
Subnet Mask . . . . . . .: 255.255.255.0
Default Gateway . . . . .: 221.54.213.145
Host Name . . . . . . . . :
        computer4.capstonetechnology.com
IP Address. . . . . . . . .: 221.54.213.213
Subnet Mask . . . . . . .: 255.255.255.0
Default Gateway . . . . .: 221.54.255.145
```

In this sample scenario, the subnet mask appears to be the same for the two computers, but the default gateway for one of the computers is incorrect. For Computer4, the correct default gateway of 221.54.213.145 was not entered.

Spotting an incorrect default gateway

I guarantee you will see a question that can be easily figured out if you can spot the incorrect default gateway. (I cover the default gateway in more detail in Chapter 7.) You need to remember a couple of important things about the default gateway:

- The default gateway is usually a router that routes packets to another subnet or network.
- The default gateway must be on the same network as your computer.

For example, if your computer's IP address is 2.2.2.2, and your subnet mask is 255.0.0.0, you must be on the 2.0.0.0 network. The default gateway must be on that network; therefore, the default gateway must begin with 2 (for example, 2.100.110.120).

Here's another example that illustrates how the default gateway must be on the same network as your computer: If your computer's IP address is 205.27.46.113, and your subnet mask is 255.255.255.0, then you are on the 205.27.46.z network. The default gateway must be on this network, so it must begin with 205.27.46.

Prep Test

1 What is the binary representation of the decimal number 215?

2 What is the decimal representation of the binary number 10001110?

3 What address class does 129.34.73.112 belong to?

4 Which subnet mask gives you 62 available subnets?

A ○ 255.255.240.0

B ○ 255.192.0.0

C ○ 255.255.255.252

D ○ 255.255.248

5 You have a franchise that consists of 18 stores. You are predicting growth at a pace of five new stores a year for the next five years. Which custom subnet would be the logical choice for your company?

A ○ .224

B ○ .240

C ○ .248

D ○ .252

6 You have been issued the IP addresses 216.24.78.119, 216.24.78.114, and 216.24.78.110 from your Internet Service Provider. The ISP also assigned you a subnet mask of 255.255.240.0. The ISP says these IP addresses are valid for the subnet mask. True or False?

7 You are manually configuring TCP/IP on a user's computer. You assign the user an IP address of 197.74.91.112 and a subnet mask of 255.255.255.0. You are confused about the default gateway because you have four routers on your network. Which default gateway is correct for the user's computer?

A ○ 197.74.91.1

B ○ 197.1.1.1

C ○ 197.75.1.1

D ○ 197.74.191.1

8 You are having trouble communicating with one computer on the network, even though you can communicate with the other hosts. You print out the results of the `ipconfig /all` command on the computer giving you trouble, and you also print the results of your own computer.

Your computer:

```
Host Name . . . . . . . . . . . . . . :
        host1.mycompany.com
IP Address. . . . . . . . . . . . . . :
        198.113.201.137
Subnet Mask . . . . . . . . . . . . : 255.255.255.0
Default Gateway . . . . . . . . . : 198.113.201.1
DHCP Server . . . . . . . . . . . .: 198.113.201.23
Secondary WINS Server . . . . : 198.113.201.32
```

The nonfunctioning computer:

```
Host Name . . . . . . . . . . . . . . :
        host2.mycompany.com
IP Address. . . . . . . . . . . . . . :
        198.113.202.109
Subnet Mask . . . . . . . . . . . . : 255.255.255.0
Default Gateway . . . . . . . . . : 198.113.201.1
DHCP Server . . . . . . . . . . . .: 198.113.201.23
Primary WINS Server . . . . . . : 198.113.201.27
Secondary WINS Server . . . . : 198.113.201.32
```

What appears to be the problem?

A ○ The IP address of host2 is invalid.

B ○ The default gateway of host2 is invalid.

C ○ The subnet mask of host2 is invalid.

D ○ Something else must be the problem. Everything appears fine.

9 Garth is trying to communicate with a host on his subnet but is unsuccessful. He is receiving his TCP/IP configuration from the DHCP server. He also uses his machine as an internal Web server for the company. Which of the following is most likely the problem?

A ○ The default gateway from the DHCP server is incorrect.

B ○ The Web server's default gateway is incorrect.

C ○ Garth's computer is using a manually configured default gateway.

D ○ None of the above.

10 Which of the following custom subnet masks can be used to accommodate a network with up to 50 subnets? (Choose all that apply.)

A ❑ 254

B ❑ 224

C ❑ 255

D ❑ 252

Answers

1 The binary representation of the decimal number 215 is 11010111. You could have done the conversion by hand or with the calculator provided by Windows. *Review "A Bit of Preliminary Information on IP Addresses."*

2 The decimal representation of the binary number 10001110 is 142. You could have done the conversion by hand or with the calculator provided by Windows. *Review "A Bit of Preliminary Information on IP Addresses."*

3 The IP address 129.34.73.112 is a Class B address because it falls between 128.x.y.z and 191.x.y.z. *Review "Assigning Network Classes."*

4 *C.* The .252 subnet mask provides 62 networks. When it is used as a Class C subnet mask, as it is here, it yields only two hosts per subnet. *Review "Defining custom subnet masks."*

5 *D.* Although the .248 subnet mask can supply enough subnets for the current stores, the expected rate of growth for the company makes this subnet mask choice unsuitable for the future. The .252 subnet mask allows room for future stores to be added. *Review "Defining custom subnet masks."*

6 *False.* The increment value of the .240 subnet mask is 16. By calculating, you find the increments of 16, 32, 48, 64, 80, 96, 112, and so on. One of the IP addresses you've been given (216.24.78.110) falls within another subnet. The addresses 216.24.78.114 and 216.24.78.119 both fall within the other subnet. *Review "Defining custom subnet masks."*

7 *A.* The rule regarding the default gateway is that it must be on the same network as the IP address issued to the computer. The network ID for this subnet mask is 197.74.91.1. *Review "Spotting an incorrect default gateway."*

8 *B.* The default gateway must be on the same network as the network ID of the IP address of the host. Don't forget that! *Review "Spotting an incorrect default gateway."*

9 *D.* Garth is trying to communicate with a host on the *same* subnet as his computer; he doesn't need to use the default gateway. The default gateway is used for routing to remote networks. *Review "Diagnosing and Resolving IP Addressing Problems."*

10 *A, C, D.* The 244 custom subnet mask only allows for a maximum of six subnets. The 252, 254, and 255 subnets are the only custom subnet masks you can use if your network consists of more than 50 subnets. *Review "Defining custom subnet masks."*

Chapter 7

IP Routing

Exam Objectives

▶ Configuring TCP/IP on an NT server to support multiple network adapters

▶ Configuring a Windows NT Server computer to function as an IP router

*I*n order for packets of information to arrive at their proper destination, they may need to be routed through a gateway. *IP routing* (the subject of this chapter and the focus of a good seven to ten questions on the exam) is the method by which those packets are routed and delivered between networks.

You need to be familiar with how and why packets are routed in order to answer those complicated IP routing questions that may be thrown at you. This chapter is designed to help you tackle those questions. (If you're rusty on any IP addressing issues, I recommend reviewing Chapter 6 before digging into this chapter.)

In this chapter, I cover those topics related to the Microsoft exam objectives — configuring TCP/IP to support multiple network adapters and configuring a Windows NT Server to function as an IP router. I also tell you how to diagnose IP routing problems and walk you through the steps of solving a text-based and scenario-type routing question, such as you'd see on the exam.

Quick Assessment

1 Routers can connect physically different types of networks, such as Ethernet and Token Ring networks. This connection and how it's laid out is known as the _____.

2 Packets that are not on the local network will be sent to the _____.

3 The _____ is checked before the default gateway to determine whether a path is known.

4 _____ routing should be used for slower WAN links.

On a Windows NT Server computer, configure MS TCP/IP to support multiple network adapters

5 A Windows NT computer with two network cards installed to connect to separate networks is referred to as _____.

6 Windows NT configured as a router can use the _____ protocol to exchange route information with other routers on the network.

Configure a Windows NT Server computer to function as an IP router

7 The _____ command displays the current routing table for your computer.

8 The _____ command verifies connectivity by attempting to contact the destination host.

9 The _____ utility can determine the time it takes for a packet to be sent to each router.

Answers

1   *Topology.* Review *"Defining routers."*

2   *Default gateway.* Review *"IP routing on a remote network."*

3   *Routing table.* Review *"Checking the default gateway."*

4   *Static.* Review *"Integrating static and dynamic routing."*

5   *Multihomed.* Review *"Configuring TCP/IP on an NT Server to Support Multiple Network Adapters."*

6   *Routing Information Protocol (RIP).* Review *"Examining dynamic routing."*

7   *route print.* Review *"Using the route print command."*

8   ping. Review *"Using the ping command."*

9   tracert. Review *"Using the tracert utility."*

Heading in the Right Direction: IP Routing Basics

The Internet layer of the TCP/IP network model, of which the IP protocol is a part, is solely concerned with where packets of information are going and where they came from. A *packet* is a network message that includes data and has a source and addressing information appended to it. The destination addresses enable a packet to be sent along its way via a router.

Defining routers

A *router* is a networking device that routes packets that are destined for a network other than the local network. The *subnet mask* determines which network a host is located on (see Chapter 6 for more information on subnet masks). If the host is not on the local network, a packet is sent via the *default gateway*. Both the subnet mask and default gateway, as they apply to IP routing, are mentioned throughout this chapter. In the Internet world, routers are called *gateways*.

Routers can interconnect physically different types of networks, such as Ethernet and Token Ring networks, which are known as *topologies.* This term is important to remember because on the exam you may be presented with a diagram displaying networks with several different topologies. An exam question may trip you up if you think that IP packets can't be sent to dissimilar networks by a router.

Routers tend to be expensive items because they are very efficient at routing packets to different networks (after all, that's their sole job). The Internet is filled with routers, but you can configure your Windows NT computer to route packets to different networks and save yourself the expense of purchasing routers.

Because Windows NT is capable of IP forwarding, you will undoubtedly see many questions on the TCP/IP exam concerning configuring Windows NT as a router. A Windows NT machine that functions as a router requires two network interface cards: one card for the local network and one for the remote network. An NT computer configured in this way is called a *multihomed* computer. You find out more about multihomed computers in the section, "Configuring TCP/IP on an NT Server to Suppport Multiple Network Adapters," later in this chapter.

IP routing is one of the most challenging areas of the exam. The IP routing process can become very complicated, and you must understand the basics before you can take on the more-complex issues. Expect the exam to have complex illustrated and text-based routing scenarios for both local and remote networks (both of which I cover in this chapter so you can be well prepared come test time).

Delivering packets on a local network

Although routing isn't involved with a LAN, you should understand the way packets are sent on a local network versus the way they're routed to a remote network because not every question involves routing to remote networks. You can determine whether a packet will have to be routed to a remote host by using the subnet mask, which is covered in Chapter 6.

If another host is determined to be on the same network as the source host, the packet does not have to be routed. The following information identifies two hosts that are on the same network:

IP address = 134.36.23.118	Subnet Mask = 255.255.0.0
IP address = 134.36.46.22	Subnet Mask = 255.255.0.0

Because the destination shown here is on a local network, another member of the TCP/IP protocol suite in addition to the IP protocol goes to work. The Address Resolution Protocol (ARP) must determine the hardware address that corresponds to the destination IP address before the packet is sent out on the network. After that, the source and destination hosts can communicate with each other on the local network.

Even though a packet's address is visible to every computer on the local network, only the computer that matches the hardware address processes the packet. Therefore, each computer's network interface card inspects every packet sent to determine whether that packet is meant for that particular computer.

Having each computer inspect every packet on the network is fine for small to midsized networks, but traffic on the network can get heavy and performance begins to decline. This situation can be remedied by placing some computers on another subnet by using a technique known as *subnetting* the network, which you can read about in Chapter 6. Larger networks that make use of subnetting have routers to route the packets to other subnets. This process doesn't seem too complicated, until you begin routing packets to remote networks.

IP routing on a remote network

If the subnet mask determines that the destination address is on a remote network, the packet has to be routed to that network. The process of *routing* to a remote network makes use of the default gateway, which is configured for the computer in the TCP/IP Properties dialog box in the Network window of the Control Panel or is assigned via Dynamic Host Configuration Protocol (DHCP). The subject of routing — which includes the default gateway, the route table, and configuring your computer to route packets — gets ample coverage on the exam. I talk about each of these topics in this chapter.

You can think of the default gateway as a router. Although they're not exactly the same thing, imagining the default gateway as a router helps you to remember that the default gateway is used to route packets to remote networks. The *router* is the actual hardware device that routes the packet, and the *default gateway* is the address of the router that the hosts point to in order to have their packets routed.

After a packet is sent to the default gateway, it is either on the correct network or it has to be routed again. If the packet needs to be rerouted, it is sent to yet another router via the first router's default gateway, or by a route in the routing table (see the section "Building a static routing table with the route utility," later in this chapter for more information). If the packet takes too long to reach its destination, the *time-to-live* (TTL) expires, which prevents packets from being routed indefinitely. The TTL decreases each time the packet passes a router. Eventually the TTL reaches zero, and the packet is no longer routed but is discarded.

I've heard some test-takers complain that the complex network diagrams that appear on the test aren't completely legible on some testing centers' 15-inch monitors. I recommend finding a testing center equipped with 17-inch monitors. Your ability to read a complex mass of information can make the difference between your correctly answering a question or not.

Figure 7-1 illustrates a scenario you may see presented in an exam question. It depicts a packet reaching a destination host on a remote network via a router.

In a more complicated routing example shown in Figure 7-2, the destination host couldn't be found on the first network to which the packet was routed. Therefore, the router had to send the packet to its own default gateway.

By just looking at Figure 7-2, you should be able to determine the default gateway for Router1, even though it is not specified. (In this example, Router1 has a default gateway of 107.25.120.1.) However, you can't be certain about Router2's default gateway. Not enough information is available to determine the default gateway of Router2. (The default gateway is, however, a router on the 107.25.130.0 network.)

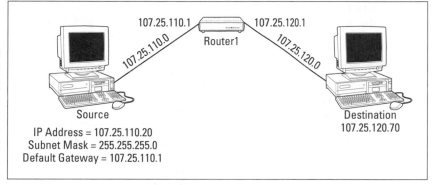

Figure 7-1:
An example
of routing
via a local
computer's
default
gateway.

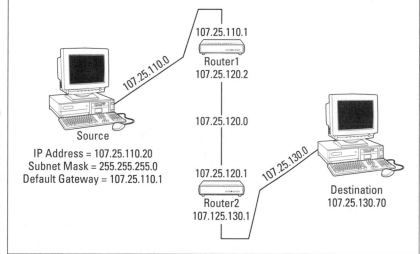

Figure 7-2:
An example
of a packet
being sent
via a
router's
default
gateway.

Configuring a Windows NT Server Computer to Function as an IP Router

During my exam, I saw a reference (more than a few times, in fact) to the option "Enable IP Forwarding." (You select Enable IP Forwarding if you have set up your Windows NT system to route packets between different networks, a process called *multihoming*.) I hadn't used Windows NT enough to know the exact name of the box you click to enable IP routing (illustrated in Figure 7-3).

I thought I was being tricked whenever an exam answer stated, "Click the Enable IP Forwarding check box in TCP/IP Properties." I thought the check box was clicked for *IP routing* (not IP forwarding), so I didn't choose "IP Forwarding" *every* time that was a possible answer. Now I realize that oversight cost me a few right answers. The "IP Forwarding" questions can quickly eliminate MCSE hopefuls who haven't spent enough time with Windows NT.

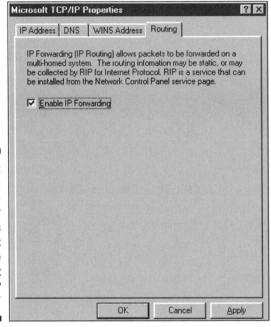

Figure 7-3:
The Routing page of the TCP/IP Properties dialog box is where you select "Enable IP Forwarding."

Routers are responsible for routing packets to different networks through one of two methods: *dynamic* or *static* IP routing. The exam focuses more heavily on static IP routing, which involves administrator intervention through use of the route command, which is covered in the section "Building a static routing table with the route utility" later in this chapter.

Examining static routing

Be prepared for a few questions regarding static routing. They can be a challenge because they likely involve the route command, which is one command that's not used very often. (I demonstrate how to build static routes with the route command later in this chapter in the section "Building a static routing table with the route utility.")

Static routing, as you can imagine, is much more limited than dynamic routing. The Internet is made up of dynamic routers that can share information with each other regarding the limitless number of paths that packets can travel along on the Internet. A network administrator (you) has to create, maintain, and delete static routes for your networks. This process isn't much of a chore, unless the network is extremely large and has multiple subnets. That's because static routing involves updating route tables on each routing device.

On a small network with only two subnets, connections are likely made with one router. This type of connection does not require an addition to the route table for the remote subnet because the local computer's default gateway can route the packets adequately.

Static routing is fine for a very small network, but when you begin adding additional remote networks, you can't get by with just the default gateway. If these additional networks are connected by routers with static route tables, you have to add the exact static route in order to get the networks to communicate with each other.

Using a default gateway address in a static router

When more than two networks are involved in static routing, you need to use the default gateway of one router to connect to the next router. If you imagine a router having two addresses (which, in fact, it does), the concept becomes clearer. You have to imagine each side of the router as different networks.

Figure 7-4 provides an example of how to configure default gateways with more than two networks. In this example, if a host on Network A wants to send a packet to another host located on Network B, specifying Router2 as the default gateway gets the packet to the proper destination without any problems.

Figure 7-4:
An example of routing via default gateways with more than two networks.

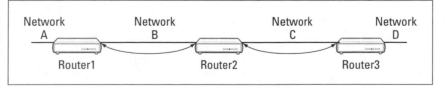

You are likely to spot an exam question with a scenario involving a host on Network A wanting to send a packet to another host located on Network C (refer to Figure 7-4). This type of situation shouldn't be difficult to deal with because it involves the default gateway. In this case, the default gateway of Router2 routes the packet to Network C, through its (Router2's) default gateway.

Continuing with this example, what if a host located on Network A wants to send a packet to another host located on Network D? (You are likely to see this sort of scenario presented on the exam.) It would seem that the default gateway of Router3 simply sends the packet as the other routers did earlier. The only problem with this scenario is that the default gateway for Router3 may not lead to Network D (again, check out Figure 7-4). It may lead there, or it may take a completely different path that does not lead to Network D at all.

You can't rely on the default gateway to perform accurate routing when more than two routers are in use, which means you have to use another method to route packets to remote networks that have more than two routers. The routing can be done dynamically if the router supports it; otherwise, you have to configure the *route table,* which is explained in the next section in this chapter, "Building a static routing table with the route utility."

You need to keep a number of aspects about default gateways in mind for the exam:

- ✔ The default gateway is used only when an entry is not found in the route table.

- ✔ It doesn't matter whether you have more than one default gateway specified; the first gateway found is used.

- ✔ The default gateway is used quite often because most networks do not have a route entry for every other network they communicate with.

- ✔ You can specify more than one default gateway, but for fault tolerance purposes only. The first default gateway is used to route information unless that gateway proves unacceptable, in which case, the next default gateway specified is used.

- ✔ You can't use multiple default gateways to route packets to the appropriate network as you would with a routing table. For that, you use the `route add` command, which is covered in the next section.

Building a static routing table with the route utility

One of the more challenging aspects of routing with your Windows NT Server that you'll find tested on the exam is the use of *routing tables*. You can expect to be asked to create a *static routing table* that must be absolutely accurate, right down to the syntax, to work properly. The test is likely to measure your ability to add a correct entry in a routing table in order to reach a remote host. And don't rule out the possibility of a question regarding proper syntax.

Adding, modifying, viewing, and deleting route entries is done with the route utility. You can use this utility to modify the routing table on your local computer. Keep in mind that a routing table can specify only the next router to use to get to a remote network, and not one beyond that point. The syntax for the route command utility follows, along with Table 7-1, which lists the available parameters for the route command:

```
route [-f, -p] [command [destination] [mask netmask] [gate-
       way]]
```

Table 7-1   Available Parameters for the Route Command

Parameter	Purpose
-f	Clears the routing table.
-p	Makes the route persistent, which means that the routes remain stored in memory, even when the computer is restarted.
Command	One of four commands: print, add, delete, or change.
Destination	Specifies the host to be used for the command.
mask	Signifies that the next parameter to be used is the subnet mask.
Netmask	Determines the subnet mask for the route entry; if Netmask is not present, the default of 255.255.255.255 is used.
Gateway	Specifies the gateway.

Lab 7-1 is an example of how to use the route add command, based on the information presented in Table 7-1.

Lab 7-1   Using the Route Add Command to Add a Route Entry

1. **Assume that you want to enter a route to a remote network of 116.21.78.0 with a subnet mask of 255.255.0.0 that uses the gateway of 116.21.1.1. Enter the following command:**

```
route add 116.21.0.0 mask 255.255.0.0 116.21.1.1
```

To help remember the `route` syntax, just keep in mind the following simple phrase: "To get to Network X, first go to Router Y. . . ." If the exam reverses the syntax of the `route` command, you won't get tripped up. For instance, using the example in this step, to get to the `116.21.0.0` network, you have to go to the `116.21.1.1` router. In short, the router is specified *last* in the `route` command.

2. **Don't forget to add trailing zeros after a network address.**

   For example, the 116.21 network (which is assumed to be 116.21.0.0) must be entered as `116.21.0.0` on the command line for the route to work properly. If you don't include the trailing zeros and just use `116.21`, for example, the `route` command doesn't know whether you mean the network address of 116.21.0.0 or the host address of 0.0.116.21.

In order to display your computer's current route table, use the `route print` command. (You can find more on this command in the section "Diagnosing IP Routing Problems" later in this chapter.)

Examining dynamic routing

If you are using dynamic routing, you don't have to worry about adding, modifying, or deleting route tables. Dynamic routing enables routers to communicate among one another and share routing information. Routers can query other routers for updated route information, which can create more efficient paths for sending packets or locate an alternative route if the original route fails. Dynamic routers, however, cannot update the static route tables of nondynamic routers.

The exam deals only slightly with dynamic routing, with the exception of one area: You may be asked which routing protocols are supported by a Windows NT machine that's acting as a router. The *Routing Information Protocol (RIP)* is used, which provides dynamic routing capability. A *RIP router* broadcasts routing information, such as network addresses, and directs data packets. RIP routers broadcast the routes they have discovered to keep neighboring routers up to date on the most efficient paths available.

Windows NT does not support more advanced routing protocols such as Open Shortest Path First (OSPF). Advanced routing protocols such as OSPF are used by dedicated hardware routers.

✔ If you have only one network interface card on a system with RIP enabled, the card listens for routing information updates only. Your system doesn't advertise (broadcast) more efficient routes that it has discovered through the process of normal routing throughout the network.

✔ When you add more than one network interface card to a system, RIP routing is enabled, and your computer functions as a *dynamic router,* listening for route updates from neighboring routers and broadcasting routing information to other RIP routers.

When your Windows NT computer is configured as a dynamic router, you can use the `route print` command to view the dynamic routes that your computer knows about. (See the section "Using the route print command" later in this chapter.)

When I took the test, I wasn't certain whether or not Windows NT can support dynamic routing. I had read an older test preparation guide and a TechNet article that said Windows NT does *not* support dynamic routing. This information is, of course, wrong. The moral of the story: Make sure you're reading up-to-date information when you're studying for the exam.

Integrating static and dynamic routing

You aren't required to use just one of the two routing types — static or dynamic. You can integrate both static and dynamic routing on a network. The exam is likely to test you on how to properly configure your network for routing, using a combination of static and dynamic routing. For example, which is the most efficient routing type for the internal LAN? Which is the most efficient for the external WAN? Your network uses static routes to connect to some networks and dynamic routes to connect to others. The following is what Microsoft recommends when it comes to configuring routing on the network:

✔ Static routing should be used for slower WAN links to reduce network traffic.

✔ You manually configure the static route to reach a destination network. Whenever packets travel to this remote network, they use the static route that you configured.

✔ Dynamic routing should be used when you want to reduce administrative overhead involved with modifying route tables.

If you configure your Windows NT static IP router to point to a dedicated *dynamic hardware router,* such as a Cisco, 3Com, or Bay router, you can take advantage of all the benefits those dedicated hardware routers provide. Because you can't dynamically update routes on your static Windows NT router, the next best thing is to point to a router (via the default gateway on your Windows NT static router) that is able to discover the most efficient routes.

Your packets get to their destinations sooner and provide some fault tolerance if a link in the network goes down. When your static Windows NT router sends a packet to the dedicated dynamic hardware router, the router discovers new paths around any congestion to get your packets where they need to go.

By the way, using RIP, the most efficient route to any destination is determined by the number of *hops* it takes to reach the destination. Each router is considered to be a hop. The fewer the number of hops to the destination, the more efficient the route is.

Answering Text-Based and Scenario-Type Routing Questions

The exam presents questions as both illustrated scenarios and as purely text-based problems. The text-based questions are more difficult to answer because you have to visualize the layout of the network. I strongly recommend that you use the paper and pen you are given to sketch out the network layout as you read the question to make answering these questions easier.

Example text-based question

The text-based scenario questions during the exam are more difficult than scenarios with illustrations because you have to imagine the layout of the network. However, you should sketch a diagram as you read the question to help clarify everything. You'll see what I mean about the usefulness of sketching out a diagram when you encounter a question such as the following:

> A network has four different subnets, which are represented by HostA, HostB, HostC, and HostD. Three Windows NT computers, acting as multihomed gateways, are represented by Router1, Router2, and Router3. Every host on each subnet must be able to communicate with every other host. Your subnet mask is 255.255.248.0.

My advice is to go through the analytical process step by step on a piece of scratch paper to arrive at the correct answer. Lab 7-2 describes the process.

Lab 7-2	Answering Text-Based Scenario Questions on IP Routing

The following steps show you how to proceed when confronted with a text-based scenario question on the exam:

1. Sketch a diagram based on the network and router information given.

The diagram can be as simple as the one shown in Figure 7-5. The subnets are represented by 1.0, 2.0, and so on. (They stand for 160.32.1.0 and 160.32.2.0.)

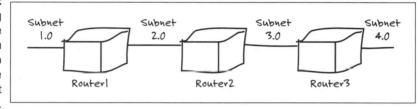

Figure 7-5:
Sketching out a simple diagram can help you arrive at a correct answer.

2. Add the IP addresses to each of the router interfaces, as shown in Figure 7-6.

The arrows in Figure 7-6 stand for the default gateway for the interface. For example, Router1's interface of 160.32.2.1 has a default gateway of 160.32.2.2. The Router3 interface of 160.32.3.2 has a default gateway of 160.32.3.1, which sends the packets back the other way.

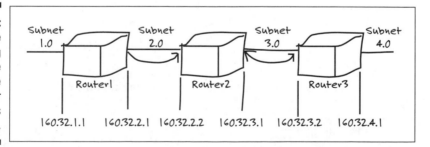

Figure 7-6:
The drawing from Figure 7-5 with the router addresses added.

3. **Determine which subnets can already communicate with each other by asking yourself the following:**

Can the 1.0 subnet communicate with the 2.0 subnet? Most likely, but the default gateway hasn't been specified in the scenario.

Can the 2.0 subnet communicate with the 3.0 subnet? Most likely, but again, the default gateway hasn't been specified in the scenario.

Can the 1.0 subnet communicate with the 3.0 subnet? You don't know for certain because the default gateway hasn't been specified.

I think you can safely assume that the packet routing process continues from left to right, meaning that all the options just listed do work. What may just crop up as a test question involves what happens next.

Example scenario-type question

Consider the following scenario question. I modeled it after a question that test-takers tell me they've seen on the TCP/IP exam:

Host Name	IP Address	Default Gateway
HostA	160.32.1.80	160.32.1.1
HostB	160.32.2.70	160.32.2.1
HostC	160.32.3.60	160.32.3.1
HostD	160.32.4.50	160.32.4.1
Router1	160.32.1.1	(blank)
(Router1)	160.32.2.2	(blank)
Router2	160.32.2.2	(blank)
(Router2)	160.32.3.2	(blank)
Router3	160.32.3.2	160.32.3.1
(Router3)	(blank)	(blank)

What should be done, if anything, to make sure everyone can communicate?

With the sample scenario presented above, you have a problem when a host on the Subnet 3.0 wants to communicate with the Subnet 1.0. Following along with Figure 7-6, you see that Router3 sends the packet back to its default gateway of 160.32.3.1, as shown by the far-right arrow in the figure.

The problem is that Router2 determines that the packet is destined for a remote network and sends it back to Router3 via its default gateway. Doing so makes the packet loop until the time-to-live (TTL) expires. Therefore, no packets can reach Subnet 1.0 when they are being sent by Subnet 3.0. How do you remedy this situation? Some possible solutions follow:

- ✓ What happens if you add a static route on Router1 to send packets that are destined for Subnet 1.0 through the 2.1 interface of Router1? This alternative would send packets destined for Subnet 1.0 in the opposite direction of where they need to go, so this idea won't work.

- ✓ What happens if you add a static route on Router3 to send packets that are destined for Subnet 1.0 through the 2.1 interface of Router3? This option won't work because it specifies an interface on Router1 that Router3 doesn't even know about.

- ✓ What happens if you add a static route on Router2 to send packets that are destined for Subnet 1.0 through the 2.1 interface of Router2? This option sends packets destined for Subnet 1.0 in the correct direction they need to go while avoiding a loop situation.

Therefore, the third option is the one you want. Router2 can send packets in both directions, which is desirable because this route is placed between two routers.

Ignore any extraneous information that won't help you answer a question. Try to ignore details such as the domain you are in, the type of computer (Pentium, UNIX) you're using, the name of the user, and so on. (The domain, user name, and computer name *may* be important for other questions on the exam, just not this type of question.) Jot down the most important facts on some scratch paper so you can keep them uppermost in your mind.

Yet another tactic helped me greatly on the exam when it came to adding static routes. Keep this rule in mind: Always bind the outer subnet to the far side of the middle subnet. This rule works for two routers connecting three subnets (illustrated in Figure 7-7) and for three routers connecting four subnets (illustrated in Figure 7-8).

The key to answering the routing questions correctly is in visualizing the network and diagramming it on paper, which is a whole lot easier than trying to keep all those addresses and networks in your head while you're trying to work out the problem.

After you draw the network layout, apply the binding rule. Find out which network you want to reach. For example, in Figure 7-7, Router2 needs to send information to the 1.0 subnet. The binding rule suggests that in order to get to the 1.0 subnet, you should send the information via the Router1 interface that is on the 2.0 subnet.

Figure 7-7:
Diagramming
the proper
binding for
static
routes with
two routers.

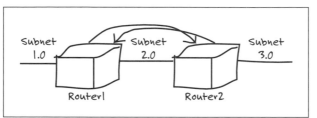

Figure 7-8:
Diagramming
the proper
binding for
static
routes with
three
routers.

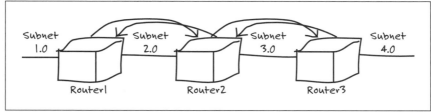

Configuring TCP/IP on an NT Server to Support Multiple Network Adapters

Because the exam is called "Internetworking with Microsoft TCP/IP on Microsoft Windows NT 4.0," I can guarantee that you will see a number of questions regarding the use of Windows NT as an IP router.

A few requirements must be met in order to route packets with a Windows NT computer. First, you must have more than one network adapter installed on the system. At that point your computer is considered *multihomed*. Two network interface cards (NICs) are typically installed in a multihomed computer in order to connect to separate networks, but you can have more than just two NICs installed.

If you plan on using Windows NT to route information between two networks, a few *multihomed configuration* requirements must be met. These requirements are worth noting because they're prime candidates for test question material:

✔ You must be running Windows NT Version 4.0 (or higher).

✔ You must have two network cards on the computer.

After you meet the hardware and software requirements for routing, you have some configuration tasks that you must attend to:

🖊 The network cards must have valid IP addresses and subnet masks assigned to them for the network they're on.

🖊 The Enable IP Forwarding option on the Routing page of the TCP/IP Properties dialog box must be selected.

🖊 You need to create a static routing table with entries to remote networks that the interface cards are not attached to.

🖊 You can create a route entry to a dynamic router in order to benefit from its capability to exchange routing information with other routers. If you do not have access to a dynamic router on your network, this isn't possible.

Diagnosing IP Routing Problems

Plenty of opportunities exist in IP routing for your making errors that can leave you scratching your head. Of course, Microsoft loves to include plenty of troubleshooting questions in the exam to exploit your weaknesses.

With the IP routing information I provide throughout this chapter and the troubleshooting procedures I introduce in this section, you should have no problems with IP routing troubleshooting questions on the exam. A few utilities are used to diagnose problems related to IP routing. However, I don't describe every feature of these utilities, just the features that relate to IP routing.

Using the route print command

The route print command displays the current routing table for your computer on screen (Figure 7-9 shows the output from this command). In the route print information, you find routes to other networks. If you have trouble communicating with a particular subnet, you can verify that a route exists to the network through the data supplied by route print.

If you need to examine the current routes that your computer is using, you can enter the route print command at the command prompt. What you get is a tabular display similar to the one shown in Figure 7-9. For example, a route entry with the value of 2 under the Metric column of the route print command output (refer to the figure) indicates that the route has been obtained from the router listening to dynamic routing updates from neighboring routers.

```
Shortcut to Cmd.exe                                              _ □ X
F:\>route print

Active Routes:

 Network Address          Netmask   Gateway Address        Interface   Metric
       0.0.0.0            0.0.0.0   207.149.40.236   207.149.40.236        1
     127.0.0.0          255.0.0.0         127.0.0.1        127.0.0.1        1
   207.149.40.0    255.255.255.0   207.149.40.236   207.149.40.236        1
 207.149.40.236  255.255.255.255         127.0.0.1        127.0.0.1        1
 207.149.40.255  255.255.255.255   207.149.40.236   207.149.40.236        1
       224.0.0.0          224.0.0.0   207.149.40.236   207.149.40.236        1
 255.255.255.255  255.255.255.255   207.149.40.236   207.149.40.236        1
F:\>
```

Figure 7-9:
Sample
display from
the route
print
command.

Checking the default gateway

The default gateway has almost the same effect as static routing: to route
packets to remote networks, except that the default gateway is used if none
of the routes in the routing table can get the packet to where it should go. If
a path is found in the routing table, the packet is sent and the default
gateway isn't used.

If a static route doesn't exist to a remote network in the routing table and
the packet still isn't arriving, check for the proper default gateway in the
TCP/IP configuration. If the packet is not arriving, you can determine that
both the route table and default gateway are not correct.

Using the default gateway without a static route for a remote network is very
common. A static route in the routing table is for a specific network entry;
the default gateway is used for *all* remote networks. For the test, remember
that the route table is checked *before* the default gateway to determine
whether a route exists.

Using the ping command

The ping command verifies connectivity by trying to contact the destination host. It sends packets to the destination host and listens for the echo
replies.

If the `ping` command is something new to you, you can open up a command prompt window by choosing Start➪Programs➪Command Prompt. At the command prompt, enter the `ping` command, followed by the name of the computer *or* the IP address of the computer. You either receive a response from the host or the request times out, which indicates that the host could not be contacted. (More information on troubleshooting with the `ping` command is in Chapter 16.)

Using the tracert utility

The `tracert` (trace route) utility is used to trace the route a packet takes in real time as it travels to its destination. The output from this command includes the routers (or hops) it passes along the way. `tracert` is important for three reasons:

- ✔ It can determine whether the destination is not being reached.
- ✔ It can determine which router was the last one the packet passed before failing.
- ✔ It can determine how long the packet travels between routers.

You may not see a question directly related to the `tracert` utility; nevertheless, it may appear in a scenario-type question involving packets being incorrectly routed. The fact that `tracert` is mentioned does not necessarily mean the question is about `tracert`. The question is likely to concern basic IP addressing issues covered in Chapter 6.

For example, a question involving the `tracert` utility may go something like this: "You are unable to communicate with Host X on Network Z. You used the `tracert` command to determine that the packet continues to take an incorrect path, and therefore does not reach its destination," and so forth.

Examine the output of the `tracert` command, as illustrated in Figure 7-10. You can see the path the packet takes as it travels across the network, the time between hops, and the router address that routed the packet. The trace is complete when the packet arrives at the destination.

For the exam, you should be able to identify problems requiring troubleshooting with the `tracert` command. Figure 7-11 shows an example of a packet having difficulty reaching its destination. The destination can't be contacted and begins to time out.

```
C:\WINNT\System32\cmd.exe                                              _ □ ×
Microsoft(R) Windows NT(TM)
(C) Copyright 1985-1996 Microsoft Corp.

C:\>tracert mcse.com

Tracing route to mcse.com [38.250.143.30]
over a maximum of 30 hops:

  1    131 ms    130 ms    130 ms  portmaster.Direct-Source.com [207.149.40.2]
  2    130 ms    130 ms    130 ms  br1.Direct-Source.com [207.149.40.1]
  3    130 ms    150 ms    140 ms  s2-6.c1.pdx.ixa.net [204.194.10.57]
  4    140 ms    140 ms    140 ms  s10-4.c2.sea.ixa.net [199.242.24.5]
  5    140 ms    140 ms    141 ms  905.Hssi5-0.GW1.SEA1.ALTER.NET [137.39.136.5]
  6    140 ms    241 ms    140 ms  103.ATM3-0-0.XR2.SEA1.ALTER.NET [146.188.200.
]
  7    181 ms    150 ms    140 ms  100.ATM3-0-0.TR2.SEA1.ALTER.NET [146.188.200.
]
  8    190 ms    180 ms    180 ms  110.ATM9-0-0.TR2.SCL1.ALTER.NET [146.188.137.
]
  9      *       200 ms    180 ms  100.ATM9-0-0.XR2.SCL1.ALTER.NET [137.39.197.1

 10    170 ms    180 ms    170 ms  194.ATM1-0-0.BR1.SFO1.ALTER.NET [146.188.145.
]
 11    170 ms    170 ms    171 ms  204.6.117.33
 12    230 ms    240 ms    241 ms  sse.sc.psi.net [38.1.3.14]
 13    240 ms    271 ms    300 ms  rc2.south-southeast.us.psi.net [38.1.27.2]
 14    270 ms    451 ms    340 ms  38.1.47.233
 15      *       761 ms    370 ms  winterpark2.fl.isdn.psi.net [38.146.233.111]
 16    311 ms    481 ms    420 ms  38.250.143.1
 17    340 ms    331 ms    300 ms  38.250.143.30

Trace complete.

C:\>
```

Figure 7-10: The `tracert` command output tracing the route to `mcse.com`.

```
C:\WINNT\System32\cmd.exe - tracert nbc.com                            _ □ ×
  7    140 ms    141 ms    150 ms  sl-bb1-sea-8-0-0-155M.sprintlink.net [144.232.
93]
  8    171 ms    150 ms    150 ms  sl-bb11-stk-2-1.sprintlink.net [144.232.8.29]
  9    160 ms    150 ms    160 ms  sl-bb2-stk-0-0-0-155M.sprintlink.net [144.232.
70]
 10    160 ms    160 ms    161 ms  sl-w1-mae-4-1-0-T3.sprintlink.net [144.228.10.
]
 11    160 ms    161 ms    180 ms  f0.mae-west.verio.net [198.32.136.80]
 12    231 ms    250 ms      *     mae-west.mae-east.verio.net [205.238.56.6]
 13    230 ms    250 ms    241 ms  mae-east.mae-east1.verio.net [205.238.56.114]
 14    250 ms      *         *     mae-east1-0.phl1.verio.net [205.238.56.122]
 15    200 ms    210 ms    211 ms  jvnc.phl.verio.net [205.238.52.18]
 16    221 ms    230 ms    210 ms  ge.jvnc.net [130.94.40.251]
 17    210 ms    220 ms    221 ms  192.35.39.75
 18      *         *         *     Request timed out.
 19      *         *         *     Request timed out.
 20      *         *         *     Request timed out.
 21      *         *         *     Request timed out.
 22      *         *         *     Request timed out.
 23      *         *         *     Request timed out.
 24      *         *         *     Request timed out.
 25      *         *         *     Request timed out.
 26      *         *         *     Request timed out.
 27      *         *         *     Request timed out.
 28      *         *
```

Figure 7-11: An example of a request that timed out during a trace.

Prep Test

1 You are at host 101.36.118.200 and you want to connect to host 101.37.143.13. Your local gateway is 101.36.1.1, the subnet mask is 255.255.0.0, and the remote host's gateway is 101.37.1.1 with a subnet mask of 255.255.0.0. Which command would you use?

A ○ `route add 101.36.118.200 mask 255.255.0.0 101.37.143.13`
B ○ `route add 101.37.143.13 mask 255.255.0.0 101.37.1.1`
C ○ `route add 101.37.0.0 mask 255.255.0.0 101.36.1.1`
D ○ `route add 101.36.0.0 mask 255.255.0.0 101.37.1.1`

2 (True/False). The default gateway is used before the routing table when routing packets to remote networks.

3 Which `route` command parameter clears the route table?

A ○ `-p`
B ○ `-c`
C ○ `-d`
D ○ `-f`

4 Which of the following are possibilities for the default gateway for a host with the IP address of 134.21.85.211 and a subnet mask of 255.255.255.0? (Choose all that apply.)

A ❑ 134.221.85.1
B ❑ 134.21.85.255
C ❑ 134.21.85.1
D ❑ 134.21.85.127

5 The rule to remember when adding static routes is:

A ○ Bind the outer subnet to the near side of the last subnet.
B ○ Bind the inner subnet to the far side of the middle subnet.
C ○ Bind the outer subnet to the outer side of the last subnet.
D ○ Bind the outer subnet to the far side of the middle subnet.

6 What must be enabled to properly route packets with your Windows NT multihomed computer?

A ○ Enable IP Routing must be checked in TCP/IP Advanced Properties under the Forwarding page.
B ○ Enable IP Forwarding must be checked in TCP/IP Properties under the Routing page.
C ○ Enable IP Forwarding must be checked in TCP/IP Advanced Properties under the Routing page.
D ○ Enable IP Routing must be checked in TCP/IP Properties under the Forwarding page.

7 (True/False). You have a static route configured to reach the remote network 100.20.10 that uses a router IP address of 100.20.10.1. You have discovered a more efficient route that uses the router at IP address of 100.50.90.1. The command `route change 100.20.10.0 100.50.90.1` correctly changes the route.

8 (True/False). A route table can only specify the next router to use to get to a remote network.

9 You are trying to use your Windows NT computer to route packets between two networks. You have checked the IP Forwarding box in the Routing page, given the network cards an IP address to share, and created a static route for each network you need to route to. What else do you need to do to configure this computer as a router?

A ○ Nothing. It will work fine.

B ○ Give each of the network cards a unique default gateway.

C ○ Give each of the network cards a unique subnet mask.

D ○ The configuration is invalid and must be reconfigured.

10 You would like your Windows NT router to advertise the routes it has learned. How do you configure this to happen?

A ○ It will always happen when you install the Routing Information Protocol.

B ○ You have to select IP Forwarding on the Routing page.

C ○ You need at least two network cards installed on the system.

D ○ You have to select the option for RIP broadcasting in the Network window of the Control Panel.

Answers

1 *C.* You are adding a static route to the network that the destination host is on, which is 101.37.0.0. You get to this network by specifying the default gateway of the local network, which is 101.36.1.1. *Review "Building a static routing table with the route utility."*

2 *False.* The routing table is checked for the network entry before the default gateway is checked. *Review "Using a default gateway address in a static router."*

3 *D.* -f is the parameter to clear the route table. The parameter to make the routes persistent is -p. *Review "Building a static routing table with the route utility."*

4 *C, D.* The default gateway must always be on the same network as the host. Therefore, the default gateway address of 134.21.85.1 and 134.21.85.127 are the only answers listed that are on the same network as the host. Although the default gateway of 143.21.85.255 is on the same network, the last octet of the IP address is invalid. Review *"IP routing on a remote network."*

5 *D.* This option eliminates the looping situation in which packets can't travel back through the network. *Review "Example scenario-type question."*

6 *B.* This is the correct method for enabling IP routing in Windows NT 4.0. Prior versions used the IP Routing check box in the Advanced TCP/IP Properties dialog box. *Review "Configuring a Windows NT Server Computer to Function as an IP Router."*

7 *True.* The route change command uses the same syntax as the route add command. However, you are specifying the new address to the network, which changes the existing route to the new route. *Review "Building a static routing table with the route utility."*

8 *True.* The route table can only specify the next router to use. It can't specify a router to use that is beyond another router. *Review "Building a static routing table with the route utility."*

9 *D.* Having the IP addresses that are valid for their own particular network is essential for configuring a Windows NT machine as a router. They can't share the same IP address. Review *"Configuring an Windows NT Server Computer to Function as an IP Router."*

10 *C.* With only one network card in your system, you can listen for new routes from RIP routers. But with two network cards installed, you can not only listen to new routes but also broadcast the routes you have learned to other RIP routers. *Review "Examining dynamic routing."*

Part III
Installation and Configuration

The 5th Wave   By Rich Tennant

CLIENT/SERVER
SOLUTIONS

"ODDLY ENOUGH, THIS HAS BEEN THE LEAST DISRUPTIVE PART OF OUR MOVE TO CLIENT/SERVER COMPUTING."

In this part . . .

The most heavily tested sections on just about any
Microsoft exam involve installation and configuration.
In the first part of this book, I cover some installation and
configuration fundamentals, including ARP, Host Name
Resolution, and NetBIOS. In this part of the book, I delve
into the Dynamic Host Configuration Protocol, the
Windows Internet Name Service (WINS), the Domain
Name Service (DNS), and the Simple Network Management Protocol (SNMP). These topics can cover a lot of
territory, so to save you some precious time, I call your
attention to what you definitely need to study for the
exam, and what you can safely skip.

Chapter 8

Dynamic Host Configuration Protocol

● ●

Exam Objectives

▶ Configuring scopes by using DHCP Manager

▶ Installing and configuring the DHCP Relay Agent

● ●

*T*he Dynamic Host Configuration Protocol (DHCP) is a fairly significant portion of the exam, and this chapter gives you the information you need to nail those DHCP test questions. The most important area to study for the exam, in addition to installing and configuring the DHCP Relay Agent, is configuring the DHCP scopes with the DHCP Manager. The following is a rundown of what you need to know for the exam, which also happens to be areas covered in this chapter:

✔ You absolutely need to know how the DHCP Relay Agent works and how it's used for fault tolerance.

✔ You should be familiar with the WINS and DNS server settings and configurations (also known as *values*) that are sent to DHCP clients.

✔ You should definitely know what a DHCP scope is and what configuration options are available when you're defining scopes.

If you have any questions on the subnet mask, default gateway, or configuring an IP address — the basic TCP/IP configuration parameters that must be provided to a DHCP client — those elements of the TCP/IP technology are covered in Chapters 6 and 7. You may want to review those chapters before diving into the subject of DHCP.

Quick Assessment

1 The _____ command is very useful when combined with DHCP to determine the current configuration.

2 A source address of _____ is used when a DHCP client is initializing on the network.

3 (True/False). After 87.5 percent of the lease has expired, the client tries to renew with any DHCP server on the network.

4 DHCPDISCOVER is an example of a(n) _____ type.

5 Setting the lease _____ is required when configuring your DHCP server.

6 (True/False). You should have only one scope per subnet.

7 You should _____ an IP address for special nodes on the network.

8 The Unique Identifier for the Add Reserved Clients dialog box is the _____ address.

9 The _____ forwards information to the remote DHCP server.

10 The _____ may not be capable of forwarding DHCP messages.

Configuring scopes by using DHCP Manager

Installing and configuring the DHCP Relay Agent

Answers

1 *ipconfig*. Review "Using ipconfig with DHCP."

2 *0.0.0.0*. Review "Phase one: The IP lease request."

3 *True*. Review "Renewing an IP address lease."

4 *Message*. Review "DHCP message types."

5 *Duration*. Review "Installing and Configuring a DHCP Server."

6 *True*. Review "Defining DHCP scopes."

7 *Reserve*. Review "Reserving DHCP client IP addresses."

8 *MAC*. Review "Reserving DHCP client IP addresses."

9 *Relay Agent*. Review "Installing and Configuring the DHCP Relay Agent on Multiple Subnets."

10 *Router*. Review "Zeroing in on the DHCP essentials."

Scoping It Out: Some DHCP Basics

Configuring TCP/IP can be a challenging undertaking. Every computer on a TCP/IP network must have a unique IP address as well as the correct subnet mask and default gateway. In the past, an administrator had to configure each computer manually, but now the Dynamic Host Configuration Protocol (DHCP) makes the task of configuring each TCP/IP-based computer much easier.

Using DHCP to configure TCP/IP on a client computer lets you reap certain benefits:

- Additional TCP/IP information, such as the IP addresses of other important servers on the network (for example, the WINS and DNS servers), can also be entered and sent to a client computer.
- An administrator doesn't have to visit each client to configure TCP/IP.
- The DHCP server doesn't assign the same address twice.
- The server doesn't make clerical mistakes as humans do, such as misspelling a computer name or forgetting to include a period in the IP address.
- DHCP can automatically reconfigure a client that moves to another subnet.
- An administrator can control which IP addresses are used.

A DHCP server can't detect which addresses are already being used on a network. If a host has a manually configured IP address that falls within a DHCP *scope* (an IP address pool), the chances are great that the DHCP will assign a duplicate of that address to another host. You can prevent this scenario from occurring by excluding already existing, manually configured IP addresses from the scope when you create the scope.

Configuring a client for DHCP

For the exam, you should know how to configure a client for DHCP, which is a fairly simple process. The steps in Lab 8-1 describe how to configure a Windows NT Workstation client to obtain TCP/IP information from a DHCP server.

Lab 8-1   Configuring a TCP/IP-Based Client for DHCP

1. **Click Start, choose Settings, and then choose Control Panel.**

2. **Double-click the Network icon in the Control Panel.**

3. **Click the Protocols tab.**

   You get a list of installed network protocols.

4. **Double-click the desired TCP/IP protocol, or select the TCP/IP protocol and click the Properties button.**

   The IP Address Property page appears, which is where you need to configure the client to use DHCP.

5. **Select Obtain an IP Address from a DHCP Server.**

   You are prompted to restart your computer for the changes to take effect. If you don't have a DHCP server on your network, your computer continues to search for a DHCP server on startup, which causes delays when you first start Windows NT.

Other exam preparation books go on for pages about how the DHCP client and server send and receive TCP/IP information. But I don't remember seeing questions that detailed on my exam, and I haven't heard that anyone else has, either. Therefore, I won't waste your time by making you study stuff that won't be on the exam. I just stick to the essentials.

Requesting an IP address

The following sections of this chapter provide a brief overview of the communication process between the DHCP client and the server when TCP/IP initializes on a client. The process results in the client receiving an IP address from the server. Four phases make up the request for an IP address:

1. The host makes an IP lease request.

2. The server responds with an IP lease offer.

3. The client makes an IP lease selection.

4. The server responds with an IP lease acknowledgment.

Phase one: The IP lease request

The IP lease request happens the first time a computer starts as a DHCP client, or when a client is denied a request for a specific IP address, or when the client requires a new lease, or when an existing DHCP client moves to a new subnet. The following are the steps for issuing an IP lease request:

1. The host contacts the DHCP server with an *IP lease request* when the client initializes on the network.

   The lease request is a broadcast message because the host has no knowledge of the DHCP server's IP address or name. The destination address of the lease request, therefore, is 255.255.255.255, the broadcast address. The DHCP server must listen for the broadcast message on the network.

   The host also has no IP address yet; therefore, the requests come from the source address of 0.0.0.0. This source host also includes its hardware address in the broadcast message so that the DHCP server knows which host sent the broadcast.

2. When the DHCP server hears the IP lease request, it responds with an *IP lease offer*.

   The IP lease offer contains an IP address and the configuration information for the host that sent the request. (I explain the IP lease offer more fully in the next section.)

3. If the host doesn't receive a response from the DHCP server, it rebroadcasts the IP lease request four times every five minutes until it receives a response from the DHCP server.

Phase two: The IP lease offer

After the host sends the IP lease request, it receives an *IP lease offer* from the DHCP server. The IP lease offer contains IP configuration information meant for the host. The IP lease offer also contains the IP address and subnet mask for the DHCP server that sent the request to the client. The DHCP client can receive responses from multiple DHCP servers. However, the DHCP client usually selects the first IP lease offer it receives. If the DHCP client previously leased an IP address from this server, the client requests the previous address, which is granted if available.

Phase three: The IP lease selection

After the client accepts the IP lease offer, it broadcasts to all DHCP servers that it has made a *lease selection* by accepting an offer. This lease selection broadcast contains the IP address that the client has just accepted. More than one DHCP server may have offered an IP address to the client, and the broadcast enables the other DHCP servers to see that the client has not accepted their offered IP addresses. These other DHCP servers that weren't selected by the client can use their offered IP addresses for other DHCP clients in the future.

Phase four: The IP lease acknowledgment

The DHCP server that received the IP lease selection from the client responds with an *IP lease acknowledgment*, which is a broadcast that contains the IP address that the client has accepted. The IP lease acknowledgment also includes the terms of the lease and the valid configuration parameters for the client. When the client receives the IP lease acknowledgment, it can complete the startup phase with the newly received IP address.

Releasing an IP address lease

You release a lease if you no longer want that IP address to be used by a client, or if you want the client to lease a different IP address. If you decide that you need to reserve an IP address that is already being used, you can release the IP address from the client to make it immediately available for the new machine.

You can't exclude a range of addresses that includes an active lease, so you must delete the active lease before you can continue.

The lease for the IP address either expires or is released manually by the administrator. An IP address can be manually released in one of two ways:

✔ By the server, through the DHCP Manager

✔ By the client, through the `ipconfig /release` command

You should know the differences between these two lease release methods for the exam:

✔ **Releasing a lease through the DHCP Manager.** You can delete an active lease on the server within DHCP Manager by selecting the lease you want to release and clicking the Delete button. This method removes the IP address lease but doesn't inform the client that the lease has been removed. The client still uses the IP address, but any attempts to renew the lease fail. The DHCP Manager method of releasing IP addresses is not immediate; actual release of the address can take days.

✔ **Releasing a lease through the** `ipconfig /release` **command.** To immediately release an IP address, you can use the `ipconfig / release` command from the client. The client sends a `DHCPREQUEST` message to the DHCP server indicating that it no longer requires the IP address lease. The server returns the IP address to the pool of available IP addresses on the server. The client can then start a new IP address lease with the IP lease request.

The following is the output of the `ipconfig /release` command:

```
Windows NT IP Configuration IP address 198.113.201.109
         successfully released for adapter "El90x2"
```

Renewing an IP address lease

An IP address lease has an expiration date; the DHCP administrator sets the length of the lease. As the expiration date on the lease approaches, the client attempts to renew it. In the following three IP lease renewal situations, take special note of the percentage of time expired and the server that renews the lease:

- ✔ After 50 percent of the lease has expired, the client tries to renew the lease with the original DHCP server that offered the lease.

- ✔ If the client is unable to renew the lease with the original server when 87.5 percent of the lease has expired, the client attempts to renew the lease by broadcasting the request to any of the DHCP servers on the network.

- ✔ If the IP address lease expires, the client has to discontinue use of the IP address and begin a new lease, starting with the IP lease request.

You may be asked a question on the test about renewing and releasing IP addresses from the client. This releasing is through the use of the ipconfig command, which forces the client to renew the current IP address, regardless of how much time has expired on the lease. A DHCPREQUEST message is sent to the DHCP server, asking for the new lease and any modifications that have been made to the scope. If the DHCP server doesn't respond to the client renewal request, the client continues to use the existing lease information.

If you get a question that asks why you would use the ipconfig /renew command, just remember this: You *renew* a lease if you make changes to the scope options on the DHCP server that you want to be reflected on the clients.

DHCP message types

Microsoft has documented message types that are passed between the client and server during the DHCP process. If you see a question on the exam about the communication process between the DHCP client and server, it most likely involves the types of messages. Table 8-1 provides a description of the DHCP message types, which you should memorize for the exam:

Table 8-1	DHCP Message Types between the Client and Server	
Message Type	*Phase When Used*	*Description*
DHCPDISCOVER	Used in the IP lease request phase	A packet that's broadcast the first time a DHCP client computer attempts to start on the network. The client requests IP address information from the server from a source address of 0.0.0.0 because the client does not yet have an IP address.
DHCPOFFER	Used in the IP lease offer phase	An offer from the DHCP server containing an IP address from the range of available IP addresses. The DHCP server also returns additional TCP/IP configuration information, such as the subnet mask and default gateway.
DHCPREQUEST	Used in the IP lease acknowledgment phase	A packet that contains the offered IP address that is broadcast when the client receives the DHCPOFFER packet.
DHCPDECLINE	Used in the IP lease selection phase	A message to the server from the DHCP client indicating that the offered configuration parameters are invalid.
DHCPACK	Used in the IP lease renewal phase	An acknowledgment from the DHCP server for the client's DHCPREQUEST.
DHCPNACK	Used in the IP lease renewal phase	A negative acknowledgment to the client if the address can't be used or is no longer valid.
DHCPRELEASE	Used in the IP lease renewal phase	A message to the server from the DHCP client that releases the IP address and cancels any remaining lease.

Installing and Configuring a DHCP Server

For the exam, you should know that you install the Windows NT DHCP server through the Network window in the Control Panel.

Lab 8-2 describes the process of installing the DHCP Server Service.

Lab 8-2	Installing the DHCP Server Service

1. Open the Control Panel window and double-click Network.

2. Select the Services tab and click Add.

A list of available network services is displayed.

3. Select Microsoft DHCP Server.

Files are copied to your hard drive. A message appears saying that any adapters in the system using DHCP to obtain an IP address are now required to use static IP addresses (unless the IP address has already been assigned).

4. Reboot.

Configuring a client to use DHCP is fairly simple, but configuring a DHCP server takes some extra work. You need to complete several tasks to get your DHCP server rolling:

✔ Create a scope of IP addresses.

✔ Exclude certain IP addresses (optional).

✔ Set the lease duration.

✔ Reserve certain IP addresses (optional).

✔ Set the DHCP options, such as router, DNS, and WINS server addresses (optional).

Using the DHCP Manager to Configure Scopes

The DHCP Manager is the graphical interface that you use to configure and monitor the local and remote DHCP servers on the network. You find the DHCP Manager under the Administrative Tools (Common) program group in the Start menu. Figure 8-1 shows the main screen of the DHCP Manager.

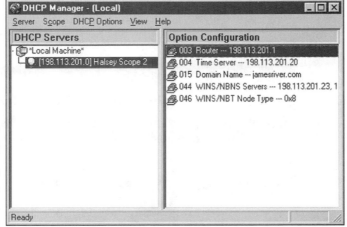

Figure 8-1:
The main
window of
the DHCP
Manager.

From the figure, you can see the DHCP servers (or, in this case, the single DHCP server) listed in the left half of the DHCP Manager window, and the option configurations that are set for each server in the right half of the window. The DHCP options in the right half are settings, such as the router and WINS server addresses, that are going to be used to configure the client. In "Assigning advanced DHCP options," later in the chapter, I show you how to configure these DHCP options that are used to configure the client.

Defining DHCP scopes

The DHCP scope is second in importance only to DHCP over multiple subnets for the exam. You should definitely know what a DHCP scope is and what options, such as the duration of the lease, are available to create a scope.

A *DHCP scope* is a grouping of IP addresses and configuration information made by an administrator for computers that require the same configuration on each subnet. The scope contains a range of valid IP addresses that the server assigns to the clients. A scope must be created before the clients are able to receive TCP/IP configuration information from the DHCP server. You need a few required elements in order to create a scope, and these elements make great material for exam questions:

   ✔ A range of IP addresses

   ✔ A subnet mask for the IP address

   ✔ The duration of the lease before a client must renew its configuration

The scope name or comments are not required, but they're helpful if you have more than one scope. Lab 8-3 lists the steps to creating a scope with the DNCP Manager.

Lab 8-3   Creating a Scope in the DHCP Manager

1. Choose Scope⇨Scope Properties in the DHCP Manager window.

The Scope Properties dialog box appears. Figure 8-2 shows the dialog box with all the required scope elements specified.

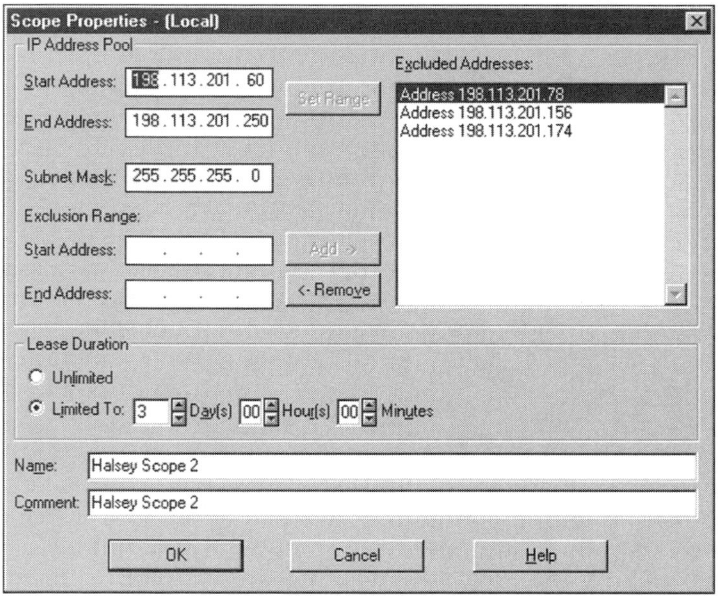

Figure 8-2: The required scope property elements.

2. Enter the starting IP address for the scope.

3. Close the range of IP addresses in the scope by including the ending address for the IP address range.

This step creates one large range of IP addresses that are available to be leased to the DHCP clients.

4. Specify the subnet mask to be used for these IP addresses; one subnet mask is specified for the entire range of IP addresses.

5. If you need to exclude any range of IP addresses, enter the starting address and ending address in the space provided and click Add to exclude these addresses.

6. If you don't want to accept the default lease duration of three days, change the lease duration in the spaces provided.

The properties set in these steps make up the required DHCP scope properties.

A few pieces of important information on scopes appeared on my exam; you should be aware of this information:

✔ Each subnet can have only one scope of addresses.

✔ The scope of addresses in a subnet can be one large continuous range or a group of smaller ranges within the subnet. If you need to have a number of smaller ranges within one subnet, you have to create one large scope that includes all these addresses, and then exclude the addresses that fall between the ranges you want to use.

✔ The scope can't be reduced, but it can be extended. If you need to reduce the scope, you have to exclude addresses within the range that you no longer need, instead of changing the beginning or ending IP address of the scope boundary.

The questions on these subjects may seem difficult at first because they typically include extraneous information to confuse you. Just think about the basics of the situation and you should do fine.

Setting DHCP scope properties

In addition to the required properties for the DHCP scope, you may find some other scope properties on your exam. These additional properties are detailed in Table 8-2. They can be found by choosing Active Leases from the Scope menu.

Table 8-2	Setting Additional DHCP Scope Properties
Option	**Description**
Deactivate	You can deactivate an IP address if a client is no longer using it.
Renewal	You can change the renewal period for the IP address renewals. By default, the time at which a client begins renewing IP addresses is when 50 percent of the lease time has expired.
Reserve	You can reserve addresses for certain DHCP clients so that they continue to receive the same IP address. Reservations are important for some machines on the network, especially servers that clients expect to find at certain IP addresses.

Assigning advanced DHCP options

In addition to assigning the required TCP/IP configuration specifications to DHCP clients, you can also assign more advanced TCP/IP specifications, such as the address of routers and DNS, WINS, or Internet Web servers on the network. When you assign these DHCP options, you can assign them for every scope as a *global* option or for a specific scope. These settings are not required. You should keep the following important rules in mind for the exam:

✔ Settings in the global options always apply to every scope on the server, unless they are overridden by specific scope options or a manual configuration of the client.

✔ Settings in the active scope apply to every computer in the scope, unless they are overridden by manual configuration of the client.

Because configuration information that you manually specify on a client overrides any of the DHCP settings that the DHCP server gives the client, you must be sure that you don't have incorrect settings configured at the client. If you forget that a client has been manually configured and then move that client to a DHCP network, the manual settings still override the DHCP options, and those manual settings may cause problems.

Table 8-3 lists predefined configuration parameters, or options, available to assign to Microsoft DHCP clients. A number of other options are available, but you're not likely to be tested on them.

Consider the DHCP options in Table 8-3 as *values* that can be sent to the DHCP client. Thinking of the options in this way makes understanding the purpose of DHCP options easier for the exam.

Table 8-3	Default DHCP Options
Configuration Option	*Purpose*
001 Subnet mask	Specifies the subnet mask to be used for the client
003 Router	Specifies the IP addresses for one or more routers on the network
006 DNS servers	Specifies the IP address of the DNS server for host name resolution on the network
044 WINS/NBNS servers	Specifies the IP address of a NetBIOS Name Server (WINS) for NetBIOS name resolution on the network
046 WINS/NBT node type	Specifies the resolution method to be used for NetBIOS name resolution
051 Lease time	Specifies the length of the IP address lease for the client

Specifying different options for two different groups of computers is best accomplished by using separate scopes. You would not specify global scope options, because global options apply to every scope on the DHCP server. Overriding the options by manually configuring the clients doesn't ensure that every member of the group receives the same options and is difficult to maintain. If you receive a question concerning multiple groups of computers that use DHCP, choose "specify separate scopes" as the answer.

Reserving DHCP client IP addresses

You can reserve addresses for special machines on the network. Microsoft recommends that you reserve IP addresses for the following computers on the network:

- ✔ Domain controllers, if the network uses LMHOSTS files for static IP addresses
- ✔ Clients that use IP addresses assigned using another method for TCP/IP configuration
- ✔ IP addresses used by the RAS server to issue to dial-in clients
- ✔ DNS servers
- ✔ WINS servers
- ✔ Routers

The rule to keep in mind for the topic of IP address reservation is that any time clients are hard-coded to find a server by the server's IP address, that server is a candidate for reservation. Hard-coding server IP addresses is done in LMHOSTS and HOSTS files, as well as in the Network window of the Control Panel. Hard-coding can also be done in the WINS and DNS databases.

If you have multiple DHCP servers that are using the same pool of IP addresses, the reserved addresses should be identical on all the servers. If these addresses are not identical, one DHCP server may assign an IP address that is marked as reserved in another DHCP server's database.

Lab 8-4 demonstrates how to add a reservation in the scope for a server.

Lab 8-4	Adding an IP Address Reservation in DHCP Manager

1. **In the DHCP Manager, click the server to which you're adding a reservation.**

2. **Click the scope to which you're adding a reservation.**

3. **Choose Scope⇨Add Reservations.**

The Add Reserved Clients dialog box, shown in Figure 8-3, lists the properties for reserving an IP address for a computer. Only the IP Address and Unique Identifier are required to add a reservation for this IP address. The other options, Client Name and Client Comment, are for the administrator to document the name of the computer for which the IP address is being reserved and why this IP address is being reserved.

Figure 8-3:
You can
add an IP
address
reservation
for a
computer
here.

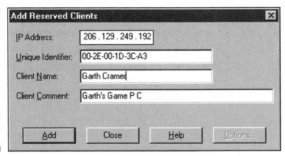

Add Reserved Clients	☒
IP Address:	206 . 129 . 249 . 192
Unique Identifier:	00-2E-00-1D-3C-A3
Client Name:	Garth Cramer
Client Comment:	Garth's Game P C

Add   Close   Help   Options...

Two entries in the Add Reserved Clients dialog box make likely candidates for exam material:

✔ **Unique Identifier:** The Unique Identifier is the Media Access Control (MAC) address for the DHCP client, which can be found by typing the `ipconfig /all` command at the command prompt on the client. (Chapter 6 covers using the `ipconfig` command.)

✔ **Client Name:** The Client Name should be the computer name of the DHCP client so that you can easily identify the computer that the reservation is for.

Installing and Configuring the DHCP Relay Agent on Multiple Subnets

Using DHCP over multiple subnets is probably the most important portion of the exam as far as DHCP goes. You need to know that you can span multiple subnets with one DHCP server. A server can still assign IP addresses to clients that don't exist on the same subnet as the DHCP server, but the process requires using the DHCP Relay Agent.

On a subnet that doesn't contain a DHCP server, a DHCP Relay Agent must be installed to forward the IP lease information to the DHCP server on the

remote subnet. When a client begins broadcasting IP lease request information, the DHCP Relay Agent forwards this information to the DHCP server.
The server then examines the relay IP address field to determine whether it
has an IP address in one of its address pools for the client. In this way, a
DHCP server can have multiple scopes for assigning IP addresses.

Creating a *multihomed computer* that has two network cards connected to
separate networks makes using Windows NT as a DHCP Relay Agent possible. (You can expect to see questions about Windows NT as a DHCP Relay
Agent on the exam.) The multihomed computer has the DHCP server on one
network, and listens for client IP lease requests that are broadcast on the
subnet that doesn't have the DHCP server.

If you don't use a multihomed computer, you must have a router that is
capable of acting as a relay agent. If the router isn't capable of passing
messages to the remote subnet, you have to have a DHCP server on each
network — which isn't a bad idea anyway. If you have a DHCP server on
each subnet, the servers can provide fault tolerance with a second scope of
IP addresses that are valid on each other's subnet. You can find out more
about configuring multiple DHCP servers in the section "Allowing for fault
tolerance" later in this chapter.

Installing the DHCP Relay Agent

Like the DHCP Server Service, the DHCP Relay Agent is installed through the
Network window in the Control Panel. Lab 8-5 demonstrates the installation
of the DHCP Relay Agent.

Lab 8-5   Installing the DHCP Relay Agent

1. **Open the Network window from the Control Panel.**

2. **Click the Services tab and then click Add.**

   A list of available network services appears.

3. **Select DHCP Relay Agent.**

   The files that are required for the DHCP Relay Agent are copied to your
   hard drive.

4. **Reboot.**

You receive a message saying that the DHCP Relay Service can't start unless
at least one DHCP server's IP address is listed. Requiring a static IP address
for the DHCP server shows you how important these addresses are for the
DHCP servers themselves, as well as other important servers on the network.

When you're finished installing the DHCP Relay Agent, a new page tab appears in the Network window called DHCP Relay. The DHCP Relay page is where you specify the IP addresses of the DHCP servers on the network. Keep this page in mind if you get a question on the exam about where to configure the DHCP Relay Agent.

Allowing for fault tolerance

A topic that is almost guaranteed to appear on your exam is fault tolerance with multiple DHCP servers. Microsoft recommends that you place your DHCP servers on multiple subnets for fault tolerance, rather than have them all on one subnet.

All DHCP servers on your network should *not* have the same IP addresses in their scopes. Each server should have a unique pool of IP addresses available.

If a DHCP server were to fail in a remote subnet, the Relay Agent can forward the messages to another DHCP server located in a different subnet. This server can respond with an IP address for the client request only if the server maintains a scope for the subnet that the source host belongs to. For example, if the source host is on the 101.32.0.0 network, and the DHCP server on a remote subnet maintains a scope for just the 101.33.0.0 and 101.34.0.0 networks, then the server can't provide a valid address for the requesting host.

To remedy the situation I just described, your clients should maintain a small number of valid IP addresses in a scope for each subnet for which the client may provide fault tolerance. For instance, in the preceding example the client from the 101.32.0.0 network can't receive a valid address from a remote DHCP server. If the server maintained a small scope for the 101.32.0.0 network, in addition to the 101.33.0.0 and 101.34.0.0 scopes that it already maintains, it could respond to the client's request with a valid address.

A rule that you should keep in mind for questions on fault tolerance is this: Make sure that 75 percent of the addresses are on the subnet that your DHCP server is on, and 25 percent of the addresses are on the remote subnet, in order to provide fault tolerance for the remote subnet. **Remember:** You can't have duplicate addresses on the network. The remote subnet that has 25 percent of the valid IP addresses isn't specified in the remaining 75 percent of the addresses.

Zeroing in on the DHCP essentials

Questions on the exam covering the DHCP Relay Agent may seem convoluted and difficult to understand at first. In order to make sense of these questions, just keep the following basic rules in mind, and you should do well on questions regarding multiple subnets and DHCP:

- ✔ **If you have two subnets and only one DHCP server:** Install a DHCP Relay Agent on the subnet without the DHCP server.

- ✔ **If your router isn't capable of forwarding DHCP messages:** Install a DHCP server on that subnet.

- ✔ **If you want fault tolerance between two DHCP servers:** Maintain a small pool of valid IP addresses for every subnet other than your own.

Using ipconfig with DHCP

The `ipconfig` command is useful to DHCP clients because TCP/IP configuration information can change quite often, especially if you lease IP addresses for only a few days. The `ipconfig` command enables clients to renew the same IP address many times before it changes.

You can use the `ipconfig` command to view and modify IP lease information. You want to keep this in mind because you can expect to receive a question on the exam about how to renew or release IP addresses that have been obtained from a DHCP server.

To view the most essential configuration information, enter the `ipconfig` command with no parameters at the command prompt. Be aware that entering this command gives you information on three required TCP/IP elements only: IP address, subnet mask, and default gateway. Although a default gateway isn't required on a single network with no remote subnets, it's nevertheless one of the three key TCP/IP elements.

The `ipconfig /all` command tells you when the lease was obtained and when it expires, as the following sample partial output from the `ipconfig/all` command shows:

```
Lease Obtained. . . . . . . . : Wednesday, February 25, 1998
        6:46:34 PM
Lease Expires . . . . . . . . : Saturday, February 28, 1998
        6:46:34 PM
```

In this example, you can see that the lease is for a period of three days. You can check your IP address often and find that you still retain the same address because you renew the lease long before the lease ever expires.

Maintaining the DHCP database

The questions concerning maintenance of the DHCP database shouldn't be all that difficult — this topic constitutes only a small portion of the DHCP picture, and one that I haven't heard discussed in newsgroups. You don't have to do much to maintain the DHCP database because backing up the database is done at regular intervals by Windows NT. However, you should understand the DHCP database and the components involved.

The database stores everything related to DHCP issues, including scope options and lease and renewal information. The DHCP database is created automatically when the DHCP service is installed on a Windows NT Server. Information in the database is constantly being added, deleted, and modified.

A number of files make up the DHCP database. Table 8-4 shows the components of the DHCP database that you should memorize for the exam.

Table 8-4	Components of the DHCP Database
File	*Description*
Dhcp.mdb	The DHCP server database file
Dhcp.tmp	A temporary file used by the DHCP database during database index maintenance operations
J50.log and J50#####.log	A log of all database transactions; used by the DHCP database for recovery
J50.chk	A checkpoint file

The files that make up the DHCP database have changed slightly from Windows NT 3.51 to Windows NT 4.0. Make sure that you don't memorize any lists of files from the previous version of NT, which can be easy to do if you are searching through TechNet or reading outdated exam materials.

Prep Test

1 Which of the following is a benefit of DHCP? (Choose all that apply.)

A ❑ DHCP servers can be used across routers.

B ❑ DHCP servers can communicate with each other for fault tolerance.

C ❑ Leases can be configured to never expire.

D ❑ Addresses can be excluded from the current scope.

2 After the client accepts the IP lease offer, what does it respond to the server with?

A ○ DHCPOFFER

B ○ DHCPACK

C ○ IP lease acknowledgment

D ○ IP lease selection

3 You have two different groups of machines that have TCP/IP configured differently. One group contains engineering department computers, which require access to the DNS server, and the other group contains sales department computers, which require shorter leases. How should you fulfill the needs of both groups?

A ○ Create a global option for each group.

B ○ Override the configuration information at the client.

C ○ Create two scopes.

D ○ Configure one global scope, and deactivate the DNS server for the sales group's scope.

4 What is the best way to ensure fault tolerance when more than one DHCP server is present on a subnet?

A ○ Configure the clients to access the second DHCP server in the event that the first DHCP server can't be reached.

B ○ Make sure that the DHCP servers have the same IP addresses in the pool so that the second server can renew the existing server's active leases.

C ○ Make sure that the DHCP servers have different IP addresses, in case one server can't be reached.

D ○ Configure the clients to access the Relay Agent in the event that the first DHCP server can't be reached.

5 You have moved one client computer from one DHCP-enabled subnet to another. The computer worked fine on the first subnet, but now it can't connect with any other computers on the network. What is most likely the problem?

A ○ The computer has manually assigned TCP/IP settings.

B ○ The DHCP server is not assigning the correct default gateway.

C ○ The DHCP server is not assigning the correct IP address.

D ○ The client needs to change the address for the new DHCP server in the Network window.

6 You have only one server on your network that is currently a file server and a WINS server. You want to enable DHCP on the network. Which of the following statements is true regarding this situation?

A ○ You must install the DHCP server on the WINS server.

B ○ You can't install the DHCP server on the same server as the WINS server.

C ○ You must configure clients with the DHCP-assigned WINS information.

D ○ You need to install the DHCP Relay Agent on a computer on the network.

7 Which of the following is not part of the DHCP database?

A ○ Jet.log

B ○ J50.chk

C ○ Dhcp.tmp

D ○ J50.log

8 You have discovered that you are running out of valid IP addresses on your network. Some of the machines are UNIX machines that don't receive an IP address from the DHCP server. Your DHCP scope has almost 30 IP addresses that are not being used. What should you do in this situation?

A ○ Drop the last few IP address numbers in the scope.

B ○ Reserve some IP addresses for the UNIX machines.

C ○ Install a DHCP Relay Agent.

D ○ Exclude some of the IP addresses in the scope.

9 You have a DHCP server enabled on one of your three subnets. You have found that your router is not capable of passing DHCP messages. Which of the following is not true in this situation?

A ○ You can install DHCP servers on each of the remote subnets.

B ○ You can include a scope of valid IP addresses for each subnet for fault tolerance.

C ○ You can configure your Windows NT computer as a multihomed host.

D ○ You can configure the other two subnets manually.

10 Which of the default DHCP options have the correct code specified? (Choose all that apply.)

A ❏ 46 WINS/NBT node type

B ❏ 006 DNS servers

C ❏ 042 WINS/NBNS servers

D ❏ 003 Router

Answers

1 *A,C,D.* One of the disadvantages of DHCP is that the servers can't communicate with each other to determine whether an address has already been assigned by another DHCP server. *Review "Scoping It Out: Some DHCP Basics."*

2 *D.* This IP lease selection is the IP address that the client accepted, also known as a DHCPREQUEST. *Review "DHCP message types."*

3 *C.* Anything that involves two separate groups of computers requires two separate scopes. Managing two scopes is easier and is the recommended course because you can make changes to each scope without affecting any other scopes. *Review "Assigning advanced DHCP options."*

4 *C.* You must remember not to duplicate IP addresses between DHCP servers. They can't communicate among themselves, and they will undoubtedly lease a duplicate IP address. *Review "Allowing for fault tolerance."*

5 *A.* Manually configured TCP/IP settings on the workstation overriding the settings received from the DHCP server is a common cause of failure when moving machines to a different subnet. *Review "Assigning advanced DHCP options."*

6 *C.* The DHCP option of 44 WINS/NBNS servers and 46 WINS/NBT Node Type has to be assigned in order for DHCP clients to use the services of the WINS server. *Review "Assigning advanced DHCP options."*

7 *A.* A log of all database transactions is kept by the J50.log and J50#####.log. *Review "Maintaining the DHCP database."*

8 *D.* You can't reduce the size of the scope. You have to exclude the IP addresses in order to free up these IP addresses for other uses. *Review "Defining DHCP scopes."*

9 *B.* Your routers must be capable of forwarding DHCP messages. If a DHCP server goes down on one subnet, a DHCP Relay Agent can pass messages to another remote DHCP server. *Review "Installing and Configuring the DHCP Relay Agent on Multiple Subnets."*

10 *A, B, D.* The code for WINS/NBNS (NetBIOS Name Server) is 44. Many more codes exist for DHCP options, but you don't need to study those for the exam. *Review "Assigning advanced DHCP options."*

Chapter 9

Windows Internet Name Service

· ·

Exam Objectives

▶ Installing and configuring a WINS server

▶ Running WINS on a multihomed computer

▶ Configuring static mappings in the WINS database

▶ Configuring WINS replication

▶ Configuring LMHOSTS files

▶ Configuring HOSTS files

▶ Importing LMHOSTS files to WINS

· ·

*T*he Internetworking with Microsoft TCP/IP on Windows NT 4.0 exam addresses many aspects of WINS (the Windows Internet Name Service), largely because WINS is a Microsoft Windows-based technology. The contents of this chapter, therefore, will prove especially useful come exam time. In this chapter, I tell you what you must remember about WINS for the exam and also what you can skip in the interest of time.

I start with an overview of WINS and then cover the installation and configuration of a WINS server — a subject that is guaranteed to be featured in a few exam questions. Running WINS on a multihomed computer is covered in this chapter, too, as is configuring LMHOSTS files and importing them to WINS. Other aspects of WINS, such as replication and static mappings, are also examined in detail.

Heed my advice: The exam tests heavily on the following topics regarding WINS:

✔ Installing a WINS server and the requirements for the installation.

✔ How and where to add static mapping for a non-WINS client.

✔ The use of the WINS proxy, which is also required for non-WINS clients.

✔ Database replication, including the concept of push and pull partners and when to configure a WINS server as either a push or pull partner.

Quick Assessment

Installing and config- uring a WINS server

1 A WINS server resolves _____ to IP addresses.

2 WINS is a dynamic replacement to _____.

3 A WINS server can be queried if a(n) _____ server can't resolve a name.

4 (True/False). A WINS server must be some type of domain controller, such as a primary or backup.

Configuring static mappings in the WINS database

5 The type of static address mapping that permits only one address per name is called _____.

6 A non-WINS client must have a static mapping or use a(n) _____ to use the WINS service.

Configuring WINS replication

7 The replication partner that "forces" its updates to another partner is called the _____ partner.

8 The replication partner on the opposite end of a WAN link should be the _____ partner.

Running WINS on a multihomed computer

9 When running WINS on a multihomed computer, you have to disable the _____ service on one of the adapters.

10 The _____ page in the TCP/IP Properties dialog box is where you can import LMHOSTS from other computers into your local LMHOSTS file.

Importing LMHOSTS files to WINS

11 (True/False). Importing an LMHOSTS file through the Network window accomplishes the same goal as using the #BEGIN_ALTERNATE tag in the LMHOSTS file.

Answers

1   *NetBIOS names.* Review "Understanding Some WINS Basics."

2   *LMHOSTS.* Review "WINS and the LMHOSTS file."

3   *DNS.* Review "WINS and DNS."

4   *False.* Review "Adding a secondary WINS server."

5   *Unique.* Review "Changing static mappings."

6   *WINS proxy.* Review "Using a WINS proxy."

7   *Push.* Review "Examining the push partner and pull partner concepts."

8   *Pull.* Review "Configuring push and pull partner replication."

9   *Browser.* Review "Running WINS on a Multihomed Computer."

10   *WINS Address.* Review "Importing LMHOSTS Files to WINS."

11   *True.* Review "Importing LMHOSTS Files to WINS."

Understanding Some WINS Basics

To explain how and where the Windows Internet Name Service (WINS) fits into the whole Microsoft networking scheme, I need to explain the evolution and purpose of WINS.

NetBIOS computer names are required to enable communication with other machines on a network. (In Chapter 5, I cover the Network Basic Input/Output System [NetBIOS] interface and explain its importance to Microsoft Windows-based operating systems.) NetBIOS networks are traditionally broadcast-based, which works well for smaller networks.

Broadcasts, however, are not recommended for larger networks, especially WANs, because routers, by default, don't pass broadcast messages. Also, the more computers you have broadcasting on a network, the more precious becomes the bandwidth that those broadcasts gobble up.

WINS and the LMHOSTS file

The *LMHOSTS file* solves the NetBIOS broadcasts problem that occurs on large networks and WANs. Being a *static text file,* it maps NetBIOS computer names to IP addresses, a system that limits broadcasts on the network but adds a great deal of work for an administrator in configuring and maintaining the files for each computer on the network. Whenever a computer has a change of name or IP address, the LMHOSTS file has to be updated manually by the administrator to reflect the new configuration. On the up side, the LMHOSTS file, unlike the HOSTS file, can be centrally managed, decreasing the amount of time and effort needed to maintain the file.

To eliminate the need for maintaining static configuration files, the *Windows Internet Name Service* (WINS) was developed as a means of dynamically resolving NetBIOS names to IP addresses on the network. You can think of WINS as a dynamic, centralized LMHOSTS file.

The exam covers a number of the benefits of WINS, which you should remember for the test:

- ✔ WINS is a dynamic database that minimizes maintenance required by the administrator.
- ✔ WINS is a centralized NetBIOS name management system.
- ✔ WINS eliminates the need for static LMHOSTS files, unless they are used in addition to the WINS server for fault tolerance.
- ✔ WINS decreases broadcast traffic.
- ✔ WINS can be used with clients on remote subnets.

Client hardware and software requirements

Questions about minimum hardware and software requirements for Microsoft products are on every Microsoft certification exam. WINS client requirements are no exception; therefore, you should make a point to remember the following WINS client system requirements for the exam:

- ✔ Windows NT 3.5 or higher, server or workstation
- ✔ Windows 95 or Windows for Workgroups 3.11 with TCP/IP services installed
- ✔ MS-DOS network client 3.0 or higher
- ✔ LAN Manager Server 2.2c or higher

You must specify the use of a WINS server, either manually at the client or through the use of DHCP. If you're receiving WINS configuration through the use of DHCP, just select the option called Obtain an IP Address from a DHCP Server, which is in the Network dialog box.

If you're manually configuring the client to use a WINS server, you enter the IP address for the WINS server in the WINS Address property page. To reach this page, do the following:

1. **Choose Start⇨Settings⇨Control Panel.**
2. **Double-click the Network option and then click the Protocols tab.**
3. **Select TCP/IP Protocols from the list of Network Protocols and then click Properties.**
4. **Click the WINS Address tab and enter the IP address of the WINS server in the text box labeled Primary WINS Server.**

Almost every Microsoft exam I have taken had questions about integrating different operating systems, such as UNIX and Novell NetWare, with Microsoft products. You can expect to see questions on integrating non-WINS clients into a network on your TCP/IP exam.

Keep this in mind: You must configure non-WINS clients to use one of two methods in order to resolve NetBIOS names on the network:

- ✔ The method of using the WINS Manager utility to create a static mapping, consisting of a NetBIOS name and IP address mapping, for the non-WINS client in the WINS server database.

✔ The method of installing a WINS proxy, which listens for NetBIOS broadcasts and relays those messages to the WINS server, on the subnet that has non-WINS clients.

B-node broadcasts can't pass through routers, so the non-WINS clients must be on the same subnet as the WINS proxy. You may also need a WINS proxy for each subnet of non-WINS clients.

Information on static mappings is in the section "Configuring Static Mappings for WINS Clients," and information on the WINS proxy is in the section "Using a WINS proxy," both of which are later in this chapter.

WINS and DNS

You can use a WINS server to resolve names for a DNS (Domain Name Service) server. (For more on DNS, see Chapter 10.) If a DNS client issues a request in which the server must resolve a DNS host name, the client can query the WINS server if the DNS server is unable to resolve the name itself. The WINS server resolves the name and returns it to the client.

A DNS database is not dynamic like the WINS database, which is why the integration between WINS and DNS is so important.

Using WINS for registering, renewing, and releasing names

To understand WINS name registration and resolution for the exam, you need to know how clients interact with the WINS server. Clients must register, renew, and sometimes release their registered names through the WINS server. The following sections cover some important details that occur in each step of the process.

Registering names

When a NetBIOS computer connects to the network, it must register its name. The process of registering NetBIOS names began with broadcasts, but with the WINS service, the *name registration query* messages are sent directly to the WINS server and registered in the database. The registration query includes the source IP address and the NetBIOS name to be registered, along with the destination computer's IP address.

Configuring your client to use a WINS server is all you need to do in order to register your computer's NetBIOS name with the WINS server. Review the section "Client hardware and software requirements" earlier in this chapter for a description of how and where to configure your client to use a WINS server.

The WINS server checks the database to determine whether an entry already exists for the computer name that the WINS client is trying to register. After that, one of two things happens:

- ✔ If the name has no entry, the server sends a *positive name registration response,* designating a time at which the client needs to renew its registration.

- ✔ If an entry already exists in the database, the server challenges the holder of the current registration to respond. If the current holder responds successfully, a *negative registration response* is sent to the computer that tried to register the existing name. The server knows the address of the source computer because it was sent in the registration query message.

Renewing names

The registered name for a computer has to be reregistered after a certain period of time known as the *time-to-live (TTL).* The WINS server, which time-stamps the entries in the database as they are added and deleted, enforces the TTL. The reason for renewing the registered names is to purge expired entries. Entries that are not renewed are marked as released in the WINS database.

You have control over the length of time before a computer name has to be renewed. The default TTL is 96 hours, or four days. If you increase the amount of time, the WINS database can become outdated and incorrect. If you decrease the amount of time, you have more traffic on the network, because computers attempt to renew their names more often.

When the client must renew its name, it sends a *name refresh request* to the server, asking to refresh its registration. This request includes the IP address and name of the source computer that wants to be renewed. The WINS server responds to the name refresh request with *a name refresh response* that has a new TTL.

Releasing names

A name is released through an orderly system shutdown, as follows:

1. When a client computer is shutting down, it informs the WINS server that the name that had been registered for the client can be removed from the database. The client accomplishes this task by sending a *name release request* to the server with the IP address and name that should be released.

2. When the WINS server receives the name release request, it searches the WINS database for the entry.

3. The server removes the entry from the database and sends a *name release response* back to the client. The name release response contains the name that the client requested be released.

This response doesn't mean much, because a positive or negative response doesn't affect the client computer shutting down.

 Broadcasting plays no part in this process. The WINS client and server know each other's addresses from the registration requests and responses that began the process and from the IP address for the WINS server that you specify on the client computer.

Name query and response

A WINS client attempts to register its name with the WINS server upon initialization (when a computer boots up) by using the following steps:

1. The WINS server checks the database for any existing entries with that WINS client's name.

2. If the name already exists, a name query request is sent to the existing computer (the one that already has that name registered on the network).

3. If the existing computer responds with a name query response, the server rejects the name request by the second computer.

4. If the existing computer doesn't respond to the name query request, the new name is accepted.

Planning for a WINS Implementation

You must consider a number of planning issues in a WINS implementation. After taking many Microsoft tests, I've found that planning is given significant emphasis on every MCSE exam. The TCP/IP test is no different.

Although you may not be tested on the specific answers to the following questions, you should keep the following in mind when implementing WINS:

- ✔ How many WINS servers are needed for the number of clients on a network?

- ✔ How many WINS servers are needed for fault tolerance, backup, or recovery?

- ✔ What about name registration and renewal for non-WINS clients?

I talk about the traffic generated by the WINS servers and clients for name registration and renewal in the section "Understanding Some WINS Basics" earlier in the chapter. The configuration of the WINS server to support non-WINS clients is covered later in this chapter in the section "Using a WINS proxy."

WINS generates considerably less traffic than broadcast-based implementations. Estimating the amount of network traffic that WINS generates is possible, but you probably won't see any exam questions addressing the subject.

Microsoft has recommendations for the number of WINS servers required on a network based on the number of clients. For every 10,000 clients on a network, you should have one primary WINS server and another secondary WINS server — but that's just a rough estimate. For example, if you're asked how many WINS servers should be used for a network with 50,000 clients, the answer is 10 (five servers and five backups).

With multiple WINS servers, *replication* of the WINS database, which contains the NetBIOS-name-to-IP-address mappings, is important. If the primary WINS server becomes unreachable, the secondary WINS server can have a current database to maintain the client registrations and renewals. The secondary WINS server is only used in the event that the primary WINS server is down. Later in this chapter, in the "Configuring WINS Database Replication" section, I discuss various methods for maintaining a WINS server database on multiple servers.

Depending on a network's topology type, you must determine how much WINS traffic can be supported on the network. But that's not something you have to worry about on the exam. The test questions don't address physical network implementation and WINS traffic.

Installing and Configuring a WINS Server

The topic of installing and configuring a WINS server can cover plenty of territory. In the following sections, I narrow the subject down to those elements of installation and configuration that are most likely to be tested.

Installing WINS

Configuring your Windows NT server as a WINS server requires you to install WINS first. You add this service from the Services page under Network. (I talk about installing other services — for example, the Dynamic Host Configuration Protocol service and the DHCP Relay Agent — in Chapter 8.) Lab 9-1 explains how to install the WINS service on your Windows NT server.

Lab 9-1   Installing the WINS Service

1. **Open the Network window from the Control Panel.**

2. **Click the Services tab to get the Services page.**

3. **Click Add.**

4. **Select Windows Internet Name Service from the list of available services.**

   You may receive a dialog box from Windows NT that asks you to insert the Windows NT Server 4.0 CD so that the files required by the WINS service can be copied to the `<systemroot>\system32\wins` directory.

5. **Restart the computer in order for the installation changes from the newly installed WINS service to take effect.**

   When the computer is restarted, an icon for the WINS Manager appears in the Administrative Tools program group under the Start menu.

Configuring the WINS server

You use the WINS Manager utility that was installed during the WINS installation to configure the WINS server. To add a WINS server by using the WINS Manager, follow these steps:

1. **On the WINS Manager Server menu, click Add.**

   The Add WINS Server to Server List dialog box appears.

2. **In WINS Server, enter the IP address of the server to be added to the list.**

   After you add a WINS Server to the list, you can configure the server.

You can repeat this process to add any additional servers that you want to configure.

A list of such servers is shown in the left pane of the WINS Manager window, which is the main screen that you see when you open the WINS Manager from the Administrative Tools program group. Statistics concerning the WINS server, such as the total number of queries received and the last replication times, are displayed in the right side of the screen. (See Figure 9-1.)

After you add the WINS servers, you can configure them with the WINS Manager graphical interface. To do so, you must do the following:

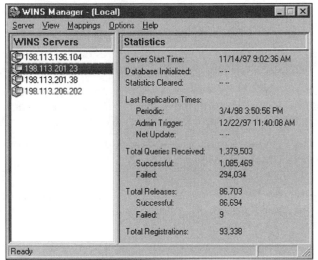

Figure 9-1:
The WINS
Manager
window.

1. **Become a member of the Administrators group.**

   This requirement prevents unauthorized users from wreaking havoc on your network. In order to become an Administrator, you must have your user account placed in the Administrators group.

2. **Choose the desired configuration options by specifying them in the WINS Server Configuration dialog box, as shown in Figure 9-2.**

Which configuration options you need to be familiar with for the exam is difficult to predict. Therefore, I cover each of them briefly and focus on what I think are the most important details. It's safe to say that the test doesn't delve too deeply into these options (with the exception of push and pull partners, which are covered later in this chapter).

Figure 9-2:
The WINS
Server
Configuration
dialog box.

The following default configuration settings are the ones most commonly seen in Microsoft exam questions:

- ✓ **Renewal Interval:** The duration before WINS clients must renew their leases. Default is 96 hours.

- ✓ **Extinction Interval:** The amount of time between when an entry is marked as released and when the entry is marked as extinct. The default is the same as the renewal interval — 96 hours.

- ✓ **Extinction Timeout:** The length of time that must pass before extinct entries are scavenged from the database. Default is the same as the renewal interval, 96 hours.

- ✓ **Verify Interval:** The amount of time that must pass before the server verifies whether entries from other WINS servers are still active. Default is 576 hours (24 days).

- ✓ **Pull Parameters:** Determines whether the server pulls information from the replicating WINS servers. Also includes the number of times the server retries connecting to a remote WINS server. In Figure 9-2, the default is selected with a retry count of 3.

- ✓ **Push Parameters:** Determines whether the server notifies the pull partners that the local database has changed.

- ✓ **Initial Replication:** Specifies whether the server notifies the replication partners about the status of the WINS database when this system is initialized.

- ✓ **Replicate on Address Change:** Specifies whether the server notifies other partners when a name registration changes.

Adding a secondary WINS server

One WINS server can handle all the name registration and renewal for an entire network, even a network with remote subnets. WINS packets can cross routers, unlike broadcast-based name registration methods.

Even though you can support a whole network with one WINS server, you should add a second server for fault tolerance. A *secondary WINS server* replicates the primary server and can continue the registration and renewal process if the primary server goes down. The secondary WINS server is contacted only if the first server doesn't respond to a request.

The steps for adding a secondary server are simple:

1. On the client for which you want to configure a secondary WINS server, double-click Network in the Control Panel.

2. **Click the Protocols tab and select TCP/IP Protocol from the list of Network protocols.**

3. **Click Properties and then click the WINS Address tab in the TCP/IP Properties dialog box.**

4. **In the Secondary WINS Server text box, enter the IP address of the secondary WINS server.**

Some of the hardware and software requirements for implementing a WINS server are likely to turn up in the exam questions. Make sure you have the following WINS server requirements memorized for the exam:

✓ The WINS service must be running on a Windows NT Server 3.5 or higher.

✓ The WINS server does not have to be a domain controller.

✓ The WINS server must have static TCP/IP information, such as the IP address, default gateway, and subnet mask, but can receive its TCP/IP information from a DHCP server. However, receiving settings from a DHCP server is not recommended.

Configuring a WINS client to use a WINS server

You can configure a client to use WINS in either of two ways — by manually configuring the client or by using the Dynamic Host Configuration Protocol (DHCP), which is covered in greater detail in Chapter 8.

Configuring a non-DHCP client

Clients that aren't DHCP-enabled must be manually configured. For manual configuration of the client, you have to

1. **Click the WINS Address tab in the Microsoft TCP/IP Properties dialog box to get the WINS Address page.**

2. **Enter the IP address of the primary WINS server in the Primary WINS Server text box.**

   Optionally, you can also enter the IP address of the secondary WINS server in the Secondary WINS Server text box.

The client is then configured to use the primary WINS server for name registration and resolution, and the secondary WINS server is only used when the primary WINS server is down.

Configuring a DHCP-enabled client

For a DHCP-enabled client, you don't have to do the configuration manually. Instead, you must specify two DHCP options in the DHCP Manager by following these steps:

1. **On the Windows NT Server, launch the DHCP Manager by selecting Start➪Programs➪Administrative Tools (Common)➪DHCP Manager.**

2. **Select the following two options from the DHCP Manager Options menu:**

   • 044 WINS/NetBIOS Name Service Servers

   • 046 WINS/NetBT Node Type

3. **Move to the client machine, open the Network window, and click the Protocols tab.**

4. **Select TCP/IP Protocols from the list of Network Protocols and then click Properties.**

5. **Click the IP Address tab and select the option button Obtain an IP Address from a DHCP Server.**

You should be aware of the reason for having primary and secondary WINS servers. You can configure clients to use both servers, but only the primary server is used most of the time. The secondary server is used only if the primary server becomes unresponsive. Even though a client may be registering and renewing with the secondary server, the client continually checks the primary server until that server comes back online.

Using a WINS proxy

Non-WINS clients don't need to be configured to take advantage of the WINS server for name registration and resolution; however, it's critical that you realize that non-WINS clients require a WINS proxy.

A *WINS proxy* intercepts the name-query broadcast messages that it hears on the local subnet. The WINS proxy is the intermediary between the non-WINS client and the WINS server. Figure 9-3 shows the relationship between the WINS and non-WINS clients and the WINS server.

The WINS proxy must listen for requests from the non-WINS clients and then forward those requests to the WINS server. The WINS client, on the other hand, can send requests to the WINS server directly and doesn't need the WINS proxy.

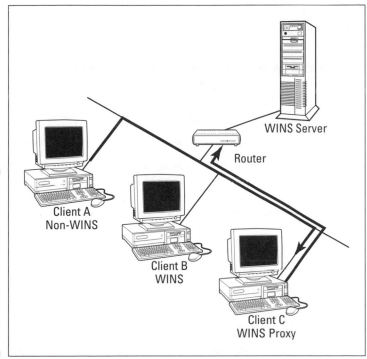

Figure 9-3:
An example
of how non-
WINS
clients use
the WINS
proxy to
communicate
with the
WINS
server.

Running WINS on a Multihomed Computer

With earlier versions of Windows NT Server, such as Windows NT 3.51, browsing resources across remote subnets wasn't possible if your primary domain controller (PDC) was configured as a Windows NT multihomed router with WINS installed. Having the Windows Browser service bound to multiple network adapters confused NT, which made maintaining one browse list for the entire network difficult. (You can find out more about the Browser service in Chapter 12.)

You can configure Windows NT 4.0 to overcome the limitation of not being able to browse remote networks by adding a new Registry entry with the Registry Editor tool. This new Registry entry enables the Windows NT server with WINS installed to disable the Browser service on one of the network adapters.

To add this Registry entry, follow these steps:

1. **Start the Registry Editor by selecting Start⇨Run⇨Regedt32.**

2. **Under the** HKEY_LOCAL_MACHINE **subtree, find the subkey**
   SYSTEM\CurrentControlSet\Services\Browser\Parameters\.

3. **Choose Edit⇨Add Value and enter the following:**

```
Value Name: UnboundBindings
Data Type:  REG_MULTI_SZ
String:     NetBT_<name of network adapter driver to be
            disabled>
```

If you don't know the name of the network adapter driver to be disabled,
follow these steps:

1. **Open a command prompt window by clicking Start⇨Run and
   typing** cmd.

2. **Type** ipconfig /all.

3. **Find the line that says "Ethernet Adapter."**

   This line tells you the name of the network adapter driver. For example,
   mine says "Ethernet Adapter EPRO01."

In order for browsing to work correctly, you should have every network
adapter in the system configured to use the same primary and secondary
WINS servers. The following example output from the ipconfig /all command
demonstrates this requirement in action:

```
Ethernet adapter LECARD5:


IP Address. . . . . . . . . : 112.37.200.1
Subnet Mask . . . . . . . . : 255.255.255.0
Default Gateway . . . . . . : 112.37.200.200
Primary WINS Server . . . . : 112.37.200.1
Secondary WINS Server . . . : 112.37.200.1


Ethernet adapter NETFLX32:


IP Address. . . . . . . . . : 112.37.100.1
Subnet Mask . . . . . . . . : 255.255.255.0
Default Gateway . . . . . . :
Primary WINS Server . . . . : 112.37.200.1
Secondary WINS Server . . . : 112.37.200.1
```

Every network adapter in the multihomed computer that specifies the primary and secondary WINS server must point WINS queries to the same IP address — specifically, to the network adapter that has the browser service enabled. In the preceding example, the adapter with the Browser service enabled is 112.37.200.1, which is the IP address that both network interface cards are configured to use for WINS queries.

That's everything you need to know about running WINS on a multihomed computer for the exam. Other WINS settings, such as those for replication and mappings, are not affected by whether the WINS server is multihomed.

Configuring Static Mappings for WINS Clients

WINS is designed for Microsoft Windows-based machines that use NetBIOS names to establish and maintain sessions between computers. Because some computers on your network may not be Windows-based or are not configured as WINS clients, you must do some additional configuring to accommodate those clients by manually adding a NetBIOS-name-to-IP-address mapping on the server. This process is what Microsoft calls *configuring static mapping.*

Adding static mapping in the WINS database for clients is a fairly easy task (and is one of the study requirements that Microsoft lists for this exam). You use these static mappings because a non-WINS client can't dynamically update its NetBIOS name and IP address in the WINS database like a WINS client can.

Recognizing the benefits of static mappings

You can use LMHOSTS to achieve the same results as a NetBIOS-name-to-IP-address mapping; however, the static mapping method is much more efficient for a few important reasons:

- ✔ **The WINS server is queried before the LMHOSTS file is *parsed* (that is, read one line at a time).**
- ✔ **LMHOSTS files must be manually maintained for non-WINS clients.** For more information on LMHOSTS, see the section "Configuring an LMHOSTS File" later in this chapter.

> ✔ **You can create a static mapping for clients in order to reserve a name for an important machine, such as a server that must continually maintain the same name.** For example, assume that a machine registers a name that was previously used by a server, and that server is down for repair. When the server reinitializes, it can't use its existing name because the name has been taken. Using static mapping lets you avoid this situation.

Changing static mappings

You add, modify, or delete static mappings from the WINS Manager. Just follow these steps:

1. **Launch the WINS Manager by clicking Start and then choosing Programs⇨Administrative Tools (Common)⇨WINS Manager.**

2. **In the WINS Manager window that appears, choose Mappings⇨ Static Mappings.**

   The Static Mappings dialog box appears.

3. **Click the Add Mappings button to access the Unique, Group, and other mapping options.**

You can create different types of WINS database mappings when you add the static mapping. Some types of mappings can permit more than one IP address, as you can see in Table 9-1. The table shows the available mapping types and what can be defined with each type. How those mapping types differ is probably the most important aspect of static mappings you need to remember for the exam. For example, you may encounter a question that asks which type of static mapping to use in a particular situation.

Table 9-1	Static Mapping Types
Mapping Type	*Description*
Unique	A type of address that permits only one address per name. The *unique* name is the name of the computer.
Group	Used to group computers for broadcasts and for browsing the domain. IP addresses are not stored for the computers in the group.
Internet Group	Used to enable domain controllers to communicate with each other. The Internet group contains IP addresses for up to 25 primary and backup domain controllers.
Multihomed	Similar to the Unique mapping type, up to 25 addresses can be used for multihomed systems (computers with more than one network interface card and IP address).

You must choose the static mapping type when you're adding a new static mapping. Lab 9-2 demonstrates how to add static mappings to a WINS database.

Lab 9-2	Adding Static Mappings for Non-WINS Clients

1. **Open the WINS Manager and choose Mappings⇨Static Mappings.**

2. **Click Add Mappings.**

3. **Enter the name of the computer for the mapping.**

4. **Enter the IP address of the computer you want to add.**

5. **For the mapping type, select Unique.**

6. **Click Add and then click Close.**

   You see that three entries are generated automatically for the mapping you just made in the WINS Manager window. The three entries are for the NetBIOS service types of Redirector, Messenger, and Server (see Chapter 5 for more information on NetBIOS).

Configuring WINS Database Replication

The exam is sure to address the subject of replication between two or more WINS servers. *Replication* between WINS servers maintains current mappings for clients so that any computer in the enterprise network can resolve any other computer's NetBIOS name. NetBIOS name registrations in the WINS database are replicated to other WINS servers by configuring WINS servers to be either push partners or pull partners.

Examining the push partner and pull partner concepts

The scenario questions in which you must determine the best combination of push and pull partners on the network make the database replication portion of the exam especially challenging. An understanding of how to configure a server as a push partner or pull partner (or both) is very important for the exam.

Think of push partners as "forcing" their updates to the pull partners. A *push partner* notifies its replicating *pull partner* that the WINS database has changed. The pull partner then responds to the push partner's notice with a replication request. When the push partner receives the replication request, it sends the new, updated entry to its pull partner in one of the following two ways. The WINS administrator specifies which of these two methods is to be used in the WINS Manager.

✔ Waiting until a predetermined number of WINS updates have collected (every *x* hours)

✔ Immediately replicating the updated entries (on demand)

Pull partners also use these methods when notifying the push partner that replication is needed.

Pull partners receive updated entries from the push partners by requesting entries that have higher version numbers than those entries already existing in the database.

Configuring push and pull partner replication

When determining whether a server should be a push or pull partner, the two most important considerations are

✔ Whether or not the partner crosses a WAN link

✔ How important it is that the database remains current

When a WINS server is on the other end of a WAN link from the local network, that server makes a good pull partner candidate. By configuring the servers at the other end of the WAN links as pull partners, you can control when the pull partner requests updates from the push partner on the local side of the WAN link. If a server on the other side of the WAN link is configured as a push partner instead, you have no control over when that server pushes its updated entries across the WAN link.

Configuring a WINS server as a push or pull partner is done by using the following steps:

1. **Launch the WINS Manager utility.**

2. **In the WINS Manager window, choose Server⇨Replication Partners.**

   In the Replication Partners dialog box that appears (see Figure 9-4), you see a list of IP addresses for WINS servers and, to the right of the list, columns marked Push and Pull.

3. **For each selected WINS server, click Push Partners, Pull Partners, or Other in the area labeled WINS Servers to List.**

   A check mark under the corresponding columns in the WINS Server list means that the server is configured as a push or pull partner.

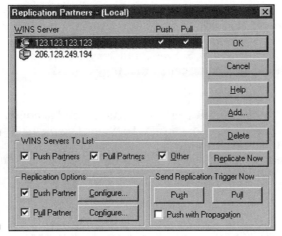

Figure 9-4:
The
Replication
Partners
dialog box.

4. **Under Replication Options, click Configure for each of the appropriate settings.**

   The Push Partner Properties of Pull Partners Properties dialog box appears.

In Figure 9-5, Server 2 is configured as a pull partner to request updated entries every 12 hours because it's on the opposite side of the WAN link. You can set the pull partner to request updates at whatever interval you want.

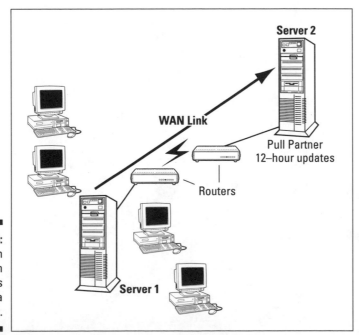

Figure 9-5:
Replication
between
servers
across a
WAN link.

If both WINS servers are on a much faster link, such as a LAN, you should configure replication so that both servers act as push and pull servers for each other. This setup ensures that the entries in the database are as current as possible. In Figure 9-6, Server 1 and Server 2 are configured to be push and pull partners for each other so that they can take advantage of the faster LAN link.

Keep in mind one very important fact about primary and secondary WINS servers, as far as replication is concerned: They *must* be push and pull partners to each other. This arrangement ensures that the client can continue with the secondary WINS server if the primary server becomes unavailable. The client also continually checks to see whether the primary server has become available.

Determining replication frequency

If you're faced with a question on the exam about the placement of WINS servers for replication, remember this rule: The longer the distance from WINS server to WINS server (which most often equals the slowest link), the less frequent are the updates.

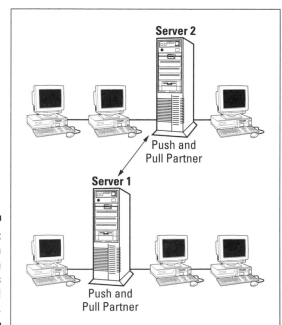

Figure 9-6:
Replication between servers across LAN links.

Server 2

Push and Pull Partner

Server 1

Push and Pull Partner

For example, if you have links between two schools in the same city, the replication frequency can be higher — for example, every 15 minutes or more often. If those schools must replicate with another server across the country, the replication frequency is lower — for example, every hour or less often.

You can expect to have exam questions based on illustrations of replication scenarios. If you remember the placement of the servers in relation to the WAN link, these types of questions should be no problem for you.

Maintaining the WINS Database

You must perform a number of maintenance tasks on the WINS database that are similar to the activities required for maintaining the Dynamic Host Configuration Protocol database (see Chapter 8 for more on DHCP). Those tasks include backing up, restoring, and compacting the database. A great deal of activity occurs within the WINS database, such as adding and updating leases, resolving names, and housekeeping, so you can see how maintenance tasks may show up as the subject of a test question.

Table 9-2 shows the components that make up the WINS database. Memorize these components just in case you get an exam question that asks what constitutes a WINS database, as well as what it takes to maintain it.

Table 9-2	Components of the WINS Database
Component	**Description**
Wins.mdb	The WINS server database
Winstmp.mdb	A temporary file created by the WINS database for maintenance purposes
J50.log and J50#####.log	A log with database transactions for use in recovering data if necessary
J50.chk	The checkpoint file

Backing up the database

WINS Manager has tools for backing up the WINS database. In the WINS Manager, you specify a directory for the database to be backed up to, and then the database is automatically backed up at intervals that you also specify in WINS Manager (every three hours is the default in Windows NT 4.0). For a complete backup, you should also back up the Registry entries for the WINS server, which are located in a folder with the following path:

```
Hkey_local_machine\System\CurrentControlSet\Services\Wins
```

Backing up the Registry is possible with most backup software on the market. However, don't worry about backing up for the exam.

I found that the installation default for the automatic backup of the Registry for Windows NT 4.0 is every three hours, but the default for Windows NT 3.5 is every 24 hours — just another example of how using outdated materials to study for a certification exam can be disastrous. Be sure that you use only the specifications for the newest product, Windows NT 4.0, to study for the exam.

Restoring the database

If you have an exam question that addresses restoring the WINS database, you should know the two ways to do it:

- ✔ You can use the WINS Manager.
- ✔ You can move the database files manually.

When you use WINS Manager for restoring the WINS database, simply click the directory in which the "good" database files are located. These "good" files are the backup directory that you specified when backing up the WINS database. Backing up simply copies the database files to another directory on a regular basis. If you determine that your current WINS database is corrupt, you can use the backup database in the alternate directory.

Manually moving the database files involves deleting the J50.log, J50#####.log, and Winstmp.mdb files from the WINS directory, and then copying only the Wins.mdb file to a new directory. When the WINS service is restarted, new log and temp files are created automatically. Alternatively, if a corrupt database is detected when stopping and restarting the WINS service, the WINS service automatically restores a backup copy.

Compacting the database

Although Windows NT 4.0 automatically compacts the WINS database, you may need to compact the database manually. The WINS database may become fragmented, just as hard drives become fragmented. When WINS database entries are removed, they leave gaps in the database that may not be filled with new entries.

Compacting the database not only decreases the size of the database, it speeds up transactions as well. Microsoft recommends compacting the database when it grows larger than 30 megabytes. Manual or automatic compaction accomplishes the same task.

Using the Jetpack utility

The Jetpack utility is used to compact the WINS database manually. If you get an exam question regarding compaction, the question most likely is about the command-line syntax of this utility. The Jetpack.exe syntax is as follows:

```
jetpack <database name> <temp database name>
```

The `temp database` is used for the compaction process and is deleted after compaction is complete.

You must stop the WINS server before the compaction process, either by using the Services dialog box or the `net stop wins` command at the command prompt.

Good news! The syntax for the Jetpack utility is the same for the DHCP database as it is for the WINS database. Everything you see in this section works for the DHCP database. In the instructions, just substitute stopping the DHCP service for stopping the WINS service. Check out Chapter 8 for more information on compacting the DHCP database.

Removing obsolete database entries

An entry in the WINS database is in one of three states:

- ✔ Active
- ✔ Released
- ✔ Extinct

The process of removing obsolete database entries is called *scavenging*. From the names of the three states I just listed, you can guess that the extinct entries are the ones that need to be scavenged from the database. The only thing you probably need to know about the scavenging process is that it occurs automatically, based on the settings in the Renewal and Extinct intervals in the WINS Server Configuration dialog box (refer to Figure 9-2) that I describe earlier in this chapter. You can also force a scavenging in the WINS Manager. Obsolete entries are removed more quickly if you configure entries to become extinct more rapidly.

Configuring an LMHOSTS File

Table 9-3 shows the LMHOSTS tags that are most likely to be on the exam. More LMHOSTS tags exist than those listed in Table 9-3, but they probably won't show up on the exam.

Table 9-3	LMHOSTS Extensions
Extension	*Description*
#PRE	Preloads an entry into the name cache
#DOM	Specifies a remote domain controller for logon requests
#INCLUDE	Parses an LMHOSTS file from another computer
#BEGIN_ALTERNATE	Specifies the beginning of a group of entries to be searched
#END_ALTERNATE	Specifies the end of a group of entries to be searched

The terms *tag, keyword,* and *extension* are all used to refer to these special entries in the LMHOSTS file, such as #PRE and #DOM.

The #PRE extension

Following a NetBIOS name mapping entry in the LMHOSTS with the keyword #PRE loads the entry into the name cache, which eliminates the need to parse the LMHOSTS file one line at a time — the entry is resident in memory. Entries with the #PRE tag should be placed at the end of an LMHOSTS file because entries with the tag slow up the parsing of the file while the #PRE entry is being loaded into memory. The #PRE tag is also required for some of the other extensions to work properly, such as #DOM and #INCLUDE.

LMHOSTS entries are not loaded into the name cache by default; they are parsed only when a NetBIOS name is in the process of being resolved and the dynamic resolution has failed.

The #DOM extension

Of all the LMHOSTS tags, I recommend spending the most time studying #DOM, including the purpose of the #DOM tag and its format.

Following an entry in the LMHOSTS file with the #DOM:<domain> tag associates the entry with the domain name that you specify. The specified domains should have domain controllers, which are the servers that authenticate users in the remote domain. (Various Windows NT services direct information, such as logon entries, to these domain controllers.) If you don't use the #DOM keyword and you have hosts on different subnets, the hosts won't be able to communicate with the domain controller.

Specifying the #DOM keyword in the LMHOSTS file of a domain controller also enables this server to replicate account information with the other domain controllers that are located on different subnets. For example, say that you're currently in a domain called SALES. You see the following entry in your LMHOSTS file specifying the domain controller for the ENGINEERING domain:

```
110.27.211.13      mustaine          #PRE #DOM:ENGINEERING
                  #Engineering's DC
```

Domain controllers should have entries similar to the preceding example only if the domain controllers are on different subnets. If they are on the same subnet, they can communicate via broadcasts without the need for the #DOM keyword. Having a WINS server on your network eliminates the need for the #DOM keyword because the domain controller's name and IP address are automatically added to the WINS database and are used for communicating to the remote subnet.

The #PRE tag must also be used when the #DOM tag is present. The #PRE tag loads this entry into the cache, where it must remain. Any entries with the #DOM tag are ignored unless they are preceded by the #PRE tag.

#INCLUDE <filename>

An LMHOSTS file can be centrally located in a network so that more than one computer can use it. (The concept of centrally locating an LMHOSTS file for multiple computers is a likely candidate for exam questions.)

The LMHOSTS file can also include other LMHOSTS files from different hosts, so that you don't have to update every computer's LMHOSTS file manually when another computer on the network changes its NetBIOS name or IP address. The #INCLUDE <filename> keyword forces the system to look for a filename and parse it as local.

For example, if your mail server's IP address changes, you have to update the mail server's entry in the LMHOSTS file on every computer in the network if not for the #INCLUDE tag. In this way, the #INCLUDE tag can save you some time and effort.

The filename that is included is most likely another LMHOSTS file. It can also be another text file that contains NetBIOS-name-to-IP-address mappings similar to the LMHOSTS file.

The following entry parses an LMHOSTS file on another computer just as if it were the local computer's file. In order for the local computer to parse the remote computer's LMHOSTS file, you have to insert the #PRE keyword before the #INCLUDE statement to load the entry into the name cache.

```
142.24.74.137        server1           #PRE          #needed for
               the include
#INCLUDE       \\server1\share\lmhosts
```

If the LMHOSTS file fails to resolve the NetBIOS name, the name is stripped of its 16th service type character and stripped of any zeros used to pad the name to 15 characters. The result now becomes the host name. The next three name resolution methods — local host name, HOSTS file, and DNS — attempt to resolve the host name. (More information on the name resolution sequence and the methods used to resolve a host name can be found in Chapter 4.)

Configuring HOSTS Files

Another area you're likely to see tested on the exam is the proper format for the HOSTS file. You may be given a HOSTS file that is incorrect in some way — maybe the syntax is wrong, or the case of the host name is not exactly correct, or a wrong IP address was used in the HOSTS file. You then have to determine why the entry in the HOSTS file won't work. Figuring it out is easy if you know how the HOSTS file is constructed. (For more information on HOSTS files, turn to Chapter 4.)

In a HOSTS file, the IP address and host name are separated by at least one space. The IP address consists of four octets separated by periods. Standard rules apply for the IP address, such as the use of valid classes. (Refer to Chapter 6 for more information on the proper formatting of an IP address.)

The most important thing to remember in formatting a HOSTS file entry is that the IP address is listed first, followed by the host name(s) on the same line. (Watch out for any exam question that lists a HOSTS file entry with the host name first and then the IP address. You'll know right off it's incorrect; the IP address is listed first.)

Troubleshooting the format of a HOSTS file entry is somewhat difficult because you have to contend with the order of the mappings and separation of the entry's elements. (*Remember:* A HOSTS file is not case-sensitive. You'll likely receive a question on this point.) For example, if you have a mapping for 127.33.102.200 RUBY, and you ping Ruby, you don't receive a response. This situation can be remedied by entering another alias for the IP address on the same line to guarantee that you always reach the host regardless of the case being used. Pinging either RUBY or Ruby, such as in the following single line in the HOSTS file, gets you a response from the 127.33.102.200 host:

```
127.33.102.200      RUBY      Ruby
```

The HOSTS file can also contain Fully Qualified Domain Names, such as the following:

```
86.128.21.114  host.domain.com
```

Comments to explain the purpose of a mapping can be inserted in the HOSTS file and are preceded by a # (pound) sign. These comments are usually on the same line as the IP-address-to-host-name mapping to the right and never to the left of the mapping. Longer comments can be on a line above the mapping. For example, examine the following comment:

```
# This mapping is for the main SQL server at Capstone
192.31.154.22 sqlserver    SQLServer
```

Because a HOSTS file is parsed line by line until a mapping is found, the most heavily used mappings should be listed near the top of the text file.

Get used to the look and feel of the HOSTS file. At least one exam question will give you the name of a HOSTS file and you'll have to determine whether it is valid or not.

Importing LMHOSTS Files to WINS

In the WINS Address page of the Microsoft TCP/IP Properties dialog box, you can opt to import an LMHOSTS file from a remote computer. Clicking the Import LMHOSTS button brings up the dialog box shown in Figure 9-7, which you can use to browse to find the LMHOSTS file on the remote computer that you want to include. The file doesn't have to be located in the `<systemroot>\system32\drivers\etc.` directory on the remote computer, but most likely it is because the remote computer is using the LMHOSTS file for its own NetBIOS name resolution.

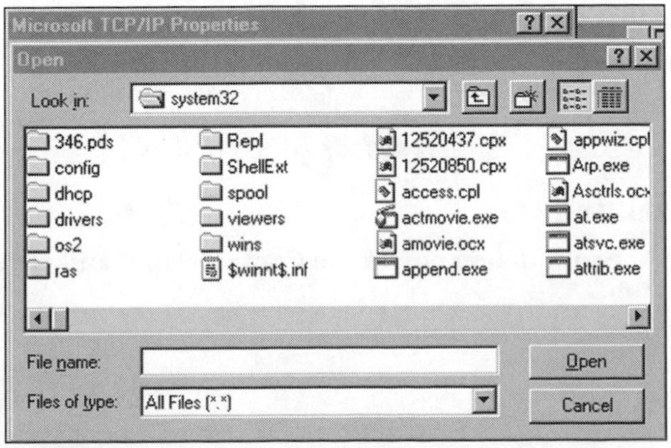

Figure 9-7:
Here's where you go to import an LMHOSTS file from a remote computer.

Including and *importing* a remote LMHOSTS file accomplishes the same thing: An LMHOSTS file on a remote computer is parsed just as the local LMHOSTS file is parsed on your machine. Because they have different names, you should remember that you do the *including* in the LMHOSTS file, and you do the *importing* under the WINS Address page of the Microsoft TCP/IP Properties dialog box.

Configuring an entry to be loaded into the cache

Lab 9-3 provides the steps for configuring an entry in the LMHOSTS file to be loaded into the cache. You can verify that the entry has been loaded in the cache by issuing the nbtstat -c command.

The lab provides information on the syntax of the LMHOSTS file, enabling the LMHOSTS file in Windows NT, preloading an entry into the NetBIOS name cache, and viewing the results with the nbtstat command. Knowing this stuff is helpful when you receive a question on the exam concerning the LMHOSTS file (notice that I said *when,* not *if*).

Lab 9-3 Viewing Preloaded Entries in the NetBIOS Cache

1. **Go to the** <systemroot>\system32\drivers\etc **directory.**

2. **Rename the LMHOSTS file from LMHOSTS.SAM to LMHOSTS.**

   You may have to choose Options➪View to display the file extension. The LMHOSTS file should not have an extension.

3. **Open the LMHOSTS file.**

   Select the Notepad option if you are prompted to choose an application in order to open the file.

4. **Remove the** # (comment) **from the beginning of one of the sample mappings that contain the keyword** #PRE.

   For example, I removed the # (comment) from the line that contained this entry:

   ```
   102.54.94.117      localsrv              #PRE
   ```

5. **Save the LMHOSTS file.**

6. **Open the Network dialog box in the Control Panel and click the Protocols tab.**

7. **Under Network Protocols, select the TCP/IP protocol and click the Properties button.**

8. **Click the WINS Address tab and then select Enable LMHOSTS Lookup if it's not already checked (see Figure 9-8).**

9. **Open a command prompt window by selecting Run from the Start menu and then typing** cmd **in the space provided.**

10. **In the command prompt window, enter the following command:**

```
nbtstat -R
```

This step purges and preloads the NBT Remote Cache Name Table.

11. **Enter the following command:**

```
nbtstat -c
```

This step displays the Remote Cache Name Table, which contains the mapping in the sample LMHOSTS file from which you removed comments in Step 4.

The LMHOSTS file has successfully preloaded an entry, which you view with the nbtstat command.

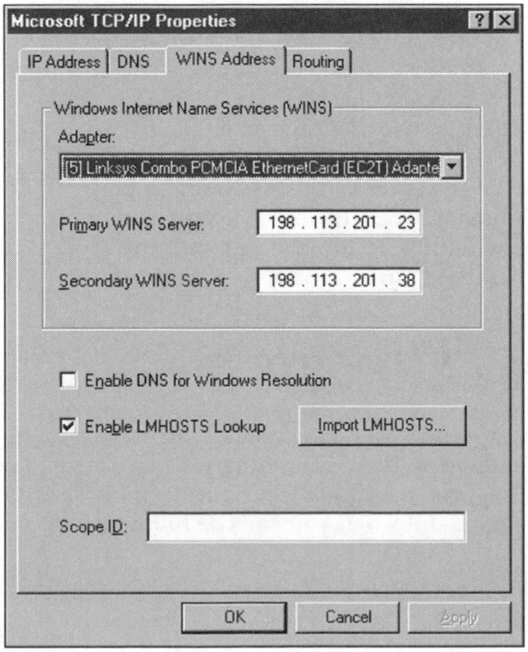

Figure 9-8:
The dialog box you use to enable LMHOSTS lookup on the local machine.

Using #BEGIN_ALTERNATE and #END_ALTERNATE to fix including problems

If you're including a file from a different host by using the #INCLUDE keyword and the computer holding the file suddenly malfunctions, you can no longer parse the file. This snag in the process can be remedied through the use of the #BEGIN_ALTERNATE and #END_ALTERNATE keywords, a method known as *block inclusion*. The syntax for these keywords looks something like the following:

```
server1    #PRE      #required for include
107.62.88.55 server2 #PRE       #required for include

#BEGIN_ALTERNATE
     #INCLUDE \\server1\sharename\LMHOSTS
     #INCLUDE \\server2\sharename\LMHOSTS
#END_ALTERNATE
```

In order for the *include statement* to work, the entries must be loaded prior to entering the statement. The alternate locations for the LMHOSTS files are parsed until a successful include is found. Not every include file is added; only the first successful include. This process is similar to the one used with primary and secondary WINS servers. For example, the secondary server is used only if the primary WINS server is down. (For more information, see "Configuring a WINS client to use a WINS server.")

The number of entries in the LMHOSTS file should be limited because the files are parsed one line at a time. The most heavily used entries should be located at the top of the LMHOSTS file. Entries with the #PRE tag should be located at the bottom of the LMHOSTS file.

Reloading the LMHOSTS file

After you modify the LMHOSTS file, you can use the nbtstat -R command to reload the file into memory. The parameters for the nbtstat command are case-sensitive, so -R produces a different output than -r. You know that the reload has been successful when you see the following command:

```
Successful purge and preload of the NBT Remote Cache Name
        Table.
```

Prep Test

1 What is the default interval before a computer name has to be renewed?

A ○ Two days

B ○ Three days

C ○ Four days

D ○ Six days

2 What must be configured to enable WINS packets to cross routers to remote WINS clients?

A ○ IP Forwarding must be enabled.

B ○ A WINS proxy must be on the same subnet.

C ○ An entry in the routing table must be specified.

D ○ Nothing.

3 You have eight subnets with 500 computers on each subnet. This is a DHCP-enabled network with non-WINS clients on some of the subnets. How many WINS servers would you recommend, and why?

A ○ Only one WINS server because that's all you need for a network of this size.

B ○ One primary and one secondary WINS server because that's all you need for a network of this size.

C ○ Two primary and two secondary WINS servers, because you've reached the limit of just one server.

D ○ One primary server, with a secondary server for each remote subnet that contains non-WINS clients.

4 If you're manually restoring the WINS database, which step would you take next after deleting the files in the WINS directory?

A ○ Stop the WINS service.

B ○ Copy the backup Wins.mdb file to a new directory.

C ○ Start the WINS service.

D ○ Copy the backup Wins.mdb, J50.log, J50#####.log, and Winstmp.mdb to a new directory.

5 At your corporate headquarters in Atlanta, you have four WINS that are configured to replicate with a WINS server in Boston and another in Seattle. How should you configure replication for these servers?

   A ○ Atlanta's WINS servers on the LAN should be configured as push and pull partners of each other, with Boston and Seattle configured as pull partners.

   B ○ Atlanta's WINS servers on the LAN should be configured as push and pull partners of each other, with Boston and Seattle configured as push partners.

   C ○ Atlanta's WINS servers on the LAN should be configured as push partners of each other, with Boston and Seattle configured as push partners.

   D ○ Atlanta's WINS servers on the LAN should be configured as pull partners of each other, with Boston and Seattle configured as push partners.

6 Which of the following are factors to consider when configuring a WINS server as a push or pull partner? (Choose all that apply.)

   A ❑ Whether the database must be updated often for accuracy.

   B ❑ Whether you have remote subnets with non-WINS clients.

   C ❑ Whether a WAN link is involved.

   D ❑ Whether the server is a primary or secondary server.

7 For a DHCP-enabled client that is configured to use the WINS server, what DHCP options have to be configured at the server?

   A ○ 046 WINS/NetBIOS Name Service Servers, and 048 WINS/NetBT Node Type

   B ○ 044 WINS/NetBIOS Name Service Servers, and 046 WINS/NetBT Node Type

   C ○ 046 WINS/NetBT Node Type, and 045 WINS/NetBIOS Name Service Servers

   D ○ 045 WINS/NetBT Node Type, and 046 WINS/NetBIOS Name Service Servers

8 What information is required when adding a static mapping entry in the WINS database for a non-WINS client?

   A ○ IP address, mapping type, and name

   B ○ Name and unique mapping type

   C ○ IP address, node type, and group name

   D ○ IP address, mapping type, node type, and name

9 Which is a requirement for a WINS server on a remote subnet with non-WINS clients?

   A ○ It must use the Internet Group mapping type.

   B ○ It must have the WINS Relay Agent installed.

   C ○ It must have a unique IP address.

   D ○ It must have the WINS proxy installed.

10 Which entries should be placed at the end of an LMHOSTS file because they slow down the parsing while the entry is being loaded?

A ○ #PRE keywords.

B ○ #DOM keywords.

C ○ #INCLUDE keywords.

D ○ Every keyword should be placed near the end of an LMHOSTS file.

Answers

1 C. This default value can be adjusted but does affect the database by either creating too much renewal traffic or leaving outdated entries in the database. *Review "Renewing names."*

2 D. Although you must have a WINS proxy on the same subnet as non-WINS clients, you don't have to configure the WINS server in any way for the packets to reach the remote clients. *Review "Using a WINS proxy."*

3 B. Using a secondary WINS server for fault tolerance is always recommended, even when you haven't exceeded the limits of one WINS server. *Review "Adding a secondary WINS server."*

4 B. The backup Wins.mdb file is the only file that needs to be copied to the WINS directory after the other files have been deleted or moved. The WINS service automatically creates the other files. *Review "Maintaining the WINS Database."*

5 A. Remote WINS servers make excellent candidates for pull partners because you can configure them to pull information at certain intervals. *Review "Configuring push and pull partner replication."*

6 A, C, D. Remote subnets with non-WINS clients make no difference as far as push or pull partners are concerned, unless the remote subnets are across WAN links. *Review "Configuring WINS Database Replication."*

7 B. If the client is configured via DHCP, you have to specify the IP address of the WINS server(s) at each client manually. *Review "Configuring a DHCP-enabled client."*

8 A. The IP address, mapping type, and name are all you need for the static mapping. *Review "Changing static mappings."*

9 C. A unique IP address is a requirement for every TCP/IP computer on the network. The WINS server needs Windows NT Server 3.5 or higher installed, and it must be configured with static information. *Review "Understanding Some WINS Basics."*

10 A. These commands should be as close to the bottom of the LMHOSTS file as possible; however, other keywords, such as #DOM, require that the entry be preloaded into cache before the line executes. Therefore, the #PRE tag should precede these keywords. *Review "Configuring an LMHOSTS File."*

Chapter 10

Domain Name Service (DNS)

● ●

Exam Objectives

▶ Configuring DNS server roles

▶ Installing and configuring DNS on a Windows NT Server computer

▶ Integrating DNS with other name servers

▶ Connecting a DNS server to a DNS root server

● ●

*M*any test-takers who frequent the newsgroups have noted their surprise at the relatively few exam questions on the Domain Name Service (DNS), and I've heard it said that some of the DNS questions seem almost like no-brainers. Nevertheless, you still need to be familiar with a number of DNS features so you won't be lulled into thinking that this is one area you can safely dismiss.

This chapter focuses primarily on the Microsoft exam objectives, especially in the areas of installing DNS, integrating DNS with other servers, and configuring DNS. When you've absorbed the material in this chapter, you should be able to breeze through the DNS exam questions. But first make sure to study the following information that's included in this chapter — you'll definitely be tested on it:

- ✔ The DNS terminology, including the meaning of *zones, domains, resolver, distributed database,* and *name servers*
- ✔ The different types of name servers and what each type is used for
- ✔ The query types
- ✔ The various types of DNS files
- ✔ The basics of integrating WINS and DNS

Quick Assessment

Configuring
DNS server
roles

1 The four types of name servers are _____, _____, _____, and master servers.

2 A secondary name server can be configured as a _____.

Installing
and
configuring
DNS on a
Windows NT
Server
computer

3 DNS is a replacement for the _____ file.

4 Domains can be grouped into _____ for administrative purposes.

5 The DNS database files are located in the _____ directory.

Connecting a
DNS server
to a DNS
root server

6 The _____ file has names and IP addresses of the root name servers on the Internet.

Integrating
DNS with
other name
servers

7 WINS lookup can be enabled from the DNS Manager or through a _____ in the DNS database.

8 A secondary name server downloads the DNS database information from a _____ name server.

9 (True/False). Check the box titled "Use a WINS Server for NetBIOS Resolution" to enable WINS Lookup.

Answers

1 *Primary, secondary, caching-only.* Review "Configuring DNS Name Server Roles."

2 *Master Server.* Review "Master name server."

3 *HOSTS.* Review "At the Top of the List: The DNS Hierarchy."

4 *Zones.* Review "Zones."

5 `<systemroot>\system32\Dns directory`. **Review "Installing and Configuring the Microsoft DNS Server."**

6 *Cache.* Review "Connecting a DNS Server to a DNS Root Server."

7 *Resource record.* Review "Integrating DNS and WINS."

8 *Master.* Review "Master name server."

9 *False.* Review "Integrating DNS and WINS."

At the Top of the List: The DNS Hierarchy

Domain Name Service (DNS) provides a way to resolve host names to IP addresses. Before DNS came along, static HOSTS files were used to resolve host names. (For the exam, you should have a good understanding of what a host name is and why it needs to be resolved. For more information on host names, see Chapters 4 and 6.)

Domain names

DNS contains a database of domain names that are organized hierarchically into *domain name spaces*. A domain that's below another domain within the hierarchy is called a *subdomain*. The hierarchy allows domains in the name space to be parents to domains as well as subdomains. Domains and subdomains are grouped into *zones* for administrative purposes. (More on the subject can be found in the section "Zones," coming up next.)

A domain's position in the DNS hierarchy can be identified by the placement of periods in the domain name. In Figure 10-1, you can see how the host `sapphire` within the `capstonetechnology` domain name space relates to the root domains (`.com`, `.edu`, and the rest), which are managed by the Network Information Center (InterNIC).

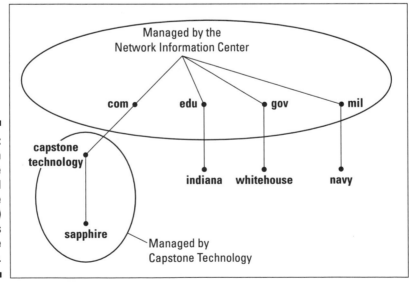

Figure 10-1:
A domain name space (managed by Capstone Technology) and its place on the Internet.

The host name and the domain name constitute the *fully qualified domain name* (FQDN) of `sapphire.capstonetechnology.com`. The FQDN uniquely identifies a host on the Internet (or company intranet). DNS resolves the name from right to left — that is, from the least-specific to the most-specific part of the domain name.

Zones

A *zone* is an administrative unit for DNS. It is a portion of the DNS domain that can separated from the entire domain. This segmenting of the DNS domain into zones can make an administrator's life much easier.

Be sure not to confuse a zone with a DNS domain. A *zone* is an actual database that can be managed for a whole domain or just portions of a domain. A zone doesn't have to contain the entire domain hierarchy.

The exam preparers may try to trick you into thinking that you have to have one zone for an entire domain, but it isn't true. Breaking up the domain into multiple zones makes network management easier because you can manage distributed portions of the domain rather than one large domain. A Microsoft DNS Server can contain and manage a single zone or multiple zones.

For example, a domain such as `capstonetechnology.com` can be split into multiple zones for ease of administration and greater networking efficiency. Two zones are shown in Figure 10-2. A second zone shown in the figure — `eng.capstonetechnology.com` — was created beneath the zone `capstonetechnology.com`. The figure further illustrates that a zone is named for the highest point of the hierarchy that it maintains.

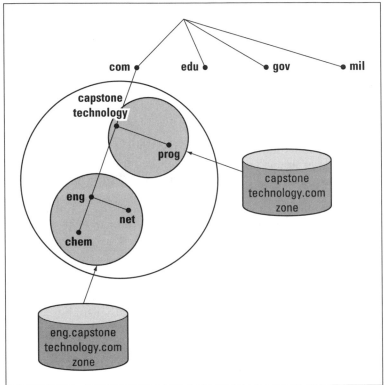

Figure 10-2:
Multiple
zones
created for
administration
purposes.

Configuring DNS Name Server Roles

DNS servers dominate the Internet. They are used all day, every day, for nearly everything you do on the Internet. The top level domains, as well as the domains and zones that are administered by private companies, use DNS servers.

Name servers are DNS servers that store information for the zone or zones for which they are responsible. A name server is considered the "authority" for the zone because it keeps track of the other servers. The vast majority of test-takers agree that you must be able to differentiate the DNS name servers and be familiar with the purpose of each server for the exam.

Primary name server

A server that gets its information for a zone from a local file stored on a machine is a *primary name server*. As you can guess, the primary server is the most important of the name servers because any additions, modifications, and deletions of DNS database information occurs on this server.

A *zone transfer* is the method by which information gets transferred from server to server across the network. Secondary name servers (which are covered in the next section) are configured with an IP address for the primary name server to download information in a zone transfer when the secondary name server initializes.

Secondary name server

A server that receives its information from another name server through a zone transfer is called a *secondary name server*. Secondary servers are very important for a few reasons, which you should definitely know for the exam:

- ✔ **A secondary server provides fault tolerance for the zone.** You should have at least two name servers for each zone in case one fails. (Chapter 9 has information on primary and secondary servers and Windows NT primary and backup domain controllers.)

- ✔ **Secondary name servers should be used for DNS name servers communicating across remote locations.** Secondary servers should be placed at remote locations so that clients do not have to cross slow WAN links for name resolution.

- ✔ **Secondary name servers provide load balancing.** If the demand for host name resolution overloads the primary name server, you can add a secondary server to reduce the load.

The terms *primary* and *secondary* are also used to describe WINS servers. However, in DNS, a secondary server can participate in host name resolution as extensively as a primary server, instead of simply being on hold until the primary server goes down, as is the case with WINS servers.

A name server can be a primary server for one zone and a secondary server for another zone, because the zone information is stored in different databases that do not conflict.

The main difference between primary and secondary DNS servers is that the primary DNS server has the local database (the database on the hard drive of the primary DNS server) to itself. The primary server can modify this database, whereas secondary servers must download the zone information.

Lab 10-1 demonstrates how to configure your DNS server as a secondary name server for a new zone that's being created. (Refer to Lab 10-2 for directions on installing a DNS server.)

Lab 10-1	Configuring a DNS Server as a Secondary Server for a New Zone

1. **Launch the Domain Name Service Manager, which is under the Administrative Common Tools group.**

2. **Right-click the server name and select New Zone, as shown in Figure 10-3.**

   A dialog box called "Creating New Zone for <servername>" appears.

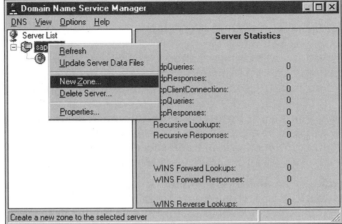

Figure 10-3:
The first step in creating a new zone for your server to administer.

3. **Select either the Primary or Secondary zone type option.**

   If you select Primary, no further configuration is required. If you select Secondary, you need to continue with the following steps.

   Primary zones store information locally, whereas secondary zone information must be transferred from a master name server.

4. **While still in the Creating New Zone for <servername> dialog box, enter** testzone **in the text box labeled "Zone," and in the text box labeled "Server," enter** testserver.

5. **In the "Zone Info" area of the Creating New Zone for <servername> dialog box, you can accept the default zone name and zone file that are created, or you can enter new ones.**

   If this were a real-life situation, and you needed to contact a master zone, you would have to enter the correct zone name and file for that zone in order for the zone transfer to be successful. You can get those settings from the primary zone server that you contact by the IP address in Step 6.

6. **Enter** 123.123.123.123 **as the IP address for the master zone in the space labeled IP Master(s), and then click Add.**

   If this were not an exercise, you would enter the IP address for the master zone server to be contacted for the zone transfer to take place. Remember, the master zone is a primary zone server that contains the *master copy* of the DNS database.

The new zone called `testzone` is added to the zone hierarchy and is visible in the left pane of the DNS Manager window (see Figure 10-4). The server is now a secondary name server for this zone. If desired, you can add subdomains under the newly created zone.

In addition to the new server name (that is, the new zone), several default zones are created by using the steps in Lab 10-1. Those zones are listed in the DNS Manager window (see Figure 10-4):

- `Cache` — The cache contains the records needed to connect to the Internet root DNS servers.

- `0.in.addr.arpa` — This domain is used to prevent reverse lookups from the address of `0.0.0.0` from being sent to the root DNS server.

- `127.in.addr.arpa` — This domain is used for reverse lookups of IP addresses starting with `127`.

- `255.in.addr.arpa` — This domain is used to prevent broadcasts from reaching the root DNS server.

Of the four zones that have been automatically created, (`cache`, `0.in-addr.arpa`, `127.in-addr.arpa`, `255.in-addr.arpa`) only the cache file is important to remember for the exam. It contains the records needed to connect to the Internet root DNS servers.

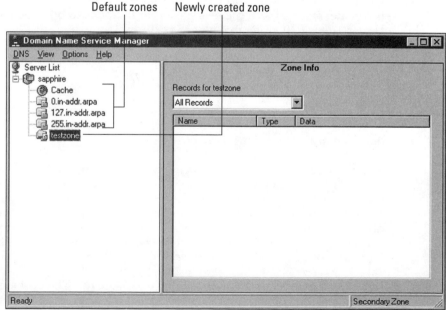

Figure 10-4: A newly created zone administered by the local server is highlighted.

It may not be immediately apparent to you, but when you are creating a secondary zone, you are configuring your computer as a secondary name server. If you were creating a primary zone, your server would then be a primary name server. A tip-off that you're creating a secondary name server is in Step 6 of Lab 10-1, which asks for the IP address of the master server.

Master name server

The master name server can be primary or secondary, and it is charged with transferring information to other servers. When a secondary server initializes on the zone, it requests the zone information from the master server.

A master name server is *not* the most important server in the zone. The most important server in the zone is the primary server. Don't let the names confuse you.

Microsoft recommends using a secondary server configured as a master server in two scenarios:

- ✔ When the primary server is overloaded
- ✔ When the path that exists between secondary servers is more efficient

Because a secondary server that comes up on a network contacts a master name server for zone information, the name server that is contacted should be the nearest server. If the nearest server happens to be a secondary name server, then configuring that server as the master is fine.

Caching-only name server

I still recall the buzz around the TCP/IP exam newsgroups about having to know the purpose of a *caching-only server*. The test-takers were right. I had a question myself about this type of server.

A caching-only server's sole job is to perform queries and to store the results in a cache for a period of time in case another identical query is made shortly thereafter. Because the results are in a cache, they are returned much more quickly. These servers do not contain any information other than the results received when performing a query. A caching-only server starts with no information in its cache, but the cache continues to grow as more queries are performed.

Don't confuse a caching-only server with a cache file. The caching-only server performs queries and caches the results. A cache file has names and IP addresses of the root name servers on the Internet.

Query Types and Name Resolution

A DNS server resolves host names to IP addresses — a basic concept you definitely need to know for the exam. (For more information on the name resolution process and the steps involved in resolving a host name, see Chapter 4.) In the name resolution process, three types of queries are used — *recursive, iterative,* and *inverse.* This section of the chapter covers those types of queries a client can make to a DNS server, and also explains the concept of *time-to-live,* which comes into the picture after the queries are sent out. (By the way, the client computer doing the querying is called a *resolver.*)

Recursive queries

A *recursive query* typically occurs between a DNS client (the resolver) and a DNS name server (see Figure 10-5). The DNS server must respond to the client with the requested data or with an error stating that a specified domain or host does not exist. The server cannot refer a client to another DNS server.

If a DNS server is configured to use a *forwarder,* the queries it receives are considered recursive queries. A *forwarder* is a DNS server on the network that has been configured to communicate with DNS root servers if the DNS servers on the local network fail to answer a query.

Iterative queries

An *iterative query* is one in which the DNS server that is being queried gives the best answer it can to the server making the query. Iterative queries are seldom used in client-to-DNS server situations. They typically occur in queries between name servers that are trying to resolve recursive queries.

The diagram in Figure 10-5 compares the recursive query and iterative query process. The numbers in the figure, and in the following steps, represent the order in which queries take place.

1. The client (resolver) asks for the IP address for `blueskyz.com`.

2. The name server queries the root server for the IP address.

3. The root server fails to find the IP address.

4. The `.com` name server is queried for the IP address for `blueskyz.com`.

5. The `.com` name server fails to find the IP address.

6. The `blueskyz.com` name server is queried for the IP address.

7. The `blueskyz.com` name server finds the IP address and responds to the local name server with the IP address.

8. The name server sends the IP address for `blueskyz.com` back to the original resolver, which can now provide the IP address for `blueskyz.com`.

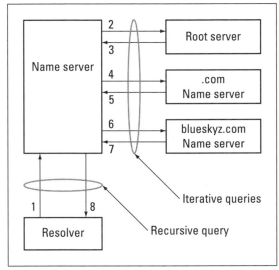

Figure 10-5:
Comparing
the
recursive
and
iterative
query
processes.

A recursive query gets more absolute results than an iterative query because a recursive query requires a response. On the other hand, if a name server is contacted with an iterative query, it can respond: "I don't know, I'm going to go and ask so and so." At that point, the name resolution process is done in bits and pieces.

Inverse queries

Inverse queries are handled a little differently than recursive and iterative queries. With an inverse query, the resolver attempts to resolve the Internet domain name for a known IP address, which is the opposite of resolving an IP address for a known host name. IP address information is spread over the DNS in no particular order, so in order to resolve an IP address to a host name successfully a special domain, called `in-addr.arpa.`, was created for this very reason. The names in this domain are organized by IP addresses.

In order for the DNS server to search for an IP address, the addresses have to be entered in the DNS database in reverse order, to accommodate the way DNS resolves names. (IP address information gets more specific as you read it from left to right; whereas, a DNS domain name gets more specific as you read it from right to left.) This process is known as *reverse lookup*. For example, an IP address of 201.58.114.31 is built as 31.114.58.201. for `in-addr.arpa` and is resolved from right to left.

Caching and time-to-live

Because a name server can send out many iterative queries for one recursive query, the results from the recursive queries are cached for future use and given a *time-to-live* (TTL). The term TTL refers to how long the cached item has before it expires and is discarded. The information in the recursive query is stored in the cache just in case the information is needed again a short time later, saving the server the trouble of going through another lengthy round of iterative queries.

The primary name server of a zone is responsible for setting the TTL for objects. As TTL values increase, the more out of date the cached information becomes. With TTL values, the information is more up to date and consistent; however, the server's workload increases due to additional traffic.

Differentiating DNS Files

As with every Microsoft product, configuration settings are selected through a graphical user interface. Configuring DNS on Windows NT 4.0 is no exception. Without a GUI, you'd have to edit the DNS database manually. Although you do not have to interact directly with the DNS database, you do need to be familiar with the components of the DNS files because there's a good chance you'll see one or two exam questions on DNS files.

I found that simply knowing what the database file, cache file, reverse lookup file, and boot file are used for was enough information to remember about them for the exam. It's highly unlikely you'll receive a detailed question concerning the files.

The database file

The *database file,* commonly known as the *zone file,* contains the records for a particular zone. This database can be edited on a primary server and then replicated to the secondary servers.

Within the database file are resource records of certain types, most of which are not covered on the exam *except* for the CNAME record, which has caught many test-takers off-guard. *CNAME* is short for *canonical name,* which is an alias for a host (a host can have more than one alias). The CNAME record is used most often to host an FTP and WWW server on the same machine.

Figure 10-6 illustrates how you can use either FTP or WWW services and still be communicating with the same server — in this case, the server `sapphire.capstonetechnology.com`. So if a user were to request `www.capstonetechnology.com`, that user would communicate with the `sapphire.capstonetechnology.com` server.

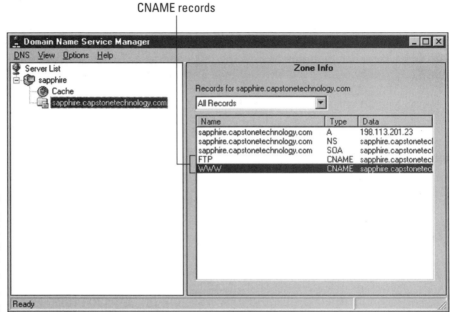

Figure 10-6:
CNAME
records
in the
database
file.

The reverse lookup file

Inverse queries return host names when you provide an IP address in a query. The *reverse lookup file* is what makes inverse queries possible. In your particular DNS zone, you configure this file with *pointer records* that work the same way that a HOSTS file works: You provide the IP-address-to-host-name mapping. When a host name needs to be determined for a particular IP address, the file is parsed. (You can find out more about the HOSTS file in Chapter 6.)

The boot file

The *boot file* provides startup information for configuring a DNS server. A boot file can point to the location of required files, load cache files, specify which domain the server is responsible for, specify the name of a database file to be used, and specify the location of other DNS name servers, such as the master server, from which the zone database can be downloaded.

The boot file is created automatically in Windows NT 4.0. Windows NT informs you that the boot information is located in the Registry, rather than in a text file as it was in the previous version of Windows NT.

Connecting a DNS Server to a DNS Root Server

In order to connect your DNS server to a DNS root server on the Internet, you need a *cache file*. This type of file is used to resolve names that are outside the domain for which you're responsible. The cache file contains names and IP addresses of root name servers on the Internet.

When you install the DNS service on a Windows NT computer without any modifications, your server becomes a caching-only name server for the Internet root servers.

Microsoft has provided a default cache file, called `cache.dns`, with the names and IP addresses of the DNS root servers on the Internet. By default, the cache file is required to connect a DNS server to a DNS root server. This cache file works fine for resolving host names just as it is. Therefore, don't expect to see any questions on the exam concerning customizing the cache file.

Installing and Configuring the Microsoft DNS Server

The Microsoft DNS server is fully compatible with other DNS servers but includes many features not found on other DNS server platforms. Those features include tight integration with the Windows Internet Name Service (a Windows-based technology) and a graphical user interface. The Microsoft DNS server can query a WINS server for resolving names that DNS cannot resolve with information contained within the DNS database.

You can administer other Microsoft DNS servers with the DNS administrative tool, but you can't use it to administer non-Microsoft DNS servers. You can, however, configure your DNS server as a primary or secondary server to another DNS server platform, such as UNIX.

Installing the Microsoft DNS Server

Before I cover the installation of the DNS server, I need to mention the DNS page of the TCP/IP Properties dialog box. You access it by doing the following:

1. **Click the Start button, point to Settings, and select Control Panel.**

2. **Double-click the Network option and then click the Protocols tab.**

3. **Select TCP/IP Protocol from the list of Network protocols and click Properties.**

4. **Click the DNS tab to get the DNS page shown in Figure 10-7.**

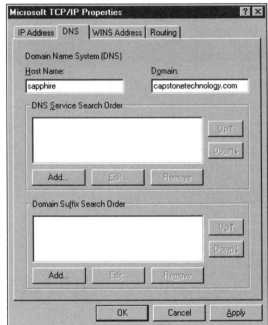

Figure 10-7:
You can configure DNS properties here.

Most of the default information (such as the host name and domain name) used during the DNS server installation is taken from this spot. If the host name and domain name are specified on this page, DNS installation makes records for them in the DNS database. Lab 10-2 demonstrates the installation of the DNS server on your Windows NT server.

Lab 10-2   Installing the Microsoft DNS Server

1. **Click the Start button, point to Settings, and select Control Panel.**

2. **Double-click the Network icon.**

3. **Click the Services tab of the Network dialog box.**

   A list of installed network services appears.

4. **Click Add.**

   A list of available services appears.

5. **Select Microsoft DNS Server from the list.**

6. **Insert the Windows NT Server CD when prompted.**

   Windows NT copies the files needed for the DNS server service to the `<systemroot>\system32\Dns` directory.

Administering and configuring the DNS server

The remaining text in this chapter covers the administration and configuration of the DNS server. DNS servers are configured to communicate with each other to resolve host names. Pay special attention to this stuff, because it's all fair game for the exam.

You can administer and configure the DNS server through the Domain Name Service Manager, which is started from the Administrative Tools (Common) program folder. Using the DNS Manager, you have to add a new server and zones for that server to administer because the DNS Manager lacks any specifications when you open it up. This process involves just a couple of steps:

1. **To add a server, select New Server from the DNS menu in the Domain Name Service Manager window.**

2. **In the Add DNS Server dialog box, enter the name of your local server.**

   If you enter any other name, you are unable to connect or configure the DNS server.

By configuring your DNS server with the name of your local server only, your DNS server becomes a caching-only server for the Internet (see the section, "Caching-only name server," earlier in this chapter).

Manually configuring zones

Zones are physical portions of a domain that are stored on a number of DNS servers in order to be more easily managed. You should know how you want to distribute your zones before you continue with the configuration process because you have to configure the zones before you do anything else.

For example, if you want to have each department in your company administer its own zone, then you can configure the zones accordingly. Of course, you can have one DNS server store the information for the entire zone, which requires that the zone be administered centrally. Put simply, you have to create a zone before you can continue with creating the domain.

The zone must be created before the domain because the zone is what holds the information for the domain. The domain itself can't hold any information, so it first needs a zone to contain it.

Adding DNS domains and zones

After an administration zone is in place, you can create domains under the zone by using the steps listed earlier in the chapter in Lab 10-1. You can do this for any other zones that need to be created for the server.

A single DNS server can be a primary or secondary server for one zone, while simultaneously maintaining other zones. So don't get confused during the exam if a question cites one server as the authority for many different zones.

Adding subdomains

In order to add a subdomain under a zone that you have created, follow these steps:

1. **Open the Domain Name Service Manager.**

2. **Right-click on the name of the desired zone and select New Domain.**

3. **Enter the name of the new domain in the dialog box that appears.**

Not only can you create subdomains underneath zones, you can create subdomains of a domain by right-clicking the desired parent domain and selecting New Domain.

Adding resource records

After your zones and subdomains are created and configured, resource records need to be added to each zone's database file. For example, assume that you add another zone underneath the testzone zone created earlier in this chapter in Lab 10-1. You call this new zone secondzone. You need to add a resource record in the testzone database that will enable the original zone to see the new zone you just created. You also need to add a resource record to the secondzone database to inform other name servers that secondzone.testzone.com can be searched to resolve names.

To add a resource record, follow these steps:

1. **Open the DNS Manager and right-click the name of the zone to which you're adding the resource record.**

   The New Resource Record dialog box appears.

2. Select the Record Type you want to add.

The most popular resource records are

- A (Address) — Used for specifying the address of a host in the DNS database.

- NS (Name Server) — Used for specifying a name server in the database file.

- SOA (Start Of Authority) — Defines the authoritative name server for the zone.

- The other resource record types are more advanced, and are unlikely to turn up on the exam.

Any further information you specify depends on the type of resource record you're adding. For example, if you add an NS record, you need to supply the DNS Name Server name.

You can see the various record types listed under the Type column in the Zone Info area of the Domain Name Service Manager window (refer to Figure 10-6). The record types were added automatically to the DNS server during the installation process. The records were created from information entered into the DNS page of the TCP/IP Properties dialog box during installation.

Integrating DNS and WINS

DNS and Windows Internet Name Service (WINS) can be integrated for greater functionality. The DNS server can query a dynamic WINS server in order to resolve a host name it wasn't successful at resolving itself. The DNS server resolves the leftmost portion of the fully qualified domain name, which is the unique host name, and if necessary, passes the host name to the WINS server for resolution.

This resolution process is transparent to the client that issued the request, which operates under the assumption that the whole process was accomplished by the DNS server. However, the host name must be the same as the NetBIOS machine name for this process to work (see Chapter 5 for more information on NetBIOS). The host name is set to the NetBIOS machine name by default when Windows NT is installed.

For example, if your NetBIOS name is sparky, Windows NT calls your host sparky unless you change it to something else. If you change the default host name from sparky to george, what happens when DNS asks the WINS server to look in its database for a computer named sparky? WINS says: "I don't have an entry for a computer named sparky. Sorry DNS, you can't resolve the name." Meanwhile, there exists an entry for george, which is what you changed your computer's host name to. (See Chapter 4 for a more thorough explanation of what happens when a WINS server is asked to resolve a host name that the DNS server can't resolve.)

One way to integrate DNS and WINS is by adding a resource record to the zone database file for the DNS server. The WINS record instructs the name server to use WINS for any reverse lookup requests for IP addresses that are not statically defined in the DNS database. The record is added manually by the administrator in the DNS database and looks like this:

```
<domain> IN WINS <IP address of WINS server>
```

Enabling WINS lookup can also be accomplished through the DNS Manager utility. The following steps enable WINS lookup on your DNS server:

1. **Right-click the zone you want to configure for WINS lookup.**

2. **Select Properties from the menu that appears.**

3. **Click the WINS Lookup tab.**

4. **Select the Use WINS Reverse Lookup check box and enter the IP address for the WINS server that you want to use.**

5. **Click Add.**

Using the nslookup Command for Troubleshooting

A DNS monitoring utility that you should know something about is nslookup. You don't have to know every detail concerning the command, just what it's used for. The nslookup command utility is used to troubleshoot DNS problems, such as host name resolution, by querying a DNS name server for information. For example, with nslookup you can find the IP address of a host in a specific domain. If you're quizzed on nslookup in the exam, most likely you'll be asked about the two modes that nslookup runs in:

- **Interactive:** Use this mode when you need to look up information about various hosts or domains or print a list of hosts in a domain.

- **Non-interactive:** Use this mode when you need to look up requested information on a single host or domain. If you want more information, you have to enter the nslookup command again.

The nslookup command has the following syntax:

```
nslookup [-option...][hostname | - server]]
```

A number of parameters are available with the nslookup command, and it is most likely they will *not* be on your exam. Microsoft rarely tests on specific parameters.

The following example is output from the nslookup command in which all the records for a specified domain, capstone.com, are listed:

```
> nslookup -d capstone.com
[capstone.com]
capstone.com.          SOA     capstone.com
         hostmaster.capstone.com. (97110901 2592000
         86400)
capstone.com.          NS      CAPSTONE.COM
capstone.com.          MX      10    capstone.com
capstone.com.          A       198.68.28.62
hds100                 A       198.68.28.130
hds101                 A       198.68.28.131
hds106                 A       198.68.28.137
news                   CNAME   capstone.com
gopher                 CNAME   capstone.com
ftp                    CNAME   capstone.com
```

In this example, you can see the resource record types A, NS, SOA, and CNAME that were covered earlier in this chapter in the section "Adding resource records." Also included are CNAME entries that create aliases for the capstone.com name (see the section "The database file" earlier in this chapter).

The host name parameter is, by default, the name of the DNS server that is configured for the local system. This is convenient because the local host is most likely the DNS server you're checking if you're having DNS problems. (You'll likely be at that machine doing your troubleshooting.) If you need to look up the IP address of a host, just enter the host name at the nslookup prompt and press Enter. If you want to use a different DNS server than the one configured for the local machine, then enter *server servername.*

Prep Test

1 Which of the following is true for zones and domains? (Choose all that apply.)

    A ❑ A zone cannot have another zone underneath it in the hierarchy.

    B ❑ You can control multiple zones with one Windows NT DNS server.

    C ❑ A zone does not have to cover the whole domain.

    D ❑ The zone is named after the highest point in the zone hierarchy.

2 When should a secondary server *not* be configured as a master name server?

    A ○ When it is also a caching-only server

    B ○ When the primary server is overloaded

    C ○ When it is over a slower link

    D ○ When it is not authoritative of any zone

3 A DNS client makes a request to a DNS server with a host name. The server had the information in cache and returned the request to the client. What type of request was this?

    A ○ Inverse

    B ○ Reverse Lookup

    C ○ Recursive

    D ○ Iterative

4 You would like the information found in cache to be more consistent. How do you go about making this happen?

    A ○ Increase the TTL on the primary name server.

    B ○ Decrease the TTL on the primary name server.

    C ○ Increase the extinction parameter in the cache file.

    D ○ Decrease the extinction parameter in the cache file.

5 What makes possible the process of returning a host name when an IP address is given?

    A ○ The reverse lookup file

    B ○ The WINS lookup file

    C ○ Reverse queries

    D ○ The CNAME record

6 You would like to configure your DNS server with information on where to load the cache files. Where is this information stored?

A ○ `<systemroot>\system\Dns directory`
B ○ `<systemroot>\system32\drivers\Dns directory`
C ○ `<systemroot>\system32\Dns directory`
D ○ The Registry

7 Which of the following should you create first in DNS Manager?

A ○ The master name server
B ○ The primary name server
C ○ The zone
D ○ The domain

8 What is needed to resolve names outside the authoritative domain?

A ○ A master name server
B ○ A recursive query
C ○ A reverse lookup file
D ○ A cache file

9 What is required to enable WINS reverse lookup?

A ○ Check the box for "Enable WINS Lookup" and enter the IP address of the WINS server.
B ○ Check the box for "Use WINS Reverse Lookup" and enter the IP address of the WINS server.
C ○ Check the box for "Enable WINS Lookup" and enter the host domain name.
D ○ Check the box for "Use WINS Reverse Lookup" and enter the domain name to append to WINS responses.

Answers

1 *B,C,D.* Distributing zones that grow too large into multiple zones for adminis-tration is common. *Review "Manually configuring zones."*

2 *C.* The master server downloads the zone information to servers when they initialize, and therefore you do not want this downloading to take place over a slow link. *Review "Master name server."*

3 *C.* This type of query is used most often when a client requests information from a server. The server must provide either the information or an error message stating that the information cannot be found. *Review "Recursive queries."*

4 *B.* Making the TTL shorter on the name server causes older, possibly inaccu-rate information in the cache file to be purged more often. *Review "Caching and time-to-live."*

5 *A.* When a host name needs to be determined for a particular IP address, the reverse lookup file with pointer records is parsed. *Review "The reverse lookup file."*

6 *D.* Information on loading cache files used to be found in the boot file, which was located in the `<systemroot>\system32\Dns directory`, but now this file is no longer parsed. The Registry is now used to store this information. *Review "The boot file."*

7 *C.* Because you administer the domain by using zones, you need to create a zone. After the zone is created, you can create additional zones or begin adding domains and resource records to the zone. *Review "Administering and configuring the DNS server"* and *"Adding DNS domains and zones."*

8 *D.* This file contains names and addresses of root name servers on the Internet, which is outside your authoritative domain. *Review "Connecting a DNS Server to a DNS Root Server."*

9 *D.* This dialog box is reached by right-clicking the appropriate `in-addr.arpa` zone and selecting Properties. *Review "Integrating DNS and WINS."*

Chapter 11
SNMP Services

● ●

Exam Objectives

▶ Configuring SNMP

▶ Choosing the appropriate services to install on an NT server, given a scenario

● ●

*B*ecause the Simple Network Management Protocol (SNMP) is part of the TCP/IP protocol suite, it deserves your attention (and, obviously, the attention of the folks who write the exam). Although you probably won't see more than three exam questions on the subject of SNMP, those questions may be ambiguous and somewhat tricky. Therefore, your best defense lies in a solid understanding of SNMP as a whole and a familiarity with some SNMP specifics.

This chapter begins with an overview of the SNMP protocol and some information on installing SNMP. I focus largely on configuration in this chapter because most, if not all, of the SNMP questions you get probably address this topic.

In addition to the "big picture" topics that I just mentioned, I recommend that you also concentrate on the following areas (which are covered in this chapter). Then you should be in good shape for the exam as far as Simple Network Management Protocol goes.

- ✔ The basics elements of SNMP, including communities, traps, and security.
- ✔ Configuring an agent to accept requests only from specific computers.
- ✔ What Windows NT can and can't do when it comes to managing agents with SNMP. I'll give you a hint up front: Windows NT can only function as an SNMP agent, not as an SNMP management console.
- ✔ When to install the SNMP service. The exam presents you with a scenario, and you must decide whether SNMP is the right service to install in the given situation.

Quick Assessment

1   SNMP uses management consoles that gather information from the
_____.

2   A(n) _____ is a grouping of hosts for management purposes.

3   The descriptions of objects and information on values are stored in a
database called the _____.

4   You can specify up to _____ hosts for trap destinations.

5   The default community is called _____.

6   Windows NT can function only as an SNMP _____.

Configuring
SNMP

7   Your SNMP host can belong to a maximum of _____ communities.

8   You can use the _____ to verify that the SNMP configuration is correct.

9   Clicking the _____ tab in the SNMP Properties window displays the
text box in which you specify the community name.

Choosing the
appropriate
services to
install on an
NT server,
given a
scenario

10 You can install the _____ service on your NT Server if you want this
server to report its hardware and software information to a management console.

Answers

1 *Agents.* Review "Examining SNMP agents."

2 *Community.* Review "Configuring SNMP Communities."

3 *Management Information Base (MIB).* Review "Defining Management Information Bases (MIBs)."

4 *Five.* Review "Configuring SNMP Communities."

5 *Public.* Review "Configuring SNMP Communities."

6 *Agent.* Review "Examining SNMP agents."

7 *Five.* Review "Configuring SNMP Communities."

8 *SNMPUTIL utility.* Review "Testing the Configuration with the SNMPUTIL Utility."

9 *Traps.* Review "Configuring SNMP Communities."

10 *SNMP.* Review "Selecting the Appropriate Services to Install, Given a Scenario."

Making It Simple: Some SNMP Basics

Simple Network Management Protocol (SNMP) is a system that includes software and protocols designed to monitor and manage devices on a network. At one time, SNMP could be used only to monitor TCP/IP networking hardware such as routers, hubs, and bridges. Since then, SNMP has gone through some extensive changes. It can now be used to monitor more than just the basic networking components. Its usage has been extended to include gateways, servers, hosts, or any device installed with an SNMP agent (the concept of SNMP agents is covered later in this chapter).

In the following few sections, I describe the installation of SNMP and define SNMP agents and the Management Information Bases (MIBs) that the SNMP agents use. Then I get into the meat of the matter, as far as the test is concerned — configuring SNMP and managing SNMP communities.

Installing Microsoft SNMP

You should know a few things for the exam about installing SNMP on a Windows NT computer. Because SNMP is a service, it is installed through the Services dialog box in the Network window of the Control Panel. Lab 11-1 demonstrates the installation of the SNMP agent software on a Windows NT Workstation computer.

Lab 11-1   Installing the SNMP Agent Software

1. **Open the Network window from the Control Panel.**

2. **Click the Services tab to get the Services page with the list of network services that are installed on the computer.**

3. **Click Add.**

   A Select Network Service dialog box appears.

4. **Select SNMP Service from the list of network services.**

5. **Insert the Windows NT 4.0 CD into your CD-ROM drive to copy the files needed for the SNMP service from the CD to your computer.**

   After the files are copied, the Microsoft SNMP Properties dialog box, shown in Figure 11-1, appears.

6. **Restart your computer to make sure that the SNMP service installed correctly.**

7. **Go to the Control Panel, double-click the Network icon, and click the Services tab of the Network window.**

   SNMP Service and SNMP Trap Services have been added to the list of available services.

After the SNMP agent software is installed, the SNMP service accepts requests from the SNMP management console. The SNMP Trap service receives *traps* from the SNMP agent and forwards them to the SNMP management console. A *trap* is a message generated spontaneously by an SNMP agent and sent to an SNMP manager when an event defined by the agent occurs on a host — for example, when an unauthorized user to tries to tap into your physical network.

Before you install the SNMP agent, you need to gather together some essential pieces of information:

- ✔ **The contact individual and location for the agent computer.** You'll need this information in case you have to make a phone call or pay a visit to a computer after having viewed the agent information.

- ✔ **The available communities.** If you know the available communities before you begin installing the SNMP service on agent computers, you can configure the SNMP agent with the appropriate community during the installation.

- ✔ **The IP address of the central management console.** When you are installing the SNMP service on agent computers, you are then able to specify the IP address of the central management console to which the agent reports its information when queried. You can also use the host name, which must then be resolved to the IP address.

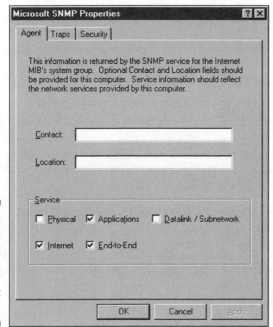

Figure 11-1:
You use this dialog box to configure the SNMP agent properties.

Many test-takers have noted that questions regarding the central management console (also called the *trap destination*) appear on the exam. Remember that you need to specify the IP address of the management console to which the agent sends information when queried.

Examining SNMP agents

SNMP uses a client/server technology that involves a central host that acts as the SNMP manager and numerous agents that are polled for information. The Windows NT 4.0 Server and Workstation currently can be used only as SNMP agents, not as management servers — which makes the material in this chapter and the exam questions less complex than you may have expected.

An important distinction between SNMP agents and SNMP management consoles to remember for the exam is that you can't use Windows NT to manage SNMP agents. If you keep this fact in mind, you can eliminate any answers to questions about SNMP that mention monitoring or managing clients from within Windows NT. All you need to remember is how Windows NT is managed as an SNMP agent. Managing a Windows NT SNMP agent involves the SNMP community, which is described later in this chapter in "Configuring SNMP Communities."

This point bears repeating (so I will repeat it): Windows NT can act only as an SNMP agent. A question on the exam may try to convince you that you can use Windows NT to manage other SNMP clients, which is incorrect.

The Microsoft SNMP agent consists of three important components:

- ✔ The SNMP service
- ✔ SNMP agent software, which is installed when the SNMP service is installed and that enables your Windows NT computer to act as an SNMP agent
- ✔ The Management Information Bases (MIBs), which are data files that contain information about object descriptions and object values for all manageable items on the SNMP agent computer

TCP/IP must be installed prior to installing the SNMP service on the agent. After the SNMP service is installed, SNMP Service is added to the list of available services that can be stopped and started from the Services icon in the Control Panel. In addition to the SNMP service, a number of files that make up the agent portion of SNMP are installed. The MIBs are also installed for the object information.

Defining Management Information Bases (MIBs)

All SNMP agents maintain a database of information that contains descriptions of the objects and values for any hardware and software installed on the SNMP agent that are manageable by SNMP. This information, known as the *Management Information Base (MIB)*, together with the SNMP agent software, makes up the entire SNMP client software. Every entity, including the hardware and software, that is manageable on the SNMP agent resides in the MIB. Any vendor can provide MIBs for its products, and Microsoft includes some MIBs with the SNMP service.

Specific details on the contents of the SNMP MIBs probably won't turn up on the exam, but you should have at least a general idea of what the MIBs contain. Basically, the following information is defined in the MIBs for each object that can be managed:

- ✔ A definition of the object's data type
- ✔ A text description of the object
- ✔ The read or write access allowed on the object

The SNMP management program can send requests to the agent asking for information about a specific object in the MIB. For example, the management program can query an agent with the WINS MIB about how many NetBIOS name resolution requests have been successful. (For more information on WINS, refer to Chapter 9.)

Configuring SNMP Communities

An *SNMP community* is a grouping of hosts for management purposes. The community contains at least one management console and a number of client hosts running the agent software. You can configure an agent to belong to one or more communities, up to five.

Communities are configured on the Services page in the Network dialog box (the same place where you install SNMP). By selecting SNMP Service from the list of installed network services and clicking Properties, you get the Microsoft SNMP Properties dialog box (refer to Figure 11-1). Clicking the Traps tab in the dialog box displays the page in which the community name is specified (see Figure 11-2).

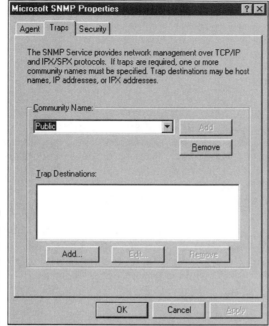

Figure 11-2:
Use this
page to
specify an
SNMP
community.

By default, the community name is Public. You can specify up to five community names in which this SNMP agent is included. These community names are case-sensitive, most likely to accommodate UNIX management consoles.

For each community to which an SNMP agent belongs, the agent can send trap information to five hosts within that community. The agents generate trap messages for normal occurrences, such as shutting down or starting the computer, or for queries from the management consoles.

What if a trap destination is used with multiple communities? In that case, what should be configured as the trap destination? The trap destination has to be in one of the communities to which the agent belongs. Any SNMP host that is running management software can be the trap destination, and up to five hosts can be specified.

You should be familiar with a few points on community configuration for the exam:

> ✔ **The default community of** Public **should include** *every* **SNMP agent on the network.** By using this community, you can gather information from every SNMP agent on the network.

> ✔ **Agents should also belong to another community that specifies the location or purpose of the agent computer.** For example, you can configure a computer to belong to the `sales` community in addition to the `Public` community. If a management console must gather information from every agent on the network, it uses the `Public` community. If a management console must gather information from every agent in the `sales` community, the `sales` community is specified.

After the management console is in place, the agent software is installed on the clients, and the communities are defined, you can begin to focus on managing the SNMP communities. For example, you can configure security for a SNMP community and then test the SNMP configuration.

Specifying SNMP Agent Services

You can set up your computer with any one of several agent service configurations, depending on the role that you want your computer to play. These services are not as likely to be on your exam as configuring communities, but they may show up.

You can specify the type of service that an agent performs — for example, whether the agent acts as a physical TCP/IP device such as a router. Figure 11-1 shows the selection of available service options — which include Physical, Applications, Datalink/Subnetwork, Internet, and End-to-End — under Service in the SNMP Properties dialog box. The default services are selected in the figure.

I remember wondering whether the exam would ask which of the agent services were selected by default. Just in case you get handed such a question, try this trick to remember the default services: Of the five available services, the three default services all begin with a vowel.

Establishing SNMP Security Services

This section of the chapter covers an area that several test-takers in the TCP/IP newsgroup encountered on their exams: security between SNMP agents and the management console.

SNMP security is based on an authentication service used for verifying messages between the management console and the host. If a message can't be authenticated, it simply doesn't get processed. A community name, which provides the authentication for these messages, is used in every message.

If a message contains a community name that is not specified in the list of available communities on the host, the message isn't processed and an optional trap can be sent to the management console for that community. This trap message informs the management console that this agent rejected a host and caused an authentication failure.

If you remove the default community name `Public` from the list of communities and don't add any other community name, the host accepts messages from any community. This is not recommended because specifying a community name provides security from unwanted messages from another management console. In addition, the whole purpose of using SNMP to help manage your SNMP agents on the network is to manage SNMP clients in logical groupings similar to domains.

Figure 11-3 shows the available security options for sending traps and accepting SNMP packets. A trap message is sent when a failed authentication is encountered. Selecting the Send Authentication Trap option ensures that failed authentication attempts are sent to the management console for the community.

Trap agents don't send SNMP communications to other trap agents; only to trap destinations (the SNMP management consoles). Therefore, the agents can't talk to each other — only the agents and managers that are configured with the same community name can communicate with each other.

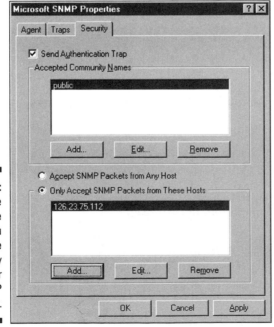

Figure 11-3:
This is the place where you configure security options for the SNMP host.

Figure 11-4 helps put the community name and trap destination configuration in perspective. The figure illustrates how only members of the `public` community can send messages to each other; the members of the `sales` community don't receive those messages.

The Accepted Community Names frame of the Security page (refer to Figure 11-3) lists communities from which the SNMP agent will accept requests. If someone else were to bring a management console onto the network with a community name other than the one listed under Accepted Community Names, he or she would not be able to query your SNMP host for information.

To further tighten SNMP security, you can specify which hosts you will accept SNMP packets from. You can enter the IP address or host name of selected SNMP hosts if you don't want to accept SNMP packets from any other host. Keep in mind that you specify hosts in order to establish a greater degree of security.

Figure 11-4:
The relationship between community names and trap destinations in an SNMP network.

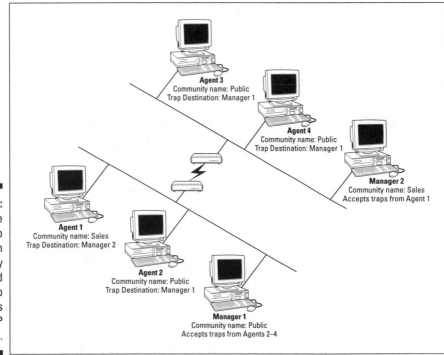

The topic of specifying which hosts you will accept SNMP packets from is very likely to be on your exam. The exam may test you on this concept with a question similar to the following:

You have three management consoles in your SNMP community: console1, console2, and console3. You are responsible for management console2, and you would like to have a smaller group of computers respond to only your requests. How can you configure the clients for this purpose?

A. Create another community.

B. Configure the clients to send authentication traps to your console.

C. Configure the clients to accept messages only from your console.

D. Specify your computer as the community name for the clients that you want to manage.

The correct answer is *C.* The actual question may be trickier, but the rule of accepting requests from only certain hosts still holds true. Keep an eye out for a question such as this one.

Lab 11-2 demonstrates how to configure an SNMP agent to accept SNMP packets from only one host. You need to have the SNMP service installed prior to trying this exercise.

Lab 11-2   Configuring an SNMP Agent to Accept SNMP Packets Only from a Specific Host

1. Open the Network window and click the Services tab.

2. Select the SNMP Service option and click Properties.

The Microsoft SNMP Properties dialog box appears.

3. Click the Security tab.

The Security page lists the accepted community names and the hosts that the SNMP agent will accept SNMP packets from. By default, the list of hosts that the agent will accept packets from is empty.

4. Select the Only Accept SNMP Packets from These Hosts option.

5. Click Add.

The Security Configuration dialog box appears where you can enter the IP address of the host you will accept packets from.

6. **Enter the IP address of 123.123.123.123, which is the IP address of the only host that this agent will accept SNMP packets from, and click Add.**

   The IP address now appears, in the Only Accept SNMP Packets from These Hosts portion of the Microsoft SNMP Properties dialog box.

Testing the Configuration with the SNMPUTIL Utility

After your SNMP configuration is in place, you can test it with SNMPUTIL, which is an application designed to obtain information from your SNMP Windows NT-based hosts.

SNMPUTIL mimics the requests that a management console sends to the agents to query them for information. (**Remember:** Windows NT does not provide a management console for you to send and receive messages to the SNMP agents on the network.)

The SNMPUTIL command syntax looks like this:

```
snmputil command agent community objectID
```

In this example, the command parameter stands for the request — for example, get, get-next, or set; agent refers to the target for the query; community refers to the community that the target agent belongs to; and objectID specifies a very long and complicated ID number for a specific object — for example, 1.2.6.1.5.1.221.1.7.2.1.1.1. The results returned are the object variable and the value of that variable.

```
snmputil getnext 131.107.subnet_id.host_id public
         .1.3.6.1.4.1.311.1.3.2.1.1.1
```

Selecting the Appropriate Services to Install, Given a Scenario

Many test-takers (including myself) will tell you to expect scenario-type questions that involve installing the appropriate service on your Windows NT Server computer. I myself encountered a couple such questions in regard to the SNMP service. Answering a question regarding which service to install on an NT Server may, at first, seem simple to answer but can quickly become more complex, as this scenario demonstrates:

You have a mixed network of Windows NT servers and Novell NetWare servers. Each client on the network is configured with the appropriate protocol for connecting to one of the server types, but not both. You would like to begin migrating the NetWare clients to Windows NT, but you need to gather information from the clients before the migration. You want to cluster the network clients into two groups — one called WindowsNT and one called NetWare. What service should you install on the Windows NT Server to assist you?

A. DHCP

B. SNMP

C. WINS

D. DNS

The answer is, of course, SNMP. Now that you have this chapter under your belt, scenario questions on SNMP should be a snap.

Prep Test

1 You have a mixed network with Windows NT servers, workstations, and UNIX machines. You are configuring the network for SNMP. Which is the most valid SNMP implementation?

A ○ A Windows NT Server as a manager for UNIX and Windows NT agents.

B ○ A Windows NT Workstation as a manager for UNIX and Windows NT agents.

C ○ A UNIX machine as a manager and Windows NT and UNIX machines as agents.

D ○ This configuration is invalid.

2 Which of the following are included in a Management Information Base (MIB)? (Choose all that apply.)

A ❑ Community name

B ❑ Permissions

C ❑ Data type

D ❑ Description

3 Which service is added to the list in the Services dialog box when installation of SNMP is complete?

A ○ SNMP Agent Service

B ○ SNMP Community Service

C ○ SNMP Message Service

D ○ SNMP Trap Service

4 Which page of the Microsoft SNMP Properties dialog box is used to specify the community name?

A ○ Community

B ○ Traps

C ○ Security

D ○ Agent

5 You have two groups of computers that need to be managed separately. What is the best way to configure these groups?

A ○ Create two different communities.

B ○ Create two different communities and a third community for all members.

C ○ Create two different communities and have each community respond to requests from only one management console.

D ○ Create only one community and configure members of one group to respond to requests from only one management console.

6 Which is not a default service when SNMP is installed?

A ○ Physical

B ○ Applications

C ○ End-to-End

D ○ Internet

7 You have just installed the SNMP service on a Windows NT computer and removed the default public community. You try to query the machine from the management console but nothing happens. What may be the problem?

A ○ No community is specified.

B ○ A community that is common to the managing computer and agent is not specified.

C ○ A trap destination has not been specified.

D ○ The SNMP services have not been started on the client.

8 Which page in the Microsoft SNMP Properties dialog box do you use if you want to configure your agent to send authentication traps?

A ○ Traps

B ○ Agent

C ○ Security

D ○ Community

9 You have been made responsible for a group of SNMP agents. You don't want the agents to respond to requests from other managers. However, the group of agents must remain in the same community. How should you configure the clients?

A ○ To accept packets only from the host name of your computer.

B ○ Create a new community and configure the agents for both communities.

C ○ Create a new community, configure the agents for both communities, and send authentication traps to only your computer.

D ○ Configure the agents to send authentication traps to your computer.

10 What type of information does the SNMPUTIL utility return on an SNMP network with only the community name of public specified?

A ○ Trap information

B ○ Community information

C ○ Packet information

D ○ Object information

Answers

1 *C.* A Windows NT machine can't act as an SNMP manager. It can only act as an SNMP agent. *Review "Examining SNMP agents."*

2 *B,C,D.* Only manageable objects and their values are contained within an MIB, not the community name. *Review "Defining Management Information Bases (MIBs)."*

3 *D.* Only SNMP Service and SNMP Trap Service are added to the list of available services when installation is complete. *Review "Installing Microsoft SNMP."*

4 *B.* The community name and the trap destination are configured on the Traps page in the Microsoft SNMP Properties dialog box. *Review "Configuring SNMP Communities."*

5 *B.* You should definitely have two different communities, but including every member in the network in one community, such as Public, enables you to query the entire network as a whole. *Review "Configuring SNMP Communities."*

6 *A.* Remember this: Only services that begin with vowels are part of the default installation. *Review "Specifying SNMP Agent Services."*

7 *D.* If you remove the Public community and don't specify another community name, the agent accepts requests from any community. However, the SNMP service must be started before any SNMP activity can occur on the client. *Review "Establishing SNMP Security Services."*

8 *C.* Although it may seem that configuring an agent to send authentication traps should be configured on the Traps page, it's actually configured on the Security page. *Review "Establishing SNMP Security Services."*

9 *A.* This is the tightest security option available. You can configure clients to accept packets only from specific computers by adding the management computer's IP address or host name. *Review "Establishing SNMP Security Services."*

10 *D.* SNMPUTIL returns the object variable and value. This utility is used to determine whether SNMP agents are receiving requests from management consoles. *Review "Testing the Configuration with the SNMPUTIL Utility."*

SNMP Services

Part IV
Connectivity

In this part . . .

The chapters in this part of the book zero in on some areas of TCP/IP technology you can bet will appear on the exam — internetwork browsing and TCP/IP utilities. In Chapters 12 through 14, I cover topics such as configuring browsers, internetwork printing (which is heavily tested on the exam), identifying the utilities you need to connect to non-Windows hosts, and working with the Microsoft utilities Performance Monitor and Network Monitor.

Chapter 12

Internetwork Browsing

● ●

Exam Objective

▶ Configuring and supporting browsing in a multiple-domain routed network

● ●

A number of elements are at work in the browsing process, any one of which may turn up on the exam. In this chapter, I cover that all-important Microsoft exam objective — configuring and supporting browsing in a multiple-domain routed network — plus, how to go about configuring a Windows NT computer as a browser.

The questions you're likely to see regarding internetwork browsing will also address the following material, which just happens to be featured in this chapter:

- ✔ The various roles assumed by browsers in a Windows-based network
- ✔ The differences among the master, domain master, and preferred master browsers
- ✔ Which type of computer will win if an election for the role of master browser is held, and why that computer does win
- ✔ How and where browsers are configured for one of the roles in the browsing process
- ✔ The configuration involved in a multiple-domain routed network when you need to browse remote subnets
- ✔ The different ways in which remote networks are browsed

Quick Assessment

Configuring
and
supporting
browsing in
a multiple-
domain
routed
network

1 The _____ keyword is required when using the #DOM keyword when loading an LMHOSTS entry into cache.

2 The domain master browser is always the _____.

3 The master browser sends a list of network resources to the _____.

4 You can use the _____ file to locate domain controllers in other domains for browsing.

5 (True/False). Every computer on the network must maintain a browse list.

6 A client contacts the _____ browser when it must obtain a list of available backup browsers.

7 An election is forced when a _____ browser comes online.

8 (True/False). A backup browser does not maintain a browse list unless instructed to do so by the master browser.

9 A Windows NT Workstation is configured as a _____ browser by default.

10 (True/False). You can configure a computer to maintain the browse list by using the Registry.

Answers

1 *#PRE.* Review "The LMHOSTS file and domain functions."

2 *Primary domain controller.* Review "Domain master browser role."

3 *Backup browsers.* Review "Backup browser role."

4 *LMHOSTS.* Review "The LMHOSTS file and domain functions."

5 *False.* Review "No Thanks, I'm Just Browsing."

6 *Master.* Review "Servicing Client Requests."

7 *Preferred master.* Review "Master Browser Criteria and the Election Process."

8 *False.* Review "Potential browser role" and "Backup browser role."

9 *Potential.* Review "Configuring Browsers."

10 *True.* Review "Configuring Browsers."

No Thanks, I'm Just Browsing

Windows NT provides the Computer Browser service, which enables you to view and find available network resources. The service works by managing what are called *browse lists* of all available domains, workgroups, and servers on a network. Computers that have been assigned with the task of performing browsing functions then distribute the browse lists. Having a specified number of computers maintain a browse list of resources has several advantages:

- **Every computer on the network does not have to maintain the browse list.** Because only a few computers on the network are designated to maintain the browse list, the other computers don't have to exhaust valuable resources updating and maintaining the list.

- **The list can be maintained by the most reliable computers.** The browse list is most often located on the computers that are guaranteed to be on the network, such as servers. This setup also provides a centralized location for the browse list.

- **Network browsing traffic is minimized.** Because only a few browser computers participate in creating and maintaining the browse list, browsing traffic is reduced.

Examining Browser Server Roles

More important than any other information in this chapter are the various roles for which you can configure the select few computers that create and maintain the browser list. A surprising number of browser roles constitute the browse system:

- Master browsers
- Preferred master browsers
- Domain master browsers
- Backup browsers
- Potential browsers
- Non-browsers

You should make sure that you understand the differences among the first three browser roles in particular because they're easily confused — and make for tricky exam questions. You should understand how browsers are configured by default. Default settings in general seem to be very popular items for Microsoft test questions, and default browser settings are no exception. I tell you about the various browser roles in the following sections.

Master browser role

The *master browser* maintains the master copy of the resource list of computers and is responsible for creating, maintaining, and distributing that list to the backup browsers. The master browser must listen for server announcement packets from the clients on the network, and then add them to the browse list.

Just because they're called *server announcement packets* doesn't mean that they're sent only by servers. Every Windows-based client, such as a Windows 95, Windows NT, or Windows 3.11 machine, sends server announcement packets to the master browser.

As this chapter explains later, a computer that is configured as a potential browser receives a message from the master browser informing it to begin maintaining a browse list if the number of browsers on the network becomes too low.

Only one master browser is maintained per subnet, but your domain can have multiple subnets, each with its own master browser. These master browsers are then responsible for reporting their subnet's list of network resources to the domain master browser.

Preferred master browser role

If you want to ensure that a certain computer always performs as a master browser on the network, you should configure that computer as a *preferred master browser*. When that computer is started on the network, it is considered to be the master browser of the workgroup or domain.

What if a master browser is already in place? In that case, an *election* is forced to determine which machine is the master browser. This isn't a democracy, however. The computers on the network can't vote to determine the master browser; the computer with the highest-ranking criteria wins the election. (See "Master Browser Criteria and the Election Process," later in this chapter, for more information.)

Domain master browser role

The *domain master browser* is responsible for providing a list of the domain's resources to the master browser. The domain master also receives browse announcements from master browsers on remote subnets.

The *primary domain controller* (PDC) always becomes the domain master browser for a domain. (Keep in mind that a computer may be the domain master browser as well as a master browser.) The domain master browser must receive a list of resources at 12-minute intervals from the master browser for each subnet.

Because the domain master browser can't maintain the entire browse list across subnets, the master browsers are required to collect and maintain a browse list for each of their respective subnets and forward this information to the domain master browser. After the domain master browser receives the list of network resources for each of the remote subnets, it can then maintain a master browse list for the entire domain. The domain master browser can also send the compiled list of network resources back to each local master browser, which can then distribute the list to its clients.

Backup browser role

The *backup browser* receives a copy of the current browse list from the master browser. The backup browser must then service any client requests for the browse list. The backup browser contacts the master browser every 12 minutes to receive the browse list.

Be aware that the clients receive a current browse list from the backup browser and *not* from the master browser. This tidbit makes for great exam question material!

Potential browser role

A *potential browser* has the capability to maintain a browse list, but it doesn't do so unless instructed by the master browser. The potential browser is only used if there develops a shortage of computers needed to maintain the browse list for the network. Windows NT workstations are configured as potential browsers by default. The section "Configuring Browsers," later in this chapter, explains how to configure a potential browser.

Non-browser role

As you may imagine, a *non-browser* doesn't maintain a browse list, nor will it ever, unless you change its configuration to that of a potential browser or master browser. Even if the master browser detects a shortage of browsers, a non-browser doesn't maintain a browse list. Client computers are most often non-browsers.

Master Browser Criteria and the Election Process

Before I list the criteria for determining the master browser, I first have to tell you what occurs during the election process. An election is forced in any of the following situations:

- ✓ **When a master browser can't be located by a client computer.** In this case, the client initiates the election.

- ✓ **When a computer that has been configured as a preferred master browser comes online.** In this case, the preferred master browser initiates the election.

- ✓ **When a backup browser attempts to update its browse list and can't locate the master browser.** In this case, the backup browser initiates the election.

- ✓ **If the computer configured as the master browser initializes on a network that already contains a master browser.** In this case, the master browser initiates the election. It does so because only one master browser is permitted for each workgroup or domain.

An election is forced after the client or browser broadcasts a special packet called an *election packet* over the network. The election process roughly follows this sequence:

1. When a browser receives an election packet, it checks the election packet's criteria for electing a master browser against its own operating system version and browse settings. (A description of those criteria follows these steps.)

2. If the receiving browser has higher-ranking criteria than those specified in the election packet, the receiving browser broadcasts another packet over the network, which causes the network to go into an *election in progress* state.

3. All browsers on the network once again check the packet's election criteria against their own and respond with higher-ranking criteria if they have it.

4. If no other browser can respond with higher-ranking criteria, the election is over, and the browser with the top-ranked criteria assumes the role of master browser.

During an election, a set of criteria is used to determine the master browser for a workgroup or domain. The relative importance of the criteria is ranked in the following order:

1. The operating system itself

2. The operating system version

3. The system's current browse settings

Some operating systems take priority over others in the event that an election for master browser is held. The following is a list of operating systems in order of priority:

1. Windows NT Server 4.0 (PDC)

2. Windows NT Server 3.51 (PDC)

3. Windows NT Server 3.5 (PDC)

4. Windows NT Server 3.1 (PDC)

5. Windows NT Workstation 4.0

6. Windows NT Workstation 3.51

7. Windows NT Workstation 3.5

8. Windows NT Workstation 3.1

9. Windows 95

10. Windows For Workgroups

If the master browser candidates have identical operating systems, then they are ranked as follows, depending on which factor applies:

1. Preferred master browser

2. Current master browser

3. Maintains the server list

4. Running backup browser

Delusions of grandeur?

I remember seeing an event in the Windows NT Event Viewer on our network that involved a computer on the network that would force an election every time it initialized. I tracked down the computer — a Windows 95 laptop. It was configured as a master browser, but it didn't stand a chance in an election against a Windows NT 4.0 primary domain controller. I reconfigured the laptop so that it no longer maintained a browse list, and after that, everything was fine.

Don't worry about memorizing the hierarchy of factors that determine which computer wins an election. It's almost intuitive if you keep in mind the relative sophistication and power of the various operating systems — that is, servers over workstations, newer operating systems over older ones, and so forth. For example, a Windows NT Workstation beats a Windows 95 machine if an election is held (and not just because a Windows NT system costs more).

Configuring Browsers

For the exam, you should know something about configuring browser settings, but don't expect any really tough questions in this area. In Windows NT, you configure browsers through the Registry, which is the central repository for configuration information. A question probably won't ask you to supply the exact registry entry needed to modify a browser's configuration, but it may ask you *where* to configure the browser. The answer is, the Registry.

Figure 12-1 shows the area in the Registry Editor window that you use to configure a computer for the `MaintainServerList` value. You arrive at this place in the Registry Editor window by following the complete path for `My Computer\HKEY_LOCAL_MACHINE\SYSTEM\ControlSet001\Services\Browser\Parameters`. (Following the path shown at the bottom of the window is similar to using the File Explorer in Windows 95/NT.) You navigate through the Registry using its *keys,* which are similar to directories. The entries on the right side of the Registry window are similar to files contained within the directories.

Clicking on the `MaintainServerList` entry enables you to enter a new value. Then when the computer initializes, it checks the `MaintainServerList` entry to determine which browser role it should assume, if any. The following list describes the possible values for the `MaintainServerList` entry in the Registry Editor to determine whether the computer maintains a browse list.

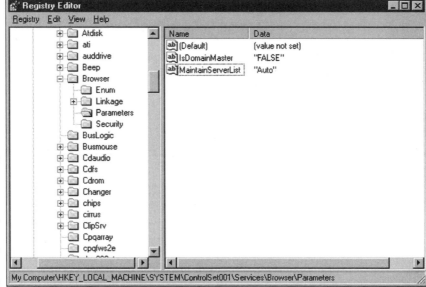

Figure 12-1:
You can
modify the
browser
roles from
the Registry
Editor.

✔ **A value of** No **for the** MaintainServerList **entry indicates that the computer never participates as a browser.**

✔ **A value of** Yes **for the** MaintainServerList **entry indicates that the computer attempts to obtain a current browse list from a backup browser on startup.** If a backup browser is not found, then the machine forces an election on the network. This computer may then become the master browser, or become a backup browser if another computer on the network has higher-priority criteria. Yes is the default for Windows NT Server domain controllers.

✔ **A value of** Auto **for the** MaintainServerList **entry indicates that the computer does not function as a browser unless instructed by a master browser.** This type of computer is also referred to as a *potential browser*. Auto is the default for Windows NT Server non-domain controllers and Windows NT Workstations.

In Lab 12-1, I demonstrate the steps required to configure your Windows NT computer as one of the browsers listed in the section "Examining Browser Server Roles" earlier in this chapter.

Lab 12-1   Configuring a Windows NT Computer as a Browser

1. **Open up the Registry Editor by clicking Start, choosing Run, and entering** Regedit.

2. **Choose Edit⇨Find.**

3. **Enter** `maintainserverlist` **in the Find What edit box of the Find dialog box that appears.**

   You see the area shown in Figure 12-1, with the `MaintainServerList` entry on the right half of the Registry Editor window.

4. **Double-click the** `MaintainServerList` **entry.**

   The Edit String dialog box appears.

5. **In the Value Data edit box of the Edit String dialog box, type the word** Yes.

   Your computer is configured to obtain a current browse list from a backup browser upon startup.

The preferred master browser is also configured in the Registry Editor by adjusting the value of the `IsDomainMaster` entry. Clicking the `IsDomainMaster` entry and typing **Yes** or **True** configures the computer to force an election on the network if another master browser is present when the computer initializes. The preferred master browser wins the election and then becomes the master browser.

Servicing Client Requests

In addition to being aware of the roles of the various browsers, you need to understand how a client makes requests for network resources from a browser. Questions testing your knowledge of this topic may crop up on the exam.

A master browser creates and maintains the browse list. However, when a client makes a request for the browse list, the list does *not* come from the master browser; the client computer requests the browse list from a *backup browser.* (Backup browsers are used to prevent the master browser getting inundated with numerous browse list requests simultaneously.)

A client needs to make a request for a browse list in certain situations:

✔ When the `net view` command is run from the command line

✔ When the Network Neighborhood is browsed

✔ When the Mapping a Network Drive dialog box is displayed

Sometimes, the client must contact the master browser. If a client has not accessed a browse list before, it needs to determine which computers on the network are configured as backup browsers. This task is achieved through the `QueryBrowserServers` broadcast on the local subnet. When a master browser hears the `QueryBrowserServers` broadcast, it returns a list of current backup browsers on the workgroup or domain. The client can then use this list of backup browsers for subsequent browse attempts.

Configuring and Supporting Browsing in a Multiple-Domain Routed Network

Computers must communicate transparently with other computers that are outside the local network. Therefore, the computers on a local network must receive a browse list for the computers in that remote workgroup or domain. Computers get such a list from the master browser of a domain, which broadcasts a DomainAnnouncement datagram to build a list of resources available in each workgroup or domain.

The *DomainAnnouncement datagram* is a message that contains the name of the workgroup or domain, the name of the master browser, information on whether the master browser is running a Windows NT server or workstation, and the primary domain controller for the domain. The master browser is responsible for receiving these DomainAnnouncement datagrams for the workgroup or domain it represents.

The announcement is broadcast over the network at every minute for five minutes, at ten minutes, and at 15 minutes. After that, the broadcasts occur every 15 minutes. If a workgroup or domain has not announced itself for three broadcasts in a row, the workgroup or domain is removed from the browse list. In this case, the workgroup or domain may still appear on the browse list for up to 45 minutes after either of them has left the network and is no longer available.

The list of network resources for the workgroup or domain is transferred to the backup browsers so that they can provide the list to the clients in their particular workgroup or domain. An example of the browser roles employed in a network with subnets is illustrated in Figure 12-2. Each subnet has its own collection of master, backup, and potential browsers. They all work separately, but each subnet also sends its information to the domain master browser. The domain master browser is responsible for receiving the browse list from the master browser for each of the remote subnets and consolidating this information into a browse list containing the entire domain's resources.

If you haven't already noticed, browsing a network involves plenty of broadcasts. In a larger TCP/IP network, like a Wide Area Network (WAN) with multiple subnets, like the network shown in Figure 12-2, broadcasting is not possible because broadcasts, by default, do not pass through routers.

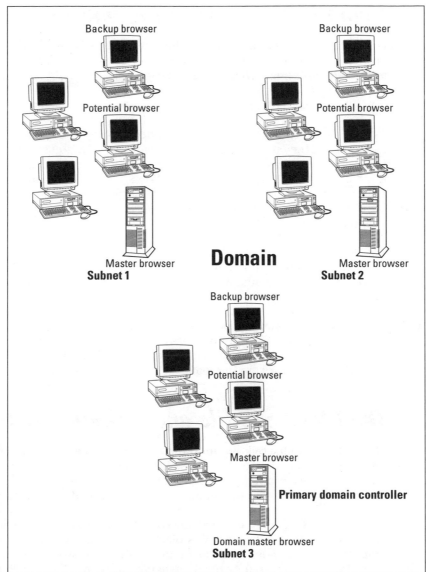

Backup browser

Backup browser

Potential browser

Potential browser

Domain

Master browser
Subnet 1

Master browser
Subnet 2

Backup browser

Potential browser

Master browser

Primary domain controller

Domain master browser
Subnet 3

In order to achieve browsing in a multiple-domain routed network, you have one of two choices: Use the Windows Internet Name Service (WINS) or the LMHOSTS file. After a client is configured to use WINS or an LMHOSTS file, both of which I talk about in the next two sections, the client can then browse remote subnets.

Using WINS for browsing multiple domains

One of the features of the Windows Internet Name Service (WINS) is that it enables a client to browse remote networks transparently. This capability is achieved by placing a WINS server on each remote subnet or by placing a WINS proxy agent on each remote subnet that doesn't have a WINS server. The WINS proxy agent forwards information to the WINS server.

The WINS server and WINS proxy agent don't take part in maintaining browse lists; they resolve the NetBIOS names to IP addresses for the computers on the remote subnets so that each subnet can communicate with the domain master browser. Without a WINS server, the master browser for a subnet is unable to resolve the NetBIOS name of the domain master browser and, therefore, can't provide the list of network resources for the subnet.

The WINS server is also responsible for maintaining a list of available domains. Using this list of domains, a client queries the master browser on a particular domain to obtain a list of available network resources for that domain.

On the exam, you can expect a question regarding the placement of the WINS server or WINS proxy on a network with multiple subnets. You have to use a WINS server on each subnet or have a WINS proxy on subnets without a WINS server to forward the requests to the WINS server.

The LMHOSTS file and domain functions

In Chapter 6 and 9, I talk about how the LMHOSTS file is used to map NetBIOS names to IP addresses. This file also has some other important uses for internetwork browsing. With the LMHOSTS file, you can map computer names and IP addresses for computers that are outside your local network.

The LMHOSTS file uses the #DOM keyword to designate domain controllers. An entry with the #DOM keyword is placed in a *domain name cache*. Domain requests, such as those for logon authentication, password changes, and browsing, are processed by the domain name cache, which contains domain controllers.

When you have a remote domain that you want to browse, you should include a mapping for the name and IP address of the primary domain controller for that domain. Backup domain controllers can also be added to the LMHOSTS file with the #DOM tag for additional fault tolerance if the primary domain controller is down.

In order for the #DOM keyword to work, it must be preceded by the #PRE keyword, which loads the entry into cache *before* the #DOM keyword is reached.

The following is an example of an LMHOSTS entry that demonstrates the proper order of keywords:

```
122.12.94.203     saxon          #PRE #DOM:domain1  #domain1
            Domain Controller
```

Although using a WINS server is the preferred method of internetwork browsing, using the LMHOSTS for internetwork browsing is still done. WINS is preferred because the administrator is not required to do much configuring, whereas configuring and maintaining the LMHOSTS file can take time and effort. In Lab 12-2, you configure the LMHOSTS to designate domain controllers on a remote domain for internetwork browsing.

Lab 12-2   Configuring the LMHOSTS File to Support Internetwork Browsing

1. **Open the LMHOSTS file from the** <systemroot>\system32\drivers\etc **directory.**

   You may be prompted by Windows NT to choose the application with which you want to open the file because this file doesn't have an extension. I just use Notepad to open the file.

2. **Remove the # sign from the beginning of the following line:**

```
102.54.94.97  rhino    #PRE #DOM:networking  #net group's
            DC
```

   This line is included by default in the LMHOSTS file for all installations of Windows NT 4.0.

3. **Save the LMHOSTS file, but make sure that you save the file with no extension.**

   If you're using Notepad, make sure you don't save the LMHOSTS file as LMHOSTS.TXT.

4. **Open a command prompt window.**

5. **Type the following command at the command prompt:**

```
nbtstat -R
```

   Note that you have to use a capital R because the command is case-sensitive. This step reloads the LMHOSTS file and places your entry into the NetBIOS name cache. You know that the command was successful when you see the following message:

```
Successful purge and preload of the NBT Remote Cache
          Name Table.
```

6. Type the following command at the command prompt:

```
nbtstat -c
```

This command displays the contents of the NetBIOS Remote Cache
Name Table. Look for the entry for rhino, which is the entry in the
LMHOSTS file that you preloaded into the cache.

After you configure a workstation with the LMHOSTS entry, you can
browse the networking domain, which is the domain specified in the
entry in the LMHOSTS file. You can contact the rhino server in the
networking domain for the browse list of network resources.

Supporting the LMHOSTS file means adding, modifying, or deleting entries
that pertain to browsing remote networks. If you add another remote
domain to the network, you may find yourself adding another entry in the
LMHOSTS file to support browsing in the domain you just added. You can
add the entry in the LMHOSTS file just as you did in Lab 12-2.

At some point, you may need to modify an existing entry in the LMHOSTS
file, maybe because the host name or IP address has changed. Simply
configure the entry in the LMHOSTS file with the new settings and reload the
NetBIOS Remote Cache Name Table as described in Lab 12-2. If you no
longer need a mapping for a specific domain controller in the LMHOSTS file,
simply delete it.

Prep Test

1 The master browser must listen for what type of packets from clients on the network?

A ○ Server query

B ○ Browse query

C ○ Server announcement

D ○ Browse announcement

2 If you have four subnets, how many master browsers (including domain master browsers) should you have?

A ○ 1

B ○ 2

C ○ 3

D ○ 4

3 Which situation will force an election? (Choose all that apply.)

A ❑ A client computer can't locate a master browser.

B ❑ A preferred master browser comes online.

C ❑ A master browser can't locate a remote master browser.

D ❑ A backup browser can't locate the master browser.

4 Which is most likely to win an election?

A ○ A current master browser

B ○ A Windows NT 4.0 server

C ○ A primary domain controller

D ○ A Windows NT 4.0 server configured as a master browser

5 Which Registry Editor setting configures a computer to obtain a current browse list from a backup browser upon startup?

A ○ MaintainBrowseList **set to** Auto

B ○ MaintainBrowseList **set to** Yes

C ○ MaintainBrowseList **set to** True

D ○ None of the above

6 Which of the following are contained in the DomainAnnouncement datagram? (Choose all that apply.)

A ❑ Name of the master browser

B ❑ IP address of the master browser

C ❑ Name of the workgroup or domain

D ❑ Name of the backup browser

7 Which command displays the contents of the NetBIOS Remote Cache Name Table?

A ○ nbtstat -R

B ○ nbtstat -c

C ○ nbtstat -r

D ○ nbtstat -s

8 What type of broadcast causes the master browser to return a list of current backup browsers that are on the workgroup or domain?

A ○ QueryBrowseMaster

B ○ QueryBrowserServers

C ○ BrowserServerList

D ○ QueryBrowseList

9 A workgroup or domain can appear on the browse list even if it is not accessible for a maximum of how many minutes?

A ○ 20 minutes

B ○ 30 minutes

C ○ 40 minutes

D ○ 45 minutes

10 You want to make a list of available resources for another network. However, you currently do not have a WINS server available. In addition to being able to browse this remote network, you would like some additional fault tolerance, just in case the PDC isn't available. What is the best way to achieve these goals?

A ○ Create a mapping in the LMHOSTS file for each master browser and backup browser.

B ○ Create a mapping in the LMHOSTS file for the primary domain controller and every backup browser.

C ○ Create a mapping in the LMHOSTS file for the primary domain controller and every backup domain controller.

D ○ Create a mapping in the LMHOSTS file for the primary domain controller and every master browser.

Answers

1 *C.* Although they are named server announcement packets, every client on a Windows-based network announces its presence to the master browser. *Review "Master browser role."*

2 *D.* A master browser must be present on each subnet in your domain. The master browsers then forward the list of network resources to the domain master browser. *Review "Master browser role."*

3 *A,B,D.* A master browser has no need to contact another master browser. However, it must remain in contact with the domain master browser. *Review "Master Browser Criteria and the Election Process."*

4 *C.* A primary domain controller is always the domain master browser, and it's most likely to win an election, so it can become the master browser as well. *Review "Master Browser Criteria and the Election Process."*

5 *D.* The correct Registry string is `MaintainServerList`, and it should be set to `Yes` or `True` in order to obtain a current browse list from backup browser on startup. *Review "Configuring Browsers."*

6 *A, C.* The *DomainAnnouncement datagram* contains the name of the workgroup or domain, the name of the master browser, information on whether the master browser is running Windows NT Server or Workstation, and the primary domain controller for the domain. *Review "Configuring and Supporting Browsing in a Multiple-Domain Routed Network."*

7 *B.* The `nbtstat -c` command is used in Lab 12-2 to view the contents of the NetBIOS Remote Cache Name Table to verify that the LMHOSTS entry was successfully preloaded into cache. *Review "The LMHOSTS file and domain functions."*

8 *B.* If a client has not accessed a browse list before, it needs to determine which computers on the network are configured as backup browsers. *Review "Serving Client Requests."*

9 *D.* The master browser of a domain broadcasts a DomainAnnouncement to build a list of resources available in each workgroup or domain every 15 minutes. *Review "Configuring and Supporting Browsing in a Multiple-Domain Routed Network."*

10 *C.* Use the `#DOM` keyword in the LMHOSTS file and precede it with the `#PRE` keyword to load the entry into cache. *Review "The LMHOSTS file and domain functions."*

Chapter 13

TCP/IP Utilities

. . . .

Exam Objectives

▶ Identifying which utility to use to connect to a TCP/IP-based UNIX host

▶ Configuring a Windows NT Server computer to support TCP/IP printing

. . . .

*T*he most noteworthy feature of the TCP/IP protocol is its ability to interconnect many diverse clients — including UNIX, Macintosh, OS/2, Windows NT, and mainframe computers. Machines running the TCP/IP protocol can seamlessly integrate with a network to take advantage of the network's file and print servers and to share their own resources with other machines.

Many TCP/IP utilities are available, but this chapter zeroes in on the various utilities that are important for the exam. This chapter covers the utilities for connecting to remote hosts, especially UNIX hosts in certain situations, and explains how TCP/IP utilities enable you to run commands on remote computers, transfer files, and print to remote printers. A significant portion of the chapter's coverage is given over to TCP/IP printing, a topic that is guaranteed to be tested on the exam.

In addition, you want to pay particular attention to the following information covered in this chapter because it's sure to be on the exam:

✔ **The purpose of each of the connectivity utilities:** But don't bother to memorize the extra switches used with a command, such as `nbtstat -c` or `arp -a`. The test questions won't be that detailed.

✔ **The purpose of the LPD, LPQ, and LPR printing utilities.**

✔ **How to configure a Windows NT client to print to a UNIX print server and how to configure a UNIX host to print to a Windows NT print server.**

Quick Assessment

1 If you can't reach the host through the host name but you can with the IP address, you should check the _____ file.

2 RCP is an example of a(n) _____ command.

Identifying which utility to use to connect to a TCP/IP-based UNIX host

3 The _____ and _____ commands are used for running commands on remote servers.

4 RSH is an acronym for _____.

5 TFTP uses the _____ protocol.

6 Windows NT can print to _____ hosts running the LPD service.

7 Microsoft uses the term _____ to describe the physical printer.

Configuring a Windows NT Server computer to support TCP/IP printing

8 _____ is the print server that accepts print requests.

9 You can view the contents of TCP/IP printers with the _____ utility.

10 Windows NT clients can print to a UNIX host by using the _____ command.

Answers

1 *HOSTS.* Review "File Transfer Protocol (FTP)."

2 *Connectivity.* Review "Distinguishing between Diagnostic and Connectivity TCP/IP Commands."

3 *RXEC, RSH.* Review "Identifying Which Utility to Use for Connecting to a UNIX Host."

4 *Remote Shell.* Review "The Remote Shell (RSH) utility."

5 *UDP.* Review "Trivial File Transfer Protocol (TFTP)."

6 *UNIX.* Review "Configuring a Server to Support Internetwork Printing."

7 *Printer Device.* Review "Configuring a Server to Support Internetwork Printing."

8 *Line Printer Daemon (LPD).* Review "The Line Printer Daemon (LPD) service."

9 *Line Printer Queue (LPQ).* Review "The Line Printer Queue (LPQ) command."

10 *Line Printer (LPR).* Review "The Line Printer (LPR) utility."

Distinguishing between Diagnostic and Connectivity TCP/IP Commands

The exam covers the Microsoft implementations of the common TCP/IP utilities and diagnostic commands. For the most part, the TCP/IP diagnostic commands work just as they do in an environment such as UNIX. Nevertheless, even if you're an experienced user in TCP/IP and UNIX, you need to pay special attention to utilities used with Microsoft-specific features, such as the Windows Internet Name Service (WINS) and the Dynamic Host Configuration Protocol (DHCP), that may be unfamiliar to you.

An important distinction must be made among the large number of TCP/IP utilities that are available. You need to know which utilities are *diagnostic* commands and which are *connectivity* commands:

✔ The diagnostic commands are `ping`, `tracert`, `nbtstat`, `netstat`, `ipconfig`, `ARP`, `hostname`, and `route`. The diagnostic commands are covered in Chapter 16.

✔ The connectivity commands covered in this chapter are Telnet, File Transfer Protocol (FTP), Trivial File Transfer Protocol (TFTP), Remote Shell (RSH), Remote Execute (REXEC), Remote Copy (RCP), Line Printer (LPR), and Line Printer Queue (LPQ).

Telnet, FTP, and TFTP are covered in the section "Universal Connectivity Utilities," coming up next. REXEC, RSH, and RCP are covered in the section "Identifying Which Utility to Use for Connecting to a UNIX Host," later in this chapter. LPR, LPQ, and the Line Printer Daemon (LPD) are covered in the section "Configuring a Server to Support Internetwork Printing."

The connectivity commands are client-side utilities that require a server running the appropriate service.

Universal Connectivity Utilities

Although most of the connectivity utilities are used to make connections to a UNIX host, a few utilities do not require a UNIX host. Those utilities include Telnet, FTP, and TFTP, which are described in the next few sections.

Telnet

Telnet provides terminal emulation to a remote host running the Telnet server service (a Telnet daemon). Unlike most of the TCP/IP utilities, Telnet is run from a window and not from a command prompt, although Telnet *can* be brought up from a command prompt (if you enter the Telnet command at the prompt, Windows NT starts the graphical Telnet program).

In order to connect to the Telnet server, a client must have a valid user account. Windows NT provides only a Telnet client utility, not the server component. An example of how a Telnet session looks is shown in Figure 13-1.

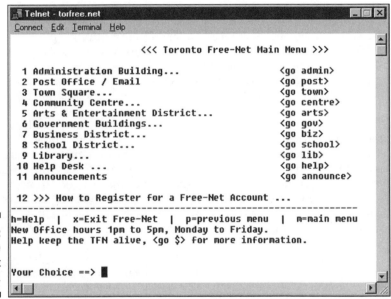

```
Telnet - torfree.net                                          _ □ ✕
Connect  Edit  Terminal  Help

                  <<< Toronto Free-Net Main Menu >>>

   1 Administration Building...              <go admin>
   2 Post Office / Email                     <go post>
   3 Town Square...                          <go town>
   4 Community Centre...                     <go centre>
   5 Arts & Entertainment District...        <go arts>
   6 Government Buildings...                 <go gov>
   7 Business District...                    <go biz>
   8 School District...                      <go school>
   9 Library...                              <go lib>
  10 Help Desk ...                           <go help>
  11 Announcements                           <go announce>

  12 >>> How to Register for a Free-Net Account ...
  -----------------------------------------------------------------
  h=Help  |  x=Exit Free-Net  |  p=previous menu  |  m=main menu
  New Office hours 1pm to 5pm, Monday to Friday.
  Help keep the TFN alive, <go $> for more information.


  Your Choice ==> █
```

Figure 13-1:
A sample
Telnet
session.

The topic of Telnet and name resolution may turn up on the exam. If you receive a question describing a scenario in which you can't connect to a Telnet server with the host name but you can connect with the IP address, then you have a name resolution problem. (See Chapter 4 for more information on the process of resolving host names.)

Another exam question concerning Telnet may involve a problem with an incorrect host name appearing in the Telnet banner, even when the IP address is correct. You can correct this problem by doing either of the following:

✔ **Make sure that the HOSTS file or the entry in the DNS database is current.** An incorrect host-name-to-IP-address mapping may cause Telnet to connect to the incorrect host.

✔ **Make sure that a duplicate computer doesn't exist on the network.** Another computer may be responding before the target host has a chance to respond. You may have to examine the ARP cache to determine whether the MAC address corresponds to the correct IP address for the host you're trying to contact. (See Chapter 3 for more information on the ARP cache.)

File Transfer Protocol (FTP)

File Transfer Protocol (FTP) is commonly confused with Telnet. The difference is that Telnet uses terminal emulation to enable a user to log on to another site's central computer, typically a mainframe computer networked with dumb terminals, whereas FTP is provided with Windows NT in order to connect to and download information from an FTP server to an FTP client. You must have a valid logon name and password to access resources on an FTP server, although you can configure the server to accept anonymous logon requests.

FTP uses name resolution to resolve a host name to an IP address when the host name is specified at the command prompt. For example, if you were to type the command `ftp microsoft.com` at the command prompt, the host name `microsoft.com` must be resolved to an IP address; otherwise an error message is returned. (I had a question covering this very topic on my exam. In that question, the host could be contacted when the IP address was used instead of the host name. This situation suggests a host name resolution problem, which you can troubleshoot with the HOSTS file and DNS, as I explain in Chapter 4.)

FTP is not covered in much depth on the exam. The most likely area for an FTP question is in regard to the FTP client. However, you may see a question on the exam in which FTP is presented in any one of the following situations:

✔ As a protocol

✔ As an FTP client

✔ As an FTP server

Many test preparation books and self-test software go on at length about the commands available with FTP, as well as the syntax. I was horrified at the thought of having to memorize more than 50 FTP commands, parameters, and syntax for the exam. To my surprise, the exam did *not* cover FTP commands and barely covered the FTP protocol itself.

Trivial File Transfer Protocol (TFTP)

The *Trivial File Transfer Protocol* (TFTP) connectivity utility, like FTP, transfers files between computers. TFTP is recommended for small file transfers when user-level security is not needed. (I purposely don't cover TFTP syntax; if you see a question on TFTP, it probably won't go into that level of detail.)

Remembering a couple of basic differences between the TFTP and FTP utilities is sufficient for the exam:

- **TFTP does not provide user authentication.** TFTP does not present you with a dialog box for logging on with a user name and password. However, you must have read and write permissions for any files being transferred.

- **TFTP uses the UDP protocol.** The connectionless User Datagram Protocol (UDP) is used because a session is not maintained between two TCP/IP computers. In that regard, TFTP is unlike FTP, which maintains a connection for the duration of the session.

Identifying Which Utility to Use for Connecting to a UNIX Host

Questions on integrating TCP/IP and UNIX are guaranteed to be on your exam. You can definitely expect to see a few questions asking for the correct utility for connecting to a TCP/IP-based host. Acing those questions shouldn't be difficult after you cruise through the following sections of this chapter, which describe three connectivity utilities that enable you to connect to UNIX hosts.

The Remote Execute (REXEC) utility

The Remote Execute (REXEC) connectivity utility lets you run commands on a server that is running the REXEC service (daemon) on the UNIX host. The REXEC service processes the commands you enter at the remote host on the remote server. The server prompts the user for authentication for each remote command that is run, such as commands to delete or move files.

The syntax for the `rexec` command is as follows:

```
rexec host [-1 username] command
```

In this example, the host parameter specifies the remote computer on which you want to execute the command. The last portion of the syntax is the command you want to run on the remote UNIX host. You can use the -1 username parameter to specify a user other than the user who is currently logged on. The REXEC server then prompts the user for a password. If the password is correct, the user is able to run the command.

The Remote Shell (RSH) utility

The Remote Shell (RSH) connectivity utility enables you to run commands on a remote server at the command prompt. The rsh command doesn't require user authentication in the same way the rexec command does, which means that you don't need to provide credentials such as user name and password to use the rsh command. This is the most important distinction between the two commands, and one you should remember for the exam.

The syntax for the rsh command is as follows:

```
rsh host [-1 username] command
```

The host parameter specifies the remote computer on which you want to execute the command. The command you want to run is specified by the command parameter. You can use the -1 username parameter to specify a user that is listed in the .rhosts file on the server. The .rhosts file contains a list of users who have permission to run commands on the server.

If you receive a question on the exam concerning which is the proper utility to use, either RSH or REXEC, the question must also specify what authentication is being used, and the type of authentication should tip you off to the correct answer. The rexec command requires user authentication.

The Remote Copy (RCP) utility

The Remote Copy (RCP) connectivity utility enables a user to copy files between a client and a server that is running the RSH service (daemon), the same daemon used for the RSH connectivity utility. The Windows NT computer can act as an RCP client but can't run the Remote Shell (RCP) service. As with the RSH utility (described in the previous section), the user must be a valid user specified in the .rhosts file on the server.

RCP has a number of parameters and the syntax can be very confusing, but test questions on those details are extremely unlikely; therefore, I don't cover them.

Configuring a Server to Support Internetwork Printing

This section covers the TCP/IP printing topics that are most likely to appear on the test. But first, I begin with a quick overview of TCP/IP printing specifics that may be new to you. As you may guess, TCP/IP printing requires TCP/IP to be installed and configured. As long as one client has TCP/IP and Microsoft TCP/IP printing service installed, all the clients on the network can use any protocol that is common to both the server and the client.

Microsoft uses the term *printer* to refer to the print queue and the term *printing device* to refer to the actual physical device that does the printing. A physical printing device can be connected to network in a number of ways:

✔ A printing device can be directly attached to a computer via the serial (COM) port or parallel (LPT) port.

✔ A printing device with a network interface card can be connected directly to the network.

✔ A printing device can be directly attached to a UNIX host that is running the Line Printer Daemon (LPD) service (which is covered in the next section of this chapter).

Where the printing device is located or how the print server has to communicate with the printing device doesn't matter to the client. The exam concentrates primarily on printing devices connected to a UNIX host running the LPD service.

You install Microsoft TCP/IP printing from the Services page in the Network window. The TCP/IP printing service is also known as the Line Printer Daemon (LPD), which is the print server that accepts print requests. Clients print by using the Line Printer (LPR) service.

You can monitor the status of the TCP/IP print queue with the Line Printer Queue (LPQ) utility. The LPR and LPD utilities enable a Windows NT computer to print to UNIX machines, as well as receive from any client TCP/IP print jobs to be processed on the Windows NT computer.

Had enough of the printing utilities alphabet soup? The following sections cover these topics in more depth.

The Line Printer Daemon (LPD) Service

You need to be familiar with some very important details about the Line Printer Daemon (LPD) service when it is used with a Windows NT host. LPR clients print to the LPD service. Those clients must use the *printer name*, and not the *printer share name*, when printing to the Windows NT LPD server.

Figure 13-2 gives an example of a printer name and share name listed in the Properties dialog box of the printing device. The printer name — *HP4si* — is the name that should be used when LPR clients print to this printing device. The share name — *HPLaserJet4si* — is the name used by Windows-based clients that print to the device. (The LPR utility is covered in the next section of this chapter.)

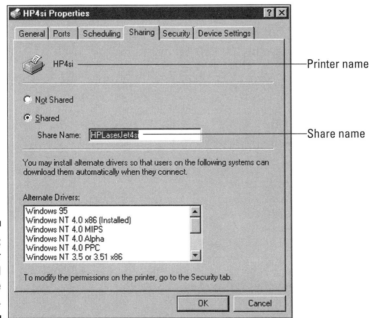

Figure 13-2:
A printer name and its share name.

After the Microsoft TCP/IP printing service (the LPD daemon) is installed on your computer, your computer acts as an LPD server that accepts requests from an LPR client. A new port becomes available when you add a new printer. When adding a new printer, you must select the port the printer will be installed on. The sequence to do that is as follows:

1. **Click Start⇨Settings⇨Printers.**

2. **Double-click Add Printers, and the Add Printer Wizard dialog box appears.**

   After you specify that the printer is to be managed on your own machine, not on a network server, you see the Available Ports dialog box of the Add Printer Wizard utility.

3. **Click Add Port, and the Printer Ports dialog box opens.**

   A listing of available ports is shown in the Printer Ports dialog box. The new LPR port is available, as illustrated in Figure 13-3.

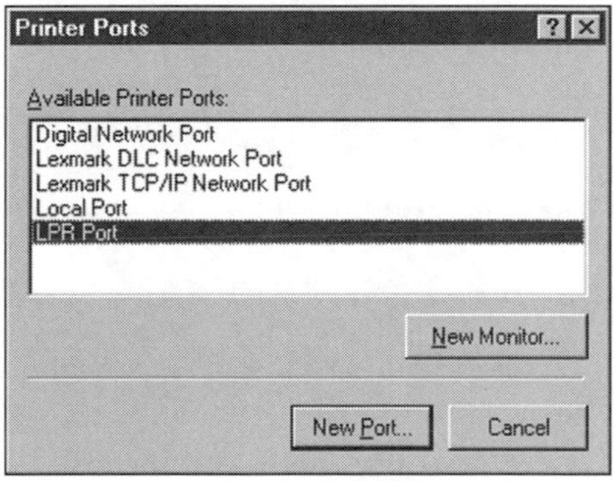

Figure 13-3:
The LPR
Port is
added by
installing
the TCP/IP
printing
service.

After you select the LPR port in the Printer Ports dialog box and click the New Port button, you enter the name or address of the server providing LPD and the name of the printer or printer queue on that server in the Add LPR Compatible Printer dialog box, as shown in Figure 13-4.

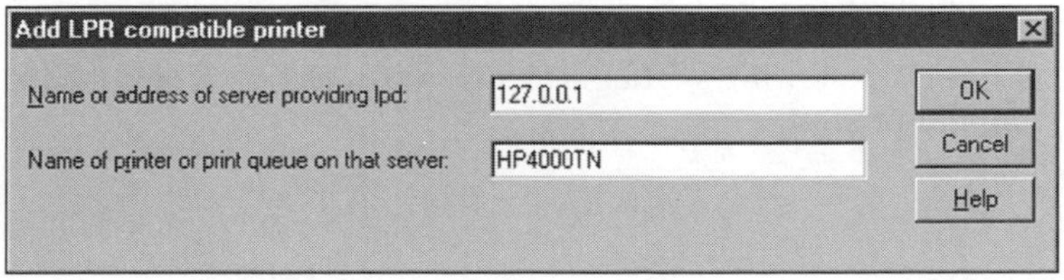

Figure 13-4:
This is the
place
where you
specify the
LPD server
and printer.

The Line Printer (LPR) utility

After you install the Microsoft TCP/IP printing service (LPD daemon), you can then print to the print server that has the service running by using the Line Printer (LPR) client printing utility. The LPR utility permits UNIX hosts to print to a newly created LPD server. It also enables Windows NT clients to print without having to set up a separate printer under Windows NT. A Windows NT client can simply open up a command prompt window and send the job to print by using the lpr command.

The Line Printer utility is available only after you install the Microsoft TCP/IP printing service.

The lpr command has the following syntax:

```
lpr -S Server -P Printer [-o Options] [-J Jobname] filename
```

Given this syntax, the following is an example of an lpr command:

```
lpr -S gemini -P laserjet4si IcedEarth.txt
```

With this command, IcedEarth.txt prints to the HP LaserJet 4si printer, which is located on the Gemini server.

The Line Printer Queue (LPQ) command

Just as you can view the contents of a print queue for a Windows NT printer by opening the Printers window and double-clicking the name of the printer you want to view, you can also view the contents of the TCP/IP printer queue by using the Line Printer Queue command. (You must have the Microsoft TCP/IP printing service installed before you can view the TCP/IP print queues.)

LPQ has the following syntax, which you can see by typing lpq at the command prompt:

```
Displays the state of a remote lpd queue.
Usage: lpq  -Sserver -Pprinter [-l]
Options:
-S server    Name or ip address of the host providing lpd
             service
-P printer   Name of the print queue
-l           verbose output
```

Notice that the command syntax doesn't show a space between the -S parameter and the server name, nor between the -P parameter and the printer name. This space is optional, and the command works the same whether or not you leave a space between the two, as the next example illustrates. The LPQ command *is,* however, case sensitive.

Given the preceding syntax, the following is an example of the Line Printer Queue command:

```
C:\>lpq -S nevermore -P deskjet870c
Windows NT LPD Server
      Printer deskjet870c
Owner      Status     Jobname Job-Id     Size Pages Priority
-----------------------------------------------------------\
Cbrandon   Printing   C:\ironmaiden.txt  74   275   1
```

This LPQ command displays the contents of the HP DeskJet 870c printer queue, which is located on the Nevermore server. Notice that the job information, such as status and size, looks the same as information in Windows-based print queues.

You can do just fine on the exam if you know the basics of each of the TCP/IP printing utilities. Keep in mind that UNIX and Windows NT hosts can print to each other through the LPQ command.

Lab 13-1 gives you an example of installing the Microsoft TCP/IP printing service and viewing the output from the LPQ command. For this exercise to work, you have to create a local printer, or you can use a printer that is already configured locally on your system.

Lab 13-1	Installing the Microsoft TCP/IP Printing Service and Examining TCP/IP Print Queues

1. Double-click the Network icon in the Control Panel.

The Select Network Service dialog box appears. The list of available services appears in the dialog box, as shown in Figure 13-5.

2. Click on Microsoft TCP/IP Printing and click OK.

3. Close the Network dialog box.

You may be prompted to restart your computer, which you don't need to do for this exercise.

4. Make sure a local printer is available.

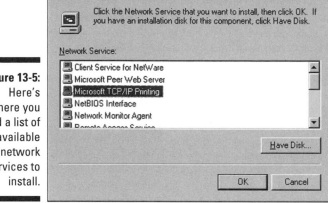

Figure 13-5:
Here's
where you
find a list of
available
network
services to
install.

5. **Double-click the Services icon in the Control Panel to get the Services dialog box.**

   The TCP/IP Print Server that was installed with the Microsoft TCP/IP printing service is highlighted, as shown in Figure 13-6.

6. **Click Start if the printing service isn't started already.**

7. **Open a command prompt window and enter the following command:**

   ```
   lpq -S <your computer> -P <your printer>
   ```

   You see the Windows NT LPD Server status for the printer on the next line immediately after executing the command.

   If you don't see the printer status information, either the service is not started, or the computer or printer name is not correct, or the printer is not a local printer.

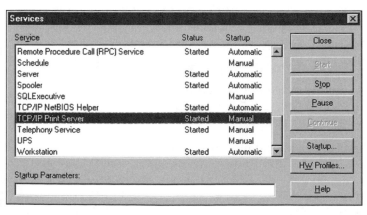

Figure 13-6:
In the
Services
dialog box,
you can find
out whether
the TCP/IP
Print Server
is installed.

To see how the LPD command behaves when erroneous information is entered, try the steps in Lab 13-1 again, except when you open the command prompt window in Step 8, enter the following command:

```
lpq -S wrong_server -P wrong_printer
```

The status of the printer is not displayed because the (misspelled) printer doesn't exist.

If you're on a network, try installing the Microsoft TCP/IP service on your machine and practice the Line Printer Queue command with remote print servers.

1 Which connectivity utility does not require some sort of user authentication, such as an entry in a file?

A ○ FTP

B ○ RSH

C ○ LPR

D ○ REXEC

2 Which connectivity utility prompts you for a password every time in order to process the command?

A ○ REXEC

B ○ RSH

C ○ LPR

D ○ Telnet

3 Which of the following is not a step for enabling LPR clients to print to a newly created Windows NT LPD server?

A ○ Specify the name of the printer queue.

B ○ Add an LPR port.

C ○ Specify the name of the printer share name.

D ○ Specify the name of the LPD Server.

4 Which of the following is an incorrect statement concerning the TFTP protocol?

A ○ It requires user authentication.

B ○ It uses a connectionless delivery method.

C ○ It is used when user security is not an issue.

D ○ It works best when used with small file transfers.

5 A print server is configured with the Microsoft TCP/IP Print service. You return to your workstation to test the printer by entering the following command:

```
lpq -S <server> -P <printer>
```

You have verified that the server and printer are correct, but an error message is returned. What is the most likely cause?

A ○ The LPQ syntax is wrong.

B ○ The printer has not been set up as a TCP/IP printer.

C ○ Your workstation has not been set up with Microsoft TCP/IP printing.

D ○ This response is normal. The queue is empty.

6 You have a mixed network of Windows NT, Windows 3.11, UNIX, and Novell machines. Each of these clients must be able to print to Windows NT print servers. While you are configuring the NT print servers, your boss tells you that permitting every computer to print to these print servers is impossible. Is your boss correct?

A ○ Yes, because the Novell machines aren't able to print using the IPX protocol.

B ○ Yes, because not every machine can have Microsoft TCP/IP printing services installed.

C ○ No, because every machine can have Microsoft TCP/IP printing services installed.

D ○ No, because the NT server can have other protocols installed.

7 You're trying to connect to a Telnet server with an IP address, but the banner at the top of the screen reflects a different host name. You try the command on another user's computer, which is DHCP-enabled, and the correct host name appears. What is a likely cause for this scenario?

A ○ The LMHOSTS file has an incorrect entry.

B ○ The other user's computer received the correct mapping from the DHCP server's LMHOSTS file.

C ○ The HOSTS file has an incorrect entry.

D ○ The other user's computer received the correct mapping from the DHCP server's HOSTS file.

8 Which of the following utilities is a graphical utility with Windows NT, in addition to being a command-line utility?

A ○ TFTP

B ○ FTP

C ○ Telnet

D ○ LPR

9 Which of the following utilities can be used to copy files from a remote UNIX host running the appropriate daemon? (Choose all that apply.)

A ❑ Telnet

B ❑ FTP

C ❑ TFTP

D ❑ RCP

10 You have just configured an LPD server and restarted the computer. Now you're going to check the printer queue for a printer. You enter the following command:

```
lpq -s Odyssey -p hp4si
```

Assuming that the computer name and printer name are correct, what response do you receive?

A ○ Error: No response from Odyssey.

B ○ Error: unsupported argument '-s'.

C ○ Error: specified printer does not exist.

D ○ The print queue is displayed.

Answers

1 *C.* The Line Printer (LPR) utility requires no user authentication. The other connectivity utilities require a user name and password, or an entry in the server's `.rhosts` file, in order to be successful. *Review "The Line Printer (LPR) utility."*

2 *A.* The server prompts the user for authentication for each command that is given. If the password is correct, the command is run. *Review "The Remote Execute (REXEC) utility."*

3 *C.* LPR clients shouldn't specify the printer share name; they should specify the printer name or printer queue name. *Review "The Line Printer (LPR) utility."*

4 *A.* The biggest differences between TFTP and FTP are that TFTP doesn't require user authentication and that TFTP uses the UDP protocol. Review "Trivial File Transfer Protocol (TFTP)."

5 *C.* Each computer that's supposed to print to a TCP/IP printer requires the Microsoft TCP/IP printing service to be installed. *Review "The Line Printer Queue (LPQ) command."*

6 *D.* Every client doesn't have to have the TCP/IP protocol installed to print to a Windows NT TCP/IP print server. The client only has to have a protocol that is common to the print client and print server. Windows NT accepts its clients' print requests in their native protocol. *Review "Configuring a Server to Support Internetwork Printing."*

7 *C.* You have an incorrect entry for the Telnet server in your HOSTS file, whereas the other user does not. A correct mapping on the DHCP server doesn't matter; the DHCP server doesn't assign HOSTS file mappings. *Review "Telnet."*

8 *C.* Although graphical FTP programs are available, Windows NT provides only the Telnet TCP/IP utility as a graphical utility in addition to being a command-line utility. *Review "Telnet."*

9 *B,C,D.* Telnet is not used to copy files from one host to another; it is used for terminal emulation. Use one of the three universal connectivity utilities (Telnet, FTP, TFTP) listed in this chapter to copy information from a remote UNIX host. *Review "Identifying Which Utility to Use for Connecting to a UNIX Host."*

10 *B.* The LPQ command is case-sensitive, so not capitalizing the S in the parameter results in an error message. *Review "The Line Printer Queue (LPQ) command."*

Chapter 14

Non-TCP/IP Utilities
That Run on TCP/IP

- -

Exam Objectives

▶ Configuring a RAS server and Dial-Up Networking for use on a TCP/IP network

▶ Identifying which tool to use to monitor TCP/IP traffic, given a scenario

- -

Some utilities aren't TCP/IP utilities but run on TCP/IP nevertheless. As such, questions on what those utilities are and how they work are a sure bet for test material. If you've taken other Microsoft certification exams, such as those for Windows NT Server or Windows NT Workstation, you may already be familiar with these utilities. They include Microsoft's Internet Information Server (IIS), Remote Access Service (RAS), Performance Monitor, and Network Monitor.

If you're up to speed on the following topics (which I cover in this chapter), you can definitely handle that handful of questions you're likely to get on non-TCP/IP utilities.

✔ Pay special attention to the information in the section "Configuring a RAS Server." Make sure that you're familiar with server and client security and configuration for TCP/IP technologies such as WINS and DNS. These subjects are guaranteed to be on the exam.

✔ Be sure you know when and why to choose the Performance Monitor and Network Monitor over other utilities such as NETSTAT and nbtstat. (Performance Monitor and Network Monitor are used for real-time monitoring at certain intervals.)

✔ Although you don't have to spend a great deal of time cramming on the Internet Information Server, you do need to know how to restrict a computer from accessing the Internet based on the computer's IP address.

Quick Assessment

1 You must install _____ prior to installing Internet Information Server (IIS).

2 By specifying the _____ and _____ , you can grant or deny access to the Internet for a group of computers.

3 (True/False). PPP is responsible for encryption during a PPTP session.

4 Broadcast name resolution does not work with _____.

Configuring a RAS server and dial-up networking for use on a TCP/IP network

5 If a RAS Server is configured to use _____ and _____, the clients will also use this information.

6 The RAS Server can be configured to enable the _____ to assign clients IP addresses from the server's pool of available IP addresses.

7 The _____ protocol is used to create a secure channel between a remote client and an enterprise server over a TCP/IP network.

8 You need to enable IP _____ on your Windows NT RAS server/router.

Identifying which tool to use to monitor TCP/IP traffic, given a scenario

9 If you want to gather protocol information at specific intervals, use _____.

Answers

1 *TCP/IP.* Review "Some IIS installation preliminaries."

2 *Network ID, subnet mask.* Review "Configuring IIS with the Internet Service Manager."

3 *True.* Review "Point-to-Point Tunneling Protocol."

4 *RAS.* Review "Configuring a RAS Server."

5 *WINS, DNS.* Review "Configuring a RAS Server."

6 *DHCP server.* Review "Configuring a RAS Server."

7 *Point-to-Point Tunneling.* Review "Point-to-Point Tunneling Protocol."

8 *Forwarding.* Review "Routing with RAS."

9 *Network Monitor.* Review "Choosing the Tools Used to Monitor TCP/IP Traffic."

Serving Up the Basics on the Microsoft Internet Information Server

A couple of questions on the exam will probably deal with Microsoft's *Internet Information Server* (IIS). Don't expect anything too detailed in this area, because another MCSE exam is devoted entirely to IIS. Any questions that you do see on IIS should be fairly easy to answer. In this section of the chapter, I tell you about the elements of IIS that are likely to show up on your exam.

The IIS is a Web server that uses the TCP/IP protocol to publish and transfer information on the Internet or on an intranet. IIS contains World Wide Web (WWW), File Transfer Protocol (FTP), and Gopher services. Each of these services has properties that must be configured. For purposes of the exam, the most important of these services is FTP, because it's a part of the TCP/IP protocol.

Gopher isn't covered on the exam, and questions about the WWW service are unlikely to appear.

Some IIS installation preliminaries

A few TCP/IP-related issues must be taken care of before you can install IIS. Prerequisites for installing software frequently turn up in Microsoft certification exam questions. (Microsoft wants to make sure you know the requirements for its software before you attempt to install any of it.) In the following sections of this chapter, I cover the system elements you must configure on an IIS server.

TCP/IP must be installed prior to the installation of IIS. You need to configure basic TCP/IP settings, which include the IP address, the subnet mask, and the default gateway. Your Internet Service Provider (ISP) can most likely provide this configuration information for you.

IIS uses the default gateway that is the ISP's router for all your Internet traffic. Questions about the default gateway are scattered all over the exam, so be sure that you understand it. Check out Chapter 7 for more information on the default gateway.

Configuring IIS with the Internet Service Manager

The Internet Information Server is configured using the Internet Service Manager (see Figure 14-1), which is the graphical utility that comes with the Internet Information Server for configuring IIS.

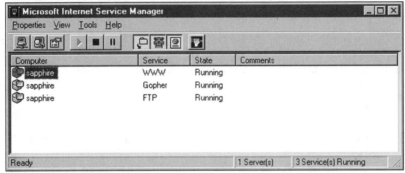

Figure 14-1:
The main window of the Internet Service Manager 3.0.

The specific features of the Internet Service Manager probably won't be on the exam, with one exception — how this utility can be used to grant or deny access to the Internet based on the IP address of a computer. You can configure Internet access in either of two ways.

Figure 14-2 displays the dialog box you use for granting or denying access to all users except a specific subset of computers. To get to this dialog box, double-click the icon for the computer on the WWW Service line in the Internet Service Manager window (refer to Figure 14-1). Clicking Advanced brings up the Web Site Properties dialog box. Then click the Directory Security tab. The access restrictions are empty by default.

After *granting* access to all computers on a network, you can then restrict access to certain individual computers or a group of computers by clicking the Add button (see Figure 14-2) and adding the single computer or group of computers you would like to restrict. Conversely, after *denying* access to all computers, you can then grant access to certain individual computers or a group of computers. In Figure 14-3, you can see that the option Group of Computers has been selected in the Deny Access On dialog box (which would be titled Grant Access On if you were granting access to some computers after denying access to all).

Figure 14-2:
Here you can grant or deny access to the Internet to all computers in a network by default, and deny access to certain user groups.

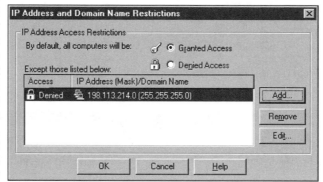

The approach makes is easier for you (the administrator) to make exceptions for a small number of users. If everyone in your company needs access to the Internet except one person, it makes no sense to grant Internet access to each person individually — just grant everyone access and then single out certain users later.

Whether you're granting or denying access to an individual computer or group of computers, you can set the specifications in the text boxes of the Deny Access On or Grant Access On dialog box (except for the titles, the two dialog boxes look the same — whether you grant to all, deny a few, deny to all, or grant to a few). You enter the IP address to specify one computer, or you can enter the network ID *and* subnet mask to specify a group of computers (see Figure 14-3). For example, by specifying the network ID of `101.38.0.0` with a subnet mask of `255.255.0.0`, you grant access to all computers in the `101.38.x.x` group. You can expect the exam to have a question related to this aspect of the IIS.

Figure 14-3:
Use this dialog box to deny access to a single computer or a group of computers after you've granted access to them all.

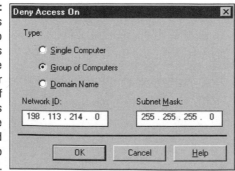

In addition, you can deny access to a certain domain name, as Figure 14-3 indicates. However, this is one feature of the IIS 4.0 that is not covered on the exam.

Configuring a RAS Server

You need to be familiar with a few aspects of the TCP/IP-related *Remote Access Service* (RAS) for the exam. RAS provides remote networking for system administrators who monitor and manage servers at multiple locations. Users with RAS on a Windows NT computer can remotely access their networks for file and data sharing, e-mail, and so on. Although RAS is not covered in depth on the exam, you do need to be familiar with a few specifics that are likely to turn up on the test.

A RAS server has two groups of settings that need to be configured:

✔ The TCP/IP settings for the RAS server itself on the network
✔ The TCP/IP settings that are supplied to the RAS clients

As with any other TCP/IP computer on a network, you must configure the RAS server with a valid IP address, subnet mask, and default gateway (if applicable). You also want to assign the RAS server a static IP address or reserve an IP address in the pool of Dynamic Host Configuration Protocol (DHCP) addresses, to ensure that the RAS server is always found at the correct IP address. (You can find more on DHCP in Chapter 8.)

Figure 14-4 shows the Network Configuration dialog box on the RAS server. This is where you configure the RAS server protocols and authentication to be used when communicating with RAS clients. Don't expect anything on the exam regarding authentication; that's a topic for Windows NT exams, not the TCP/IP exam. Nevertheless, you should be familiar with the TCP/IP server settings.

If you are configuring the RAS server with TCP/IP, you need to specify some additional settings. Figure 14-5, the RAS Server TCP/IP Configuration dialog box, shows the TCP/IP client settings that must be configured on the RAS server. To get to the RAS Server TCP/IP Configuration dialog box, follow these steps:

1. **Double-click Network in the Control Panel and click the Services tab in the Network window to display the list of installed services.**

   Because you have installed the Remote Access Server, RAS is on the list.

2. **Select Remote Access Service and click Properties.**

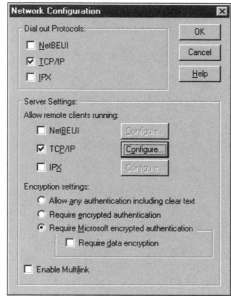

Figure 14-4:
The RAS
Network
Configuration
dialog box.

3. **On the Remote Access Setup dialog box that appears, click the Network icon.**

   A Network Configuration dialog box appears (see Figure 14-4), with the TCP/IP protocol selected by default.

4. **Click the Configure button next to the TCP/IP protocol.**

   This step brings up the dialog box seen in Figure 14-5.

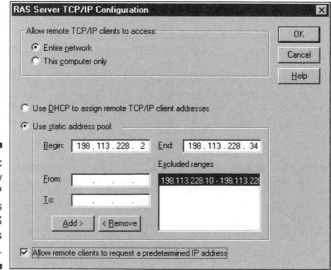

Figure 14-5:
You specify
TCP/IP
properties
for the RAS
clients
here.

Knowing that you can restrict TCP/IP clients to only the RAS server or, instead, give them access to the entire network is important to remember. (See the Allow Remote TCP/IP Clients to Access options in Figure 14-5.) You can make some essential network resources available on the RAS server and deny clients access to the rest of the resources.

Another key RAS server configuration option can enable DHCP to dynamically assign IP addresses to the RAS clients or require the RAS server to assign IP addresses from a static pool of addresses. Having the RAS server assign addresses offers a number of possible benefits:

✔ The clients can receive an IP address from the pool of available addresses on the RAS server from a specified range, similar to a DHCP IP address pool. The RAS server IP address pool of valid IP addresses to assign to the RAS clients can be used when a DHCP server is not available.

✔ You can specify a range of IP addresses within the scope that you want to exclude — for example, IP addresses for important computers such as servers.

✔ The RAS server can be configured to enable the DHCP server to assign clients IP addresses from the server's pool of available IP addresses.

✔ RAS clients can request a specific address to be given each time they connect using the RAS server.

A few specifics concerning RAS clients and name resolution are very valuable to remember for the exam. Expect to see a question that you can easily answer if you keep the following points in mind:

✔ If a RAS server is configured to use WINS and DNS, the clients also use the same settings for WINS and DNS. Configuring RAS clients is easy because they simply inherit the RAS server's WINS and DNS configuration settings.

✔ RAS clients can also use LMHOSTS and HOSTS files for name resolution instead of WINS and DNS servers. (See Chapter 9 for more on the LMHOST and HOSTS files.)

✔ If the RAS server is *multihomed* (see Chapter 7 for more information on multihomed computers), the RAS clients use the first adapter specified for WINS and DNS information.

✔ RAS clients can also specify WINS and DNS servers on a per-computer basis using the TCP/IP Dial-Up Networking settings for the connection you are configuring. Those configuration settings can be found by double-clicking the Dial-Up Networking icon under My Computer and then selecting the connection you want to configure.

✔ Broadcast name resolution doesn't work with RAS. Clients must use WINS or DNS or have properly configured LMHOSTS and HOSTS files.

Configuring Dial-Up Networking

Dial-Up Networking (DUN) is the client side of RAS. You can expect to see a couple of questions on the exam that involve configuring a DUN client. Naturally, a TCP/IP configuration is required for the DUN connection. When you elect to use TCP/IP protocol to configure Dial-Up Networking, you have to specify a few TCP/IP settings in the PPP (Point-to-Point) TCP/IP Settings dialog box, which is shown in Figure 14-6:

 ✓ Select the Server Assigned IP Address option if you're configuring the RAS server to assign an IP address from its pool of addresses when you connect to it.

 ✓ Select the Server Assigned Name Server Addresses option if the RAS server is configured with addresses for the WINS and DNS servers that the client inherits. Otherwise, select the Specify Name Server Addresses option and enter the IP addresses of the name servers.

 ✓ Select the Use Default Gateway on Remote Network option to enable packets to use the default gateway on the network you're connecting to, rather than leaving the packets to run around your local network looking for a way out.

Because this is a test on TCP/IP, don't expect any questions on configuring RAS to use NetBEUI or IPX/SPX (NWLink). NetBEUI and IPX/SPX are completely different protocols from TCP/IP, and therefore won't be tested.

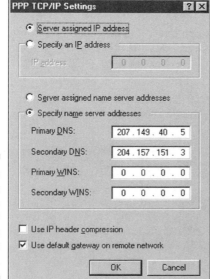

Figure 14-6: Here you configure TCP/IP properties for RAS clients.

Lab 14-1 shows you how to configure TCP/IP on a Dial-Up Networking client for Windows NT Workstation. For this exercise, you need NT Workstation and a modem with RAS already installed.

Lab 14-1	Configuring TCP/IP for Dial-Up Networking in Windows NT Workstation

1. **Open the My Computer window and double-click the Dial-Up Networking icon.**

   The main Dial-Up Networking window comes up, possibly with an existing DUN connection if you're already configured to dial up the Internet.

2. **Click New.**

   A dialog box appears, in which you can enter the information about the new Dial-Up Networking connection you're going to make, such as the name of the connection, the phone number to dial, and the modem to use to make the connection.

3. **Click the Server tab.**

   You get the page shown in Figure 14-7, where you can specify the Dial-Up Server Type, Network Protocols, and a few other options.

4. **Select TCP/IP under Network Protocols and then click TCP/IP Settings.**

   You get a dialog box like the one in Figure 14-6.

Figure 14-7:
The Server page is where you specify network protocols and other options.

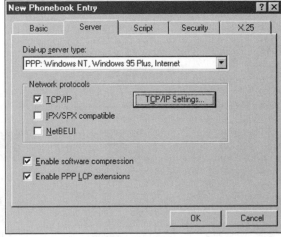

5. **Click the Specify an IP Address radio button, and in the text box enter a fictitious IP address — for example** `123.123.123.123`.

6. **Click the Specify Name Server Addresses radio button, and enter fictitious IP addresses for the Primary DNS server and Primary WINS server.**

Specifying an IP address yourself should be done only after your Internet Service Provider has assigned you a valid IP address. You should also have your Internet provider supply you with the correct IP addresses for the DNS and WINS servers. (For the purposes of the exercise in this lab, the server IP addresses don't have to be valid.)

Routing with RAS

A question concerning routing with the RAS server may appear on your exam. In Chapter 7, I note that a *multihomed* Windows NT computer can act as an IP router between networks. You can configure a multihomed computer to route packets to and from your LAN and the Internet. (Figure 14-8 shows a diagram of the layout of a network with the Windows NT RAS server routing packets to the Internet.)

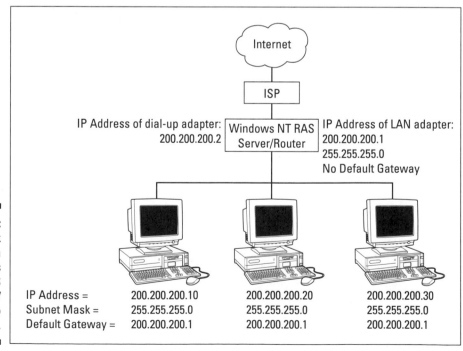

Figure 14-8: A network using a Windows NT RAS Server/ Router to the Internet.

In order to configure the sort of routing shown in the figure with your Windows NT RAS server, you need to satisfy the following hardware and software requirements:

✔ A Windows NT 3.51 or higher computer with a network adapter connected to the LAN and a dial-up adapter.

✔ A Point-to-Point Protocol (PPP) connection to the Internet.

✔ Valid IP addresses for the clients and one valid IP address for the local machine.

✔ Correct TCP/IP configuration for the computer that is acting as a router. This configuration information must include the IP address, subnet mask, and default gateway.

The Windows NT RAS server routing to the Internet is basically the same configuration as that for a Windows NT computer configured to route between two networks, except that the routing is between the LAN and the Internet.

The following steps provide a general overview of how a Windows NT machine needs to be configured in order to route packets between two subnets. This process is crucial to remember for the exam.

1. **Install TCP/IP on the computer that will act as a router.**

   You need to have one IP address for the LAN adapter on the network and one IP address for the dial-up adapter to the ISP's network.

2. **Enable IP Forwarding on the Windows NT router.**

   You can do this on the Routing page of the TCP/IP Properties dialog box.

3. **Configure the hosts on the LAN with valid Internet IP addresses.**

   The hosts on the LAN are visible on the Internet; therefore, they can't have randomly assigned IP addresses. Using DHCP to assign valid addresses avoids assigning IP addresses that are not valid. (Check out Chapter 8 for more on DHCP.)

4. **Configure the default gateway setting on each of the hosts on the LAN to point to the LAN adapter of the Windows NT router.**

   You need to know the IP address of the Windows NT router that is routing the packets for you.

5. **Enter the IP address of the Windows NT router in the Default Gateway text box of the IP Address page in the TCP/IP Properties dialog box.**

6. **Configure DNS for name resolution for each of the hosts on the LAN.**

   You can do this by entering the IP address of the DNS server in the DNS Service Search Order text box on the DNS page of the TCP/IP Properties dialog box.

7. **Dial into the ISP from one of the RAS clients using your Dial-Up Networking connection.**

The Windows NT computer now routes between the LAN and the Internet.

On the exam, you may be presented with an illustration that displays a network configuration with IP addresses for various devices. If you're asked to provide the correct IP address for the default gateway to be configured for a RAS client, select the router that's connected to the Internet. However, the router has two interfaces — one on the network and another on the Internet. You would configure the RAS client to use the interface that is on the network, which is where you reside. The router then passes packets across to the Internet. Key items to remember for the exam are the settings that directly relate to TCP/IP, such as those for the IP address, subnet mask, DNS server, and especially the default gateway.

Point-to-Point Tunneling Protocol

Point-to-Point Tunneling Protocol (PPTP) is used to create a secure channel between a remote client and an enterprise server over a TCP/IP network. PPTP creates a Virtual Private Network (VPN) that tunnels encrypted information through a public network. The tunneling begins at the source host and ends at the destination host. PPTP can be used over LANs, WANs, dial-up lines, or the Internet.

If you already use the TCP/IP protocol, you don't have to configure PPTP any differently than it already is. PPTP uses the existing TCP/IP settings, such as the IP addresses of WINS and DNS servers. You do, however, have to configure RAS with Dial-Up Networking on both the PPTP clients and servers, and you must also use the PPP protocol, which encrypts the information. PPTP is installed like most TCP/IP services — by using the Services page found in the Network window in the Control Panel.

Choosing the Right Tools to Monitor TCP/IP Traffic

Test-takers have commented on seeing a few questions regarding Performance Monitor and Network Monitor. These real-time monitoring utilities can be very complicated, but luckily the exam doesn't cover them in much detail. One user had this to say about the monitoring questions: "The really easy questions asked for the charting and logging capabilities, which can only be supported by Performance Monitor and Network Monitor."

If you have taken other Microsoft tests such as Windows NT Server 4.0, you've probably already studied Performance Monitor and Network Monitor. You probably won't even need to review this section!

When you open Performance Monitor, you're in Chart mode by default, which is illustrated in Figure 14-9. This mode uses an X and Y axis to display data to continually monitor the network at an interval you specify. You can add specific objects, counters, and instances to be monitored and viewed on the chart. You can also save and load charts that you have configured to monitor specific events. These items aren't tested on the exam, however, and therefore aren't covered in this section.

For Performance Monitor logging, you can have the object information saved to a file at the interval of your choice. You can create alerts that are logged when the information has exceeded your determined threshold.

The Network Monitor utility captures packets from the network in realtime. As with Performance Monitor, you can graphically display statistics as they are being collected, as shown in Figure 14-10. You can also save the data to a capture file to be loaded and examined at a later date.

Don't expect questions concerning Network Monitor on the exam except for a possible question where you are to determine whether Network Monitor is the best utility for a given scenario. The next paragraphs can give you a good understanding of when to choose Performance Monitor or Network Monitor.

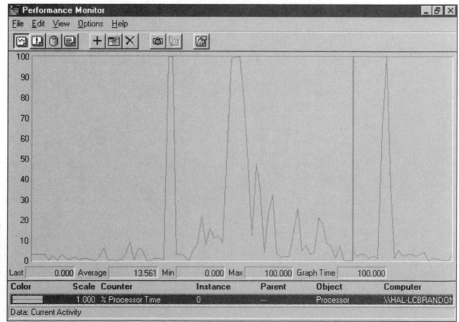

Figure 14-9:
Performance
Monitoring
in Chart
mode.

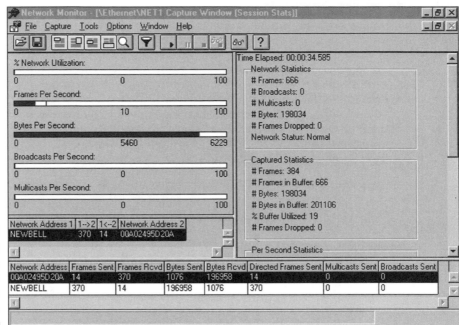

Figure 14-10:
Capturing
packets with
the Network
Monitor.

When the exam asks you which utility you should use to monitor TCP/IP information, choose Performance Monitor or Network Monitor when you need to monitor the network *continually*. The other utilities display information as of that given moment. You also choose these two utilities when information must be logged at certain intervals, which is not possible with the other utilities.

Here is a breakdown of when to use the various utilities:

- ✔ If you want to gather protocol information at specific intervals, use **Network Monitor.**

- ✔ If you want to display protocol statistics since the computer was started, use NETSTAT.

- ✔ If you need to monitor a TCP/IP object continually, use **Performance Monitor.**

- ✔ If you need to log information to a text file, use **Performance Monitor** or **Network Monitor.**

- ✔ If you need to configure alerts when thresholds are reached, use **Performance Monitor** or **Network Monitor.**

- ✔ If you want to display current TCP/IP connections, use nbtstat.

To get a better understanding of which utility to use to monitor TCP/IP information, take a look at the following scenario that's similar to one you may see on the exam:

> Your company is going to upgrade three Web servers from Windows NT 3.51 to NT 4.0. Before you upgrade the servers, you want to monitor their performance for a few days to create a baseline of performance in order to determine the effect of the operating system upgrade. Which utility would you use to establish this baseline for comparing results when you perform the same test with the new operating system?
>
> The answer is *Performance Monitor*.

With the Performance Monitor, you can monitor a number of different counters and objects before and after the upgrade, and export the results to files for later viewing. You can also create reports from the information gathered to include in presentations.

Prep Test

1 Which of the following is not required when configuring your IIS server?

A ○ IP address

B ○ Name resolution

C ○ Host name

D ○ Default gateway

2 Which of the following statements are true about RAS clients and Windows NT? (Choose all that apply.)

A ❑ You can configure a RAS client to request the same IP address each time the client logs on.

B ❑ You can configure a RAS client to have access to only the resources on the RAS server.

C ❑ You can configure a RAS client to use broadcast name resolution if a WINS or DNS server is not available.

D ❑ You can configure a RAS client to automatically use the WINS and DNS server that the RAS server itself has specified.

3 Which is the easiest method of configuring RAS clients with name resolution?

A ○ Maintain an LMHOSTS file on the RAS server.

B ○ Configure WINS on the RAS server.

C ○ Configure WINS on the RAS clients.

D ○ Do nothing. Broadcast is enabled by default.

4 A number of RAS clients try to access network resources when they are not permitted to do so. How can you configure a RAS server in order to maintain tighter security?

A ○ Exclude the IP addresses of the RAS clients from the range of addresses on the RAS server.

B ○ Deny access to the RAS clients' IP addresses individually.

C ○ Configure these users to have access only to resources on the RAS server.

D ○ Place RAS client resources on the RAS server and deny access to the rest of the network.

5 You have a RAS server on a DHCP-enabled network that has WINS and DNS servers. Every RAS client can dial in to participate on the network except for one host. That host can connect and authenticate with the RAS server, but it can't participate on the network. What can possibly be wrong with this host?

A ○ The host is not configured to use IP Header Compression.

B ○ The host may have TCP/IP information that was manually configured.

C ○ The host is not using the TCP/IP protocol.

D ○ The host does not have a valid IP address.

6 Which of the following is not a step when you configure your RAS server to route packets between two subnets?

A ○ Adding the IP address of the DNS server in the DNS Service Search Order text box in the DNS page of the TCP/IP Properties dialog box.

B ○ Configuring the default gateway on each host on the LAN to point to the Internet adapter of the Windows NT router.

C ○ Assigning each of the clients a valid IP address on the Internet.

D ○ Enabling IP forwarding on the server.

7 The sole reason you use your RAS server is to enable a few contractors who work outside of your company to gain access to an online database. How should you configure the RAS server so that those contractors can use the online database only to enter product information?

A ○ Reserve the IP addresses of each contractor's machine and grant access only to those IP addresses.

B ○ Configure the RAS server to allow users access to this RAS server only, not the entire network.

C ○ Configure permissions on the server to deny the contractors' IP addresses access to everything on the server, except the online database.

D ○ Use encrypted security and allow the contractors' computers to pass only through the encrypted security firewall.

8 You have a DHCP-enabled network with WINS and DNS servers. You are configuring some clients to have access to the Internet. Access to the Internet is limited to those people in salaried positions, and hourly-position personnel are not to have access. How should the Internet Service Manager be configured to accomplish this arrangement?

A ○ Deny access to all computers and grant access to certain computers.

B ○ Grant access to all computers and deny access to certain computers.

C ○ Deny access to all computers and grant access to a group of computers.

D ○ This arrangement can't be accomplished effectively.

9 Which of the following is not required for the PPTP protocol to work effectively for a secure connection through an ISDN line?

A ○ PPTP installed on the client

B ○ PPTP installed on the server

C ○ PPTP forwarding enabled

D ○ The PPP protocol installed on the two computers

10 Which of the following is not installed through the Services page in the Network window of the Control Panel?

A ○ PPTP

B ○ PPP

C ○ RAS

D ○ TCP/IP printing

Answers

1 C. Although a host name is helpful for your users, it isn't required. You can use just the IP address if you prefer. *Review "Configuring a RAS Server."*

2 A, B, D. Of the answer choices, only answer C is not correct. Broadcast name resolution does not work with RAS. You must specify a WINS or DNS server, or use an LMHOSTS or HOSTS file for name resolution when using RAS. *Review "Configuring a RAS Server."*

3 B. This is the easiest way to configure the RAS clients with name resolution because the clients inherit the RAS server's name resolution settings. *Review "Configuring a RAS Server."*

4 D. Granting some RAS clients access to the entire network and others access only to the RAS server is not possible. Therefore, the decision must be made to restrict every RAS client from the network, which is the most secure option, or grant access to the entire network, which is less secure. *Review "Configuring a RAS Server."*

5 B. This manually configured information is incorrect and is overriding the WINS and DNS settings that can be inherited from the RAS server. *Review "Point-to-Point Tunneling Protocol."*

6 B. When you're specifying the default gateway for the host on the LAN, the network clients need to point to the LAN adapter, not the Internet adapter. The Internet adapter isn't on the same network as the hosts on the LAN, and therefore isn't visible to the hosts. *Review "Routing with RAS."*

7 B. With RAS, you can configure the server to allow access to the entire network, or only to the RAS server itself. If you have applications that you want to be made accessible to RAS clients — and only those applications should be accessible — place them on the RAS server and then deny access to the entire network for RAS clients. *Review "Configuring a RAS Server."*

8 D. Because IP addresses are assigned dynamically, granting or denying access to an IP address doesn't work because the client can receive a different IP address the next day. You have to manually configure IP addresses on clients, reserve IP addresses in the DHCP pool, or create another pool of addresses (one for IP addresses that are allowed access and another pool for those that are not allowed access). *Review "Configuring IIS with the Internet Service Manager."*

9 *C.* No such thing as PPTP forwarding exists. PPTP uses existing TCP/IP information. The PPTP protocol must be installed on both the client and the server, and both the client and server must have the PPP protocol installed. *Review "Point-to-Point Tunneling Protocol."*

10 *B.* Point-to-Point Protocol (PPP) is *not* installed from the Services page of the Network window, although Point-to-Point Tunneling Protocol (PPTP) is. PPP is installed when you install RAS, which is accomplished from the Services page. *Review "Point-to-Point Tunneling Protocol."*

Part V
Monitoring, Optimization, and Troubleshooting

The 5th Wave   By Rich Tennant

"Troubleshooting's a little tricky here. The route table to our destination hosts include a Morse code key, several walkie-talkies, and a guy with nine messenger pigeons."

In this part . . .

*L*ike the title says, in this part of the book you enter the world of monitoring, optimization, and trouble-shooting. You may want to pay particular attention to Chapter 15, which shows you how to use the utilities covered in previous chapters in order to solve TCP/IP-related problems, especially those snags you may encounter in the name resolution and IP addressing process. Chapter 16 rounds out TCP/IP troubleshooting by covering the Microsoft TCP/IP utilities you need in order to diagnose IP configuration problems.

Chapter 15

Troubleshooting IP Addressing and Host Name Resolution

. . . .

Exam Objectives

▶ Diagnosing and resolving IP addressing problems

▶ Diagnosing and resolving name resolution problems

. . . .

*M*icrosoft loves to include questions on the TCP/IP exam that demand you have a significant understanding of the topic of troubleshooting. This chapter covers the art of troubleshooting and how to use TCP/IP utilities to identify and solve networking problems. The big focus here is on two troubleshooting issues certain to be on the exam: solving problems with both IP addressing and name resolution.

In order to breeze through those troubleshooting questions, you need the following information (which this chapter conveniently provides):

- ✔ You must have a good understanding of the TCP/IP properties required for troubleshooting, including the IP address, subnet mask, and default gateway.

- ✔ You must know how to solve a networking problem when you're able to contact a host with its IP address but not with its host name, and vice versa. The most challenging troubleshooting questions you'll come across address this topic.

Quick Assessment

1 The _____ command is used to determine the current configuration.

2 To pinpoint a hardware problem, `ping` the address of _____.

3 _____ can also be examined for errors to determine whether the hardware has been configured correctly.

4 If you are having initialization problems, you should verify that _____ has been installed.

5 Creating a NetBIOS session involves using the _____ command.

Diagnosing and resolving name resolution problems

6 If you can't `ping` a computer, you can check the _____ file to see whether it is up to date.

7 Name resolution on the network can be _____ or _____ .

8 Windows NT uses the _____ name as the default name for the host.

Diagnosing and resolving IP addressing problems

9 The default gateway can be thought of as a _____.

10 Duplicate IP addresses on the network can cause a host to _____.

Answers

1 *ipconfig/all.* Review "Armed and Ready: The Basic Troubleshooting Steps."

2 *127.0.0.1.* Review "Checking TCP/IP Components and Services."

3 *Event Viewer.* Review "Checking TCP/IP Components and Services."

4 *TCP/IP.* Review "Checking TCP/IP Components and Services."

5 *Net.* Review "Troubleshooting problems with NetBIOS name resolution."

6 *HOSTS.* Review "Troubleshooting snags in host name resolution."

7 *Host name, NetBIOS.* Review "Solving Name Resolution Problems."

8 *NetBIOS.* Review "Solving Name Resolution Problems."

9 *Router.* Review "Understanding the default gateway."

10 *Hang.* Review "Detecting duplicate IP addresses."

Armed and Ready: The Basic Troubleshooting Steps

TCP/IP can be very difficult to configure, and it can be equally difficult to troubleshoot. As additional TCP/IP-related components (such as DHCP, WINS, and DNS) are added to the mix, the potential problems are multiplied. Getting at the root of a problem with TCP/IP usually requires that you follow some basic steps:

1. **Identify the symptoms of the problem.**

   Is a host unable to connect to other hosts? Does the connection hang? When did the connection stop working? What has changed since it was last working?

2. **Determine the current TCP/IP settings.**

   If the problem is believed to reside with TCP/IP and not with the physical network, then you need to determine the current TCP/IP settings by using the `ipconfig /all` command. You can begin by verifying the required TCP/IP settings, such as the IP address, the subnet mask, and the default gateway.

3. **Determine which component of TCP/IP is faulty.**

   If a route does exist between the two hosts, you can determine which component of the TCP/IP protocol is faulty by using the `ping` utility.

4. **Determine which TCP/IP utility can best diagnose the problem.**

   Depending on the situation, a number of TCP/IP utilities can be used to further diagnose and resolve a problem.

 A firm understanding of the TCP/IP basics is essential for troubleshooting. A problem can often be solved through the main TCP/IP configurations, such as the IP address, subnet mask, and default gateway. If you are experiencing TCP/IP problems, you should always verify that those configurations are correct.

Checking TCP/IP Components and Services

Figuring out why a host isn't able to connect to another host can be a real chore — whether in real life or during the exam. The TCP/IP components and services covered in the following sections are listed in the order in which they should be checked for trouble.

Because you should eliminate the networking hardware problems first, start low in the TCP/IP protocol model and continue through each layer until the problem eventually surfaces. Try testing each layer in the following order:

1. The TCP/IP configuration
2. Networking hardware
3. IP addressing
4. Subnet addressing
5. Host name resolution
6. NetBIOS name resolution

The elements in the preceding list are independent from one another in terms of troubleshooting. For example, if you're having a host name resolution problem, checking the networking hardware may be a waste of time, but it nevertheless pays to troubleshoot the most-likely culprits first. The following sections describe each of these components and services in the TCP/IP protocol model in more detail.

One: Check the TCP/IP configuration

Are you making a simple mistake in a configuration setting that should be checked before you continue any further? Make sure the IP address, the subnet mask, and the default gateway are correct. Has the host worked before? If the host has worked before but isn't working now, that's a good indication that the hardware should be checked, which is the next step in the process.

Two: Check the networking hardware

If the host suddenly is no longer able to communicate with other hosts on the network, you should check the network adapter card and cable. You should begin by troubleshooting on your local machine. If other hosts are experiencing the same problem, you should start checking network components common to all the hosts.

To determine whether you are experiencing a hardware-related problem, try the following steps:

1. Ping **the loopback address of** 127.0.0.1. **If you receive a response, then TCP/IP is installed and has initialized correctly.**
2. Ping **the IP address assigned to your host.**

3. After you have successfully pinged your IP address, try pinging another host on the network.

If that fails, you most likely have a hardware problem.

Before you begin tearing your machine apart, try pinging other hosts from a different computer. If you're successful, then you have determined that the problem resides on the local host.

If you encounter TCP/IP initialization problems on your machine, you begin by verifying that the TCP/IP configuration is correct and that the networking hardware is functioning correctly. You also need to determine whether TCP/IP is installed and verify that TCP/IP is bound to at least one adapter on the machine. You can do this in the Bindings page of the Network window under the Control Panel.

Your TCP/IP configuration that was entered manually or received from a DHCP server could also be configured incorrectly.

Three: Use the ipconfig command

The `ipconfig` command quickly determines whether TCP/IP has initialized correctly. If you receive an error, or if the configuration is blank when you issue the `ipconfig` command, then TCP/IP has not initialized correctly. (Chapter 16 covers the use of the `ipconfig` command for troubleshooting in more depth.)

Four: Use the Event Viewer

The Event Viewer can be used to examine information relating to hardware failure or TCP/IP initialization failure. If your network card cannot be found in the system, or if it is not configured correctly, an error is written in the Event Viewer log, and you see an error message stating that TCP/IP did not initialize properly.

During system startup, you may receive an error message that a device or driver has failed near the time when you're about to log on to Windows NT. If you are just starting your system, this message is usually the first indication that the hardware is at fault. You should immediately examine the Event Viewer for a more detailed description as to what the error message is referring to. When you click on an event in the Event Viewer, the Event Detail dialog box opens. Figure 15-1 shows the error message that's logged in the Description list of the Event Detail dialog box when the network adapter cannot be located.

Error message

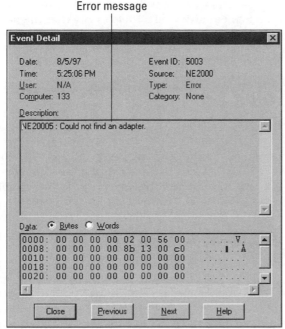

If you successfully ping the loopback address, TCP/IP is functioning properly. When packets have to be sent out on the network via the network card, you should then check for problems higher up in the TCP/IP protocol model, such as IP addressing.

Five: Troubleshoot the IP addressing

You will undoubtedly see questions on the exam regarding IP addressing problems. Because Microsoft includes "Diagnosing and resolving IP addressing problems" in its list of exam objectives, I treat this subject in more depth in the section "Solving IP Addressing Problems" later in this chapter.

Six: Troubleshoot the subnet addressing

Although questions on the process of troubleshooting subnet addressing may seem difficult to answer, the correct response generally boils down to just one problem on the network: The host may not be configured for the proper subnet.

Making a mistake in subnet addressing is very easy to do, especially when you're using a custom subnet mask. You should verify that the host has the correct subnet mask and that the IP address is valid for that particular network. (See Chapter 6 for more information on the subnetting process.)

Seven: Resolve the host name and NetBIOS name

Because Microsoft includes "Diagnosing and resolving name resolution problems" in its list of exam objectives, I treat this subject in more depth in the section "Solving Name Resolution Problems" later in this chapter.

Solving IP Addressing Problems

The most common IP addressing problems that you're likely to encounter as the subject of a test question include the following:

- ✔ A computer not being able to communicate with another host
- ✔ A connection that appears to be hung
- ✔ Receiving messages intended for another host

Checking the configuration settings

The most likely cause of a problem involves the three main TCP/IP configuration settings — the IP address, the subnet mask, and the default gateway, which must be properly configured. You can verify the settings with the `ipconfig` command, and use the `ping`, `route`, and `tracert` utilities to determine whether a host can be reached and to examine the route the packets are taking to reach the host.

Detecting duplicate IP addresses

If a connection appears to hang when you contact other hosts, you may have a duplicate IP address on the network. This is one of the most common IP addressing problems to troubleshoot. Windows NT TCP/IP fails to initialize on the network if a duplicate IP address is detected. An error message, similar to the one in the Event Detail window shown in Figure 15-2, is logged if a duplicate name is detected.

Error message

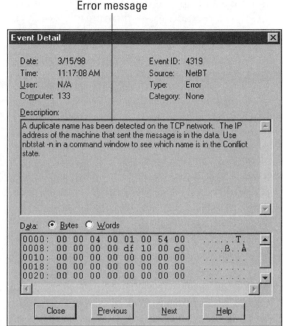

Figure 15-2:
The
message
you receive
when a
duplicate
name is
detected
on the
network.

Other operating systems are not so informative when it comes to duplicate IP addresses. They can initialize TCP/IP, but they may cause intermittent problems on the network, such as hung connections, which are very difficult to troubleshoot. With Windows NT, at least you know that a duplicate name or IP address exists because TCP/IP refuses to initialize and an error is logged in Event Viewer.

Receiving messages that are intended for another host is an obvious sign of a duplicate IP address. You want to remember this in case you see a question that reads something like: "You establish a connection to a Telnet server, but the banner indicates a different name than the host you are trying to connect to. . . ." This statement hints of a name resolution problem.

Solving Name Resolution Problems

Both the host name and NetBIOS name resolution methods involve a number of sources that can be queried to resolve a name, and any one of those sources introduces another chance for error. This section covers the areas most likely to give you trouble during the resolution process and, therefore, are topics that are likely to turn up on the exam.

The following points sum up a couple of differences between host name resolution and NetBIOS name resolution — information worth remembering for the exam.

✔ Windows NT uses the NetBIOS machine name as the default name for the host.

✔ TCP/IP utilities, such as ping and Telnet, do not connect using NetBIOS. Resources of that type use *sockets,* which are IP addresses used in conjunction with port numbers. An example of a socket connection is #103.58.221.12(132).

If you are having problems with the TCP/IP utilities ping or Telnet, you don't need to troubleshoot NetBIOS name resolution.

Troubleshooting snags in host name resolution

The process of resolving a host name to an IP address is time-consuming and complicated (Chapter 4 can provide you with more information on the subject). Even if you're able to communicate with other hosts on the network using the IP address, you may still have other TCP/IP-related problems to contend with.

If you receive the error Bad IP address *host name,* in which *host name* is the name of the host you are trying to communicate with, you definitely have a host name resolution problem. During the exam, you are almost guaranteed to be presented with a scenario in which you're able to connect to the host with the IP address, but not with the host name. The solution to the problem depends on the name resolution method being used on the network:

✔ If a Domain Name Service (DNS) server is being used, make sure you have specified the correct IP address for the DNS server. Ping the DNS server to make sure it is functioning on the network. Is there a correct mapping in the DNS database? Is the DNS database up to date?

✔ If a HOSTS file is being used, make sure there is a correct host-name-to-IP-address mapping for the host you are trying to connect to. Is the HOSTS file in the correct directory? Is it up to date?

The answer to an exam question dealing with host name resolution will be somehow related to the Domain Name Service (DNS) or the LMHOSTS file. Because they are the only two methods used to resolve a host name to an IP address, one of those two isn't configured correctly. For example, if you're using a HOSTS file for name resolution on a network, ask yourself the questions I just listed to reach a solution to a failed attempt at host name resolution. The problem lies in an incorrect mapping, an out-of-date HOSTS file, or the file not being located in the proper directory.

Lab 15-1 lists the steps involved in a failed attempt at name resolution using the HOSTS file. The steps illustrate the symptoms of having a HOSTS file in the wrong location. The lab gives you an idea of what to look for when you are having host name resolution problems with the HOSTS file. Then, if you get a question that asks you why you received a `Bad IP address hostname` error when using the HOSTS file, you can zip right through it.

Lab 15-1   Troubleshooting the HOSTS File

1. **Open the HOSTS file from the** `<systemroot>\winnt\system32\ drivers\etc` **directory.**

   The contents of the HOSTS file are listed. At the bottom of the file, find the following entry, which is added by default:

   ```
   127.0.0.1          localhost
   ```

2. **Change** `localhost` **to your first name.**

   Using your first name makes the name easier to remember later on in the exercise.

3. **Save the HOSTS file.**

   Do not save the HOSTS file with the `.txt` extension. In order for the HOSTS file to work, it must be saved without an extension. In the File Explorer, you should see `HOSTS`, not `HOSTS.TXT`, listed.

4. **Open a command prompt window by clicking Start, selecting the Run option, and entering** `CMD` **in the Run dialog box.**

5. **At the command prompt, enter the following command:** `ping <your name>`

   For example, I enter `ping cameron`.

   You see a response from 127.0.0.1, which is the IP address that was specified in the HOSTS file for your first name.

6. **Go back to the** `<systemroot>\winnt\system32\drivers\etc` **directory and move the HOSTS file to another directory, such as** `C:\` **(the root directory).**

   Moving the HOSTS file makes the `ping` utility unable to find the HOSTS file to resolve the host name.

7. **At the command prompt, enter the** ping **command used in Step 5.**

   Expect a long pause, during which all the host name resolution methods are being tried. Ultimately the ping command fails and returns a `Bad IP address <your name>` error.

8. **Return the HOSTS file to the correct directory and change the** `127.0.0.1` **entry back to** `localhost` **from your first name.**

You may see a question on the exam that presents a scenario in which you're able to connect to the host with the IP address, but not with the host name. In that case, a host-name-to-IP-address mapping is incorrect somewhere on the network, and the solution depends on whether the DNS or the HOSTS file is being used for name resolution.

Troubleshooting problems with NetBIOS name resolution

NetBIOS name resolution is just as complicated as host name resolution. Plus, you have to deal with host name resolution in addition to NetBIOS name resolution. A NetBIOS machine name must be resolved to an IP address, and NetBIOS name resolution does just that. With host name resolution, you can try the IP address if the host name does not work; with NetBIOS resolution you can't, which makes NetBIOS troubleshooting more difficult.

Remember this rule for the exam: If you can `ping` the host but you can't create a NetBIOS session, then a NetBIOS name resolution problem exists. Creating a NetBIOS session requires typing the `net` command at the command prompt with the name of the `server` and `share` you want to connect to, for example:

```
net use e: \\server\share
```

If you have verified that the computer name and the share name are correct and you still cannot connect, the solution depends on the name resolution method being used on the network:

- ✔ If a WINS server is being used, check the WINS server database to determine whether a NetBIOS name registration appears for the computer you are trying to connect to. Use the nbtstat command at the command prompt to examine the NetBIOS name cache on the local machine. This cache contains computer names that have been registered to IP addresses. (More information on the nbtstat command is in Chapter 13.)

- ✔ If an LMHOSTS file is being used, check to see whether an entry exists for the computer name you are trying to create a session with. Once again, use nbtstat to examine the NetBIOS name cache on the local machine.

Don't confuse a host name with a NetBIOS name. They each have different methods of name resolution. When you are thinking through a tough question on the exam, ask yourself: "Is this computer name a host name or a NetBIOS name?" It can make the difference in your analysis and, ultimately, in how you answer the question.

Handling Common TCP/IP Problems

Although many common TCP/IP problems exist in real life, in this section of the chapter, I'm concentrating on just that handful of TCP/IP problems that are almost 100 percent certain to be tested on the exam.

Understanding the default gateway

The default gateway sends packets to the router, which, in turn, routes them to a remote network. The following rules help you avoid any default gateway problems in real life and solve any default gateway questions on the exam.

- ✔ The default gateway must be on the same network as the host.
- ✔ The default gateway can be thought of as a router.
- ✔ The default gateway is only used when an entry is not found in the route table.
- ✔ It doesn't matter whether you have more than one default gateway specified; the first gateway found is used.

Figure 15-3 illustrates the process used in specifying the next router as the default gateway. (It's a good idea to keep this illustration in mind for the test.) In the figure, the arrow from Router1 to Router2 indicates that Router1 has a default gateway of 160.32.2.2, which is Router2's interface on the same network. The arrow from Router2 to Router3 indicates that Router2 has a default gateway of 160.32.3.2, which is Router3's interface on the same network. What do you think the default gateway for Router3 is? According to the figure, the default gateway has to be 160.32.3.1. Packets destined for remote networks are then sent back to Network 1.0 and Network 2.0.

Figure 15-3:
An example
of default
gateways
through
routers.

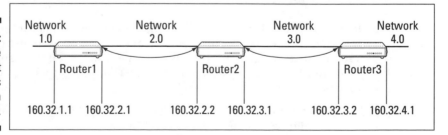

When you get an exam question about a default gateway, get ready to draw some diagrams on your scratch paper. First, quickly sketch the network based on the information presented in the question. Next, add the IP addresses or host names for the computers and routers. Having a drawing in front of you makes it much easier to solve a complex default gateway question. A picture is worth a thousand words, and those text-based scenario questions sometimes seem almost that long.

Using the route command and adding static routes

The process of adding static routes will be tested, so you should understand the concept of static routes to avoid making simple mistakes and easily identify tricky questions. What you'll probably get is a questions with incorrect syntax for the `route` command. Or the routing table may have an incorrect route, which is more difficult to detect.

In order to diagnose default gateway problems, you should `ping` a host on the local network and `ping` a host on a remote network. If you can `ping` a host on the local network (which doesn't use the default gateway) but not a host on the remote network, then you know the default gateway is not correct. The packets have no idea where to go in order to be routed to the remote network.

The following rules help you to better understand both the `route` syntax and the process for adding static routes:

- ✔ If you want to enter a route to a remote network of 116.21.0.0 with a subnet mask of 255.255.0.0 that uses the gateway of 116.21.1.1, you enter this command:

  ```
  ROUTE ADD 116.21.0.0 MASK 255.255.0.0 116.21.1.1
  ```

- ✔ Remember the phrase: "To get to this network, use this router . . ." Using the preceding example, this means that in order to get to the 116.21.0.0 network, go to the 116.21.1.1 gateway. Sound too simple? Trust me, it works. For example, assume that you get a question like the following:

  Which route table entry uses the 1.1.1.1 router when a host must communicate with the 1.0.0.0 network?

  ```
  A. ROUTE ADD 1.1.1.1    MASK 255.0.0.0    1.0.0.0
  B. ROUTE ADD 1.0.0.0    MASK 255.0.0.0    1.1.1.1
  ```

> See how confusing it can be? If you remember "to get to this network, use this router . . ." you know to select *B* because 1.0.0.0 is the network, and 1.1.1.1 is the router.

✔ Bind the outer subnet to the far side of the middle subnet, as shown in Figure 15-4.

Figure 15-4:
An example of the binding rule in action.

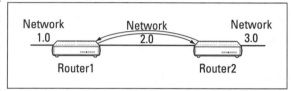

You must know the route syntax for the exam, especially the order in which entries are typed in the route command. You'll definitely see a question with entries from a routing table, and you'll have to determine whether they are correct. You also may be asked to choose the correct route table entry to type at the command prompt in order to route packets to the correct network. (See Chapter 7 for more information on IP routing.)

Checking for the correct mapping

Remember the following advice to make quick work of answering questions on troubleshooting host name resolution: Just check the DNS database or HOSTS file for the correct mapping. The host name always corresponds to an IP address in a HOSTS file or on a Domain Name Service (DNS) server.

The DNS server must be available and the mapping must be in the correct syntax. If the HOSTS file is being used instead of DNS, it must be in the correct directory. (Turn to Chapter 4 for more information on the host name resolution order, which is a likely candidate for exam question material.)

Prep Test

1 What is the first TCP/IP component you should check to determine the source of a problem?

A ○ The TCP/IP configuration

B ○ Networking hardware

C ○ Subnet addressing

D ○ IP addressing

2 You are troubleshooting an intermittent host problem. If you `ping` the loopback address of `127.0.0.1` and receive a response, what should you do next?

A ○ Check to see whether the network card or cable is bad.

B ○ Go to another host and try to ping another computer.

C ○ Ping another computer on the network.

D ○ Examine the contents of the ARP cache.

3 Which of the following gives the best indication that the problem is hardware failure?

A ○ `ipconfig`

B ○ `tracert`

C ○ `ping`

D ○ Event Viewer

4 If you have encountered TCP/IP initialization problems on your machine, what else must you verify after you have verified that TCP/IP is installed correctly?

A ○ The default gateway is specified.

B ○ The computer has a host name configured.

C ○ TCP/IP is bound to an adapter.

D ○ The computer has WINS configured.

5 Today, you receive the error `Bad IP address testament.com` when you try to connect to the FTP server using the host name. It worked last night from the same computer. What is most likely the cause?

A ○ The server is down.

B ○ The HOSTS file is outdated.

C ○ The DNS database has an incorrect mapping for this host.

D ○ The HOSTS file is in the wrong directory.

6 You `ping` a host and receive a reply. You then issue the following command to create a NetBIOS session to the `apps` share on the SQLServer:

```
net use \SQLServer\apps
```

Will this command determine whether you have a NetBIOS name resolution problem on your network?

A ○ Yes.

B ○ No.

C ○ Not enough information is supplied to answer this question.

D ○ The command will not work at all.

7 If you wanted to enter a route to a remote network of 102.77.124.0 with a subnet mask of 255.255.255.0 that uses the gateway of 102.77.124.1, you would enter which of the following commands?

A ○ `ROUTE ADD MASK 255.255.255.0 102.77.124.1 102.77.124.0`

B ○ `ROUTE ADD 102.77.124.0 MASK 255.255.255.0 102.77.124.1`

C ○ `ROUTE ADD 102.77.124.1 MASK 255.255.255.0 102.77.124.1`

D ○ `ROUTE ADD 102.77.124.0 MASK 255.255.0.0 102.77.124.1`

8 You continue to receive the `Bad IP address host name` error. You have verified there is a correct mapping in the DNS database for the destination host and have verified that you have the correct IP address specified for the DNS server. You have successfully connected to the database server by IP address. What should you do now?

A ○ Make sure the HOSTS file is in the correct directory.

B ○ `Ping` the DNS server.

C ○ Make sure there isn't an incorrect mapping in the HOSTS file.

D ○ `Ping` another computer on the network.

9 Which of the following does not support the assumption that TCP/IP has not initialized correctly?

A ○ `Ipconfig` is blank.

B ○ The Event Viewer has a network adapter error message.

C ○ The connection hangs.

D ○ The `ping` command times out.

10 You have two routers — Router1 and Router2 — connecting three separate networks. The routers have the following IP addresses for their interfaces:

Router1: 120.50.100.1 and 120.50.200.1

Router2: 120.50.200.2 and 120.50.300.1

If a host on the 100.x network needs to reach a host on the 300.x network, what should the default gateway be for that host?

A ○ 120.50.300.1

B ○ 120.50.200.1

C ○ 120.50.100.1

D ○ 120.50.200.1

Answers

1 A. Checking the required TCP/IP settings to make sure that you didn't make a simple configuration mistake before you begin the lengthy process of trouble-shooting is very important. *Review "Checking TCP/IP Components and Services."*

2 C. The fact that the loopback address responded doesn't mean that every-thing is working. You should ping another computer to make sure you have connectivity with hosts on the local network. *Review "Checking TCP/IP Components and Services."*

3 D. The other TCP/IP utilities don't function correctly if TCP/IP has not initial-ized. Therefore, the Event Viewer logs an error for the failing of the hardware and any TCP/IP services that require the networking hardware. *Review "Checking TCP/IP Components and Services."*

4 C. When you are experiencing TCP/IP initialization problems, you should check to make sure that TCP/IP is installed correctly and that it has been bound to a network adapter. You can verify binding on the Binding page of the Network Window. *Review "Checking TCP/IP Components and Services."*

5 A. When something such as a host name is working and then abruptly stops, don't spend too much time checking your configurations. If the host name worked the day before, it's likely that the server is down. *Review "Checking TCP/IP Components and Services."*

6 D. The syntax for the `net use` command is incorrect. Therefore, you won't be able to determine whether you have a NetBIOS name resolution problem on your network. The correct command is `net use X: \\SQLServer\apps`. You need to prefix the server name with double backslashes. *Review "Trouble-shooting problems with NetBIOS name resolution."*

7 B. You are trying to reach a remote network of 102.77.124.0 through the default gateway of 102.77.124.1. In order to get the correct order for the `route` command, remember the phrase: "To get to this network, use this router . . ." *Review "Using the route command and adding static routes."*

8 B. Because you have a functional DNS server on the network, troubleshooting the HOSTS file makes no sense. `Ping` the DNS server to make sure it is available on the network. You may have checked the mapping in the DNS database, but that doesn't mean it is visible on the network. *Review "Check-ing for the correct mapping."*

9 C. If TCP/IP is not initialized, you won't even have a chance to communicate with other hosts. The other possible answers indicate that TCP/IP has not initialized, most likely because of a network adapter problem. *Review "Check-ing TCP/IP Components and Services."*

10 C. In order for a host on the 100.x network to reach the 300.x network, it has to specify a default gateway of 120.50.100.1. The router then forwards the packet accordingly. *Review "Using the route command and adding static routes."*

Chapter 16

Using TCP/IP Utilities to Troubleshoot IP Configuration

• •

Exam Objectives

▶ Identifying which utility to use in diagnosing IP configuration problems

▶ Using Microsoft TCP/IP utilities to diagnose IP configuration problems

• •

*M*ost test-takers agree that the troubleshooting portion of the TCP/IP exam is the most difficult. The questions that ask you which utility to use in a given situation should be no problem for you, but those questions that require you to determine exactly what's wrong with a current configuration can be a real bear.

No doubt about it, you have plenty of material on diagnostics to review for the exam, especially concerning troubleshooting utilities. This chapter shows you which TCP/IP utilities to use to solve IP configuration problems that are likely to be on your exam, and how to use those utilities to solve those problems.

You need to know some basics and some specifics of troubleshooting an IP configuration for the exam, which I cover in this chapter:

✔ Make sure that you at least know the purpose of each utility. You can expect to see questions asking which utility is best in a given situation, which should be slam-dunks after you read this chapter! (Good news: You won't need to study the parameters and switches for each command utility.)

✔ Make sure you know the `ping` order process. You may be asked to provide the next step in the process of troubleshooting a connection.

✔ Make sure you know how to decipher the information contained within the `ipconfig` command. A question that includes `ipconfig` command output is almost guaranteed to be on the exam.

Quick Assessment

Identifying which Microsoft TCP/IP utility to use in diagnosing IP configuration problems

1 The command to check domain host aliases is _____.

2 The _____ command is the most useful TCP/IP troubleshooting tool.

3 The _____ command prints the current routing table for your computer to the screen.

4 The _____ command will display the name of the local host.

5 The _____ command can still work if there is a name resolution problem on the network.

6 The _____ command can display the machine's hardware address.

Using Microsoft TCP/IP utilities to diagnose IP configuration problems

7 (True/False). If you suspect a duplicate IP address on the network, you can check the contents of the cache for both IP addresses.

8 Ping and the _____ can determine whether the destination is being reached.

9 If the router is a multihomed Windows NT computer, make sure that IP _____ is enabled.

10 After you successfully ping the IP address of the default gateway, you should ping a _____ host.

Answers

1 *nslookup.* Review "Identifying the TCP/IP Diagnostic Utilities"

2 *ping.* Review "Using the ping command to verify connectivity."

3 *route print.* Review "Using the route utility to modify static routes."

4 *hostname.* Review "Identifying the TCP/IP Diagnostic Utilities."

5 *ping.* Review "Using the ping command to verify connectivity."

6 *ipconfig /all.* Review "Using the ipconfig command to view the current configuration."

7 *ARP.* Review "Identifying the TCP/IP Diagnostic Utilities."

8 *tracert.* Review "Using the tracert command to verify a route."

9 *Forwarding.* Review "Using the ping command to verify connectivity."

10 *Remote.* Review "Using the ping command to verify connectivity."

Part V: Monitoring, Optimization, and Troubleshooting

Identifying the TCP/IP Diagnostic Utilities

TCP/IP has numerous utilities, but only a fraction of them will be tested. Nevertheless, you need to be able to distinguish between *connectivity utilities* and *diagnostic utilities* when you see them mentioned in an exam question. (I cover the connectivity utilities in Chapter 13, and the diagnostic utilities in this chapter and in Chapter 15. In this chapter, the diagnostic utilities are approached from the angle of troubleshooting an IP configuration, and in Chapter 15 the utilities are covered from the angle of troubleshooting IP addressing and name resolution.)

No matter how you slice it, that's a lot of utilities. In order to distinguish the two types of utilities at a glance, check out the following list of connectivity utilities, and then compare it with the list of diagnostic utilities shown in Table 16-1, which I urge you to memorize. The table lists diagnostic utilities included with Microsoft's TCP/IP.

The connectivity commands (which are covered in Chapter 13) include the following:

- Telnet
- FTP
- TFTP
- RSH
- REXEC
- RCP
- LPR
- LPQ

Table 16-1	Windows NT TCP/IP Diagnostic Utilities for Troubleshooting IP Configurations
Utility	**Purpose**
ping	Verifies connectivity between two TCP/IP hosts.
ARP	Displays the ARP (Address Resolution Protocol) table of IP addresses associated with hardware addresses.
ipconfig	Displays the current TCP/IP configuration settings for the host.
tracert	Traces the route taken to a remote system.
nbtstat	Displays NetBIOS over TCP/IP (NBT) statistics.

Utility	Purpose
NETSTAT	Displays statistics for, and the current state of, the TCP/IP protocol connections.
nslookup	Checks domain information, including records, domain host aliases, and domain host services.
route	Displays the IP route table, and adds or deletes IP routes.
hostname	Displays the name of the current host.

Using TCP/IP Utilities to Diagnose IP Configuration Problems

Keep in mind that you won't be tested on parameters or switches used with TCP/IP utilities. But, you *can* expect some basic questions that ask which utility you should use in a given situation. The following sections of this chapter describe how to use each of those utilities that are most likely to turn up on the exam.

Using the ping command to verify connectivity

The ping command is the most useful TCP/IP troubleshooting tool you can use. The ping command sends IP echo request packets to the destination host to verify connectivity. You can also use ping to troubleshoot a number of problems, such as

- ✔ Whether TCP/IP is installed and has initialized correctly on the local host
- ✔ Whether the local host has a valid IP address
- ✔ Whether a host on the local network can be contacted
- ✔ Whether a host on a remote network can be contacted

You use the ping utility in a particular sequence to determine where a failure occurred. Lab 16-1 and Figure 16-1 illustrate the order in which you should ping devices on a network in order to determine the cause of a problem. You may reference the figure as you're reading the Lab steps.

You may see a question on the exam in which you are asked to provide the next host that should be tested in the ping process. The question will be a cinch if you remember the ping order.

Lab 16-1   Reviewing the Ping Troubleshooting Sequence

1. Ping **the loopback address of** 127.0.0.1 **on the local computer to verify that TCP/IP has been installed and has initialized correctly by entering the following line at the command prompt:**

```
ping 127.0.0.1
```

2. Ping **the IP address of the local host to make sure the IP address is valid by entering the following:**

```
ping ip_address_of_local_host
```

3. Ping **a host on the local network by entering the following (optional):**

```
ping ip_address_of_host_on_local_network
```

If you receive a response from a host on the local network, you can communicate with hosts on the local network.

4. Ping **the IP address of the default gateway (router) to determine whether the router is functioning correctly by entering the following:**

```
ping ip_address_of_default_gateway
```

If pinging the IP address of the default gateway returns a Request timed out message, the router may not be functioning. In this case, you can communicate with hosts on the local network but not with remote hosts.

5. Ping **the far side of the router by entering the following (optional):**

```
ping ip_address_of_far_side_of_the__router
```

Because the router has an interface for both of the networks it is connecting, you can ping the far side of the router to determine whether the router is correctly passing packets across to the remote network. If pinging a remote host fails, you can't be certain whether the problem is with the router or with the host itself. Therefore, you have one more step.

6. Ping **the IP address of a host on a remote network to verify that you can communicate across the router.**

```
ping host_name_of_remote_host
```

By pinging the IP address of the host, you eliminate the possibility of a host name resolution problem. Use the host name when pinging if you are, in fact, trying to determine whether such a problem exists. (Chapter 15 presents more information on host name resolution problems and how to troubleshoot them.)

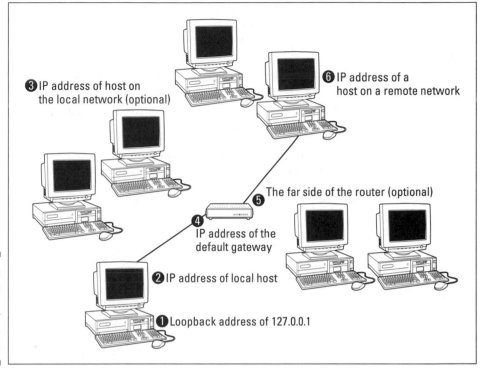

❸ IP address of host on
   the local network (optional)

❻ IP address of a
   host on a remote network

The far side of the router (optional)

❺

❹
IP address of the
default gateway

❷ IP address of local host

❶ Loopback address of 127.0.0.1

Figure 16-1:
An example
of the ping
order for
trouble-
shooting.

Pinging the host name should not be used as a replacement for pinging the IP address. If the IP address fails, then you should consider using the ping sequence in Lab 16-1, because connectivity is definitely a problem.

If the ping command fails at any step in the pinging process, a number of reasons may be to blame for the failure. In order to determine which one it is, verify the following:

✔ Make sure the computer was restarted after TCP/IP was installed.

Windows NT has to be restarted for most of the networking changes to adapters and protocols made in the Network window of the Control Panel to take effect.

✔ Make sure the computer's IP address (if not assigned by DHCP) appears in the TCP/IP Properties dialog box found under Network and that the address is valid.

Verifying the IP address may require the use of the TCP/IP Properties dialog box or the ipconfig command.

✔ If TCP/IP is manually configured, make sure the IP address is unique, and the subnet mask is the same for each host on the subnet. The proper default gateway must be specified so the packets that are destined for a remote network can be routed accordingly.

✔ If the router is a multihomed Windows NT computer, make sure that IP forwarding is enabled.

Enabling IP forwarding is done on the Routing page in the TCP/IP Properties dialog box.

Verifying connectivity from another computer is always helpful in determining whether the problem is specific to just one computer. If a second computer on the network is not having the same problems as the first computer, then you know the problem is specific to the first computer.

Using the ipconfig command to view the current configuration

For the exam, you need to know that the `ipconfig` command displays the required TCP/IP configuration settings: the IP address, subnet mask, and default gateway. If you want more information, you can issue the `ipconfig /all` command, which is an essential command for troubleshooting. The following is an example of the `ipconfig /all` command and its result:

```
C:>\ipconfig /all
Windows NT IP Configuration
Host Name . . . . . . . . . . :
            hcurtis.capstonetechnology.com
DNS Servers . . . . . . . . :
Node Type . . . . . . . . . : Hybrid
NetBIOS Scope ID. . . . . . :
IP Routing Enabled. . . . . : No
WINS Proxy Enabled. . . . . : No
NetBIOS Resolution Uses DNS : No
Ethernet adapter NdisWan4:

Description . . . . . . . . : NdisWan Adapter
Physical Address. . . . . . : 4C-AA-00-BD-5C-B3
DHCP Enabled. . . . . . . . : No
IP Address. . . . . . . . . : 195.112.31.169
Subnet Mask . . . . . . . . : 255.255.255.0
Default Gateway . . . . . . :195.112.31.1
```

The ipconfig /all command displays information for every adapter in a system. This command is especially useful for troubleshooting multihomed computers, such as a Windows NT computer configured as an IP router.

If the ipconfig results from two machines are presented in an exam question, don't panic. Review each set of results separately. The question most likely involves two hosts on different networks that can't communicate. The two computers should have *no* similarities (such as hosts on the same network would have) in terms of their IP address, subnet mask, or default gateway. The source of the problem most likely can be determined from just one host's ipconfig readout. In order to answer the question correctly, ask yourself these questions:

✔ Is the default gateway on the correct network?

✔ Is the subnet mask correct?

✔ Is the IP address valid?

Using the tracert command to verify a route

You may see a question about tracert on the exam. Lucky for you, the utility is fairly simple to use, and the results are pretty straightforward (more information on tracert can be found in Chapter 7). You use the tracert (trace route) utility to trace the route that the packet makes in real time as it travels to its destination, including the routers (hops) it passes along the way. The utility is important for three reasons:

✔ It can determine whether the destination is being reached.

✔ It can determine which router was the last one the packet passed before the transmission failed.

✔ It can determine how long a packet travels between routers.

Using the NETSTAT command to display protocol statistics

The NETSTAT command displays protocol statistics and current TCP/IP connections. The only exam question I've ever heard of that addressed the NETSTAT utility concerned the fact that NETSTAT displays statistics from the time a computer is first booted. Nevertheless, you should know what kind of results you get with the NETSTAT command.

Without parameters, the NETSTAT command doesn't provide much information other than active protocol connections, as shown in the following example:

```
Active Connections
 Proto   Local Address        Foreign Address      State
 TCP     pcbran:1025          localhost:1026       ESTABLISHED
 TCP     pcbran:1026          localhost:1025       ESTABLISHED
```

A number of other parameters can be used with the NETSTAT command to show detailed protocol statistics, but they won't be tested on the exam, so you don't need to worry about them.

Remember: The statistics displayed in the NETSTAT command are from the time the computer was started.

Using the route utility to modify static routes

You can view, add, modify, and delete route entries with the route utility, which changes the routing table on your local computer. (Chapter 4 covers the route utility in more detail, and not just from the troubleshooting perspective.) One component of the route utility you should definitely know for the exam is the route print command, which prints the current routing table for your computer to the screen. Figure 16-2 shows the output from this command.

```
⚙ Shortcut to Cmd.exe                                              _ □ ✕

F:\>route print

Active Routes:

  Network Address          Netmask  Gateway Address        Interface  Metric
        0.0.0.0          0.0.0.0  207.149.40.233     207.149.40.233       1
      127.0.0.0        255.0.0.0        127.0.0.1          127.0.0.1       1
   207.149.40.0    255.255.255.0  207.149.40.233     207.149.40.233       1
 207.149.40.233  255.255.255.255        127.0.0.1          127.0.0.1       1
 207.149.40.255  255.255.255.255  207.149.40.233     207.149.40.233       1
      224.0.0.0        224.0.0.0  207.149.40.233     207.149.40.233       1
255.255.255.255  255.255.255.255  207.149.40.233     207.149.40.233       1
F:\>_
```

Figure 16-2: An example of route print command output.

Within the `route print` information, you can find routes to other networks. If you have trouble communicating with a particular subnet, you should check the output of the `route print` command to determine whether a route to the network exists.

Using the default gateway for routing to remote networks has almost the same effect as using static routing; however, the default gateway is used if none of the routes in a routing table can get a packet to its intended destination. If a path is found in the routing table, the packet is sent and the default gateway is not used. (Static routing is covered in more detail in Chapter 7.)

If you don't have a route to a remote network in the routing table and the packet is still not being sent to its destination, check for the proper default gateway in the TCP/IP configuration.

Prep Test

1 What is the first thing you should do to verify that TCP/IP has initialized correctly?

A ○ Ping your host name.

B ○ Check the Event Viewer.

C ○ Ping your IP address.

D ○ Ping the loopback address.

2 You are trying to contact the host with the IP address 101.88.207.34 named PAdams on a remote network. You get no response. The local host has the IP address 198.21.68.115 and the name Cbrandon, and the default gateway is the IP address 198.21.68.1, with the name Router1. If you ping the default gateway at 198.2168.1 and receive the error Destination net unreachable, what should you do next?

A ○ Ping the host name PAdams.

B ○ Ping the host name Router1.

C ○ Ping the loopback address.

D ○ Ping the IP address 198.21.68.115.

3 If pinging a remote host fails, how can you determine whether the problem is with the remote host or the router?

A ○ Ping the host name of the remote host.

B ○ Ping the far side of the router.

C ○ Ping the near side of the router.

D ○ Ping the IP address of the remote host.

4 Which of the following utilities provides the current TCP/IP connections?

A ○ ipconfig

B ○ nbtstat

C ○ NETSTAT

D ○ ARP

5 If you suspect a duplicate IP address on the network, what can you do?

A ○ Examine the ARP cache.

B ○ Ping both IP addresses.

C ○ Examine the NetBIOS name cache.

D ○ Trace the route to both computers.

6 Which of the following commands displays information from the time the computer was first initialized?

A ○ ARP
B ○ NETSTAT
C ○ nbtstat
D ○ route

7 Which command produced the following output?

```
TCP     pcbran:1025     localhost:1026     ESTABLISHED
```

A ○ NETSTAT
B ○ nbtstat -c
C ○ nbtstat -n
D ○ NETSTAT -s

8 When is the default gateway used?

A ○ Always
B ○ Only when a path is not found in the routing table
C ○ Only when a path in the routing table has been tried and did not work
D ○ Only when the route table is not used

9 Which of the following is a reason that the `ping` command will fail completely? (Choose all that apply.)

A ❏ IP Forwarding is not enabled.
B ❏ The IP address is invalid.
C ❏ DNS or the HOSTS file is not correct.
D ❏ The computer has not been restarted.

10 Which of the following commands can you use to display domain information?

A ○ nbtstat
B ○ nslookup
C ○ ipconfig
D ○ netstat

Answers

1 *D.* Although most of the answers will work, you should `ping` the loopback address to determine whether TCP/IP has initialized correctly. This is the first step in the `ping` process. *Review "Using the ping command to verify connectivity."*

2 *C.* This is an example of how important it is to determine whether TCP/IP has initialized correctly on your host. Keep in mind that you should `ping` a host by its IP address before you use its host name in order to eliminate a potential host name resolution problem. *Review "Using the ping command to verify connectivity."*

3 *B.* By successfully pinging the far side of the router, you determine that the router is capable of passing packets to the remote network. You then proceed by pinging the remote host or any other host on the remote network. *Review "Using the ping command to verify connectivity."*

4 *C.* The `NETSTAT` command displays protocol statistics and current TCP/IP connections from the time the computer was first started. *Review "Using the netstat command to display protocol statistics."*

5 *A.* You can check the contents of the ARP cache for both IP addresses and verify which hardware address is being used for each IP address. `ipconfig / all` gives the hardware addresses. *Review "Identifying the TCP/IP Diagnostic Utilities."*

6 *B.* The only command listed that will display information on TCP/IP protocol statistics since the computer was first initialized is the `NETSTAT` command. *Review "Using the netstat command to display protocol statistics."*

7 *A.* The `NETSTAT` command, without any parameters, provides information on the active connections. *Review "Using the netstat command to display protocol statistics."*

8 *B.* If a path in the routing table has been specified, the information is sent there. Otherwise, the default gateway routes any packets accordingly. *Review "Using the route utility to modify static routes."*

9 *A,B,D.* Although an absence of a DNS or a HOSTS file can cause `ping` to fail, DNS or HOSTS will only affect pinging with the host name. IP addresses will still respond to the `ping` command. *Review "Using the ping command to verify connectivity."*

10 *B.* This command is very helpful for viewing DNS information. Review Chapter 10 for more information on DNS and the `nslookup` utility. *Review "Identifying the TCP/IP Diagnostic Utilities."*

Part VI
The Part of Tens

The 5th Wave — By Rich Tennant

SHERLOCK HOLMES TAKES THE TCP/IP EXAM

Hmm...ELEMENTARY!
Ah, yes...ummm...A HA!
ELEMENTARY! ELEMENTARY!
Now, let's see. Ahhhhh HA!
ELEMENTARY INDEED!!

Gimme a break.

In this part . . .

This part of the book contains top-ten lists of useful information to help you emerge victorious from the TCP/IP exam. Chapter 17 is crammed with proven test-day tips from those in the know — successful TCP/IP test-takers. Those tips include techniques for managing your time during the exam and methods for tackling complex questions. Chapter 18 lists the ten best online exam-preparation resources recommended by MCSEs — including myself!

Chapter 17

Ten Test Day Tips

In This Chapter

▶ Visualize the answer by scratching it out on paper

▶ Jot down those subnetting tables before you begin

▶ Do a last-minute cram with your study notes

▶ Stay cool and you'll do okay

This chapter provides some test-day tips that can give you that extra edge when it finally comes time for your exam. These tips have been compiled from my personal experience, as well as from the experiences of many successful Microsoft test-takers. Keep these tips in mind during the test and try to incorporate them into any Microsoft test you encounter.

Write Down the Possible Choices and Return to the Question Later

If you're not certain of the answer to a particular question, but you've narrowed it down to one of two choices, use the scratch paper they give you to write down the number of the question and the letters for the two possible answers. When you return to the question later, you can immediately pick up your thought process where you left off without having to assess every answer all over again. For example, your scratch paper notes may look something like this:

> 6. <u>A</u> or C?
>
> 22. B or <u>C</u>?
>
> 41. Is this a trick? I think it's B, maybe C.

 I usually underline or use some other way to draw attention to the answer I think is most likely to be correct. Another question you receive down the road can help you in answering that first difficult question, so keep that in mind, too.

Don't Rush — But Don't Dawdle Away Your Time Either

Having a few minutes left to review your answers is better than having to answer ten questions in two minutes. You may think you have enough time to complete the exam and then, whammo, you get a few gigantic scenario-based questions right at the end. Hopefully you won't have to feel the pinch of having to blindly select answers just seconds before the timer expires.

Did you know that even though the timer expires, you can continue working on the question you are on? Keep this in mind if you're on a mind-boggling question that requires plenty of time to answer. If you know a question will take you longer to answer than many of the others, save that one for last, and make sure you're working on it when the timer expires.

Sketch a Layout for the Complex Questions

If you're presented with a text-based scenario that involves a physical layout, draw the layout on scratch paper. While you're drawing, you may have an insight into the solution that you wouldn't have had otherwise. You'll find this technique especially helpful if you're a "visual learner." Make sure to use this technique on questions such as the following one that involve complex routing patterns:

1. You are at host 101.36.118.200, and you would like to connect to host 101.37.143.13. Your local gateway is 101.36.1.1, the subnet mask is 255.255.0.0, and the remote host's gateway is 101.37.1.1 with a subnet mask of 255.255.0.0. What command would you use?

Remember, You Can Use a Calculator!

This is the only Microsoft exam I know of that allows you the privilege of using the Windows calculator. If you've memorized each and every table in this book, you may not need the calculator, but don't count on it.

I didn't use a calculator during my exam, but I did use it at home to find out that each question (if it isn't weighted) is worth 17 points. With a minimum passing mark of 750, that means you can miss up to 14 questions and still pass. With 90 minutes and 58 questions, you can spend 1 minute and 30 seconds per question (or, five minutes on those complex scenario questions). Cool, huh?

Resist the Urge to Go Back and Change Your Answers After You're Done

Studies have shown that following your initial instincts usually produces the right answer. I've found that I tend to fool myself into thinking that I answered the question incorrectly, and then I go back change my (probably correct) answer.

If you do review your answers, make sure you have overwhelming evidence that they aren't correct before you change them. For instance, a question that appears later in the exam may provide you with information that indicates you didn't answer an earlier question correctly. In that case, go ahead and take advantage of this new information and change your response.

Some Questions Pose the Same Problem as Other Questions

One complex scenario question will sometimes present the same problem as another scenario question, but present different solutions to solve the problem. You can spot these questions right off because they're preceded by a blue screen. If you know this, you won't have to read the scenario again for every subsequent question that uses the same problem. Nevertheless, be sure to read the scenario carefully the first time!

Write Down the Subnetting Tables Before the Exam Begins

If you remember just one thing from this chapter, please let it be that you're going to jot down the subnetting charts on scratch paper before the test begins. The few minutes you spend to do this will be well worth it when you need to consult those subnetting charts later on.

I consulted my charts at least a half-dozen times for the subnetting questions. Using the charts takes some of the sting out of these nasty subnet mask questions.

Make Sure You Have Enough Space to Write On

The TCP/IP exam may involve more scribbling to reason out the answers than any other exam you've ever taken. A significant portion of your notes will probably involve the subnetting tables I urge you to memorize throughout this book. You're going to need enough paper or some clean space on the laminated markerboards they give you to write down those tables.

A Tip to Save Some Time on the Scenario Questions

On the scenario questions that include required and optional results, you can save a minute or so if the proposed solution does not meet the *required* results. You don't need to determine if the proposed solution also meets the optional results because there is no answer that says, "Meets some optional results, but not the required results."

If the solution meets the required results, you have to continue on to determine if it meets some of the optional results. If the solution does not meet the required results, just select the answer that says, "The proposed solution does *not* meet the required result or any of the optional results," and move on.

Review Your Notes Right Before the Exam

I always have my best notes in the car with me to review just before the exam. Some people say that if you don't know something by test time, you probably won't ever know it. But I have to disagree. Doing a quick review of the material that's guaranteed to be on the exam just minutes before the exam begins is an excellent strategy. It's also a good time for one more look at those subnetting charts!

Relax!

I understand how difficult these exams can be, especially if you've never taken a Microsoft exam before. Your mind can play tricks on you if you're nervous. Just take a deep breath, let your muscles loosen up, be ready with the information you acquired in this book, and you'll do fine!

Chapter 18

Ten Online Resources

*W*hen studying for MCSE exams, you can probably use all the help you can get, and some of the best resources available for acing your exam can be found on the Internet. There you'll find up-to-date information, as well as forums for sharing information with hundreds of other MCSE hopefuls like yourself. This chapter provides a collection of online resources for your edification and further enlightenment.

mcpmag.com

The best site I've found on the Internet for corresponding with others who have taken the certification tests is at www.mcpmag.com. After you get there, click the FORUMS link. Not only can you communicate with people who are studying for the test just like you are, but you'll also meet others willing to share their test-taking experiences. I visited this site nearly every day while I was studying and found that it helped to keep me on track and focused.

You can also order online back issues of *Microsoft Certified Professional* magazine, which contains test-taking hints, suggestions, and articles relating to the exam you're preparing for. The articles are written by professional certified trainers and engineers who have been exactly where you are. Then, after you've passed the TCP/IP exam, you can post your experiences for others who are preparing to take the test.

Cramsession.com

Of the many sites I've seen on the Internet on exam-related issues, www.cramsession.com has the largest amount of valuable information for last-minute cram sessions. You can use this site when you're just days away from your exam or as a guideline to the exam objectives you need to concentrate on as you study. You can find information not only on the Internetworking TCP/IP on Windows NT 4.0 exam, but also on other popular exams, such as Networking Essentials, NT Workstation, and NT Server.

LearnQuick.com

One site that I visit often for MCSE information is www.learnquick.com, which is the home page of the Accelerated MCSE Training Company. I discovered this page from one of the company's instructors, Herb Martin, who frequents the MCSE newsgroups. Herb has been an invaluable source of information for MCSE hopefuls by providing clear and accurate answers to countless questions. He's also one of the rare few who have scored a perfect 1000 on a Microsoft exam.

This site not only has information about the courses that the LearnQuick company offers, but it also has a Study Help page that contains links to many different topics related to MCSE information and exams, such as software, study guides, and white papers. The Study Help page also has several DNS documents that you may be interested in, as well as Herb's expert introductory comparison of WINS, DNS, and the DHCP server. To access the Study Help page, just click the Study Help link on the site's home page.

MCSE Mailing List

You can subscribe to an MCSE mailing list and receive e-mail, like you do in a forum. But the MCSE mailing list is even better than a forum — the information is compiled and sent to you every day. While you're reading through the various posts and brain-dumps written about the exams, you can compile your own text file for each exam you're preparing to take. Copy important test hints and paste them into your exam-specific document. After a couple of weeks, you can create a sizable document about what to expect on the exam. If you know you're going to take an exam a few months down the road, begin compiling your document now, and you'll have an invaluable resource later on!

To subscribe to the MCSE mailing list, send an e-mail message to majordomo@saluki.com with the following message in the Subject box: SUBSCRIBE mcse <your email address> (for example, SUBSCRIBE mcse cbran@capstonetechnology.com). If you're having any trouble subscribing to the MCSE mailing list, contact the mailing list administrator at saluki@saluki.com.

MCSE Mailing List Archives

If you're just now subscribing to the MCSE mailing list (see the previous section of this chapter), you may be missing some very valuable exam information. To catch up, you can visit the gigantic vault of information that includes the mailing list's archives.

Visit www.saluki.com/mcse_archive/index.html to see hundreds, if not thousands, of messages from users. If you were a member of the mailing list in the past, these messages would have arrived in your e-mail box daily as an easy-to-read digest of 20 to 30 messages.

After the Web page finishes loading, you may have to use your Web browser's Find feature to search for relevant topics, such as *TCP/IP*. After you get some hits, you can bring up the message and read the post. I encourage you to keep a text file for each exam so that you can copy and paste important information into a single handy study aid.

Microsoft Training and Certification

Head directly to *the* source at www.microsoft.com/train_cert for information on new exams, beta exams, and certification requirements. This page is a jump station to other Microsoft resources, such as information on exam objectives and study courses. This is a very important site to monitor if you're interested in taking a beta exam or if you need to find out whether any of your exams are being retired — an event that will require you to update your certification.

Microsoft Training and Certification Downloads

Another site for a number of different downloads — such as exam and course title grids, free self-test software to help you study for the exam, and case studies on how Microsoft Certified Engineer status has made a difference on the job — can be found at the following site:

```
www.microsoft.com/Train_Cert/download/downld.htm
```

The Microsoft self-test software looks exactly like the real test. In fact, the questions from the beta exams that were not included in the final exam are in these tests.

The other self-test software sample available for downloading from the training and certification page at Microsoft is put out by a company called Self Test Software. Although not as close to the real thing as the Microsoft software, it can still reliably determine your strengths and weaknesses. Use the self-test software for a couple of days before your exam to determine your weak areas, or use the software well before the exam date as a guide to the material being tested.

Breeze through Subnet Masking

One of the best resources I've used that helped me understand the concept of subnet masking was an article published by *Microsoft Certified Professional* magazine called "Breeze through Subnet Masking." You can find the article at www.mcpmag.com/members/97mayjun/oe1body.asp.

I spent plenty of time studying this article, and it made me more confident about answering questions on subnet masking — a topic that used to terrify me. Although the Windows NT 4.0 version of the exam doesn't focus on subnet masking as much as its predecessor, you can still expect to be tested on the subject.

Transcender.com

Probably the best self-test software for preparing for the real exam is Transcender exam simulation software. You can purchase Transcender software on the Web at www.transcender.com. These exams are very challenging, almost more challenging than the real Microsoft tests! For each question there's an in-depth explanation of the correct answer. As with most self-test software, you can use it to determine your weak areas a few days before the exam so you know what to cram for, or use it as a guideline early on to plan your studying.

Although the Transcender software is very helpful for becoming certified, it is expensive. As of this writing, individual simulated exams cost $179, and a package of just about every simulation product you could want is $999.

And one excellent subscription resource: TechNet

If you're not already using Microsoft's Technical Information Network (TechNet), then you should get your hands on a copy. This monthly subscription CD is packed with information on Microsoft products and technologies. It also includes resource kits that you would otherwise have to buy individually. Being able to access loads of useful and relevant information instantly is the most important feature of this product. I've used it for nearly every test I have taken.

You receive one copy of TechNet when you become a certified professional on a Windows operating system. You get a year's subscription when you become a certified engineer. Microsoft automatically mails you the copies that you earn by passing the exams.

Part VII
Appendixes

The 5th Wave   By Rich Tennant

"I assume you'll be forward thinking enough to allow '.dog' as a valid domain name."

In this part . . .

The name of this part may be "Appendixes," but I wouldn't be surprised if you turned here first for some real juicy (and useful) stuff. Included are two sample exams such as you'll see come test time — nearly 40 pages of questions and answers to test your TCP/IP knowledge. You also find an appendix of requirements for Microsoft Certified Professional status and an appendix telling you about the contents of the companion CD — which includes demo tests, a collection of test tips from the book, and an incredibly cool game.

Appendix A

Practice Exam 1

● ●

Practice Exam Rules

▶ You have 90 minutes to complete this exam

▶ This exam has 50 questions

▶ You must answer 38 questions correctly to pass

● ●

1 To which address class does the IP address of 191.31.45.197 belong?

A ○ Class A

B ○ Class B

C ○ Class C

D ○ Class D

2 You must subnet your network with five networks and you have a Class C IP address of 201.23.87.117. You have a few small groups of independent engineers, with no more than 20 per group. Which subnet mask should you use?

A ○ 255.255.255.240

B ○ 255.255.255.248

C ○ 255.255.255.0

D ○ 255.255.255.224

3 What is the correct syntax for the `route` command to reach a remote network of 202.37.112.0, with a subnet mask of 255.255.255.0, that uses the gateway of 202.37.112.1?

A ○ `ROUTE ADD 202.37.112.1 255.255.255.0 202.37.112.0`

B ○ `ROUTE ADD 202.37.112.0 255.255.255.0 202.37.112.0`

C ○ `ROUTE ADD 202.37.112.0 MASK 255.255.255.0 202.37.112.1`

D ○ `ROUTE ADD 202.37.112.1 MASK 255.255.255.0 202.37.112.1`

4 What is the function of the UDP protocol?

A ○ It provides connection-oriented data delivery.

B ○ It provides connectionless-oriented data delivery.

C ○ It provides error-checking functions.

D ○ It provides routing functions.

5 A packet is being routed from host1 to a host on a remote network called host2. It will pass router1 and router2 along the way. ARP has just obtained the hardware addresses before the packet is sent. Which addresses has ARP obtained?

A ○ host1, host2

B ○ host2, router1

C ○ host1, router2

D ○ host1, router1

6 What is the difference between the ARP cache and the routing table?

A ○ You can't add static entries to the ARP cache.

B ○ You can't modify static entries in the routing table.

C ○ The static entries in the ARP cache can be updated automatically.

D ○ The dynamic entries in the routing table can't be modified.

7 In the host name resolution process, what is checked after the DNS server is queried?

A ○ WINS server

B ○ NetBIOS name cache

C ○ HOSTS file

D ○ Broadcast

8 Which of the following is not one of the first three sources that is checked during the host name resolution process? (Choose all that apply.)

A ❑ WINS server

B ❑ DNS server

C ❑ HOSTS file

D ❑ Local host name

9 You have entered the following entry into your HOSTS file:

```
127.13.76.183          SOCKS      socks
```

You put the file in the winnt\system32\drivers\etc directory. You try to ping the host, and you receive an error. What is the problem?

A ○ The syntax is wrong.

B ○ The file is in the wrong directory.

C ○ Two host names are specified.

D ○ The problem isn't related to the HOSTS file.

10 Which NetBIOS node type needs to have LMHOSTS `lookup` enabled in order to work?

A ○ b-node

B ○ h-node

C ○ enhanced b-node

D ○ m-node

11 What is the last step in the NetBIOS name resolution order?

A ○ WINS server

B ○ LMHOSTS

C ○ Broadcasts

D ○ DNS server

12 Which of the following is the correct syntax for the `#DOM` keyword in the HOSTS file?

A ○ `110.27.211.13      aceshigh      #PRE #DOM:ENGINEERING`

B ○ `110.27.211.13      aceshigh      #PRE:ENGINEERING`

C ○ `110.27.211.13      aceshigh      #DOM:ENGINEERING`

D ○ None of the above.

13 Which of the following is optional when configuring your DHCP server?(Check all that apply.)

A ❑ Lease duration

B ❑ Excluding addresses

C ❑ Reserving addresses

D ❑ Setting router, DNS, and WINS options

14 Which of the following statements concerning DHCP scope options is not correct?

A ○ The global options can be overridden by the scope options.

B ○ The scope options can be overridden by the client.

C ○ The global options can be overridden by the client.

D ○ All of the above are correct.

15 Which is the default DHCP option code for WINS/NBNS servers?

A ○ 042

B ○ 044

C ○ 046

D ○ 016

16 What is the most effective method of fault tolerance for DHCP servers?

A ○ Have all DHCP servers on one subnet with one scope for all servers.

B ○ Have all DHCP servers on one subnet with different scopes.

C ○ Have a DHCP server on each subnet, with one scope for all servers.

D ○ Have a DHCP server on each subnet, with different scopes.

17 You are configuring an enterprise network to use WINS instead of LMHOSTS. You have four cities that will be connected: Dallas, Seattle, Las Vegas, and Portland. The corporate headquarters is located in Portland. Here is a list of the required and optional results you should accomplish:

Required results: Bandwidth usage must be controlled.

Optional results: Fault tolerance should be in effect. Reduce logon authentication times for the cities.

Proposed Solution: Configure a primary WINS server in Portland, with secondary WINS servers in Dallas, Seattle, and Las Vegas, and an additional secondary WINS server in Portland.

Which of the following is true?

A ○ The proposed solution produces the required result and produces both of the optional desired results.

B ○ The proposed solution produces the required result and produces only one of the optional desired results.

C ○ The proposed solution produces the required results but does not produce any of the optional desired result.

D ○ The proposed solution does not produce the required result.

18 Which of the following is not true of static mappings for WINS?

A ○ They are required for non-WINS clients.

B ○ They are added in the WINS Manager under Static Mappings.

C ○ They are used to reserve IP addresses for hosts.

D ○ Different types of static mappings exist.

19 What is the actual database for DNS?

A ○ Domain

B ○ Domain Name Space

C ○ Zone

D ○ Cache file

20 Which server is the most important on a DNS domain?

A ○ Master

B ○ Primary

C ○ Browse master

D ○ Secondary

21 What is the default node type for a Windows NT client using WINS?

A ○ p-node

B ○ h-node

C ○ m-node

D ○ enhanced b-node

22 You are trying to communicate with another host on the same network but you have failed. You display the `ipconfig` results for both of the computers involved:

```
Computer1: IP Address = 204.43.112.17; Subnet Mask =
           255.255.240.0; Default Gateway = 204.43.112.1
Computer2: IP Address = 204.43.12.145; Subnet Mask =
           255.255.240.0; Default Gateway = 204.43.112.1
```

What appears to be the problem?

A ○ Computer1 has an incorrect subnet mask.

B ○ Computer2 has an incorrect default gateway.

C ○ Computer2 has an incorrect IP address.

D ○ None of the above.

23 You have a Class C address of 197.25.26.81 that you're going to subnet. You're trying to create at least ten subnets, each with eight to ten process control servers, with room for a few more. Which subnet mask should you use?

A ○ 224

B ○ 240

C ○ 248

D ○ 252

24 You have just configured your network with SNMP. Previously, `Engineering` was used as the community name, but now the community name is `Central`. You are no longer able to contact every host on the network for information. What is most likely the problem?

A ○ The missing hosts aren't configured as trap hosts.

B ○ The missing hosts are configured as trap hosts.

C ○ The missing hosts have no community name specified.

D ○ The missing hosts have the old community name specified.

25 What is the `SNMPUTIL` utility used for?

A ○ To contact a trap agent

B ○ To pass silent trap messages

C ○ To mimic the management console messages

D ○ To analyze MIBs

26 If you have three subnets with 500 hosts per subnet, what is the Microsoft-recommended number of WINS proxy agents for the three subnets?

A ○ 1

B ○ 2

C ○ 3

D ○ 4

27 How can SNMP be configured to allow only one server to query the agents for information?

A ○ Configure the client to accept messages from only those servers

B ○ Configure the clients to send trap messages to only those servers

C ○ Set up one community

D ○ Remove the public default community

28 Which of the following is a diagnostic command? (Choose all that apply.)

A ❑ ARP

B ❑ rsh

C ❑ netstat

D ❑ hostname

29 What must be done prior to using the LPQ command to view TCP/IP print queues?

A ○ A share must be made for the printer.

B ○ The server must have TCP/IP printing installed.

C ○ The print server must share the TCP/IP printer.

D ○ Nothing needs to be done on the server.

30 You are considering installing a WINS server on the network to replace the LMHOSTS files. You have two subnets and non-WINS clients. Which of the following should you consider?(Choose all that apply.)

A ❑ Having one primary WINS server per subnet for fault tolerance

B ❑ Installing a WINS proxy on each subnet

C ❑ Having a secondary WINS server on a remote subnet

D ❑ Leaving LMHOSTS intact for backup

31 You are going to configure your network clients to use DHCP. Your network has one subnet, a WINS server, a DNS server, and various non-Microsoft clients. What is the minimum configuration that is required for the DHCP clients in this situation?

A ○ IP address and subnet mask

B ○ IP address, subnet mask, and default gateway

C ○ IP address, subnet mask, WINS, and DNS information

D ○ IP address, subnet mask, default gateway, WINS, and DNS information

32 A packet is routed to a host on a remote subnet. The packet must cross one router on the way to this host. How many times is the ARP cache on all computers consulted for this trip?

A ○ 1
B ○ 2
C ○ 3
D ○ 4

33 Where do you specify the IP address of the DNS server on a Windows NT machine?

A ○ In the DNS server portion of the DNS tab
B ○ In the DNS Service Search Order portion of the DNS tab
C ○ In the DNS Suffix Search Order portion of the DNS tab
D ○ In the DNS IP Address portion of the DNS tab

34 When does the DHCP client attempt to renew with any DHCP server?

A ○ After 96 hours have passed
B ○ After 50 percent of the lease time has passed
C ○ After 87.5 percent of the lease time has passed
D ○ If the original DHCP server is not reached after 50 percent of the lease time has passed

35 What is the best way to determine whether TCP/IP is functioning on a remote computer?

A ○ Ping the remote computer.
B ○ Trace the route to the remote computer.
C ○ On the remote computer, trace the route to another computer.
D ○ On the remote computer, ping another computer.

36 Which of the following statements is true regarding TCP/IP printing? (Choose all that apply.)

A ❑ Microsoft requires LPR to be installed on the print server in order to accept print requests from clients.
B ❑ The LPQ command requires TCP/IP printing to be installed on the computer.
C ❑ Windows NT clients do not require TCP/IP to be installed to print to TCP/IP printers.
D ❑ UNIX hosts can print to a Windows NT server that is running the LPD service.

37 You try to start an FTP session with the computer named Hcurtis, but you receive a `Bad IP address Hcurtis` error. Which of the following is *not* the cause?

A ○ The HOSTS file contains an incorrect mapping.

B ○ The DNS server is down.

C ○ WINS is not configured on the client.

D ○ The DNS database contains an outdated mapping.

38 Which protocol does the `ping` command use?

A ○ SNMP

B ○ ICMP

C ○ TCP

D ○ None of the above

39 You have a new server for which you want to enter an IP address manually in DHCP. You have found out that the address you want to use is already in use. What is the quickest way to make this IP address available?

A ○ Enter the command `ipconfig/release <ip_address>` from the DHCP server.

B ○ Decrease the lease time to zero to release the address.

C ○ Enter the command `ipconfig/release` or `IPCONFIG /RELEASE <ip_address>` from the client.

D ○ Enter the command `ipconfig/release` or `IPCONFIG /RELEASE` from the DHCP server.

40 Which of the following is not required for the DHCP scope?

A ○ Scope name

B ○ Range of IP addresses

C ○ Subnet mask

D ○ Duration of the lease

41 You have a non-WINS client on the network for which you need to add a static mapping. After you add the mapping in the WINS database, you realize that it was already in the LMHOSTS file. What will happen when the host is initialized on the network?

A ○ The mapping in the WINS database will be used.

B ○ The mapping in the existing LMHOSTS file will be used.

C ○ An error will be produced.

D ○ None of the above.

42 You are trying to connect to the FTP server with the `powerslave` host name, and you can't. You think you have a host name resolution problem. You use LMHOSTS and HOSTS on your network but not DNS. You found a mapping for the host in the HOSTS file as follows:

```
134.76.91.201              Powerslave
```

What is most likely the problem?

A ○ The syntax of the HOSTS file is incorrect.

B ○ The file is in the wrong directory.

C ○ The file has not been loaded into cache.

D ○ The file is case-sensitive.

43 What does it mean when the route table has the number 2 in the results?

A ○ There are two routes to this host.

B ○ The route has been added manually.

C ○ The route has been deduced from RIP updates.

D ○ None of the above.

44 How can you control the database replication for WINS partners?

A ○ You have to adjust the interval at which pull partners request information.

B ○ You have to adjust the interval at which push partners send information.

C ○ You have to edit the Registry.

D ○ You have to manually replicate information for WINS partners.

45 Which of the following is not a component of the WINS database?

A ○ Winstmp.mdb

B ○ J50.log

C ○ J50.dll

D ○ Wins.mdb

46 Which command produced the following output?

```
CBRANDON            <03>  UNIQUE      Registered
```

A ○ `nbtstat -s`

B ○ `nbtstat -c`

C ○ `nbtstat -n`

D ○ `nbtstat -m`

47 What is known as a virtual server?

A ○ A server that contains two or more network interface cards.

B ○ A server that has more than one domain name assigned to a network interface card.

C ○ A server that has more than one NetBIOS name assigned to a network interface card.

D ○ A server that has more than one Internet service bound to a network interface card.

48 For security with a PPTP connection, the data should be encrypted. How do you configure the connection to pass encrypted information?

A ○ On the Server page of the Dial-Up Networking window, you check the Require Encrypted Information check box.

B ○ On the Server page of the Dial-Up Networking window, you check the Use only Microsoft Encrypted Information check box.

C ○ You don't have to configure encryption for the PPTP connection.

D ○ None of the above.

49 Which of the following is the most secure way to connect to an FTP server?

A ○ Allow only encrypted information.

B ○ Require Microsoft CHAP authentication at logon.

C ○ Use only anonymous access.

D ○ Require every user to have a valid user name and password.

50 You are planning to install Windows NT for a firm that has four remote offices. Each remote office will be a member of the ICEDEARTH domain. They want a Windows NT Server for each remote subnet, with WINS and DHCP. However, they have only three servers. How should you configure the network to accommodate their needs?

A ○ Have a Windows NT Server at three of the remote offices and configure a WINS Relay Agent on the remote subnet without the WINS server.

B ○ Have a Windows NT Server at three of the remote offices and configure a DHCP Relay Agent on the remote subnet without the DHCP server.

C ○ Have a Windows NT Server at three of the remote offices and configure a separate pool of DHCP addresses on each of the three DHCP servers. Configure a DHCP Relay Agent on the remote subnet without the DHCP server.

D ○ Have a Windows NT Server at three of the remote offices and configure the DHCP servers to be push and pull partners of each other. Configure a DHCP Relay Agent on the remote subnet without the DHCP server.

Answers

1 *B.* The B address class starts at 128.x.x.x and extends to 191.x.x.x. *Objective: Diagnosing and resolving IP addressing problems (Chapter 6)*

2 *D.* This subnet mask gives you a total of six subnets, which leaves you one subnet for future expansion. You have only 30 hosts available on each subnet, which will work fine for your small number of engineers per subnet. *Objective: Configuring subnet masks (Chapter 6)*

3 *C.* Remember the phrase "To get to the destination network, use this router. . . ." Using the example in the question, this phrase means that in order to get to the 202.37.112.0 network, you need to use the router interface of 202.37.112.1. *Objective: Configuring a Windows NT Server computer to function as an IP router (Chapter 7)*

4 *B.* The UDP protocol, as opposed to the TCP protocol, is a connectionless data delivery system that is used for utilities such as TFTP. *(Chapter 2)*

5 *D.* ARP is used to determine the hardware address of the source host and the next router (router1 in this case), if the destination is remote. This information is appended to the TCP/IP packet. *(Chapter 3)*

6 *C.* A manually static entry in the ARP cache can be updated dynamically if a new address is found. You can't dynamically update a static routing table entry. *Objective: Configuring a Windows NT Server computer to function as an IP router (Chapter 7)*

7 *B.* After the DNS server fails to resolve the host name, the NetBIOS name cache is consulted for a resolution. After the name cache is checked, the WINS server is queried. *Objective: Diagnosing and resolving name resolution problems (Chapter 15)*

8 *B,C,D.* The first three sources checked in the host name resolution order are the local host name, HOSTS file, and DNS. This is referred to as a standard resolution, rather than a specific resolution. *Objective: Diagnosing and resolving name resolution problems (Chapter 15)*

9 *D.* The IP address begins with 127, which is not used for hosts on a network. This is either a typo, or you're trying to use an invalid IP address for the host. *Objective: Diagnosing and resolving IP addressing problems (Chapter 6)*

10 *C.* Enhanced b-node uses the LMHOSTS file if a broadcast is unable to resolve the NetBIOS name. *Objective: Diagnosing and resolving name resolution problems (Chapter 15)*

11 *D.* The last four steps for NetBIOS name resolution are LMHOSTS, local host name, HOSTS, and then the DNS server is queried. *Objective: Diagnosing and resolving name resolution problems (Chapter 15)*

12 *D.* The #DOM keyword is used in the LMHOSTS file, not the HOSTS file. *Objective: Configuring LMHOSTS files (Chapter 9)*

13 *B,C,D.* Lease duration, along with creating the scope of addresses, is not optional when configuring your DHCP server. The lease duration and address scope are required. *(Chapter 8)*

14 *D.* Global options apply for all scopes but can be overridden by scope options. Manually configured client configurations can override both the global options and the scope options. *(Chapter 8)*

15 *B.* The default scope option code for WINS/NBNS servers is 044. The subnet mask and router scope option codes are 001 and 003, respectively. *Objective: Installing and configuring a WINS server (Chapter 9)*

16 *D.* DHCP servers should have separate address scopes if more than one DHCP server is being used because a DHCP server doesn't know which addresses have already been assigned by the other servers. *(Chapter 8)*

17 *D.* WINS servers configured as primary and secondary servers must be configured as push and pull partners to each other. Because of this, you can't control when database replications occur over the WAN link. *Objective: Configuring WINS replication (Chapter 9)*

18 *A.* When you have non-WINS clients on the network, either a WINS proxy must be used or a mapping in the host's LMHOSTS file for the WINS server must be present. *Objective: Installing and configuring a WINS server (Chapter 9)*

19 *C.* A zone is an actual database, which can be managed for a whole domain or just portions of the domain. It doesn't have to contain the entire domain hierarchy. *Objective: Installing and configuring DNS on a Windows NT Server computer (Chapter 10)*

20 *B.* The primary server is the most important server in the DNS domain. A master server transfers zone information to the secondary servers when they initialize in the zone. *Objective: Configuring DNS server roles (Chapter 10)*

21 *B.* H-node directly contacts the WINS server first, and then it tries broadcasts if the WINS server can't be reached. *Objective: Diagnosing and resolving name resolution problems (Chapter 15)*

22 *C.* It appears that Computer2 is supposed to have an IP address of 204.43.112.145, but a 1 is missing in the third octet. *Objective: Diagnosing and resolving IP addressing problems (Chapter 6)*

23 *B.* The subnet mask of 255.255.255.240 creates 14 subnets with 14 available hosts per subnet. This setup gives you enough subnets, with a small amount of room for growth on each subnet. *Objective: Configuring subnet masks (Chapter 6)*

24 *D.* Messages are only processed between the server and the client if the message is sent from a source that corresponds to an entry in the client's list of community names. *Objective: Configuring SNMP (Chapter 11)*

25 *C.* Because Windows NT doesn't have the capability to function as a management console, the SNMPUTIL utility is used to mimic the management console to test your SNMP configuration. *Objective: Configuring SNMP (Chapter 11)*

26 *C.* You should have only one WINS proxy per subnet, regardless of the number of clients per subnet. *Objective: Installing and configuring a WINS server (Chapter 9)*

27 *A.* You can enter the IP address or host name of the SNMP hosts that you will only accept requests from, rather than accepting SNMP packets from any host. ***Remember:*** This arrangement is recommended for a higher degree of security. *Objective: Configuring SNMP (Chapter 11)*

28 *A,C,D.* The Remote Shell utility enables you to run commands on the remote server at the command prompt. RSH is considered a connectivity utility, not a diagnostic utility. *Objective: Identifying which utility to use to connect to a TCP/IP-based UNIX host (Chapter 13)*

29 *B.* The server requires the TCP/IP printing service to be installed, even if the workstation is just viewing the contents of the TCP/IP queue. *Objective: Configuring a Windows NT Server computer to support TCP/IP printing (Chapter 13)*

30 *B,C,D.* Having more than one primary WINS server on a network isn't possible. You should configure your network with one primary server, at least one secondary server, and WINS proxies for each subnet. Leaving the LMHOSTS file as a backup is also a great idea. *Objective: Configuring WINS replication (Chapter 9)*

31 *A.* The IP address and subnet mask are all that are ever required for the DHCP client. In a multisubnet situation, you should configure the DHCP clients with a default gateway. *(Chapter 8)*

32 *C.* The ARP cache is consulted on the source host when the packet is being constructed, on the router when the destination host hardware address must be determined, and on the destination host when the packet is being sent back to the originating host. *Objective: Diagnosing and resolving IP addressing problems (Chapter 15)*

33 *B.* In the DNS Service Search Order portion of the DNS tab is where you can enter more than one DNS server, but any other servers aren't used unless the primary DNS server is not reachable. *Objective: Integrating DNS with other name servers (Chapter 10)*

34 *C.* After 50 percent of the lease time has expired, the client attempts to renew with the original DHCP server. After 87.5 percent of the lease time has expired, the client attempts to renew with any DHCP server. *Objective: Configuring scopes by using DHCP Manager (Chapter 8)*

35 *D.* Although all the methods described work, the quickest and surest way to determine whether the remote computer has TCP/IP functioning correctly is to ping another computer from that same computer. *Objective: Identifying which utility to use in diagnosing IP configuration problems (Chapter 16)*

36 *B,C,D.* In order to accept print requests from clients, you need to have the LPD service running on the Windows NT machine — also known as the Microsoft TCP/IP Printing service. *Objective: Configuring a Windows NT Server computer to support TCP/IP printing (Chapter 13)*

37 *C.* When you're experiencing a host name resolution problem, you should check anything having to do with the HOSTS file or DNS. *Objective: Diagnosing and resolving name resolution problems (Chapter 15)*

38 *B.* The ping command uses Internet Control Message Protocol (ICMP) packets to test for connectivity between hosts. *Objective: Identifying which utility to use in diagnosing IP configuration problems (Chapter 16)*

39 *C.* This command immediately releases the address. Configure the server to use this address and exclude it from the pool if possible, or just reserve the address for this server. *Objective: Configuring scopes by using DHCP Manager (Chapter 8)*

40 *A.* The scope name, surprisingly enough, is not required when creating the DHCP scope. The scope must be created before the clients are able to receive TCP/IP configuration information from the DHCP server. *Objective: Configuring scopes by using DHCP Manager (Chapter 8)*

41 *A.* The WINS server is queried before the LMHOSTS file is parsed, so after the computer is found in the WINS database, the process stops there. You must make sure that the mapping is correct in the WINS database for this reason. *Objective: Configuring static mappings in the WINS database (Chapter 9)*

42 *D.* Remember: The HOSTS file is case-sensitive, but the LMHOSTS file is not. The HOSTS file was derived from UNIX, which is a case-sensitive operating system. *Objective: Configuring LMHOSTS files (Chapter 9)*

43 *C.* The metric of 2 means that the router has obtained the route from exchanging dynamic update information with other routers. *Objective: Configuring a Windows NT Server computer to function as an IP router (Chapter 7)*

44 *A.* With push partners, you can't control when they send information to the pull partners. With pull partners, you can specify when they are to request information from the push partner, which makes pull partners ideal for use over slower WAN links. *Objective: Configuring WINS replication (Chapter 9)*

45 *C.* The J50.dll file doesn't exist, but the transaction file of J50#####.log does, and it constitutes the fifth member of the WINS database. *Objective: Installing and configuring a WINS server (Chapter 9)*

46 *C.* The result of the command is the names of all the hosts that have been registered to the local host. The `nbtstat -c` command displays the names of the other hosts that have been resolved on your machine. *Objective: Diagnosing and resolving name resolution problems (Chapter 15)*

47 *B.* A WWW Virtual Server can also contain more than one IP address assigned to a network interface card. The domain name is optional. *(Chapter 14)*

48 *D.* Use of the PPP protocol, which is required for the PPTP connection, creates a secure channel, but you must still specify "Accept only encrypted authentication" or "Accept only Microsoft encrypted authentication" in order to take advantage of encryption between the two hosts. *Objective: Configuring a RAS server and dial-up networking for use on a TCP/IP network (Chapter 14)*

49 *C.* The most secure way to access an FTP server is through anonymous access. With anonymous access, your user name and password can't be stolen while they are traveling across the network. *(Chapter 14)*

50 *B.* Although the WINS service is able to cross subnets without the use of a relay agent, the DHCP service requires a DHCP Relay Agent to forward the DHCP requests from the remote subnet without a DHCP server to the subnet containing the DHCP server. *Objective: Installing and configuring the DHCP Relay Agent (Chapter 8)*

Appendix B
Practice Exam 2

Practice Exam Rules

▶ You have 90 minutes to complete this exam

▶ This exam has 50 questions

▶ You must answer 38 questions correctly to pass

1 To which address class does the IP address of 191.31.45.197 belong?

A ○ Class A
B ○ Class B
C ○ Class C
D ○ Class D

2 What is the decimal representation of 11110000?

A ○ 242
B ○ 240
C ○ 248
D ○ 252

3 Which of following uses an SOA?

A ○ DHCP
B ○ DNS
C ○ WINS
D ○ RAS

4 You're configuring a RAS server for routing to the Internet. The IP address for its LAN adapter is 136.76.24.119, and its IP address for the Internet adapter is 196.43.81.200. The default gateway for the Internet adapter is 196.43.81.1. What should you specify for the IP address of the LAN adapter's default gateway?

A ○ 196.43.81.1
B ○ 196.43.81.200
C ○ 136.76.24.119
D ○ No address

5 You're helping the network administrator with some computer configuration. You have a sheet of paper that lists the default gateways and subnet masks for the various subnets on the network. You don't know which subnet this computer will be placed on, but you do have the IP address that it will be given, which is 205.21.86.116. Which is the correct subnet?

A ○ Default gateway = 205.21.13.76, subnet mask = 255.255.255.0

B ○ Default gateway = 205.21.86.12, subnet mask = 255.255.255.0

C ○ Default gateway = 205.21.37.113, subnet mask = 255.255.255.0

D ○ Default gateway = 205.21.116.58, subnet mask = 255.255.255.0

6 Which protocol does not guarantee that the data will arrive in order, if it arrives at all?

A ○ NetBEUI

B ○ IP

C ○ FTP

D ○ TFTP

7 What must be done prior to creating a domain?

A ○ You must pay a fee to InterNIC.

B ○ You need to configure DNS properties for the client.

C ○ A top-level domain must be created.

D ○ A zone must be created.

8 What is the only way you can configure a DHCP server to update another DHCP server according to the addresses that have previously been assigned?

A ○ Specify the second DHCP server's IP address as the replication partner.

B ○ Configure both servers to replicate with Windows NT Replication, and place the database file in the export directory.

C ○ Edit the Registry.

D ○ You can't configure a DHCP server to do this.

9 Which utility should you use to determine how many IP packets are being sent versus UDP packets?

A ○ netstat

B ○ Network Monitor

C ○ Performance Monitor

D ○ nbtstat

10 You are configuring two WINS servers — one in Maryland and one in Virginia. Database updates should be immediate in Maryland. A WAN link connects the two cities. How should you configure the WINS servers?

A ○ Maryland = Push, Virginia = Pull

B ○ Maryland = Pull, Virginia = Push

C ○ Maryland = Push, Pull, Virginia = Pull

D ○ Maryland = Push, Pull, Virginia = Push, Pull

11 You want to configure your network to use a DNS server for Windows resolution. How do you do this?

    A ○ Add an entry in the HOSTS file for the WINS server.

    B ○ Click the check box for Enable DNS for Windows Resolution.

    C ○ Enable WINS Lookup.

    D ○ Add an entry in the LMHOSTS file for the DNS server.

12 How can you configure a group of computers to *not* be visible on the same network as other computers?

    A ○ DHCP ID.

    B ○ Deny access to all computers and grant access to those you want to include.

    C ○ NetBIOS Scope ID.

    D ○ WINS Scope ID.

13 Your network is configured with DHCP, and your clients receive WINS, DNS, and router information from the DHCP server. A few clients receive error messages when they are using FTP. Everything else appears fine. What could be the problem? (Choose all that apply.)

    A ❑ They have incorrect manually configured DNS settings.

    B ❑ No mappings exist in the HOSTS file.

    C ❑ The HOSTS file is in the wrong directory.

    D ❑ The DNS server IP address received from the DHCP server is incorrect.

14 You `ping` the computer named HCurtis and receive the response `Destination net unreachable`. Which of the following is most likely the problem? (Choose all that apply.)

    A ❑ The destination computer is down.

    B ❑ You don't have a DNS server specified.

    C ❑ TCP/IP hasn't initialized on this client.

    D ❑ You don't have an IP address.

15 Which layer provides frame sequencing, error detection, and acknowledgments?

    A ○ The Transport Layer

    B ○ The Internet Layer

    C ○ The Network Layer

    D ○ The Session Layer

16 Which is often used to host FTP and WWW servers on the same machine using pointers?

    A ○ Virtual Servers

    B ○ Multihomed computers

    C ○ The CNAME records

    D ○ Binding more than one IP address to a network interface card

17 Where do you specify which Master server the DNS information can be downloaded from?

A ○ DNS properties
B ○ The HOSTS file
C ○ The cache file
D ○ The Boot file

18 You have a multihomed Windows NT server that connects two networks. One network has 33 hosts, and the other network has 212 hosts. What is the minimum number of IP addresses required?

A ○ 245
B ○ 246
C ○ 247
D ○ 248

19 Which of the following is a valid octet for a subnet mask?

A ○ 242
B ○ 244
C ○ 250
D ○ 252

20 How can you configure a non-WINS client to use a WINS proxy?

A ○ Add a mapping in the HOSTS file.
B ○ Add a mapping in the LMHOSTS file.
C ○ Configure the WINS proxy.
D ○ You don't have to configure the non-WINS client.

21 You turn off your machine at night when you leave work. In the middle of the night, someone configures his computer to use your IP address. However, his computer is only a Windows 95 computer. What happens next?

A ○ The Windows 95 machine won't be able to take your IP address.
B ○ TCP/IP won't initialize on the Windows 95 machine.
C ○ TCP/IP won't initialize on your host tomorrow morning.
D ○ Neither host will work.

22 You're on a network that uses DNS with the HOSTS file as a backup. One day you change an entry in the HOSTS file but not in the DNS database. What happens when you try to contact this host?

A ○ The entry in the DNS database is used.
B ○ The entry in the HOSTS file is used.
C ○ DNS challenges the host with the existing name to claim the host name.
D ○ You receive an error when the host is contacted.

23 You have installed a RAS server on the network, and it's configured to assign an IP address to the clients automatically. What method of configuring DNS for the clients takes the least amount of effort?

A ○ Add a mapping in the HOSTS file of the clients.

B ○ Configure the Dial-Up Networking DNS settings for the clients.

C ○ Add a mapping in the HOSTS file of the RAS server.

D ○ Configure the RAS server to assign the proper DNS server.

24 Which of the following is part of the WINS name registration query message that is sent to the WINS server? (Choose all that apply.)

A ❑ Hardware address

B ❑ Source IP address

C ❑ NetBIOS name

D ❑ Destination IP address

25 Which of the following is a message to the server from the DHCP client indicating that the offered configuration parameters are invalid?

A ○ Dhcpreject

B ○ Dhcpdecline

C ○ Dhcpnack

D ○ Dhcpnegative

26 Which of the following is true regarding the differences between primary and secondary WINS servers, as opposed to primary and secondary DNS servers? (Choose all that apply.)

A ❑ A primary WINS server is used until it can't be reached.

B ❑ The secondary DNS server requests database information from the primary DNS server.

C ❑ The secondary DNS server is used only when the primary DNS server can't be contacted.

D ❑ A secondary WINS server is used only for fault tolerant purposes.

27 Which of the following queries returns the most complete answer to the requesting client?

A ○ Recursive

B ○ Iterative

C ○ Inverse

D ○ Reverse

28 Which of the following is true of the HOSTS file? (Choose all that apply.)

A ❑ It is case-sensitive.

B ❑ It can contain FQDNs.

C ❑ Entries can be preloaded into cache.

D ❑ A line can contain many host names.

29 Which of the following is correct when using reverse lookup to search for an IP address of 195.112.34.178?

A ◯ 195.112.34.178.in.addr.arpa

B ◯ 178.34.112.195.in.addr.arpa

C ◯ 195.112.34.178.in-addr.arpa

D ◯ 178.34.112.195.in-addr.arpa

30 You have a network with multiple subnets and DNS servers. You're dynamically assigning TCP/IP configurations through DHCP. Which of the following is true regarding non-WINS clients on your network? (Choose all that apply.)

A ❑ You have to add a static mapping.

B ❑ You have to add a WINS proxy on the subnet.

C ❑ You use WINS Manager for static mappings.

D ❑ Non-WINS clients don't require any special configuration in this setting.

31 What must you do in order to use the LMHOSTS file with Windows NT?

A ◯ Place it in the appropriate directory.

B ◯ Click the Import LMHOSTS button in TCP/IP properties.

C ◯ Enable LMHOSTS lookup in TCP/IP properties.

D ◯ Nothing. LMHOSTS is ready to be used.

32 You're at host 192.65.118.21, and you want to connect to host 202.115.66.149. Your local gateway is 192.65.118.1, the subnet mask is 255.255.255.0, and the remote host's gateway is 202.115.66.1 with a subnet mask of 255.255.255.0. What command would you use?

A ◯ `ROUTE ADD 192.65.118.21 MASK 255.255.255.0 192.65.118.1`

B ◯ `ROUTE ADD 202.115.66.149 MASK 255.255.255.0 192.65.118.1`

C ◯ `ROUTE ADD 192.65.118.1 MASK 255.255.255.0 202.115.66.149`

D ◯ `ROUTE ADD 192.65.118.1 MASK 255.255.255.0 192.65.118.21`

33 Which of the following utilities should you use if you think you have a duplicate IP address on the network?

A ◯ `ARP`

B ◯ `netstat`

C ◯ `nbtstat -n`

D ◯ `nbtstat -c`

34 You're having trouble using UNC to connect to a remote host. What is most likely the problem?

   A ○ Host name resolution

   B ○ NetBIOS

   C ○ Address resolution

   D ○ TCP/IP configuration

35 You already have a primary and secondary DNS server on your network. Which type of server should you add next if you're connecting to the Internet?

   A ○ Master server

   B ○ Caching-only server

   C ○ Another primary server

   D ○ Another secondary server

36 You have added another mapping in the HOSTS file for a host that has had its IP address changed. However, when you test the host, you still connect using the old IP address. What could be the problem?

   A ○ You must also change the LMHOSTS mapping for that host.

   B ○ You must restart the computer after changing the HOSTS file.

   C ○ You may have another mapping for the computer in the same HOSTS file.

   D ○ You need to enable HOSTS lookup in TCP/IP properties.

37 What is the increment value for the subnet mask of 224?

   A ○ 32

   B ○ 16

   C ○ 8

   D ○ 4

38 Which NetBIOS over TCP/IP (NetBT) implementation uses b-node (broadcasts) first and then p-node (point-to-point) if the name resolution fails?

   A ○ p-node

   B ○ h-node

   C ○ m-node

   D ○ n-node

39 Which subnet mask should you use if you require at least 40 subnets?

   A ○ 240

   B ○ 248

   C ○ 252

   D ○ 254

40 You want the information found in the NetBIOS name cache to be more consistent. How do you go about making this happen?

A ○ Increase the TTL on the main name server.

B ○ Decrease the TTL on the main name server.

C ○ Increase the extinction parameter in the cache file.

D ○ Decrease the extinction parameter in the cache file.

41 You have two different groups of machines that will have TCP/IP configured differently. One group contains a small number of finance computers, which require access to the DNS server, and the other group contains engineering computers, which require longer leases. How should you fulfill the needs of both groups?

A ○ Create a global option for each group.

B ○ Override the configuration information at the client.

C ○ Create two scopes.

D ○ Configure one global scope and deactivate the DNS server for the engineering group's scope.

42 What should you check first to verify that TCP/IP has initialized correctly on your machine?

A ○ ping your IP address.

B ○ Check the event viewer.

C ○ ping your host name.

D ○ ping the loopback address.

43 With only one IP address, you are configuring a network that requires three subnets. Each of these subnets only contains 15 to 20 process control machines. Which subnet mask should you use?

A ○ 192

B ○ 224

C ○ 240

D ○ 248

44 You have just installed DHCP on a Windows NT Primary Domain Controller. What must you do next to ensure that clients can receive TCP/IP information from this computer?

A ○ Enable IP Forwarding

B ○ Configure the replication partners

C ○ Configure the HOSTS file

D ○ Nothing

45 Where do you enable PPTP filtering in Windows NT 4?

A ○ The Routing page of the TCP/IP Properties dialog box

B ○ By clicking the Advanced button on the IP Address page of the TCP/IP Properties dialog box

C ○ By clicking the Advanced button on the Routing page of the TCP/IP Properties dialog box

D ○ The Server page in the Dial-Up Networking Properties dialog box for the client

46 What if the name registration database contains a different IP address for the computer name when a NetBIOS name is being registered?

A ○ The WINS server rejects the new name registration request.

B ○ The WINS server overrides the existing name.

C ○ The existing computer is challenged.

D ○ The existing computer has its name modified in the database.

47 After you install DNS, the DNS Manager appears in the Administrative Tools program group. Where are the DNS files placed?

A ○ `<systemroot>\system32\drivers\dns`

B ○ `<systemroot>\system32\dns`

C ○ `<systemroot>\dns`

D ○ `<systemroot>\system32\databases\dns`

48 What is 103.58.221.12(132) an example of?

A ○ A reverse lookup file for the IP address of 103.58.221.12

B ○ A sockets entry

C ○ A NetBIOS mapping for the IP address of 103.58.221.12

D ○ A DHCP database entry

49 What is required for the #include to work with LMHOSTS?

A ○ LMHOSTS Lookup must be enabled.

B ○ The host should have an entry prior to the #include statement.

C ○ The #include line must also have the #PRE keyword in the same line to load it into memory while it searches for the LMHOSTS file.

D ○ None of the above.

50 Which subnet mask gives you the most hosts for a Class B address?

A ○ 224

B ○ 240

C ○ 248

D ○ 252

Answers

1 B. The B address class starts at 128.x.x.x and extends to 191.x.x.x. *(Chapter 6)*

2 B. The octet that is split equally between 1s and 0s is 240 in decimal. 240 is a custom subnet mask, as opposed to a default subnet mask. *Objective: Configuring subnet masks (Chapter 6)*

3 B. The Start of Authority record is the first record in any database file, and it can't be added later like the address and name server records can. *Objective: Installing and configuring DNS on a Windows NT Server computer (Chapter 10)*

4 D. You need to leave the default gateway for the LAN adapter empty so that the packets can make it to the Internet adapter and out to the Internet. *Objective: Configuring TCP/IP on an NT server to support multiple network adapters. (Chapter 7)*

5 B. The default gateway must always be on the network that the host is on. In this case, the default gateway in B was the only gateway on the same network as the host. *Objective: Diagnosing and resolving IP addressing problems (Chapters 6 and 15)*

6 B. The IP protocol, much like the UDP protocol, doesn't guarantee that the packets will arrive in order, if they arrive at all. They rely on other TCP/IP services to reorder and reassemble the packets. *Objective: Diagnosing and resolving IP addressing problems (Chapters 6 and 15)*

7 D. Because zones are how you administer the domain, you have to create a zone before you can create the domain. *Objective: Installing and configuring DNS on a Windows NT Server computer (Chapter 10)*

8 D. One of the only drawbacks to using more than one DHCP server is that the servers can't share database information according to which addresses have previously been assigned. *Objective: Configuring scopes by using DHCP Manager (Chapter 8)*

9 B. Although `netstat` can give you this information, you may find more useful packet monitoring information, including filters and triggers, with the Network Monitor utility. *Objective: Identifying which tool to use to monitor TCP/IP traffic, given a scenario (Chapter 14)*

10 A. Because Virginia is over a slow WAN link, it makes a good candidate for a pull partner that can request updates at certain intervals that you specify. *Objective: Configuring WINS replication (Chapter 9)*

11 B. The WINS Address page in the TCP/IP Properties dialog box has a check box to enable DNS for Windows Resolution. *Objective: Diagnosing and resolving name resolution problems (Chapter 15)*

12 *C.* By entering a value in the NetBIOS Scope ID, you effectively hide your computer from other computers, unless they are configured with the same scope ID. *Objective: Given a scenario, identify valid network configurations (Chapter 6)*

13 *A.* Any client that has manually configured settings overrides the settings that are given to the client from the DHCP server. *(Chapter 8)*

14 *A,B,C.* Most of the time, you receive a `Request timed out` error when contacting a host that doesn't reply. When you receive the `Destination net unreachable` error, you should verify that TCP/IP has been initialized on the computer by pinging the loopback address. *Objective: Using Microsoft TCP/IP utilities to diagnose IP configuration problems (Chapter 16)*

15 *A.* The protocols in this layer, TCP and UDP, make the difference in how the layer inspects the received data or prepares the data to be sent. *Objective: Diagnosing and resolving IP addressing problems (Chapters 6 and 15)*

16 *C.* The CNAME record is short for *Canonical Name,* which is an alias that is used in order to have more than one name point to a host. *Objective: Installing and configuring DNS on a Windows NT Server computer (Chapter 10)*

17 *D.* The Boot file is used to configure the startup configuration of a DNS server. It can point to where required files are found, load cache files, and specify the domain the server is responsible for. *Objective: Installing and configuring DNS on a Windows NT Server computer (Chapter 10)*

18 *C.* In addition to every host on the network, you must include two IP addresses for the multihomed NT computer, one for each interface. *Objective: Configuring TCP/IP on an NT server to support multiple network adapters (Chapter 7)*

19 *D.* The decimal number of 252 equals 11111100 in binary, which is valid for use with a subnet mask to specify the network ID from the host ID. *Objective: Configuring subnet masks (Chapter 6)*

20 *D.* A WINS proxy can be on a remote subnet from the WINS server and listen for name registration requests from the non-WINS clients. *Objective: Installing and configuring a WINS server (Chapter 9)*

21 *C.* If the computer still has your IP address tomorrow morning when you start your computer, Windows NT will detect the duplicate IP address and TCP/IP won't initialize. *Objective: Diagnosing and resolving IP addressing problems (Chapter 15)*

22 *A.* The DNS server is always used before the HOSTS file, so make sure that you update the DNS server first. *Objective: Diagnosing and resolving name resolution problems (Chapter 15)*

23 *D.* The RAS clients inherit the WINS and DNS settings that are configured for the RAS server, which is the easiest way to configure the clients with WINS and DNS. *Objective: Configuring a RAS server and dial-up networking for use on a TCP/IP network (Chapter 14)*

24 *B,C,D.* This registration query includes the source IP address and the NetBIOS name to be registered, along with the destination computer's IP address. *Objective: Installing and configuring a WINS server (Chapter 9)*

25 *B.* This message indicates that the offered configuration parameters are invalid. When you receive a Dhcpnack message, the address can't be used or is no longer valid. *(Chapter 8)*

26 *A,B,D.* A secondary DNS server can participate just as much as the primary DNS server can, unlike the secondary WINS server, which is only used when the primary WINS server is unavailable. *Objective: Integrating DNS with other name servers (Chapter 10)*

27 *A.* A recursive query gets more absolute results because a recursive query requires a response from the server. *Objective: Integrating DNS with other name servers (Chapter 10)*

28 *A,B,D.* HOSTS file entries cannot be loaded into a cache as entries in the LMHOSTS file can. The LMHOSTS file has many more options than the HOSTS file. *Objectives: Configuring HOSTS files* and *Configuring LMHOSTS files (Chapter 9)*

29 *D.* When searching for an IP address rather than a domain name, use the `in-addr.arpa` domain. Because DNS resolves names backward, you have to specify an IP address of 195.112.34.178 as 178.34.112.195 for it to be resolved correctly. *Objective: Installing and configuring DNS on a Windows NT Server computer (Chapter 10)*

30 *A,B,C.* Any non-WINS clients on your network require a special mapping in the WINS database or have to use a WINS proxy located on the same subnet. *Objective: Configuring static mappings in the WINS database (Chapter 9)*

31 *C.* The LMHOSTS file is not ready to be used by your Windows NT computer until you enable LMHOSTS lookup on the WINS Address page in the TCP/IP Properties dialog box. *Objective: Importing LMHOSTS files to WINS (Chapter 9)*

32 *B.* You're adding a static entry that uses the gateway address of 192.65.118.1 in order to reach the host located at 202.115.66.149. *Objective: Configuring a Windows NT Server computer to function as an IP router (Chapter 7)*

33 *A.* If you think that you have a duplicate IP address on the network, you can use the ARP utility to view the current IP address to hardware address mappings to determine which host should keep the IP address and which host should receive a different address. *Objective: Identifying which utility to use in diagnosing IP configuration problems (Chapter 16)*

34 *B.* NetBIOS sessions are created with the `net` command and the Universal Naming Convention (UNC). If you're having problems with UNC, you should begin troubleshooting NetBIOS and the NetBIOS name resolution process. *Objective: Diagnosing and resolving name resolution problems (Chapter 15)*

35 *B.* A caching-only server's sole job is to perform queries and to store those results in a cache for a period of time in case an identical query is made shortly thereafter. *Objective: Configuring DNS server roles (Chapter 10)*

36 *C.* If an incorrect mapping exists higher up in the HOSTS file, that mapping is used, rather than the correct mapping later in the HOSTS file. *(Chapter 4)*

37 *A.* The increment value is important for the exam when you're asked to determine whether a host is on a valid subnet. Using this number, make subnets such as 1–31, 32–63, 64–95, and so on. *Objective: Given a scenario, identify valid network configurations (Chapter 6)*

38 *C.* M-node isn't the most efficient node method because it uses broadcasts first and then resorts to point-to-point when the broadcast fails to resolve the host name. H-node (the opposite of m-node) uses point-to-point first and then broadcasts, and is much more efficient. *Objective: Diagnosing and resolving name resolution problems (Chapter 15)*

39 *C.* The .252 subnet mask creates a total of 62 subnets. You can't use the subnet mask of .248 because it creates a maximum of only 30 subnets. *Objective: Configuring subnet masks (Chapter 6)*

40 *B.* Making the TTL shorter on the name server causes older, possibly inaccurate information in the cache file to be purged more often. *Objective: Installing and configuring a WINS server (Chapter 9)*

41 *C.* Anything that involves two separate groups of computers should receive two separate scopes. Even though overriding the global options with the scope options may seem easier, you can actually manage two different scopes much more easily. *Objective: Configuring scopes by using DHCP Manager (Chapter 8)*

42 *D.* Although most of the answers work, you should `ping` the loopback address to determine whether TCP/IP has initialized correctly. This is the first step in the `ping` process. *Objective: Using Microsoft TCP/IP utilities to diagnose IP configuration problems (Chapter 16)*

43 *B.* The .224 subnet mask offers six subnets, with up to 30 hosts per subnet, for a total of 180 total hosts. This subnet mask also ensures that you have ample room for more subnets. However, a maximum of 30 hosts per subnet restricts future growth for each subnet. *Objective: Configuring subnet masks (Chapter 6)*

44 *D.* You don't need to do anything special to configure a DHCP server when it is also a primary domain controller. You do need to configure the usual DHCP options, such as the scope and IP address range. *(Chapter 8)*

45 *B.* Although the PPTP filtering appears as if it's configured by using the client's DUN properties, it's enabled by checking the box for Enable PPTP Filtering on the Advanced dialog box on the IP Address page of the TCP/IP Properties dialog box. *Objective: Configuring a RAS server and dial-up networking for use on a TCP/IP network (Chapter 14)*

46 *C.* The WINS server challenges the computer with the existing name in order to claim the name that is being registered by the new computer. *Objective: Installing and configuring a WINS server (Chapter 9)*

47 *B.* Not only does DNS store its files there, but you may also see directories for the other Windows NT services, such as DHCP, WINS, and RAS. *Objective: Installing and configuring DNS on a Windows NT Server computer (Chapter 10)*

48 *B.* TCP/IP connections use *sockets,* which are IP addresses used in conjunction with port numbers. Sockets are different than NetBIOS sessions. *Objective: Diagnosing and resolving name resolution problems (Chapter 15)*

49 *D.* In order for the #INCLUDE to work, you have to use the #PRE keyword to load the entry into cache before the #INCLUDE statement. *Objective: Importing LMHOSTS files to WINS (Chapter 9)*

50 *A.* The class you're using is unimportant because the maximum number of hosts applies across all classes. The .224 subnet mask doesn't provide the most hosts possible across all address classes; the .192 subnet mask provides the most hosts possible across all address classes. *Objective: Configuring subnet masks (Chapter 6)*

Appendix C
Microsoft Certification Programs

- -

In This Appendix

▶ Microsoft Certified Professional

▶ Microsoft Certified Trainer

▶ Microsoft Certified Professional+Internet

▶ Microsoft Certified Systems Engineer

▶ Microsoft Certified Systems Engineer+Internet

▶ Online References

- -

Microsoft offers a number of certifications that you can earn to accelerate your career. These certifications are the most in-demand certifications in the industry today, owing in large part to the overwhelming acceptance of the Microsoft Windows NT operating system. The following certifications all require passing computer-based exams that thoroughly test your ability to implement and support the product.

Many exams apply to more than one Microsoft certification. This appendix includes advice on choosing exams for basic certification requirements that can also apply to advanced certification.

Microsoft Certified Professional (MCP)

On your way to your MCSE designation, you earn an additional acronym: MCP (Microsoft Certified Professional). Upon passing any qualifying exams, you achieve MCP status for that operating system.

Qualifying exams

Passing any *one* exam (except Networking Essentials) earns you MCP status. We recommend these exams while you work toward MCSE certification for Windows NT 4.0:

- ✔ Implementing and Supporting Microsoft Windows 95 (Exam 70-064)
- ✔ Implementing and Supporting Microsoft Windows NT Server 4.0 (Exam 70-067)
- ✔ Implementing and Supporting Microsoft Windows NT Workstation 4.02 (Exam 70-073)
- ✔ Implementing and Supporting Microsoft Windows NT Server 4.0 in the Enterprise (Exam 70-068)
- ✔ Implementing and Supporting Microsoft Windows 98 (Exam 70-098)

Consider working on one of the preceding exams before taking other MCSE exams. MCP-qualifying exams are required for MCSE certification, so it makes sense to earn MCP status as soon as possible.

The Windows NT Server 4.0 exam (70-067) is required for MCP+I certification. If you're planning to try for MCP+I certification, consider taking the NT Server 4.0 exam to get started on the MCP+I requirements and earn MCP certification at the same time. (The MCP+I requirements are covered in this appendix.)

Microsoft plans to retire the Windows NT 3.51 exams when Windows NT 5.0 exams come out. These exams qualify you for MCP status for six months after they are retired:

- ✔ Implementing and Supporting Microsoft Windows NT Workstation 3.51 (Exam 70-042)
- ✔ Implementing and Supporting Microsoft Windows NT Server 3.51 (Exam 70-043)

One other exam earns MCP status and counts toward MCSD certification for developers:

- ✔ Analyzing Requirements and Defining Solution Architectures (Exam 70-100)

Benefits

Johnny, tell our lucky MCPs about their fabulous prizes!

- ✔ Authorization to use the Microsoft Certified Professional logos on your resume and other promotional materials, such as business cards.
- ✔ An official Microsoft Certified Professional certificate, a wallet card, and a lapel pin — all suitable for flaunting.
- ✔ Access to a private area on the Microsoft Web site for Microsoft Certified Professionals. Here, you can find information on Microsoft products and technologies.
- ✔ A free subscription to *Microsoft Certified Professional Magazine,* which has a lot of great information on Microsoft products, new exams, new certification products, book reviews, and more.
- ✔ Invitations to Microsoft conferences and training events.

Microsoft Certified Trainers (MCT)

Microsoft Certified Trainers (MCTs) are certified, technically competent individuals who can deliver Microsoft Official Curriculum at Microsoft Certified Technical Education Centers.

Requirements

For the MCT designation, candidates must

- ✔ Pass the exam for the course they are teaching
- ✔ Prove their instruction presentation skills

You prove your presentation skills by attending approved instructional presentations from Microsoft or via instructor certification by any of the following vendors:

- ✔ Novell
- ✔ Lotus
- ✔ Santa Cruz Operation

- Banyan
- Cisco Systems
- Sun Microsystems

Benefits

Benefits for becoming a Microsoft Certified Trainer are like the benefits of becoming an MCP:

- Use of the Microsoft Certified Trainer logos on your resume and other promotional materials, such as business cards
- An official Microsoft Certified Trainer certificate
- Access to a private area on the Microsoft Web site for Microsoft Certified Trainers, where you can exchange information with other MCTs and course developers
- A free subscription to *Microsoft Certified Professional Magazine,* which can help you prepare for your courses
- Invitations to Microsoft conferences and training events

Microsoft Certified Professional+Internet

The Microsoft Certified Professional+Internet (MCP+I) certification documents your ability to plan, configure, and troubleshoot Windows NT Server systems for intranets and the Internet.

You can achieve MCP+I certification while you work toward MCSE status. All the MCP+I requirements count toward MCSE certification for Windows NT 4.0. The Windows NT Server 4.0 exam (70-067) also qualifies you for MCP status, so consider taking it first.

Qualifying exams

MCP+I certification requires an exam for each of the three subjects listed in Table C-1. Your only option is your choice of Internet Information Server versions.

Table C-1	MCP+I Exams	
Subject	**Newest Exams**	**Older Exams**
Internet Information Server	Implementing and Supporting Microsoft Internet Information Server 4.0 (Exam 70-087)	Implementing and Supporting Microsoft Internet Information Server 3.0 and Microsoft Index Server 1.1 (Exam 70-077)
TCP/IP	Internetworking with Microsoft TCP/IP on Microsoft Windows NT 4.0 (Exam 70-059)	
Windows NT Server	Implementing and Supporting Microsoft Windows NT Server 4.0 (Exam 70-067)	

Benefits

In addition to receiving all of the benefits listed for becoming an MCP, upon attaining the MCP+Internet certification, you can market yourself with an MCP+Internet logo and add another certificate to your wall.

Microsoft Certified Systems Engineer (MCSE)

Microsoft Certified Systems Engineer (MCSE) is one of the most respected certifications in the industry. The dominance of the Windows NT operating system in the market has created great demand for MCSEs skilled in planning, implementing, and troubleshooting Windows NT and the BackOffice suite of products.

Windows NT 4.0 certification requirements

To become a Microsoft Certified Systems Engineer for Windows NT 4.0, you are required to pass *six* Microsoft exams, which include

✔ Four core exams, and

✔ Two elective exams

Core exams

The MCSE core exam requirements for Windows NT 4.0 cover *four* subjects, listed in Table C-2. You must pass an exam for each subject. Your only option is your choice of desktop operating system.

Always try to take the newest exam for a subject. When Microsoft retires the older exam, you may have to pass a newer exam to maintain your certification.

Table C-2	MCSE Windows NT 4.0 Core Exams	
Subject	*Newest Exams*	*Older Exams*
Desktop operating system	Microsoft Windows NT Workstation 4.0 (Exam 70-073)	Implementing and Supporting Microsoft Windows 95 (Exam 70-064)
	Implementing and Supporting Microsoft Windows 98	
Network basics	Networking Essentials (Exam 70-058) or approved equivalent certification	
Windows NT Server (basic)	Implementing and Supporting Microsoft Windows NT Server 4.0 (Exam 70-067)	
Windows NT Server (advanced)	Implementing and Supporting Microsoft Windows NT Server 4.0 in the Enterprise (Exam 70-068)	

Microsoft recognizes that other certification programs cover the requirements of the Networking Essentials exam. After you pass any of the MCSE exams, Microsoft will give you credit for Networking Essentials if you have proof for any of these certifications:

- ✓ Novell CNE, Master CNE, or CNI
- ✓ Banyan CBS or CBE
- ✓ Sun Certified Network Administrator for Solaris 2.5 or 2.6

Elective exams

MCSE certification requires you to pass elective exams for *two* of the subjects listed in Table C-3. *Retired exams* aren't available, but they count toward certification if you passed them when they were current.

Make sure that your MCSE elective exams cover two different subjects in Table C-3. If you take two exams for the same subject, only one exam counts toward your MCSE requirements.

Table C-3	MCSE Elective Exams	
Subject	**Newest Exams**	**Older Exams**
Exchange Server	Implementing and Supporting Microsoft Exchange Server 5.5 (Exam 70-081)	Implementing and Supporting Microsoft Exchange Server 5 (Exam 70-076)
Internet Explorer	Implementing and Supporting Microsoft Internet Explorer 4.0 by Using the Internet Explorer Administration Kit (Exam 70-079)	
Internet Information Server	Implementing and Supporting Microsoft Internet Information Server 4.0 (Exam 70-087)	Implementing and Supporting Microsoft Internet Information Server 3.0 and Microsoft Index Server 1.1 (Exam 70-077)

(continued)

Table C-2 *(continued)*

Subject	*Newest Exams*	*Older Exams*
Proxy Server	Implementing and Supporting Microsoft Proxy Server 2.0 (Exam 70-088)	Implementing and Supporting Microsoft Proxy Server 1.0 (Exam 70-078)
Site Server	Implementing and Supporting Web Sites using Site Server 3.0 (Exam 70-056)	
SNA Server	Implementing and Supporting Microsoft SNA Server 4.0 (Exam 70-085)	Implementing and Supporting Microsoft SNA Server 3.0 (Exam 70-013)
SQL Server administration	System Administration for Microsoft SQL Server 7.0 (Exam 70-028, available 1999)	System Administration for Microsoft SQL Server 6.5 (Exam 70-026)
SQL Server data warehouses	Designing and Implementing Data Warehouses with Microsoft SQL Server 7.0 (Exam 70-019)	
SQL Server implementation	Implementing a Database Design on Microsoft SQL Server 7.0 (Exam 70-029 available 1999)	Implementing a Database Design on Microsoft SQL Server 6.5 (Exam 70-027) *Retired Exam:* Microsoft SQL Server 4.2 Database Implementation (Exam 70-021)

Subject	Newest Exams	Older Exams
Systems Manage-ment Server	Implementing and Supporting Microsoft Systems Management Server 2.0 (Exam 70-086)	Implementing and Supporting Microsoft Systems Management Server 1.2 (Exam 70-018)
TCP/IP	Internetworking with Microsoft TCP/IP on Microsoft Windows NT 4.0 (Exam 70-059)	Internetworking Microsoft TCP/IP on Microsoft Windows NT (3.5-3.51) (Exam 70-053)

Some of the MCSE elective exams are *core* requirements for MCSE+Internet (MCSE+I) certification. If you're interested in that level of certification, consider fulfilling your MCSE elective requirements from these MCSE+I core requirements:

- ✔ Internetworking with Microsoft TCP/IP on Microsoft Windows NT 4.0 (Exam 70-059)

- ✔ Implementing and Supporting Microsoft Internet Explorer 4.0 by Using the Internet Explorer Administration Kit (Exam 70-079)

- ✔ Implementing and Supporting Microsoft Internet Information Server 4.0 (Exam 70-087) *or* Implementing and Supporting Microsoft Internet Information Server 3.0 and Microsoft Index Server 1.1 (Exam 70-077) (only *one* Internet Information Server exam counts toward your MCSE or MCSE+I certification)

Many of the MCSE elective exams *do not count* toward MCSE+I certification. When you select an MCSE exam, check whether it applies to MCSE+I. If it doesn't apply, consider selecting another exam. (MCSE+I requirements are covered in this appendix.)

Windows NT 3.51 certification requirements

Microsoft plans to retire the Windows NT 3.51 exams after releasing the Windows NT 5.0 exams. Until then, you can earn an MCSE for Windows NT 3.51. The certification remains valid for a year after the exams are retired. At the end of that year, be prepared to requalify for a current version of Windows NT.

Table C-4 lists the required core subjects for MCSE certification on the Windows NT 3.51 track. You must pass an exam for each subject. (As with NT 4.0, the only NT 3.51 core option is your choice of desktop operating system.)

Table C-4	MCSE Windows NT 3.51 Core Exams	
Subject	*Newest Exams*	*Older Exams*
Desktop operating system	Implementing and Supporting Microsoft Windows 98 (Exam 70-098)	Implementing and Supporting Microsoft Windows 95 (Exam 70-064)
Network basics	Networking Essentials (Exam 70-058) or approved equivalent certification	
Windows NT Workstation	Implementing and Supporting Microsoft Windows NT Work- station 3.51 (Exam 70-042)	
Windows NT Server	Implementing and Supporting Microsoft Windows NT Server 3.51 (Exam 70-043)	

MCSE for Windows NT 3.51 also requires two electives, just like they are described for the Windows NT 4.0 certification.

Don't bother with NT 3.51 certification. Microsoft intends to decertify the NT 3.51 exams, and they don't count toward MCSE+I. Unless you just need *one* NT 3.51 exam to finish your MCSE requirements on the NT 3.51 track, spend your time on NT 4.0.

Benefits

In addition to receiving all of the benefits of becoming an MCP, upon attaining the MCSE certification, you enjoy these benefits:

- ✔ Marketing yourself with an MCSE logo
- ✔ Yet another certificate for your accomplishments
- ✔ One year subscription to Microsoft TechNet Plus

MCSE+Internet

This designation is known as MCSE+I. This designates Microsoft Certified Systems Engineers who have extensive qualifications for Internet system management, including

- Web sites
- Browsers
- Commerce applications
- Intranets

MCSE+I requirements

Nine different exams are necessary for MCSE+I certification, which include

- Seven core exams, and
- Two elective exams

Here's how those nine exams add up.

Core exams

The MCSE+I core exam requirements for Windows NT 4.0 cover *seven* subjects, listed in Table C-5. You must pass an exam for each subject. Your only options are your choice of desktop operating system and version of Internet Information Server.

Table C-5	MCSE+I Core Exams	
Subject	*Newest Exams*	*Older Exams*
Desktop operating system	Microsoft Windows NT Workstation 4.0 (Exam 70-073)	
	Implementing and Supporting Microsoft Windows 98 (Exam 70-098)	Implementing and Supporting Microsoft Windows 95 (Exam 70-064)

(continued)

Table C-5 *(continued)*

Subject	Newest Exams	Older Exams
Internet Explorer	Implementing and Supporting Microsoft Internet Explorer 4.0 by Using the Internet Explorer Administration Kit (Exam 70-079)	
Internet Information Server	Implementing and Supporting Microsoft Internet Information Server 4.0 (Exam 70-087)	Implementing and Supporting Microsoft Internet Information Server 3.0 and Microsoft Index Server 1.1 (Exam 70-077)
Network basics	Networking Essentials (Exam 70-058) or approved equivalent certification	
TCP/IP	Internetworking with Microsoft TCP/IP on Microsoft Windows NT 4.0 (Exam 70-059)	
Windows NT Server (basic)	Implementing and Supporting Microsoft Windows NT Server 4.0 (Exam 70-067)	
Windows NT Server (advanced)	Implementing and Supporting Microsoft Windows NT Server 4.0 in the Enterprise (Exam 70-068)	

Elective exams

MCSE+I certification requires you to pass elective exams for *two* of the subjects listed in Table C-6.

Make sure that your MCSE+I elective exams cover two different subjects in Table C-6. If you take two exams for the same subject, only one exam counts toward MCSE+I certification.

Table C-6	MCSE+I Elective Exams	
Subject	*Newest Exams*	*Older Exams*
Exchange Server	Implementing and Supporting Microsoft Exchange Server 5.5 (Exam 70-081)	Implementing and Supporting Microsoft Exchange Server 5 (Exam 70-076)
Proxy Server	Implementing and Supporting Microsoft Proxy Server 2.0 (Exam 70-088)	Implementing and Supporting Microsoft Proxy Server 1.0 (Exam 70-078)
Site Server	Implementing and Supporting Web Sites using Site Server 3.0 (Exam 70-056)	
SNA Server	Implementing and Supporting Microsoft SNA Server 4.0 (Exam 70-085)	
SQL Server administration	Administering Microsoft SQL Server 7.0 (Exam 70-028)	System Administration for Microsoft SQL Server 6.5 (Exam 70-026)
SQL Server implementation	Designing and Implementing Databases with Microsoft SQL Server 7.0 (Exam 70-029)	Implementing a Database Design on Microsoft SQL Server 6.5 (Exam 70-027)

Benefits

In addition to receiving all of the benefits listed for becoming an MCSE, upon attaining the MCSE+Internet certification, you can also market yourself with an MCSE+Internet logo. Plus, you receive another certificate as proof of your accomplishments.

Online References

If you want to find out more about Microsoft's certification programs, check out Microsoft's Training and Certification Web site:

```
www.Microsoft.com/Train_Cert/
```

Make it a practice to visit this site regularly: It's the definitive source for updated information about the Microsoft Certified Professional program. Microsoft updates and retires exams often enough that you need to make an effort to stay on top of the changes, and this Web site is your best center for the latest information on the certifications and the exams.

Appendix D

About the CD

The *MCSE TCP/IP For Dummies,* 2nd Edition, CD-ROM contains the following helpful MCSE study tools:

- ✔ The QuickLearn game — a fun way to study for the test
- ✔ Practice and Self-Assessment tests to make sure that you're ready for the real exam
- ✔ Practice test demos from Specialized Solutions, Super Software, and Transcender
- ✔ A bonus chapter about Computerized Adaptive Testing
- ✔ A Links file to help you find resources on the Web

System Requirements

Make sure that your computer meets the minimum system requirements shown in the following list. If your computer doesn't meet most of these requirements, you may have problems using the contents of the CD.

- ✔ A PC with a 486 or faster processor.
- ✔ Microsoft Windows 95 or later.
- ✔ At least 16MB of total RAM installed on your computer.
- ✔ A CD-ROM drive — double-speed (2x) or faster.
- ✔ A sound card.
- ✔ A monitor capable of displaying at least 256 colors or grayscale.
- ✔ A modem with a speed of at least 14,400 bps.

Important Note: To play the QuickLearn game, you must have a 166 or faster computer running Windows 95 or 98 with SVGA graphics. You also must have Microsoft DirectX 5.0 or later installed. If you don't have DirectX, you can install it from the CD. Just run D:\Directx\dxinstall.exe. Unfortunately, DirectX 5.0 does not run on Windows NT 4.0, so you can't play the QuickLearn Game on a Windows NT 4.0 or earlier machine.

Using the CD

To install the items from the CD to your hard drive, follow these steps:

1. **Insert the CD into your computer's CD-ROM drive.**

2. **Click Start⇨Run.**

3. **In the dialog box that appears, type** D:\SETUP.EXE.

   Replace *D* with the proper drive letter if your CD-ROM drive uses a different letter.

4. **Click OK.**

   A license agreement window appears.

5. **Read the license agreement, and then click the Accept button if you want to use the CD. After you click Accept, you'll never be bothered by the License Agreement window again.**

   The CD interface Welcome screen appears. The interface is a little program that shows you what's on the CD and coordinates installing the programs and running the demos. The interface basically enables you to click a button or two to make things happen.

6. **Click anywhere on the Welcome screen to enter the interface.**

   Now you're getting to the action. The next screen lists categories for the software on the CD.

7. **To view the items within a category, click the category's name.**

   A list of programs in the category appears.

8. **For more information about a program, click the program's name.**

   Be sure to read the information that appears. Sometimes a program has its own system requirements or requires you to do a few tricks on your computer before you can install or run the program; this screen tells you what you need to do, if necessary.

9. **If you don't want to install the program, click the Go Back button to return to the preceding screen.**

   You can always return to the preceding screen by clicking the Go Back button. This feature enables you to browse the different categories and products and decide what you want to install.

10. **To install a program, click the appropriate Install button.**

    The CD interface drops to the background while the CD installs the program you chose.

11. **To install other items, repeat Steps 7 through 10.**

12. **When you finish installing programs, click the Quit button to close the interface.**

    You can eject the CD now. Carefully place it back in the plastic jacket of the book for safekeeping.

To run some of the programs on the *MCSE TCP/IP For Dummies,* 2nd Edition, CD, you need to keep the CD in your CD-ROM drive.

What You Find on the CD

This section offers a summary of the software on the *MCSE TCP/IP For Dummies,* 2nd Edition, CD-ROM.

Dummies test prep tools

This CD contains questions related to TCP/IP. Most of the questions are TCP/IP topics that you can expect to be on the test. The CD also includes some questions on other TCP/IP topics that may not be on the current test or covered in the book, but that you will need to perform your job.

The QuickLearn Game

The QuickLearn Game is the *...For Dummies* way of making studying for the Certification exam fun. (Or at least less painful.) OutPost is a DirectX, high-resolution, fast-paced arcade game.

Answer questions to defuse dimensional disrupters and save the universe from a rift in space-time. (The questions come from the same set of questions that the Self-Assessment and Practice Test use, but isn't this way more fun?) Missing a few questions on the real exam almost never results in a rip in the fabric of the universe, so just think how much easier the exam will be for you!

Note: QUIKLERN.EXE on the CD is a self-extractor to simplify the process of copying the game files to your computer. It doesn't create any shortcuts on your computer's desktop or Start menu.

Don't forget that you need to have DirectX 5.0 or later installed to play the QuickLearn game; the game doesn't run on Windows NT 4.0.

Practice Test

The Practice Test is designed to help you get comfortable with the MCSE testing situation and pinpoint your strengths and weaknesses on the topic. You can accept the default setting of 60 questions in 60 minutes, or you can customize the settings. You can choose the number of questions, choose the amount of time, and even decide which objectives you want to focus on.

After you answer the questions, the Practice Test gives you plenty of feedback. You can find out which questions you answered correctly and incorrectly and get statistics on how you scored, broken down by objective. Then you can review all the questions — all the ones you missed, all the ones you marked, or a combination of the ones you marked and the ones you missed.

Self-Assessment Test

The Self-Assessment Test is designed to simulate the actual MCSE testing situation. You must answer 60 questions in 60 minutes. After you answer all the questions, you find out your score and whether you pass or fail — but that's all the feedback you get. If you can pass the Self-Assessment Test regularly, you're ready to tackle the real thing.

Links Page

I've also created a Links Page, a handy starting place for accessing the huge amounts of information on the Internet about the MCSE tests. You can find the page at D:\Links.htm.

Bonus Chapter: Computerized Adaptive Testing For Dummies

This special CD chapter describes computerized adaptive testing (CAT), showing you how it works and how it differs from both computerized testing in general and other types of tests. The chapter also discusses the many advantages of CATs and includes a FAQ section specifically about certification CATs. You even get a section where test takers discuss their reactions to the CATs that they've survived. A final section discusses the use of simulations in performance-based testing and shows how such tests are superior to multiple-choice and other types of questioning for certification exams. This chapter is in PDF format, and you need Adobe Acrobat Reader to view it. If you don't already have Acrobat Reader, you can install it from the CD.

Screen Saver

Don't miss the spiffy little screen saver that the Dummies team created. If you don't plan to sleep with this book under your pillow, maybe this screen saver can help you learn subliminally! Turn on the screen saver, and screen shots of test questions fill your screen. When your computer isn't doing anything else, it still quizzes you. And if you'd like to visit the *Certification ...For Dummies* Web site, all you have to do is press the space bar while the screen saver is running — your default browser launches and sends you there!

Commercial demos

The following demos are handy study tools from several companies that are at the forefront of test prep software makers.

MCSEprep TCP/IP

The MCSEprep Exam Simulator demo (from Super Software, Inc.) is designed to help you prepare for the MCSE TCP/IP exam. It gives you five practice questions — just enough to get a taste. You can get many more practice questions by ordering the software. To learn more, visit the company Web site at www.mcseprep.com.

QuickCert Exam Simulator

The QuickCert package (from Specialized Solutions) offers QuickCert practice tests for several Certification exams. Run the QuickCert IDG Demo to choose the practice test that you want to work on. For more information about QuickCert, visit the Specialized Solutions Web site at www.specializedsolutions.com.

TCP/IP Demo

TCP/IP Demo (from Specialized Solutions) is a demo of some of the training aids that you get from Specialized Solutions self-study courses. A practice quiz, video training, simulations, and an electronic dictionary give you a taste of the training module for TCP/IP.

TCP/IP-Cert

Transcender TCP/IP-Cert Demo (from Transcender Corporation) is a demo version of Transcender's TCP/IP exam simulation. You can get a feel for Transcender's other products through the Certification Sampler, which is also on the CD. To learn more about what Transcender has to offer, check out their Web site at www.transcender.com.

TCP/IP-Flash

Transcender TCP/IP-Flash (from Transcender Corporation) is a valuable piece of demo software designed to help you learn the fundamental concepts and terminology behind TCP/IP. You provide short-answer explanations to questions presented in a flash card format, and you grade yourself as you go.

Transcender Certification Sampler

Transcender's demo tests are some of the most popular practice tests available. The Certification Sampler gives you demos of many of the exams that Transcender offers.

SimDemo

The SimDemo software (from Sylvan Prometric) shows you two simulation questions and lets you work through them, quickly helping you to become comfortable with the simulation questions that you'll see on the exam.

Computer Adaptive Testing Demonstration

The Computer Adaptive Testing Demonstration program (from Galton Technologies) demonstrates how computer adaptive testing (CAT) works. When you start the Math CAT test, you receive a series of math problems. If you remember lots of high school algebra, you'll finish this test pretty quickly. If you didn't plan to ever solve for x again, you might take a little longer. Either way, this demo shows you what CAT is all about.

If You Have Problems (Of the CD Kind)

I tried my best to compile programs that work on most computers with the minimum system requirements. Alas, your computer may differ, and some programs may not work properly for some reason.

The two most likely problems are that your computer doesn't have enough memory (RAM) for the programs that you want to use, or that other programs running on your computer are affecting the installation or running of the program from this CD. If you get error messages such as `Not enough memory` or `Setup cannot continue`, try one or more of the following actions and then try using the software again:

- **Turn off any antivirus software that you have on your computer.** Installers sometimes mimic virus activity and may make your computer incorrectly believe that it is being infected by a virus.

- **Close all running programs.** The more programs you're running, the less memory is available to other programs. Installers also typically update files and programs; if you keep other programs running, installation may not work properly.

- **In Windows, close the CD interface and run demos or installations directly from Windows Explorer.** The interface itself can tie up system memory or even conflict with certain kinds of interactive demos. Use Windows Explorer to browse the files on the CD and launch installers or demos.

- **Have your local computer store add more RAM to your computer.** Admittedly, this is a drastic and somewhat expensive step. If you have a Windows 95 PC, however, adding more memory can really help the speed of your computer and enable more programs to run at the same time.

If you still have trouble installing the items from the CD, please call the IDG Books Worldwide Customer Service phone number: 800-762-2974 (outside the U.S.: 317-596-5430).

Index

●●

Notes

Notes

Notes

Notes

Notes

Notes

Notes

Notes

Notes

Notes

IDG Books Worldwide, Inc., End-User License Agreement

READ THIS. You should carefully read these terms and conditions before opening the software packet(s) included with this book ("Book"). This is a license agreement ("Agreement") between you and IDG Books Worldwide, Inc. ("IDGB"). By opening the accompanying software packet(s), you acknowledge that you have read and accept the following terms and conditions. If you do not agree and do not want to be bound by such terms and conditions, promptly return the Book and the unopened software packet(s) to the place you obtained them for a full refund.

1. **License Grant.** IDGB grants to you (either an individual or entity) a nonexclusive license to use one copy of the enclosed software program(s) (collectively, the "Software") solely for your own personal or business purposes on a single computer (whether a standard computer or a workstation component of a multiuser network). The Software is in use on a computer when it is loaded into temporary memory (RAM) or installed into permanent memory (hard disk, CD-ROM, or other storage device). IDGB reserves all rights not expressly granted herein.

2. **Ownership.** IDGB is the owner of all right, title, and interest, including copyright, in and to the compilation of the Software recorded on the disk(s) or CD-ROM ("Software Media"). Copyright to the individual programs recorded on the Software Media is owned by the author or other authorized copyright owner of each program. Ownership of the Software and all proprietary rights relating thereto remain with IDGB and its licensers.

3. **Restrictions on Use and Transfer.**

   (a) You may only (i) make one copy of the Software for backup or archival purposes, or (ii) transfer the Software to a single hard disk, provided that you keep the original for backup or archival purposes. You may not (i) rent or lease the Software, (ii) copy or reproduce the Software through a LAN or other network system or through any computer subscriber system or bulletin-board system, or (iii) modify, adapt, or create derivative works based on the Software.

   (b) You may not reverse engineer, decompile, or disassemble the Software. You may transfer the Software and user documentation on a permanent basis, provided that the transferee agrees to accept the terms and conditions of this Agreement and you retain no copies. If the Software is an update or has been updated, any transfer must include the most recent update and all prior versions.

4. **Restrictions on Use of Individual Programs.** You must follow the individual requirements and restrictions detailed for each individual program in Appendix D, "About the CD," of this Book. These limitations are also contained in the individual license agreements recorded on the Software Media. These limitations may include a requirement that after using the program for a specified period of time, the user must pay a registration fee or discontinue use. By opening the Software packet(s), you will be agreeing to abide by the licenses and restrictions for these individual programs that are detailed in Appendix D, "About the CD," and on the Software Media. None of the material on this Software Media or listed in this Book may ever be redistributed, in original or modified form, for commercial purposes.

5. **Limited Warranty.**

   (a) IDGB warrants that the Software and Software Media are free from defects in materials and workmanship under normal use for a period of sixty (60) days from the date of purchase of this Book. If IDGB receives notification within the warranty period of defects in materials or workmanship, IDGB will replace the defective Software Media.

   (b) **IDGB AND THE AUTHOR OF THE BOOK DISCLAIM ALL OTHER WARRANTIES, EXPRESS OR IMPLIED, INCLUDING WITHOUT LIMITATION IMPLIED WARRANTIES OF MER-CHANTABILITY AND FITNESS FOR A PARTICULAR PURPOSE, WITH RESPECT TO THE SOFTWARE, THE PROGRAMS, THE SOURCE CODE CONTAINED THEREIN, AND/OR THE TECHNIQUES DESCRIBED IN THIS BOOK. IDGB DOES NOT WARRANT THAT THE FUNCTIONS CONTAINED IN THE SOFTWARE WILL MEET YOUR REQUIREMENTS OR THAT THE OPERATION OF THE SOFTWARE WILL BE ERROR FREE.**

   (c) This limited warranty gives you specific legal rights, and you may have other rights that vary from jurisdiction to jurisdiction.

6. **Remedies.**

   (a) IDGB's entire liability and your exclusive remedy for defects in materials and workmanship shall be limited to replacement of the Software Media, which may be returned to IDGB with a copy of your receipt at the following address: Software Media Fulfillment Department, Attn.: *MCSE TCP/IP For Dummies,* 2nd Edition, IDG Books Worldwide, Inc., 7260 Shadeland Station, Ste. 100, Indianapolis, IN 46256, or call 800-762-2974. Please allow three to four weeks for delivery. This Limited Warranty is void if failure of the Software Media has resulted from accident, abuse, or misapplication. Any replacement Software Media will be warranted for the remainder of the original warranty period or thirty (30) days, whichever is longer.

   (b) In no event shall IDGB or the author be liable for any damages whatsoever (including without limitation damages for loss of business profits, business interruption, loss of business information, or any other pecuniary loss) arising from the use of or inability to use the Book or the Software, even if IDGB has been advised of the possibility of such damages.

   (c) Because some jurisdictions do not allow the exclusion or limitation of liability for conse-quential or incidental damages, the above limitation or exclusion may not apply to you.

7. **U.S. Government Restricted Rights.** Use, duplication, or disclosure of the Software by the U.S. Government is subject to restrictions stated in paragraph (c)(1)(ii) of the Rights in Technical Data and Computer Software clause of DFARS 252.227-7013, and in subparagraphs (a) through (d) of the Commercial Computer–Restricted Rights clause at FAR 52.227-19, and in similar clauses in the NASA FAR supplement, when applicable.

8. **General.** This Agreement constitutes the entire understanding of the parties and revokes and supersedes all prior agreements, oral or written, between them and may not be modified or amended except in a writing signed by both parties hereto that specifically refers to this Agreement. This Agreement shall take precedence over any other documents that may be in conflict herewith. If any one or more provisions contained in this Agreement are held by any court or tribunal to be invalid, illegal, or otherwise unenforceable, each and every other provision shall remain in full force and effect.

Installation Instructions

To install the items from the CD to your hard drive with Microsoft Windows, follow these steps:

1. **Insert the CD into your computer's CD-ROM drive.**

2. **Click Start⇨Run.**

3. **In the dialog box that appears, type** D:\SETUP.EXE.

   Replace *D* with the proper drive letter if your CD-ROM drive uses a different letter.

4. **Click OK.**

   A license agreement window appears.

5. **Read through the license agreement, and then click the Accept button if you want to use the CD. After you click Accept, you'll never be bothered by the License Agreement window again.**

6. **Click anywhere on the Welcome screen to enter the interface.**

7. **To view the items within a category, just click the category's name.**

8. **For more information about a program, click the program's name.**

9. **If you don't want to install the program, click the Go Back button to return to the previous screen.**

10. **To install a program, click the appropriate Install button.**

11. **To install other items, repeat Steps 7 through 10.**

12. **When you finish installing programs, click the Quit button to close the interface.**

    You can eject the CD now. Carefully place it back in the plastic jacket of the book for safekeeping.

To run some of the programs on the *MCSE TCP/IP For Dummies* CD, keep the CD in your CD-ROM drive.

For details about the contents of the CD-ROM and instructions for installing the software from the CD-ROM, see Appendix D in this book.

IDG BOOKS WORLDWIDE BOOK REGISTRATION

Register This Book and Win!

We want to hear from you!

Visit **http://my2cents.dummies.com** to register this book and tell us how you liked it!

- Get entered in our monthly prize giveaway.

- Give us feedback about this book — tell us what you like best, what you like least, or maybe what you'd like to ask the author and us to change!

- Let us know any other *...For Dummies*® topics that interest you.

Your feedback helps us determine what books to publish, tells us what coverage to add as we revise our books, and lets us know whether we're meeting your needs as a *...For Dummies* reader. You're our most valuable resource, and what you have to say is important to us!

Not on the Web yet? It's easy to get started with *Dummies 101*®: *The Internet For Windows*® *95* or *The Internet For Dummies*®, 5th Edition, at local retailers everywhere.

Or let us know what you think by sending us a letter at the following address:

...For Dummies Book Registration
Dummies Press
7260 Shadeland Station, Suite 100
Indianapolis, IN 46256-3945
Fax 317-596-5498

BUSINESS AND GENERAL REFERENCE BOOK SERIES FROM IDG

COMPUTER BOOK SERIES FROM IDG